The Learner
in Education for the Professions

AS SEEN IN EDUCATION FOR SOCIAL WORK

The Learner
in Education for the Professions

AS SEEN IN EDUCATION FOR SOCIAL WORK

Charlotte Towle

222103

THE UNIVERSITY OF CHICAGO PRESS

CHICAGO AND LONDON

THE UNIVERSITY OF CHICAGO PRESS, CHICAGO 60637

The University of Chicago Press, Ltd., London

© 1954 by The University of Chicago. All rights reserved
Published 1954. Seventh Impression 1971. Printed in the
United States of America

International Standard Book Number: 0–226–80998–6
Library of Congress Catalog Card Number: 54–11216

Foreword

Each of the professions has its own unique concerns, but all professions are recognizing increasingly certain problems in common. Particularly is this true in regard to education for the professions. How do the aims of professional education differ from the objectives sought in training for other occupations or from the goals of general education? On what basis and by what means can content and learning experiences be selected that will enable the student to attain these objectives? In terms of what criteria can students be selected that will provide a student body capable of attaining the high goals of a profession and educable in terms of the educational opportunities provided by the professional school?

Some professions, like medicine and the law, have high prestige, and opportunities to enter them are eagerly sought. Others, like teaching and nursing, are presently faced with serious shortages and find it very difficult to recruit an adequate number of students; but in both cases leaders of the professions are conscious of the need for improving the curriculum, the instructional materials and procedures, and the methods of student appraisal, as well as for making a fundamental re-examination of the student recruitment and selection processes and the counseling and guidance procedures used throughout this educational program. Because of this common concern in every profession, a significant treatment of these problems in any one profession has value for all. Miss Towle's critical and constructive analysis is based on her productive experiences in social work education. Her observations and interpretations would be helpful to us in other professions, even if she made no attempt to generalize her material beyond the field of social service. But she has, in fact, an unusually clear notion of the way in which her comments can be of value to educators in other fields, and her organization of material and formulation of suggestions are as useful for the other professions as they are for her own. Thus, in chapter 1, she faces explicitly the several controversies regarding objectives besetting educators in all the professions.

Shall we aim to teach our students the technical skills of the profession, or are these to be learned on the job? Shall we attempt to have students learn a large collection of facts and terms, or shall we try to develop principles and methods of thinking by which the professional practitioner can solve the multitude of specific problems he encounters in his daily work? Does professional education involve developing a high sense of professional ethics in students? Is our task focused solely on intellectual achievement and training in skills, or do we seek to develop appropriate feelings and attitudes in the professional student? To what extent should professional education aim at developing ability to carry on the interpersonal aspects so integral to all professions, involving, as they do, relations among the members of the profession, relations with those served (patients, clients, students, congregation), and relations with the public generally?

All efforts at education imply some notions of how learning takes place and how it can be facilitated. Some of these "theories of learning" used by teachers in professional schools are more appropriate to the training of animals or to the simple habit formation of children than they are to the demands of the complex learning involved in educating the student for the effective practice of a profession. Chapter 2 outlines basic learning principles that have much more usefulness in professional education than those implicitly followed by most of us in this field. The companion chapter 3 on personality development provides a complementary view of the developmental process in becoming a member of the profession which is extremely stimulating and should be helpful to each of us in suggesting major factors for consideration in working out an adequate conception of personality development in our profession.

The further treatment in chapter 4 of personality development and the integration of learning provides the most comprehensive view of this basic process in professional education that I have ever read. Miss Towle does not underestimate the critical and difficult nature of integration for the student preparing for a profession, but she does not confuse it with the integration process of those who are serious problems in a social-psychological sense. She points out the respects in which professional education is not therapy, as well as in what ways it is not social work. The normal student striving to become an adequate member of the profession can be aided by teachers by means appropriate to education rather than to therapy.

Professional education has its sharp reversals of fashion, as do other fields of education. One of these is the view of the teacher-student relationship. Some years ago, professional educators prided themselves on their cold, impersonal dealings with students, who were to be on their own, not "coddled" or "leaning" on teachers. Today in many professional schools the opposite view is common, namely, that a warm and close teacher-student relation is the primary, if not the sole, determinant of the educational progress of the student. In chapter 5 Miss Towle effectively demolishes both extreme views. Warmth and friendliness in the student-teacher relation are important positive values, but they do not take the place of the student's need for knowledge, the help he receives from a well-ordered sequence of learning tasks, and the stimulation and direction he obtains by identifying with the profession and the objective demands of its duties rather than identification with his teacher. Her entire treatment of this chapter is useful to educators in all professions.

The framework of analysis used in chapter 6 in discussing the selection of students gives a broad basis for considering this problem in any profession, even though the particular conditions in recruitment and selection vary markedly from one field to another. Particularly helpful is the emphasis upon the interrelation between student selection and education. What should be sought is not rightly viewed as an ideal student, capable of learning everything presented to him and one who will be highly regarded by all teachers and given marks of A in all his courses. Miss Towle defines educability both more realistically and also more constructively. The view of the selection process as a dynamic one in continuous flux also suggests problems and procedures in admission for every profession.

Currently, the role of the social sciences in professional curriculums is under discussion in many fields. The ideas developed in chapter 7 are fresh and, although directed particularly to social work education, provide constructive suggestions for every profession, because all professions are closely interwoven within the total fabric of society. To understand little or nothing about the larger society is to fail to perceive the very framework within which each profession must fashion its developing functions.

These seven chapters which comprise Part I deal with matters of general concern in all professions. So, too, does chapter 13, "Indications of Movement in Learning." Appraising the educational progress of students is an essential aspect of any educational program if it is to be intelligently guided. The choice of materials, the emphases in teaching, the nature of guidance and counseling, the efforts to improve curriculum and instruction—all require knowledge of the educational progress of students. This last chapter is applicable to other professions, both in identification of significant problems and in the methods outlined for dealing with them.

Although the other chapters of Part II are specifically directed to applications in teaching social casework, many of the points can be generalized to every profession which provides on-the-job experience as part of its education. The use of case materials, their selection and development, and their relation to actual job experience are major problems in most fields. Miss Towle's objective view, her own long experience, and her thought-provoking comments and suggestions will be welcomed by many professional educators. Hence this volume serves the whole range of professional educators, Part I most directly, but Part II in a very rewarding way. As other highly sensitive and intelligent leaders of education in their professions report their problems, experiences, and considered views, it will be increasingly possible to develop a body of theory and practice in professional education of great value in the improvement of the professions.

RALPH W. TYLER

CENTER FOR ADVANCED STUDY IN
THE BEHAVIORAL SCIENCES
CHICAGO, ILLINOIS

Preface

Out of hindsight comes foresight, and consequently an author on completing a book would rewrite it if he could. Since this often is not practicable, the Preface has been granted him, in which to prepare the reader not only for what lies before him but also for what he will not find in the book's pages.

Now that the professions, charged to educate, to help, and to heal the individual, increasingly are concerned to help him live rather than merely survive, they have in common the aim of serving people individually and collectively in ways which foster personality growth. In so far as this is true, these related professions have the shared purpose of orienting their services to the individual in the context of his social situation, with perception of what the service means to him in the light of his needs, capacities, and goals and in the light of his responses to the service. In professional education, we have the common obligation to impart certain essential knowledge and to conduct our educational processes so that they are a means to personality growth. Only thus may the student become free imaginatively to consider, understand, and relate to the needs, wants, and strivings of those whom he is to serve. Our educational systems must strengthen the student's integrative capacity, thus reinforcing his potentials for growth in order that learning may proceed rather than become constricted or break down.

It is important also that we select socially educable students, those who can become deeply committed to work for the good of others rather than largely for self-maximization. It is in relation to such aims as these that professional educators have a concern to improve their educational practices so that the educational experience may foster personality growth for the greatest integration of learning. Marked improvement in admissions practices is contingent on the attainment of this aim; for, until we have made it possible for the student to make the most of his capacities, we will not have reliable criteria of educability for the selection of the highly educable student. It is to this common concern that professional education may serve as a means to the learner's growth for the fulfilment of the profession's responsibilities that this book is addressed.

Accordingly, I have attempted to communicate with three audiences. Part I is addressed to educators and practitioners responsible for staff development in all branches of social work learning as well as to educators in related professions. I have thought it important to share the educational practices and rationale of social work with educators in other professions for two reasons: first, because our experience, which by the very nature of social work has made possible some relatively perceptive educational practices, may be used adaptively by them; and, second, if the professions are to fulfil their charge in society to make certain of the benefits of civilization generally available in ways which have a humanizing influence, it is highly essential that they collaborate rather than operate competitively as separate entities. For this, knowing one another is necessary. Basic understanding of the values and goals of a profession is perhaps attained in large part through understanding its educational ends and means.

I have addressed Part II of the book primarily to classroom teachers of social casework. It is well known, however, that the principles and processes in the several functions of social work practice have much in common. Therefore, it is conceivable that the basic principles and some of the specific measures for orienting teaching to the learner so that integration may be facilitated, may be useful to social work educators in areas other than social casework.

While the chapters in Part II focus largely on the classroom teaching of social casework, many of the general implications for field-work instruction are noted, the place of field-work instruction in the total educational experience is depicted, and the preparation of the field-work instructor is delineated. In the last analysis, professional learning really is tested as it is put to use. The final chapter on "Indications of Movement in Learning," therefore, presents more observations of student responses in practice than in the classroom. Furthermore, more weight is given to them as criteria of the outcome of learning. While I believe that the entire book will be useful to field-work instructors in schools of social work, supervisors, and others responsible for staff development in the field of practice, they may be disappointed in not finding a well-developed presentation of the specifics of field instruction comparable to that of classroom teaching. I have made it clear in the book that, while teaching and learning in classroom and field have much in common, there are decisive differences. Because of the extent of the differences, it has not been possible to cover this area comprehensively in this volume. It is hoped that in the near future someone will deal similarly with field instruction.

Whether or not Part II of the book will be useful to educators in related professions remains to be seen, but it is my belief that much is transferable if used adaptively. I first entitled this book "The Learner in Social Work Education—with Some Implications for Other Professions." I changed the title in response to the reactions of readers, who believed there would be generic implications in Part II. Reappraisal leads me to specify areas which may be of general interest.

It is possible that chapter viii, which deals with "The Place of Social Casework in Education for Social Work," will have meaning elsewhere. The teaching of the area, concerned with a profession's direct service to individuals, will inevitably contribute similarly to its total educational program. It probably will also present some of the same problems if it is to attain its aim of playing an important role in effecting those changes in the learner which enable him to become a full-fledged member of the profession rather than a technician. It is conceivable that teachers using case materials in discussion courses will feel at home in chapters x–xii and find much to affirm and supplement their experience, even though they will have to adapt the contribution to the peculiarities created by differences in subject matter and function. Since in all professions educators are concerned that their measures for evaluation be educational as well as serve as a means to test learning, the discussion of assignments and examinations in chapter xii may well have generic import. Likewise, faculty collaboration and preparation, presented in chapter xi, are common concerns which may present similar problems calling for comparable measures for their solution. Out of a conviction that growth and change in the learner will be manifested similarly in all professions where students are learning to serve people, it is my hope that members of other professions will read the final chapter on "Indications of Movement in Learning."

The multiaudience posed many problems, some of which I have not solved to my satisfaction. On the assumption that not all professional educators would find the total work equally useful, I organized it into two sections, each addressed differentially, as delineated above. Another measure to solve this problem has been that of trying to have the book be a collection of papers. Thus each chapter would stand alone not only to serve the reader's interest and purpose but also to overcome that deterrent, blocks of time for sustained reading. I believe that this aim has been attained in large measure, with the exception of chapters xi and xii, which should be read in conjunction with chapter x. The latter chapter stands alone, but the others are dependent upon it because the criteria for progression in demands on the learner are developed more fully here for the reader's use in the two subsequent chapters. As frequently occurs, the solution of a problem begets other problems, and this one inevitably heightened repetition.

The repetition stems from two other sources, first, the intricately interrelated nature of the content throughout and, second, the necessity to repeat theory as one applies it in a succession of new fact situations. I first charged the large repetitive element to more than twenty years of teaching and looked to my readers to suggest deletions. They were immensely helpful in making invaluable suggestions, but they added as much or more repetition than they took out. In order to qualify, in order not to oversimplify, in order not to burden the reader with the recall of many interrelated factors, repetition has seemed necessary. It might have been lowered, had I not applied theory in the process of presenting it through inserting many illustrations in Part I.

This seemed essential, however, for two reasons. First, distillations of theory are heady brews, which confuse and confound social workers. This may be, in part, because they are habituated to learning through putting theory to use bit by bit. Theory comes alive for them as they apply it. I suspect, however, that this may be characteristic of the professional student. His goal is learning something in order to put it to use. Intent on applying theory, he is under tension until he can use it. Hence he does not become patterned for prolonged abstract presentations. Second, in communicating with educators in other professions, it seemed essential to make known social work's use of certain concepts and ideas, both as a safeguard against misconception and in order that they might more readily see any significance of them for their work. This was demonstrated when noncasework readers inferred from chapters iii and iv that social work education entailed full-fledged clinical study of the student and that psychotherapy was implied in certain comments on the problematic learner. It was important to insert illustrations to begin to clarify the difference between the educational situation and casework practice, which might not have been required by the social casework educator.

The author's point of view on education had its origin largely in the practice of psychoanalytically oriented social casework. Prior to entering social work, I had majored in education in college. My experience was in one respect an unfortunate one, in that I was given too much of what now would be professional training at the preprofessional level. Technique courses and practice teaching presumably taught me how to teach but usurped much time which might have been given to finding what I wanted to teach. Steeped in theory with no context for its use, I was frustrated, and my motivation broke down. Consequently, I left college fired to do almost anything else and resolved never to teach. This experience was a fortunate one, however, in two respects, first, the educational point of view to which I was exposed in 1917–19 was that of "Progressive Education" in its beginnings in this country. The predecessors of the progressive educator and the forerunners of Freud—Froebel, Montessori, Rousseau—and others gave prominent place to the nature of man, arguing variously that education should play into the growth process, take account of instinctual needs and strivings at different age levels, and nurture man for total growth. Perhaps there could have been no better soil for the roots of one who was to become a social worker. I recall John Dewey's *Human Nature and Conduct* and *Democracy and Education* and William H. Kilpatrick's *Foundations of Learning,* among others, as teachings which immediately were consistent with the psychiatric point of view which was beginning to exert an influence on social casework practice. They were in harmony, in that they brought to education something of what psychiatry brought to social casework. Both emphasized individualization, the concept of the whole person, a person-centered as distinguished from a subject- or procedure-centered approach, the place of the emotions in learning, and, finally, the importance of self-activity and the freeing of the individual for expression of his capacities.

Social casework always had attempted to individualize the person and the family. Psychiatry and psychology did not contribute this focus, but they did contribute the wherewithal for more discriminating individualization in terms of knowledge with which to understand individual difference more precisely. It is my impression that the profession of education suffered a lag in this respect for some years, and it was around this lag that social caseworkers talked and worked at cross-purposes with educators in elementary and secondary schools.

The second fortunate circumstance in my college experience was that I became motivated to enter social work through observation and a bit of practice teaching, which was done in two schools, one in a poor district, the other in a private progressive school attended by economically advantaged children. In the first, I was struck forcibly by unmet needs which operated against learning. In the second, I found myself engaged in trying to understand the child for whom this fine new educational theory did not work, the problematic ones who could not use the freedom productively or who for reasons we did not understand could not learn, even though they tested high. Lack of knowledge with which to understand in order to individualize, lack of experience with which to appraise the initial distorted use of educational methods which the educator himself had not experienced, a conviction that many children needed physical and psychological nurture beyond that afforded in the schoolroom if schooling were to attain its aims, led me into social work. I well remember how irked I was, however, by prepsychiatric casework, in that it violated my concept of sound educational principles in being worker-centered and procedure-centered. At that stage, my learnings from education were fully conscious and in the foreground. In the early months of my first social casework experience psychiatric social work was born. For me, this was it.

In the subsequent years, I became absorbed in becoming a social caseworker. My early learnings in education lost their identity to the extent that I can honestly say that when I turned my hand to teaching social work I was consciously using largely my psycho-analytically oriented casework learning, into which doubtless the congruous educational component had been incorporated. White-head's formulations on principles of teaching and learning came to my attention in the late 1930's. They affirmed much that I had been doing out of my ego psychology orientation, and I was able to move ahead with greater freedom and certainty to a more precise methodology.

A social casework practitioner, I, like many of my colleagues, found myself overnight a professional educator with the task of adapting casework insights and skills to the educational process. Like many other social casework teachers, I attempted to understand learning in the light of my understanding of human needs, wants, and strivings, in terms also of my knowledge of growth and development and in relation to my knowledge of the part played by environmental pressures and cultural conditioning on personality formation. Theories of behavior were my theories of learning. Always having focused sharply on the individual in a social situation, inevitably the social casework educator focused quickly on the student in the educational regime, with an eye disposed to look for and see the effects of the regime on the learner. This led naturally to concern with educational practices. She did not turn to the educator for help partly because the usefulness of many of her casework insights in the educational situation led her to rely on her own resources to solve the problems with which she was confronted. She was slow to turn to the educator for help also, because in her contacts as a caseworker with teachers and school administrators she had not found a compatible point of view. Progressive education either had not permeated the field of practice or had not provided the knowledge and insight for understanding the exceptional child or the problematic one. To the social caseworker the educator seemed to ignore or at least fragment the learner. He seemed to feel, think, and function in relation to disembodied "I.Q.'s" and aptitudes rather than in terms of the whole person. Thus it is probable that some years back when educational experts, who might have served as consultants to social work educators, had not shaped their teaching techniques and educational measures to the learner, the two could not have worked together productively. As the educational expert has become psychologically and socially oriented, and the social work educator has become more intelligent educationally through her gleanings of palatable bits from the field of education and her trial-and-error efforts, the two now could well contribute to one another.

For the most part, however, the social worker's current educational practices have been devised through the adaptation of casework learning to the differences in the student's needs, wants, goals, and capacities from those of the client, as well as to the differences in function between professional school and social agency. This adaptation has involved a shift from the study and alleviation of conditions which impede and distort personality growth and interfere with productive living and learning, to conditions which may readily serve as a means to growth. It is not surprising that the social work educator has had an eye for the stress situation and has not been slow to place responsibility for problems in learning on the demands and pressures of the educational situation rather than on the learner. Our professional focus may even have constituted a bias which led us to overweight this factor at times.

Social work literature attests long-standing awareness of the effect of social work learning on the student. It reveals also discerning appraisals of the integrative task and recognition of the acculturation process implicit in professional education expressed in terms of the demands for change from old ways of feeling, thinking, and doing to the ways of the profession. Some measures have been devised to structure and conduct the educational experience to facilitate learning, in the light of these insights. Very recently, other professions have begun to use the social scientist to study the profession as a social system, in order to define the acculturation problem to which students are subjected and to appraise the demands made on the learner. Naturally and inevitably, social work educators through the nature of their orientation have been performing this task for themselves. It remains to be seen whether the formulations of the social scientist and those of the social worker will differ more largely in terminology than in substance.

Adaptation of casework learning to education has also implied a shift from studying and helping individuals engulfed by a life-situation beyond their integrative capacity to studying individuals with relatively high integrative capacity in a goal-striving situation. In those instances where the goal has been appropriate in terms of the student's abilities and disposition, the situation has afforded bountiful opportunity for the nurture of the ego for growth. The problem has been that of selecting, pacing, and timing the opportunities with reference to developmental norms.

Trained to see the person as central and with knowledge of human behavior to deepen perception, it is not surprising that the social work educator has been alert to the problematic learner and prone to draw on her skills in helping people meet reality demands. In this experience she gradually learned to differentiate the student from the client and the educational process of helping the individual learn from the casework diagnostic treatment process. In her attempts to orient educational methods to the dynamics of behavior, I believe that the social casework educator has arrived at some sound methodology. Her orientation to psychopathology at times has operated as a deterrent in those instances where she has been prone to see normal anxiety in learning as neurotic anxiety, and normal responses to reality stress as incommensurate to the stress. The social casework educator who has not been primarily a social worker in habitually ruling out the "situational neurosis" before assuming "character neurosis" has had a difficult time in becoming an educator. When, however, she has brought to the educational situation basic understanding of normal adult ego development and functioning in social context and when she has been patterned in her work with people to assume healthy ego development until evidence argues the contrary, she has a resource for arriving at sound educational procedures.

Out of a fortunate educational experience in my professional school, I brought this orientation to my work as field-work instructor in 1928, for the New York School of Social Work, and to my subsequent work as a social casework teacher at the Chicago school in 1932. In this I have never been completely alone, for always I have had colleagues who have shared the task of attempting to adapt casework insights and skills in the educational process. For the development of the learner, we have wanted particularly to afford an educational experience in which the student was not obsessively absorbed in a struggle for equilibrium. We have wanted a margin to permit him to become creative. Central in our thinking has been the concern lest the protective function of the ego would have to operate at the expense of its integrative function. Prominent also has been the awareness that the integrative task must be appraised in terms of the emotional demands of learning as well as of the intellectual demands. This book attempts to depict our thinking and the practices which have been gradually devised for the attainment of these and other aims.

It seems important to say that we who have been educational practitioners without professional training in education, arrived at the educational practices described in Part II of this book with little communication with the field of education. The rationale for structuring the casework sequence as we did in Chicago was formulated gradually between the years 1942 and 1947. The first two courses, essentially as described in chapter x, were structured and instituted between 1942 and 1944. It was in 1949 that we first began to check our efforts with Tyler's important work on curriculum construction and shortly thereafter that I began to cast my thinking into his frame of reference, as attested in my writings from 1949 to the present. It was immensely reassuring to us to find that his principles supported ours and that we could think and talk together.

We had proceeded alone for the reasons and misconceptions delineated earlier. We were reassured because, in spite of conviction as to our insights, we did not feel basically competent as educators. We did certain things because they made sense in the light of our orientation, but whether they were the best that could be done was a haunting question. His formulations have sharpened our thinking in part through conveying confidence but in part through supplementing our knowledge of specific ways in which to attain our aims. I think it reasonable to assume that earlier communication might have lightened the task and facilitated the movement of the casework faculty in arriving at the present stage of development. This is difficult to say, for perhaps a profession's practitioners have to develop some identity as educators through their own efforts before they can identify with the expert educator sufficiently to make productive use of his help. It is to be hoped that the time has arrived when the several fields of professional education and the profession of education will collaborate for the mutual advancement of our learning and teaching.

I attempt to present the raw material of the social casework educator's observations and tentative thinking on the individual learner in an educational process oriented, in so far as possible, to his needs and capacities, while holding to the profession's needs and responsibilities. The formulations at this stage of development of social work education are equivalent to the experience-tested ones of the clinician, unsupported by research. I do not speak for social casework educators as a whole or for all the members of the faculty with whom I have been associated. Much of the thinking of my colleagues at home and abroad is incorporated in these pages, but they might not be in full accord with my thinking on many points throughout this publication. Characteristic of the profession is the conviction that professional learning is not the profession's own to guard jealously. It belongs to the community and is to be imparted responsibly. It is in this spirit that I, who am by profession a social worker rather than an educator, share my learning and thinking on social casework education for whatever use it may have elsewhere.

CHARLOTTE TOWLE

SCHOOL OF SOCIAL SERVICE ADMINISTRATION
UNIVERSITY OF CHICAGO
CHICAGO, ILLINOIS

Acknowledgment

In the give-and-take of professional life, a book which has been more than twenty years in the making and five years in the writing bears the imprint of many minds. My first acknowledgment, therefore, is a general one to those social workers, psychiatrists, psychologists, and educators with whom I have studied and worked. Among the social workers I give prominent place to those who have studied with me and who, in giving themselves to the tasks of learning, have both motivated and given substance to this work. To the extent that my understanding of the learner in education for social work has shortcomings, they are mine through not having been able to put to full use the contribution of my teachers, colleagues, and students.

I am indebted to those with whom I first studied psychiatric social work for my disposition to transfer psychosocial learning to the educational situation with focus on the learner in this context and on the psychological import of educational practices. I owe much to Dr. Marion E. Kenworthy, a pioneer "social psychiatrist" and teacher of social workers at the New York School of Social Work. Her teaching lent itself to integration for use in social work practice because she focused sharply on the individual in his dynamic social situation. Not only did she teach students a method of case analysis which facilitated orderly thinking, but her respect for environment as treatment and her perception of the psychotherapeutic potentialities in the gamut of casework services grounded me in social work and committed me to use psychiatric insights in the helping processes of social work as differentiated from those of psychiatry. It followed naturally that I used them also in the teaching-helping processes of social work education. As an educator I owe much also to Dr. David M. Levy, with whom I worked at the Institute for Child Guidance in New York City. In contributing richly to my knowledge of child development, he focused my attention on the import of habit training for personality development and on the possible connection between the nature of

xxi

the parent-child relationships and the child's aptitudes and dis-abilities in school learning. I took into my work as an educator an eye slanted to note the part played by emotions in school learn-ing, as well as the relationship context of learning patterns and responses.

In my years as a teacher of social casework I have found the work of Dr. Franz Alexander particularly helpful. As attested in the documentation of this book and of my earlier writings on social work education, his formulations on basic learning principles and the ego and its defense system lent themselves to adaptive use in my thinking on the learning process in social work education. The problem in adaptation lay in defining the part played by seemingly defensive behavior in the goal-striving of the relatively normal young adult, as differentiated from the part played by defenses in adults encountered in psychotherapy. Throughout these years it has been my good fortune to have had the opportunity intermit-tently to discuss with Dr. Thomas M. French the problem of inte-gration in learning which is fraught with emotion. I am indebted to him for his formulations on the integration of behavior in goal-striving. Dr. French read the first four chapters of the final revi-sion of this book and helped me in defining the defenses more nar-rowly, so that their part in learning could be delineated more pre-cisely throughout the book. During the past year I have exchanged thinking on professional education with Dr. Charlotte G. Babcock, formerly of the staff of the Chicago Institute for Psychoanalysis and now professor of psychiatry in the Medical School of the University of Pittsburgh. Dr. Babcock read chapters 1 through 6 of the final revision of the book. In our stimulating discussions, she affirmed, supplemented, and at points helped me clarify my thinking beyond the credit given to her through specific documentation. I acknowl-edge also the work of Dr. Ralph W. Tyler, professor of education, University of Chicago, and director of the Center for Advanced Study in the Behavioral Sciences. His responses to my earlier writ-ings on social work education encouraged me to identify some of the generic elements in professional education.

It is not possible to acknowledge adequately the contribution of my colleagues in social work education. I owe much to Edith Abbott, dean emeritus of this school. To one who had specialized in social casework she gave historical perspective and a broadened grasp of social work as a profession, which served to enlarge my perception of the significance of psychiatrically oriented social casework for the whole. For approximately fourteen years the members of the casework faculty and Dean Helen R. Wright have worked almost continuously on structuring and restructuring the social casework courses with reference to the curriculum as a whole. Prolonged absorption in one field of study might well have led its faculty members to overweight it and thus to fail to make it an integral part of the whole. That this has not occurred is due in large measure to Dean Wright's perceptive and objective participation in the curriculum work of each field of study, as well as to her unifying leadership in this school's over-all curriculum committee. The applications in Part II of the point of view presented in Part I of this book are an outgrowth of the individual and collective thinking of the members of the casework faculty and of Dean Wright, to each of whom I am greatly indebted, but whose individual contributions I cannot specify beyond those documented throughout the book.[1] Special mention, however, is due Lois Wildy, now director of the Illinois Children's Home and Aid Society, who, when on the faculty of this school, collaborated with me in the years 1942–45 in delineating the content and focus of the basic casework courses much as presented in this book. Recognition is also due Helen Harris Perlman, who joined our casework faculty in 1945. We were immediately compatible thinkers on the whole, and particularly in our readiness to break away from the traditional specialized casework courses of the second year. Mrs. Perlman has made a creative contribution to social work education, and this book bears her imprint beyond the documentation to her writings. As we have worked together, we have affirmed and supplemented each other and, at times, differed with each other, with the end-result that my thinking has been extended and deepened.

My thanks are due to several colleagues for reading and criticizing the manuscript at several developmental stages. For this I am indebted to Helen Harris Perlman and to Mary E. Macdonald,

1. Members of the casework faculty during the writing of this book were: Dorothy Aikin, Miriam Brueckner, Dora Goldstine, Barbara Palmer, Helen Harris Perlman, Lyndell Scott, Susanne Schulze, and Bernice Kern Simon.

of our social work research faculty, for reading portions of the first draft; to Mrs. Lyndell Scott, now of the faculty of the School of Social Work, University of Minnesota, for reading the second draft with a focus on learning principles and educational concepts; to Rachel Marks, assistant editor of the *Social Service Review,* who not only edited the second draft but gave valuable comment on content and suggestions for reorganization of portions of the manuscript; to Dean Helen R. Wright for her reading and criticism of Part II of the final revision. Finally, I am indebted to my social work colleague and friend, Mary E. Rall, who has lived with the book in its making and who not only has read the whole of each revision but has put her mind to problematic bits at those moments when the author has been stymied. To Margaret W. Tafel, I owe many thanks for help in editing the final copy and for compiling the Index.

Table of Contents

PART I

Learning Process and Educational Process

CHAPTER 1

General Objectives of Professional Education

Pioneer and early industrial America was concerned that its professions educate, help, and heal the individual for survival. For this, technical skills have been essential. As modern America has moved toward the interdependence implicit in a democracy, society's aim increasingly has been to afford the individual opportunity for the development of his capacities. Professions today are intent upon their contribution to the development of the individual rather than upon services that merely assure survival. It is fast becoming the common sense that, to serve mankind for its development, one must understand man. Accordingly, in the professions directly concerned with human welfare there is a trend away from skilled services per se to concern for the individual being served. Responsible, intelligent, professional help must increasingly be oriented to the individual in the context of his social situation, with perception of what the service is doing to the person while doing something for him.

Those professions established to serve the common good through the provision and administration of services to promote individual human welfare have certain decisively important elements in common. They all serve people, individual by individual, in the interest of their welfare—physical, mental, intellectual, spiritual, or social. The professional person's services are sought because he has something to give which the applicant needs and wants. Clergyman, physician, psychiatrist, nurse, psychologist, lawyer, teacher, social worker—all are involved in a giving-taking relationship. In serving, they do things for, with, and to people. The recipient responds in terms of what he is and of what the services mean to him. His response embodies something of himself and something of the helper. Traditionally, the professional person has been concerned to give what he has to offer in ways which are helpful, in ways which enable the recipient to make good use of the contribution regardless of whether or not he pays for the services. Today there is increased awareness of the total personality involved in this relationship and growing concern as to what is being "done to" the person experiencing a professional service.

Furthermore, a professional person's services are sought because he has a competency, a mastery of knowledge and skill, which the recipient of the service does not have. In several of the professions the practitioner is needed and wanted when there is a problem to solve, when the person is in difficulty, when he may lack his normal adequacy, or may not have the specialized knowledge for the solution of his difficulty. In all of the professions people may be encountered and worked with at such times. In rendering a professional service constructively, a demand is made that professional competence shall not undermine the individual, that, in helping him in the management of his affairs, his capacity for self-management may not be decreased. Furthermore, respect for the total person in every profession implies that concern for one area of his welfare must not ignore his general welfare. Respect for the integrity of the individual implies that, in administering to his physical health, we take into account his mental and emotional needs and responses and that, in administering to his intellectual needs, we do not ignore the physical or social self. Respect for the integrity of the person implies also that his rights to self-determination within social limits be regarded, that individual difference be appreciated—in short, that the professional relationship be oriented at all times to his identity as a person with rights as well as obligations.

The function of a profession in society and the demands implicit in its practice determine the objectives of education for that profession. The responsibilities which its practitioners must assume designate the content of knowledge and skill to be attained. They determine also the character of the educational experience which students must have to become the kind of people required both to provide competent service and to contribute to the ongoing development of the profession in a changing social order. In envisaging the responsibilities and characteristics of a profession which may make for educational objectives common to all, we shall bring out some of the peculiarities of social work that differentiate its educational process.

Out of the profession's responsibility to society to maintain the common good, its educators endeavor to develop a high level of competence for immediate use throughout the ranks of its membership. It has been said: "The young man who enters a profession does not have to wait for advancement to engage in activities of the highest importance to society." He at once assumes work which calls for responsible use of all that his profession teaches.[1] In curriculum planning Ralph W. Tyler warns against confusion of professional and nonprofessional tasks that may clutter up curriculums with activity courses that can be learned on the job. He emphasizes that it is in the nature of a profession that it bases its technique of operation upon principles rather than upon rule-of-thumb procedures or simple routine skills. It is a characteristic of professional education that it teaches a body of principles and concepts for differential use. It should foster in students the inclination to understand these principles beyond the confines of the profession.[2] In short, it endeavors to set in operation a learning process that will endure and wax strong throughout the years of professional activity.

Thus professional education trains for professional self-dependence. There cannot be an admixture of limited goals and high goals. Its educational systems cannot be designed to train a few to lead, many to follow, and others permanently to serve under the guidance of more competent members. There will emerge those who will represent the profession, speak for it as a whole, act for it as a whole. There will be a group who will play an identifiable part in determining the profession's growth and in fashioning the shape of things to come, through representing it in its intra-mural and extra-mural affairs, through administering its programs, through formally teaching its future members, and through engaging in and directing its research. In the professional school, however, the basic aims of professional education are the same for all students, each one of whom is a professional person in the making. What he contributes is of the future. It is to be remembered that a profession's leaders cannot advance it beyond the level of its common practice. The educational

1. Ernest Cadman Colwell, "The Role of the Professional School," in Bernard R. Berelson (ed.), *Education for Librarianship* (Chicago: American Library Association, 1949), pp. 13–21.

2. Ralph W. Tyler, "Educational Problems in Other Professions," in Berelson, *op. cit.*, pp. 22–28.

process is aimed at developing leaders for tomorrow's practice, through producing practitioners of high caliber to provide and sustain that leadership. The members of a profession at all operating levels are charged with the responsibility to advance learning and to convey it to colleagues and students. In medicine the Oath of Hippocrates states explicitly the doctor's obligation to learn and to teach. In the field of practice as well as in the professional school, a professional person does not jealously guard his knowledge and skill. His learning is not his to have and to hold. "And gladly teach" is an attitude of mind to be instilled through professional education.[3]

The advancement of learning demands research, ingrained as an attitude of mind in all members and developed as a special skill in some. A research approach to the solution of a problem enables the practitioner to learn through experience and to convey what he learns. Certain knowledge of research and disciplined thinking will make for intelligent interpretation and use of the work of those who are specifically engaged in it. The development within a profession of its own research both improves its service and bespeaks the maturation of the field of endeavor. Sound research proceeds from and contributes to sound practice.

Our first aim is to develop in students the capacity to think critically and analytically and to synthesize and to generalize; a capacity to break a thing down in order to build it up for use; a capacity to apply knowledge and a well-established habit of seeking it, using it, testing it critically, and formulating principles—in short, the objective of developing and intrenching the spirit of scientific inquiry. Some students are keen analyzers. They can tear a situation to bits, break it down to its finest components; but they may be singularly inept at reconstruction, even being indifferent or resistant to it. Some students are slow to see the woods for the trees. They may, however, be "part-whole learners" who will come out well in the long run. Others may be "part learners" and not have the capacity to see beyond the fragments to the whole. They may give equal weight to unequal things and thus lack discrimination in terms of the significant and the trivial. Many examples of "ways of thinking" and "habits of mind" not useful in a profession could be given.

3. J. H. Means, M.D., "The Clinical Teaching of Social Medicine," *Bulletin of the Johns Hopkins Hospital*, LXXVIII, No. 2 (February, 1946), 96–111.

The decisive question is the extent to which these ways are deeply ingrained, thus fulfilling basic personality needs.

It is our impression that there are wide variations among students in their capacity to think in the way desired. This capacity can be strengthened, but, if it has not been fairly well intrenched by adult years, it is doubtful that a student can attain it at the graduate level. This ability is the product of prior habits of learning throughout school experience, certain content of learning, and whatever prior learning has been assimilated to an extent that the learning process is responded to as a pleasurable adventure rather than as an uncomfortable ordeal. It has to do also with capacity for separation of one's self from another—and all these factors relate to emotional development. The crux of the situation lies in whether or not the student's emotional development has been such as to permit him to come to grips with reality, to struggle with and face interrelationships, to think for himself apart from others. If he has been an abject learner, dependent, submissive to authority, it is doubtful whether learning will have been "taken in" or more largely annexed out of a defensive identification. Occasionally, students are so tied to past mentors through whom their thinking has been derived that they cannot accept new concepts, even intellectually. They dare not even think anew. Other students dare to think but not to act anew. They may give to new concepts intellectual acceptance but be unable to use them, because to do so would be enacting emancipation beyond their capacity, except as they replace their dependence on the old mentor with dependence on the new one.

Learning which involves transfer of loyalties may provoke anxiety, hostility, and resistance. If learning is equated with aggression and there is much hostility, learning will be hostile aggression. It may then evoke much anxiety, which will operate against smooth analytic thinking, the objectively critical attitude, and the capacity to synthesize. Such students frequently can tear down, but they may be blocked in building up for use. In these instances the individuals may lack a sense of humor but may possess, instead, a bantering attitude, a sense of fun which is expressed in witticisms. They laugh "at and off" rather than with, because *perhaps* they feel more against the world than with it. These few responses are given merely to establish the point that the emotional development of the individual must be taken into account. The direct and close bearing of the emotions upon the student's capacity to think analytically and to synthesize has many implications, a few of which will be discussed later. Thus the development of the capacity to think which the student brings to his educational experience is one realistic objective of professional education. How much growth can occur will depend in part upon whether the content and method of the professional education experience can contribute to his emotional development or only disturb his present adjustment. This leads to the next objective.

Our second aim in imparting essential knowledge for use in a profession is to develop feelings and attitudes that will make it possible for the student to think and act appropriately. More likely than not, a student will bring some feelings and attitudes, biases, and prejudices that are inappropriate to his particular profession. Educators in any one profession doubtless are familiar with a whole array of attitudes and feelings, somewhat peculiar to their particular fields, which must undergo change for disciplined and understanding services. In social work, inappropriate attitudes have been noted toward people who need help, toward the offender, toward the authority of the law, toward the dull child who learns slowly, toward certain diseases and infirmities, toward the indigent, toward the rich, toward certain groups as determined by nationality, race, religion, occupation, and the like. Many of these feelings and stereotypes, which may or may not represent the student's defenses against learning, could be said to be generally unsuitable to any and every profession. Others probably are more inappropriate in one profession than in another. The decisive fact is that in all professions some of the feelings and attitudes which the student brings must undergo change if he is to attain the critical perception, the depth of understanding, the disciplined thinking, essential for the differential action which a profession demands.

Is this objective a realistic one? Certainly, it is clear that the student's capacity for change is more important than the attitudes themselves. There are great differences in students in the attitudes brought to this learning experience. Some have been reared in a milieu where appropriate attitudes for a particular profession prevail. Others have not been reared in a favorable emotional and intellectual climate. The rigidity or flexibility of the student relates, among other factors, to the character of his prior relationships. He may be compelled to continue to feel and to think in the old ways because they meet some basic need. The important matter of capacity for change in feelings and attitudes hinges on determining the student's capacity for a new relationship. Can he give himself over freely, identify, maintain the essential separateness, be influenced without undue anxiety? How much and how compellingly is he tied to the past in the sense of being tied to past authorities? That change in feelings and attitudes is an attainable objective for many students has been proved. Professional education, by its very nature and through the fact that largely it is proffered to the young adult, is a means of achieving maturity, which is used avidly and to the utmost by the student who is emotionally ready to be emancipated from old dependency-authority ties. Every professional educator has seen, heard, and felt throughout the student's learning response the change experienced by many students and the growth attained in many ways.

Our third aim in professional education is to develop a capacity for establishing and sustaining purposeful working relationships. Working together characterizes all professional activity, whether the relationship be that of practitioner with the recipient of his services, supervisor-practitioner, administrator–staff member, or between the members of an interagency or intra-professional team. Demand for this ability may be greater in some professions than in others. One might hope that the student would bring this capacity in considerable degree to the learning situation. It is doubtful that it can be engendered in the adult through professional education. In the social work educational process it would grow and be fashioned to the ends of social work but perhaps not be brought into being by it. In social work this capacity is essential in helping relationships, in collaborative work relationships, and in group-to-group relationships. Decisive here is an intent to understand those with whom he works. This is readily distinguished from a tendency to condemn, but it is not so readily differentiated from an easy tolerance which often actually is a defense against understanding. Through tolerance, an individual may attain liking and hence leadership of a sort. Tolerance without understanding makes for troubled working relationships and at least for precarious harmony, in that often it is compounded of indifference and resistance to knowing the full import of circumstances, issues, and responses. Decisive also in establishing and maintaining purposeful working relationships will be the readiness to assume and sustain responsibility, the capacity to meet the dependency of others without taking the management of affairs out of their hands, the willingness to play a minor or subordinate role as well as a major one, and an ability to separate one's self from another so that one's own feelings, attitudes, and needs are not blindly projected onto others. In the last analysis this aptitude for collaboration again stems from the student's receptivity to self-awareness and self-understanding and from his capacity for relationships. In professional activity it represents an integration of the ability to think and to feel, as previously described. Hence the attainment of our first and second objectives will bring this third one into being. The development of this aptitude will depend on the extent to which this inclination is used throughout the educational process and on the nature of the relationships which the student experiences in professional training. It will depend also on other constituent elements, the student's intellectual capacity and his potentials for change in feeling, where inappropriate feelings and attitudes obtain.

Since a profession is a field of service established to serve the common good, professional education has as its fourth objective helping its prospective practitioners develop social consciousness and social conscience. This implies their identification with profession and agency. It also implies emotional acceptance of the profession's responsibility and authority components. "Thou shalt" was implied when society invested professional groups with certain powers, obligations, responsibilities, and privileges. It is only through identification with the conscience of the community and of the profession that the student may come to act in accordance with the rationale, the ethical system of the profession, and the regulations of its instrument—the institution or agency. Here, again, personality development has decisive importance. Important also is the place of the particular profession in society in terms of the authority accorded it and the compatibility of the aims of both.

If a profession is a field of service established to serve the common good rather than for the commonweal of its practitioners, the profit motive either in prestige or in economic gain cannot operate to the same extent as in many occupations. The profession exists to serve individuals rather than to serve the practitioner's ends. This does not mean that the practitioner should not have an adequate livelihood, nor does it mean that he does not have certain rights. It does mean, however, that the rights which he claims have as their end the community's good and that the means to the attainment of those rights can be reconciled with the profession's ethics. The obvious import of this is that there is small place for self-aggrandizement. It is clear in terms of the individual personality in relation to this demand that capacity for love for others as differentiated from self-love is requisite.

A profession has a philosophy by which its practitioners are guided to the extent that they are not free agents but, instead, are obligated to act in accordance with the rationale, the ethical system, of the profession. Of this obligation Professor Tyler states that a profession establishes some form of group discipline in support of these values. He states further that one of the indications that an occupation is becoming a profession is a concerted movement among members to establish and to maintain group discipline, that is, to uphold the ethical values involved.[4]

Not only is the professional person not a free agent, but often he also is not a free-lance worker. He may work within an agency or institution with statutory regulations and policies of administration, a program for which the administrators are accountable to a community beyond the bounds of his professional practice. When he works within the context of an agency, he is no longer just his professional self but also the agency. The agency, in turn, if it merits identity as an agent of human welfare, has procedures and policies which fulfil rather than violate the aims of its employed professions. The agency is an instrument of the profession. It is clear, therefore, that professional education does not prepare for individual self-expression, for individualistic creativity, for the independent acting-out of one's own urges in the interest of self-gratification or self-realization. An individual may have entered a profession because he likes to influence, mold, reform, punish, cure, or help people. He cannot serve them in ways that serve primarily his own need.

4. *Op. cit.*

Instead, he must subordinate his ideas and predilections to the ways of the profession and its instrument, the agency.

While the members of a profession must work within limits set by its group, they should participate in the formulation and re-formulation of its ethical system and of its operational modes. Professional education, therefore, for competent practice and for leadership should inculcate a critical, rather than a worshipful, attitude toward the profession's rationale and instruments, even that instrument, the agency. It is a professional person's right and obligation to work for change in philosophy or in agency policy and procedure in so far as either violates the basic aim of the profession—the promotion of the maximum welfare of the individuals whom the profession has been established to serve. Educators in a profession with a long and sacrosanct tradition may have a peculiar problem in inculcating this critical attitude because at the same time they must help the student accept and incorporate the imposed discipline, integrate its authority for use, and respect its traditions. Educators in professions which operate largely through agencies which express in varying degrees the aims and philosophy of the profession share a problem in helping the student work within the context of both with awareness of the identity of each. It may happen that members of these professions lose the profession in the agency. The daily impact of the authority of the latter may obliterate the former. They may compromise the basic aims of their profession rather than work to effect change, so that the agency will be truly an instrument of their profession and the profession not a cloak of respectability for the agency. The professions of social work and teaching often have a very real problem in maintaining their aims for human welfare within the rigid framework of the outworn statutes and regulations of some of their institutional systems. Professional social workers often could well question whether it is possible to perform their function in some regimes which profess a human welfare intent but resist the change implied for the attainment of that aim.

In a profession there is a recognized body of knowledge and skill to be attained for competent practice. Its practitioners must give evidence of capacity to use that knowledge and skill. Professional schools demand that students upon graduating give evidence of possessing it and of having some capacity to use it. Thereafter, evidence will be given in competent services as judged in the field of practice. Some professions have a legally constituted authority for licensing or for registration of those individuals qualified for practice. This procedure imposes a demand, but, in turn, it affords professional status and security to the membership, individually and collectively. The profession of social work lacks this legally constituted authority, and hence social work operates under the stress of being vulnerable to attack, and its members are put on the defensive when the supporting public reacts adversely to its sound practice. Social workers must assume great responsibility without the emotional support afforded to other professions through legal certification.[5] Social work lacks also the support which some professions have through their well-developed research, from which they can speak with greater authority than if they were more largely dependent on "clinical impression." Its leaders must speak for it without assurance of the respect for authority accorded members of other professions. This factor at times affects its working relationship with its more advantaged colleague professions.

Social work, by its very nature and function and because of the group it serves, as well as the nature of its relationship with its supporting public, must give great emphasis to the development of a high degree of social conscience and social consciousness. Social work is concerned with social ills. It serves a group that needs to be protected and at times actively defended. It serves society, which also seeks protection through social work. Social work exists because the community has had a conscience about the disadvantaged and an altruistic impulse to protect those who need help for survival. This conscience seemingly is a compound of many elements, several of which are discernible. First, man's propensity to feel with man, so that, as he comprehends himself in the position of the disadvantaged, he is impelled to succor them out of feelings of self-injury and guilt. When the numbers of the disadvantaged grow great, they comprise a group that threatens the peace of mind and heart of those who otherwise could be comfortable. Second, around the core of man's necessity for identification, he has developed, as he has experi-

5. Charlotte Towle, "Emotional Elements in Professional Learning," in pamphlet entitled *Professional Education* (New York: American Association of Schools of Social Work, 1948).

enced satisfying and constructive family and other group life, a feeling of obligation to others and a capacity to care for others. This is likely to occur to the extent that he has known love in his relationships and sufficient emancipation to permit him to love outside of self. Inevitably, then, the disadvantaged constitute a source of anxiety and discomfort to those who have attained this growth, thus motivating concerted action in behalf of the deprived and oppressed.

While, as democracy has grown, the community has had some impulse to help people live socially useful lives beyond a bare survival level, at the same time social work exists also because of fear. The disadvantaged become offenders through physical and mental illness and through unsocial and antisocial behavior. They thereby become a threat to the common good, thus engendering feelings of helplessness, hostility, and guilt which may beget fear of retaliation. These feelings motivate action, at times urgent and disconcerted. The profession of social work continuously operates under the impact of the mixed feelings of the community. There is fluctuating sympathy with and resentment against the groups served. This is evidenced in the varied arguments of community-fund drives which are addressed both to man's altruistic impulses and to his primitive strivings. Note that they call forth his feeling for others, appeal to his sense of social justice, and invoke his fears: Protect yourself. Poverty begets sickness and crime. "It pays to give" often is either implied or stated. Dual feeling is sometimes expressed in an attitude which says, "By all means give, but give restrictively." It is manifested through acts that give with one hand and take away with the other. It is shown also in an attitude that anybody is sufficiently well qualified to render social services.

Professional education aims to develop a constructively critical attitude both toward society's response to the profession and toward the profession's principles and instruments. The welfare of the individual in relation to the welfare of society is the purpose and test of every program and of a profession's ethical system. To think critically and objectively in order to effect change rather than to be blindly worshipful of traditional thinking and doing is the persistent aim of professional education. It is only through that degree of identification with the individual served which is implicit in understanding the person and his needs that the student may come to represent at all times the conscience of his profession and of his community.

Perhaps there is some variation among professional schools in the place that needs to be given to the last two objectives which pertain to the development of social conscience and social consciousness. In social work education the student must have knowledge of the characteristics which individualize the relationship between his profession and the community. He needs also a strong identification with the conscience rather than with the fears of the community. He must understand the fears, wherein they are realistic and wherein phobic, in order to deal with them appropriately. One educator notes that it is essential for the student to become aware that in terms of a highly developed social conscience the member of a profession, in a sense, becomes a member of a minority group. "This is because much of social conscience lies dormant, unconscious, potential, whereas the expressed conscious conscientious attitudes and motivations of the social worker often represent a minority."[6] Thus there is the necessity to understand that, while the community's conscience is a vital force to be awakened for use, the social worker's communications and activity may precipitate a threatening awareness which often is resisted, so that frequently the community conscience can be put to use only gradually. Through this understanding "the social worker may gain increased capacity to function, to maintain his perspective, to differ without personal hostility, to fight attitudes not people, and to live as a member of a minority group without developing feelings of frustration, defensiveness, or superiority."[6] For this he must also have a strong identification with the ideals and objectives of his profession as well as with the group which it serves. He must have an unwavering conviction as to the worth of the ends of his work but, withal, a critical attitude toward the profession's means to those ends.

Ambivalent conviction about social work is expressed in an almost infinite number of ways, of many of which the seasoned social worker is long and wearily aware but toward which he must have a nondespairing state of mind and heart. Community attitudes toward the group which the social work profession serves are often directed

6. Lyndell Scott in an unpublished communication to the author.

toward the profession itself. Our community feels both with and against us. Illness is socially acceptable. Sooner or later we all need medical care. The physician is highly respected, perhaps even idealized. In America we have an unwavering conviction about education and the individual's claim on society of a right to it. We are also convinced as to the individual's right to worship in his own way and to have the opportunity to do so under the religious leadership of his choice. The clergyman and teacher also are greatly respected. Perhaps it might be said that in some professions the student is under the stress of approximating the ideal which the community has of him. In social work the student must find within his profession his ideal of himself and must struggle not merely to attain it but to contend for the profession's ideals in a world which frequently contests them. He must prove not only his own worth as a professional person but his profession's worth as a profession.

A profession has a defined scope and function. It will have drawn on related fields of knowledge and skill. It will have, however, a content of knowledge and method peculiarly its own, to which other professions can contribute but for which they cannot substitute. It is a professional person's right and obligation to maintain that identity. The way is eased for him when he is a member of a profession which operates under a legally constituted authority, but, lacking this, it is all the more the professional person's responsibility to interpret his function and not to be party to misuse. Social work, by its youth and nature, has had a peculiar problem in being expected to be all things to all men. Consequently, it has served beneath and beyond its capacities. Social work education today is concerned to develop practitioners who will intelligently and responsibly define their field of practice.

The fifth objective of professional education is closely related to the preceding one. This final aim is concerned that students be oriented to the place of their profession in the society in which it operates. This implies a depth of understanding of democracy as a way of life. An eminent theologian has stated his concept of democracy in such a way as to constitute a creed in those professions concerned to educate, to heal, and to help the citizenry at large:

Democracy is first of all a faith in man, in his worth, his possibilities, his ultimate dependability. . . . Central for the democratic faith is the conviction as to the sacredness of human personality. Man is always to be treated as an end, never as property or tool as Kant pointed out and as the prophets and Jesus made plain long centuries before. Against all exploitations by class or vested privilege, against those social ends of slavery and the assumed inferiority of women and the defenselessness of childhood, against persistent feelings of race superiority, and of contempt for others, there stands this conviction of democracy, that property and government and church are here for man and not man for these institutions, that it is man as man that counts, not man as male, or white, or nordic, or rich, or wise, and that nothing less than the well being of all men can be the goal of social change.[7]

Students entering a profession by way of the American home, church, school, and college will not find a new rationale in this creed. There will be great variations, however, in the extent to which this philosophy has been experienced, integrated, and lived. Seldom has the student come to grips with the specific implications of this creed in relation to all classes and conditions of men. Certainly, he has not experienced its implications in a professional helping process. The elements of freedom and obligation as they bear upon the recipient of services, the agency, the taxpayer, the community, the profession; the extent of the individual's right to self-determination; the question of professional authority—all these and many other elements can become very troublesome to the individual who has been well blanketed in a diffuse faith in democracy. His free-floating and unanchored philosophy must now be broken down into professional beliefs and principles of conduct and be formulated for specific use.

It is clear that the educable student in a profession will be one who not only has marked intellectual ability but also has potentials for the development of a certain mark of mind and heart, the characteristics and qualities of which have been both stated and implied. The Promethean tasks of teaching, healing, and helping man in society in ways which contribute to his development as a social being entail a learning experience in which the integrative task will be heavy because of the demands for change in the learner. It is the responsibility of a professional school to select students with capacity for remotivation and reintegration of the personality as they experience learning of this nature. Considerable experimentation is

7. Harris Franklin Rall, *Social Change—Religion and Public Affairs* (New York: Macmillan Co., 1937), p. 217.

being undertaken in an effort to determine individual potentialities for professional development beyond aptitude for the mastery of specific knowledge and skills needed in particular professions.

It is the responsibility of a professional school to determine the kinds of learning, both in content and in method, which will develop the student's potentialities for the fulfilment of its educational aims. There is widespread concern in professional education with the fundamental dichotomy—the biologic versus the social—the unification of which may well be a means to the attainment of the aims of professional education. This introduces the problem of determining what knowledge and what educational process will effect essential personality change in the learner. It has been noted by professional educators that the data of the natural sciences are more readily submitted to scientific discipline than are social data. Many students can think clearly, use evidence carefully, and not conclude impulsively or distort findings when dealing with biological data. There is greater complexity in the systematic study of the interaction of man with his human environment and of the individual personality and social trends resulting from this interaction than is involved in the study of the physical world, of man as an isolate, or of his parts per se. There is greater complexity in learning to conduct a differential helping process oriented to psychological understanding and social insight than in learning skills for the manipulation of the human organism and its physical environment. A basic factor in the complexity of the science of human relations, clearly, is that the learner brings to the consideration of social-psychological problems a greater degree of emotionally determined thinking. As has been said, social work educators have noted that all students bring some unsocial, prejudiced thinking to a professional school. The decisive point is not whether they have appropriate feelings and attitudes but whether they have capacity for change. Are their prejudices rigid defenses serving some deep personality need? If so, socially and psychologically oriented professional education may lead to their intensification and often to their concealment. A recent study entitled *Anti-Semitism and Emotional Disorder* shows the pathology of anti-Semitism.[8] The findings are confirmed by impressions among social work educa-

8. Nathan W. Ackerman and Marie Jahoda, *Anti-Semitism and Emotional Disorder* (New York: Harper & Bros., 1950), Foreword by Carl Binger, M.D.

tors who have noted that such prejudices, common in students on admission, ordinarily give way as the student with aptitude and motivation to learn experiences new intellectual orientation in the context of a relationship with unprejudiced professional mentors. When these prejudices are retained, one often finds other evidences of irrational need and personality distortion which the attitudes are fulfilling and expressing. Not all people with marked intellectual abilities will be socially educable.

An impetus to the formulation of reliable criteria of educability for this learning will occur as students are offered curriculums in which objectives that are realistic in the light of the psychology of learning have been oriented to the changes desired. At all levels of education there is need for research into the learning process in order that educational systems may contribute to personality development and, in doing so, test more reliably the individual's capacity for growth.

In a maturing democracy the concept of individualism gives way to the concept of interdependence. A fully co-ordinated relationship among social institutions is essential for the attainment of democracy's aim—the welfare of the individual. Intergroup communication and collaboration for the solution of human welfare problems has become more than an abstraction in the current scene. As a profession matures in a maturing democracy, "its principles and processes must be viewed in a widening and deepening context."[9] This implies that its members see its function in relation to that of other professions and work beyond its own confines, collaborating wholeheartedly but not diffusely for the welfare of mankind rather than for the selfish interests of its own group.[10] A profession, like an individual, has come of age when it has developed capacity for interdependent relationships, notable qualities of which are readiness to give and take without anxiety and without need to dominate or to suffer loss of identity. This growth is difficult to attain. A profession's traditions, its rationale, its ethical system, its body of knowledge, its vocabulary, its special function, tend to make it a culture within a culture. It has been said that professional education as a re-educational process has to fulfil a task which is essentially equivalent to a change in culture, a means to which is the establishment of a strong

9. Tyler, *op. cit.*   10. *Ibid.*

"we feeling."[11] This important support in professional learning may produce the social problem of inbredness. By reason of its proclivity for solidarity, the profession must guard against becoming cut off from the community as a whole and from other professions concerned with the common good. When inbredness obtains, a profession may be threatened by external developments that demand change in its attitudes, working relationships, and responsibilities. In such instances it may fail to serve effectively through defending itself against social change. When this occurs in any group, the resultant isolation may breed inner tensions, which may be expressed in hostile attacks upon outsiders rather than enacted and solved within the group. The members of a group wherein "belongingness" is highly valued may not dare to threaten their status and security through disturbing its equilibrium.[12]

Applying this observation to a profession, it would seem that when this happens, change from within a profession would be slow to occur because tensions would be handled through projection outward. Resistance to and aggression against those professions receptive to social change and engaged in effecting it might occur as an expression of frustration and fear. Furthermore, it is conceivable that the frustrations, fears, and hostilities of the group as a whole might be vested in its official leadership, its members letting their leaders act in ways which they decry individually but against which they take no concerted action. Social work has not yet had to safeguard itself against the inbredness of the older sacrosanct professions. Instead, in its search for security it has had the problem of promiscuity. In achieving the aim of professional education that students develop social consciousness, a sense of the place of their profession in society, these two obstructing problems will be solved in so far as students experience multidiscipline programs in which each profession has respect for the individuality of the other. They will be decreased when the educational methods in the several disciplines give attention to the emotional growth of the learner as

11. See paper on "Conduct, Knowledge, and Acceptance of New Values" (1945), in Kurt Lewin, *Resolving Social Conflicts: Selected Papers on Group Dynamics* (New York: Harper & Bros., 1948).

12. Thomas M. French, M.D., "Psychodynamic Analysis of Ethical and Political Orientations," *American Journal of Economics and Sociology*, XII, No. 1 (October, 1952).

well as to his acquisition of knowledge and skill. The resultant concern for the recipient of the professional service will surpass self-concern, so that collaboration in the full sense of the word may replace the competitive struggle which is not favorable to the fulfilment of a profession's aims in society.[13]

In this chapter the responsibilities and characteristics of a profession have been stated and the resultant common educational objectives specified. Some of the peculiarities of social work significant for its educational process have been indicated. There is growing recognition among educators that, within a professional school, the individual and collective teaching, helping, and administering relationship with the student is the core of his preparation for professional relationship. We are becoming aware that this relationship, in the context of which knowledge and skills are conveyed, determines in large measure the learner's capacity to work purposefully with people in ways appropriate to the profession, whether in the helping relationship between practitioner and recipient, in collaborative work with colleagues, or in his relationship with subordinates and persons in authority within his own profession's hierarchy. In the report of the proceedings of the Interprofession's Conference on Education for Professional Responsibility the physician-patient relationship is described as having its own peculiar demands. Law schools are held responsible not only to help students gain knowledge and skill in basic legal processes but also to implant the peculiar characteristics of the lawyer-client relationship.[14] In social work we long have been conscious of the relationship between our educational process and the development of the learner as a professional person.[15] For the attainment of the change implied in the objectives

13. Charlotte Towle, "Discussion of 'The Significance for Social Workers of the Multidiscipline Approach to Child Development,' by Peter B. Neubauer, M.D., and Joseph Steinert," *Social Service Review*, XXIV (December, 1950), 466–68.

14. *Education for Professional Responsibility: Report of the Proceedings of the Interprofession's Conference on Education for Professional Responsibility* (Pittsburgh: Carnegie Press, 1948), papers by Dr. John Romano and S. J. Fuller.

15. Among many articles, two recent statements on social work education show agreement on this principle, even though the authors, both educators, differ in some of their means to effect growth in the professional learner. See Jessie Taft, "A Conception of the Growth Process Underlying Social Casework Practice," *Social Casework*, October, 1950 (also in *Social Work in the Current*

of professional education it is clear that the individual's potentiality for growth is a decisive factor. In order that educational systems may facilitate, rather than obstruct, learning, it is important to consider the integrative process in the adult learner. We turn, therefore, to a consideration both of basic principles of learning and of personality development and organization, for evaluation of their relationship to the integrative capacity of the individual engaged in professional learning.

Scene: Selected Papers, National Conference of Social Work [New York: Columbia University Press, 1950], and in Cora Kasius [ed.], *Principles and Techniques in Social Casework: Selected Articles, 1940–50* [New York: Family Service Association of America, 1950]); and Charlotte Towle, "The Contribution of Education for Social Casework to Practice," *Social Casework*, October, 1950.

CHAPTER 2

Basic Learning Principles

THE POINT OF VIEW OF SOCIAL WORKERS AS EDUCATORS AND SOME
PROBLEMS IN UNDERSTANDING THE HUMAN LEARNER

As social work practitioners have turned from helping individuals
learn to get along better in their life-situations to social work education, in which they are endeavoring to help students learn to help
people live more productively, they have not been grounded in
educational psychology as a foundation science. The effect that systematic attempts to use basic knowledge of learning formulated by
educational psychologists might have had on social work's educational practices is unknown. Instead, social workers have relied
heavily on the foundation sciences of their practice for understanding the learning process in social work. They have attempted to
understand learning in the light of their understanding of human
needs and strivings, in terms of their knowledge of growth and
development, in relation to their knowledge of environmental factors and forces. The literature on social work education records
noteworthy efforts to translate professional knowledge, understanding, and skill into educational practice.[1] If social work educators

1. Among many other writings note the following:
Marion E. Kenworthy, *Mental Hygiene in Social Work* (New York: Common-
wealth Fund, 1929), pp. 184–263.
Bertha C. Reynolds, *Learning and Teaching in the Practice of Social Work* (New
York: Farrar & Rinehart, 1942).
Virginia P. Robinson, *A Changing Psychology in Social Case Work* (Chapel Hill:
University of North Carolina Press, 1930); *Supervision in Social Case Work*
(Chapel Hill: University of North Carolina Press, 1936); *The Dynamics of
Supervision under Functional Controls* (Philadelphia: University of Pennsyl-
vania Press, 1949).
Sarah H. Swift, *Training in Psychiatric Social Work* (New York: Commonwealth
Fund, 1934).
Jessie Taft, "A Conception of the Growth Process Underlying Social Case Work
Practice," *Social Casework*, October, 1950; also in *Social Work in the Current
Scene: Selected Papers, National Conference of Social Work* (New York: Co-
lumbia University Press, 1950); also in *Principles and Techniques in Social*

23

were to formulate a theory of learning, they would not be grouped with those educational psychologists who make of learning "the mark of mind." Instead, they would fall with those who scarcely distinguish between a theory of learning and a theory of behavior.[2]

If professional learning is defined as "the process by which an activity originates or is changed through training procedures (whether in the classroom laboratory or in the natural environment) as distinguished from changes by factors not attributable to training,"[3] social work educators have a problem in studying the effects of the educational process. The changes they are concerned to effect may be brought about in part through concomitant life-experiences. The practice of social work is inextricably related to the life-experience of the learner, so that it is impossible to isolate the learning experience for study of its effects. There are manifestations of emotional growth in the student's performance sufficiently often to lead to the inference that professional education is a means to maturation. Repeatedly, educators note specific educational experiences in relation to specific life-events which have cumulative effect either through their nature or because of their new significance in the light of professional learning. When the educational approach is oriented to knowledge and understanding of the meaning of specific learning problems and developmental difficulties, learning frequently makes progress. Furthermore, as educators have observed and attempted to analyze learning responses in relation to learning demands and educational practice, they have noted common problems in relation to specific subject matter, specific methods, and stages of learning. Out of such experience some understanding of the learning process has been gained. Practices in social work education have

Casework: Selected Articles, 1940–50, ed. Cora Kasius (New York: Family Service Association of America, 1950).

Charlotte Towle, *Common Human Needs* ("Public Assistance Reports," No. 8 [Washington, D.C.: Government Printing Office, 1945]), Part III, pp. 95–122; *Emotional Elements in Professional Learning,* in pamphlet entitled *Professional Education* (New York: American Association of Schools of Social Work, 1948); "The Contribution of Education for Social Casework to Practice," *Social Casework,* October, 1950; also in *Principles and Techniques in Social Casework: Selected Papers, 1940–50,* ed. Cora Kasius (New York: Family Service Association of America, 1950).

2. Ernest R. Hilgard, *Theories of Learning* (New York: Appleton-Century-Crofts, Inc., 1948), p. 3.

3. *Ibid.,* p. 4.

been and are continuously being fashioned empirically through the particular orientation which educators bring to them and by results in terms of the student's performance. Even though social work educators, by the very nature of their orientation, have been alert to the connections between the factors and forces in the personal life-situation and the professional situation, the import of the education-al process is frequently obscured.

It is evident that to understand the learning process of adult learn-ers in a profession, we must study their responses to the professional education situation. Professional education must do its own research. The findings of social work educators at present are equivalent to those of the experienced clinician, unsupported by research.

Educational psychologists have long been concerned with affec-tive factors in learning.[4] The emotions brought to the learning experi-ence and the emotions produced by it, the "tension systems" which facilitate and obstruct cognitive capacity, are a central concern in social work education. Many experiments over a period of time have been conducted by educational psychologists. These experiments, whether with animal or with man, have involved relatively simple and artificial stimulus-response situations. Of the results of these experiments, Prescott states:

Very little can now be stated with assurance regarding the influence of different intensities of emotional involvement upon such mental proc-esses as reasoning, creative imagination, and the crystallization of attitudes and value concepts. This is a difficult area in which to undertake research because genuine emotions arise only when the interaction of the subject and the functional situation really justify them. To arrange situations in which the depth of emotional behavior can be controlled and in which the higher mental processes can be measured accurately at the same time is a staggering task for the experimental psychologist. Perhaps the science should be more ready than it is at present to accept the evidence of case history material in this area. At any rate, the need for more in-formation and for tentative hypotheses is quite pressing in the educa-tional world.[5]

Perhaps more will be learned about learning when it is accepted that we cannot know all there is to know about it because of its great complexity. Then, increasingly, there will be attempts to study learners at all educational levels in their natural environments as

4. *Ibid.*; Daniel A. Prescott, *Emotions and the Educative Process* (Washing-ton, D.C.: American Council on Education, 1938).
5. Prescott, *op. cit.*, p. 284.

they are engaged in the process. An inevitable limitation will be the fact that the situation cannot be isolated from the life-situation, even in academic subjects like arithmetic and reading, as psychiatry has shown. Hence there are limits to the controls that can be set in the research situation. We have the problem of studying change in a dynamic situation. As educational psychologists increasingly study learning under these conditions, it is to be expected that psychiatry and psychology will come more closely together, to provide an enriched foundation science for the use of educators at all levels. A trend in this direction is discernible.[6] This will involve conscious use of certain knowledge and insights and continuous appraisal of the rationale selected as it is tested through the learner's response to educational measures selected and shaped by the rationale. It will involve taking account of concomitant life-experiences which may promote and obstruct growth and influence learning. The complexity presented calls for a variety of evidence in the form of case-history material which records the student's development in terms of his evolving responses to the various aspects of the total educational regime, as well as psychological tests and educational measurements. On this Hilgard comments to the effect that, granted the contribution that rat psychology has made to our knowledge of learning, the recognition that cultural influences are significant means that a psychology limited to animals below man will always fall short.

As stated earlier, social workers lack grounding in educational psychology. They bring a focus on dynamics of behavior, derived largely

6. Hilgard, *op. cit.* Reference is made to the contribution of those educational psychologists who have incorporated Freudian insights into their study of human learners, notably E. C. Tolman and Kurt Lewin. See also Thomas M. French, M.D., *The Integration of Behavior,* Vol. I: *Basic Postulates* (Chicago: University of Chicago Press, 1952). Since this chapter was written, Dr. French, psychoanalytic psychiatrist, states that he has been influenced not only by his collaboration with Dr. Franz Alexander, but also by Dr. Kurt Lewin, Ivan Pavlov, Wolfgang Kohler, and E. C. Tolman, experimental psychologists. This work gives promise of making a basic contribution to education at all levels. For psychoanalytically oriented social work educators who have long been concerned with the integrative task in relation to the integrative capacity of the learner, this work affirms their insights and may well clarify, extend, and deepen them. Also for an attempt to create a psychological base for a general science of behavior through the union of the three traditions, psychoanalysis, experimental psychology, and the social sciences (cultural anthropology), see John Dollard and Neale E. Miller, *Personality and Psychotherapy* (New York: McGraw-Hill Book Co., Inc., 1950).

from Freud and his followers, and an eye to cultural influences, derived from several sources, including their own experience in the study of environment and social stress. This chapter attempts to distil some major assumptions as to human needs and wishes which motivate learning, explain the learner's responses, and illuminate the learning process. These concepts have shaped some of our educational practices, which, however, will be only fragmentarily indicated in this chapter.

LEARNING AS GROWTH PROCESS IN WHICH CHANGE INDUCES
ANXIETY FOR SURVIVAL: CONCEPTS OF GROWTH AND
REGRESSION IN RELATION TO ANXIETY

The organism's basic motive is the impulse to survive. Learning is the organism's means to survival, and hence is an enduring propensity. Learning aims at the gratification of need with the least expenditure of effort. To understand learning, therefore, it must be regarded as an organic process through which the organism strives to remain intact, to preserve itself as a whole.[7] A sense of comfort, of safety, is derived as this aim is attained. There is considerable at stake emotionally in the organism's struggle for intactness; hence anxiety would seem to be implicit in learning and even a motivating factor in the search for gratification of need. How much more often one hears the expression "anxious to learn" than "eager to learn." The educator has been aware of anxiety as an obstructing force, doubtless because when it operates effectively to motivate learning, it does not meet the eye. In such cases the educator is not presented with a problem to solve. And so the recorded concern of social work educators has largely been with that anxiety which interferes with the student's readiness to learn and with the integration of learning. He has been engrossed in devising educational measures to ease anxiety and to cultivate interest and eagerness through instilling hope. If anxiety serves as a motivating force, it might seem the more of it, the better. If this were so, the educator's task would be simple, for anxiety can be provoked with the greatest of ease. But the human organism is not simple, and certain complexities significant for education follow.

7. Franz Alexander, M.D., *Fundamentals of Psychoanalysis* (New York: W. W. Norton & Co., 1948), pp. 33–56.

If the organism survives, it must change. Growth brings change in the organism itself. Furthermore, the complex environment in which the human develops exerts different demands at different age levels and is always changing from generation to generation. Individual growth and social change require continuous learning. Learning is the process whereby the organism continually adapts to the changing self and to the changing environment and strives for mastery of both. The factor of change from within and from without threatens the survival of the organism as a whole. It feels not quite itself, particularly if change is enforced at a rapid tempo. Hence change causes discomfort and more anxiety until the organism has incorporated it through finding it useful. As this occurs, change becomes gratifying. Through it, one attains an enlargement of self, a sense of growth, unless the change involves regression. While growth occurs through change, not all change implies growth. Change may induce regression rather than development, a going backward, which, when transitory, is sometimes essential for integration and for subsequent growth. The educators' observations that plateaus and slumps in learning may be followed by marked acceleration are significant in this connection. In an educational process it is essential that regression as a phenomenon of pathology be differentiated from regression as a defense mechanism, operating against disintegration and as a means to integration. Profound regression occurs when the defenses are not working, and learning, not being reversible, is interrupted.

As the individual gradually proceeds from infancy and early childhood to adulthood, his progress, theoretically, would be smooth and uninterrupted by phases of regression, if the demands of his external world were always appropriately timed to his physical, intellectual, and psychological readiness to master the changed situation. Since throughout the course of life the individual's experiences are not so timed, fragmentary and temporary regressions are usual. If graphically described, the growth process from infancy to maturity would show marked movement forward, with slight movement backward from time to time. Except in profound regression involving the total personality, this fluctuating movement would be unevenly distributed at any one time, so that a graph would show progression in some areas and regression in other areas. When life becomes too difficult in presenting stresses which cannot be mastered or changed, the incorporation of which threatens the intactness of the personality, there is a tendency to return to earlier satisfactory life-periods. Hence each period in which an individual has had a comfortable adjustment can serve as a phase to which he may return later in life. Old behavior responses are repeated in an attempt to re-create the conditions of life in which intact survival was assured, even though the conditions may not have been favorable to growth. In the return to the past, the old may be experienced anew, so that it may serve as a solace, as an opportunity to meet need formerly unmet, or to resolve conflicts which have inhibited growth. The past way of responding, however, may become a gratifying solution and serve to obstruct growth. If obstacles continue to prevent forward movement, these past developmental phases at which the individual's responses are "frozen" may serve as a point of fixation. It is to be remembered, however, that, except in outright mental illness, regression is never complete, for it is met by the contrary growth urge. Hence regression normally produces discomfort, which motivates a struggle against it. This leads to anxiety in learning and makes it more difficult. The varied import of reaction formation against regression in professional learning will emerge later. The decisive point is that discomfort in regression often reinforces the propensity to learn in the interests of comfortable survival.

CONCEPT OF SELF OUT OF PAST EXPERIENCE
IN RELATION TO ANXIETY

Whatever the "ups and downs" of learning have been, as repeated mastery of a changing self and a changing environment has occurred, it is conceivable that, as the individual matures, anxiety in learning lessens, because out of past experience he develops an inner security, a foreknowledge, a feeling in his very bones, an expectancy that his efforts to learn will sooner or later bring order out of chaos and gratification. The decisive point for the educator is that activity in learning may ease the anxiety experienced in the process of change. When the individual's striving for mastery has repeatedly been successful, it can become relatively comfortable, habitual, and the learning process gratifying in itself, prior to the attainment of its aims. In such instances one senses interest and eagerness born of realistic hope. These learners have the wherewithal to cope with failure through flexible experimentation, by means of which they attempt new solutions. If in professional education such learning responses are few and far between, it is a commentary on many factors, several of which will emerge as this discussion proceeds.

With reference to the struggle for survival, a decisive point is that the human being from early years is not content merely to adapt himself to his life-situation. He strives for some mastery of it, in order that it may serve his purposes. The adult in civilized society is concerned not merely with the struggle for physical survival. He is absorbed in attaining certain conditions, those conditions which make survival satisfying, in terms of his needs, wishes, and concept of himself among men. Nor is he content to submit himself to the domination of circumstances or of others. He early strives for self-dependence in order to feel safe. In the last analysis, there is no real security, no deep assurance of survival, in being wholly dependent on others. One is forever uncertain if one's security rests largely outside one's self. This is the very essence of failure to preserve one's self as a whole.

Of great import in professional education is the fact that the young adult's strivings are not just bread-and-butter strivings. The educable adult in competition with his peers will not be content with marginal learning which assures him bare survival in his professional group. He will need and want to strive for mastery of skills which make it possible for him not only to carry responsibility in lives other than his own but also to contribute to his profession through leadership. His professional choice involves his concept of himself as an adequate adult, a concept which will be a composite of his needs, wishes, and strivings. His basic aims will bear the imprint of deeply influential relationships. Thus this endeavor may represent a culmination of all that he has been growing toward, at an age when he has not yet found a firm footing in the adult world. There is much at stake emotionally in survival on satisfying terms with one's self. Thus in professional learning one may expect a compelling need to attain standards of near perfection, marked anxiety, and heightened strivings. Deep frustration may occur through failure in the sense of moderate shortcomings. The resultant rage may give a cast of hostile aggression to the normal strivings. Anxiety as to what the learning will do to one, the fear of being mastered by that which one aims to master, is more prone to occur when one's shortcomings or failures repeat earlier ones or when resentment is aroused in the learning process. When hostility accompanies aggression, the unconscious fear of reprisal will have deeper import with some students than with others, an important educational differential to which we shall return. Social work educators have observed many instances in which marked aggression and hostility subside as the student becomes secure, as he gains competence, and as he sees his production in relation to developmental norms through realistic evaluation which makes conscious the learning process in which he is engaged.

There is general agreement among students of behavior, who have studied learning through various theoretical systems, that the organism has certain basic tendencies through which it adapts and assures itself an intact and relatively comfortable survival. These tendencies are regarded as the dynamic basis of learning and become learning principles. The first of these, the psychological counterpart of the physiological principle of homeostasis, has been termed the *principle of stability*.[8] Organic growth consists of a continuous cycle of supply and output of nutritive substance and of energy. There is, therefore, a continuous process of "giving off" and "taking in" which involves continuous disintegration and reintegration. The organism in a state of equilibrium is threatened with imbalance as it takes in something new and gives off the old. Alexander states: "In the higher animals the primary function of the cerebro-spinal and automatic nervous system is to maintain this dynamic equilibrium, which is upset both by external stimuli and by the process of living itself." He states further that disturbances of equilibrium appear psychologically in the form of "needs and wishes which seek gratification and serve as the motive of voluntary behavior. A basic tendency of the organism is to keep these psychological tensions at a constant level." Resistance to change, manifested in the human in many forms, represents the individual's defense against more change than he can survive, which

8. See *ibid.*, p. 35, and Walter B. Cannon, M.D., *The Wisdom of the Body* (New York: W. W. Norton & Co., 1932). Many social workers were first introduced to this principle through William A. White, *The Meaning of Disease* (Baltimore: Williams & Wilkins Co., 1926).

implies more change than he can incorporate with sufficient comfort to continue to function in accordance with his feeling or concept of adequacy.

In professional education a heavy demand for change is occurring both from within the student and from the reality pressures of the situation. The very strength of his wish to change to meet the valued demands may beget strong fears. This will occur as he and the situation, both at times, are pushing him faster than he can integrate the total experience. More new knowledge than he can immediately use under the necessity to understand and to help people whose experience is beyond his experience makes him feel helpless and confused. This both invokes fears and lowers his hope of attaining his goal. Also because throughout life his deepest wishes often have not been granted, also because often his wishes have been tabooed, it is a common human tendency to anticipate their denial as a defense against disappointment; and thus the anticipation of failure which has accompanied his hope is confirmed. The more emotional investment at stake, the greater the anxiety there may be about change, and the greater the ambivalence, as evidenced in uneven movement.

An individual, for example, may go so far as to "accept" new thinking but retreat from the use of it. He dares to think anew before he can act anew. Since the proof of growth in professional learning lies in its use, he resists the change demanded. It is as if his total being reassures itself: "Until I do differently, I am not different. I am still as I was." Until his change in feeling has caught up with his change in thinking, he cannot integrate the new intellectual content for use. Practice demands that he act anew; hence resistance to change may show up in field work when it is not discernible in the classroom.

KNOWLEDGE IN RELATION TO ANXIETY

When in the light of the principle of stability social work educators first saw anxiety as implicit in the individual's struggle for equilibrium in an educational experience, in which change was being enforced at a rapid tempo, they tended to center upon the threat of change as the major, if not the sole, factor operating against integration of learning. In some quarters this led to protective educational practices, shaped by fear of imparting knowledge freely and of traveling at too fast a tempo in teaching. Gradually, it has become clear that some of the initial anxiety in social work learning stems from not knowing rather than from the threat of change implied in learning. The learner, confronted at once with professional responsibility, needs and wants the wherewithal with which to be competent. He frequently is realistically helpless, confused, and fearful out of the lack of the know-what, know-how, and know-why for the attainment of his aims. At such moments he feels hopeless. Hence the educational task has become one of balancing giving and demanding, taking care not to give too much at once in too great detail. This entails giving first things first, with a realistic expectancy that they be mastered. It also implies helping the learner put them to use and holding him accountable for doing so. Beyond the learner's motivation, that inner pressure of need and wish to learn, intellectual grasp is a first step in learning. The feelings of hope evolved by new knowledge may quickly bring depth of comprehension and integration. They may, on the other hand, interfere with its assimilation for use, until the learner reconciles, or resolves, conflicts in feeling produced by new ideas or conflicting ideologies.

THE PRINCIPLE OF ECONOMY OR INERTIA IN RELATION
TO CONSCIOUS AND UNCONSCIOUS MIND

The second principle of learning widely recognized and agreed upon as of great importance is the principle of economy or inertia. Alexander states:

Every organism is born with automatic functions, the unconditioned reflexes which are useful for maintaining those constant conditions within the organism which are necessary for life. All internal vegetative functions . . . are examples of useful automatic mechanisms. They do not require conscious effort and with the exception of certain alimentary and excretory functions, belong to the hereditary equipment of the organism. Other functions, most of which regulate the relation of the organism to its environment, must be learned through conscious trial and error and repetition.

Alexander states further that behavior patterns which prove adequate in maintaining biological and psychological stability, that is, which reduce tensions experienced as needs and wishes by gratifying them, are repeated until they become automatic and are performed unconsciously with a minimum of effort. This whole process is called "learning." It consists of two phases: conscious attention, in which there is (1) groping experimentation through trial and error, and (2) repetition of the adequate behavior patterns which have been found useful by trial and error. Through repetition, useful behavior patterns become automatic and effortless, in that they are performed unconsciously or practically so.[9]

The reciprocal and cumulative relationship of conscious and unconscious forces in learning makes clear the importance of both for the more than marginal survival essential in professional learning. Through conscious intelligence, though a late acquisition from the evolutionary standpoint, man has created more complex conditions than automatic responses can take care of. Hence conscious intelligence comes in whenever automatic responses to familiar stimuli are not sufficient, that is, when there are new elements to master or to escape. It is needed for new experiences which require experimentation or new solutions, that is, creative activity. Professional education as a process through which the learner develops resourcefulness for the demands of professional life implies the need for reliance on energy-saving automatic behavior, so that he may be free to engage in new and creative activity which requires groping experimentation. The extent of the latter is so great that conscious intelligence continuously must perceive the new with readiness to take over from the less energy-consuming automatic system.

"Furthermore, conscious intelligence unhampered by anxiety both enriches and is enriched by the automatic system."[10] In illustration of this, Dr. Babcock comments that a social worker responding to a client's reaction may feel its import before he knows it in his head. Knowledge makes him free to use his intuition, whereas, without it, he may be fearful and uncertain. "I felt, but I did not know" is a frequent comment of the novice in explanation of failure to act on intuition. Imaginative projection of one's own consciousness onto another being, as when a social worker reflects the client's action, stems from unconscious cues, experienced automatically and then intellectually as one is stimulated to master the problem intellectually.

The line of least resistance is not the professional person's lot. He always must avoid the easy assumption that situations repeat them-

9. Alexander, *op. cit.*, pp. 36–37.
10. Dr. Charlotte G. Babcock in an unpublished communication to the author.

selves and the pitfall of stereotyped use of knowledge and skills. He must be aware that there is always something new to be learned and be ready to undergo unlearning and relearning. For the student it has become clear that professional learning brings so much that is new so fast that sufficient repetition often has not been possible for the new ways of feeling, thinking, and doing to have become ingrained as part of himself during the training period. On the other hand, it has been noted that considerable learning in social work has old elements in it. Knowing people intimately, helping people in trouble, serving as a confidante, establishing and sustaining a working relationship of a sort, being instructed, even having one's behavior or production closely surveyed and being held accountable, are not entirely new experiences to the adult entering a professional school. There is much he can carry over for use, but sometimes these old adaptive responses and learnings become problematic. This probably is in part because at any particular time a great deal of what we have learned is not conscious. Some of it may never have been conscious, or, once consciously mastered and deeply incorporated through use, it may have become automatic, so that the individual has become unconscious of his adaptive responses and learnings. He often mistakenly assigns past consciously mastered learnings to intuition.

In the initial stages of social work education, for example, students frequently comment variously to the effect that they have lost their intuitive knack in helping people or their intuitive hunches in understanding them. All that we have learned is capable of becoming conscious. When the social work learner becomes aware that his former "understanding" of people, through being composed in part of inherited assumptions which he has taken for granted, had many elements of misunderstanding in it; when he becomes aware also that his former ways of working with people are not so appropriate in the context of his professional function as they were felt to be in his personal relationships and are, therefore, subject to some modification, he may experience a sense of loss of adequacy. Unfortunately, he may depreciate not only specific knowledge but also the experiences which he has had. When this occurs, he fails to see the usefulness of past learning in the present, where it could contribute to his understanding.

Dr. Babcock has observed that this increment in learning is depreciated by teachers who fail to relate the new to the old. For example, in teaching the nature of the helping relationship in social casework, the teacher could well help students identify not only wherein it is different from helping relationships of their personal social lives but also wherein old ways of doing which do not carry over here were appropriate elsewhere. She attributes the tendency to "do social work" on and off the job to this nullification of the appropriateness of the student's conduct of other relationships.[11]

The student who has had social work experience as an untrained worker has the added problem of sense of loss of professional understanding and skill. His high hope of having less to learn than other students crashes aground as he must unlearn and relearn much that he took for granted as useful accomplishment. In fact, while he has some advantages over inexperienced students, the latter in some respects have a less difficult task as learning becomes a conscious process. It is particularly in relation to old adaptations that the conscious attention demanded in the educational situation often seems to hinder rather than to help the learning process. Of this Miss Reynolds states: "Such a complaint is not made when the activity is overwhelmingly new and no automatic functioning is thought possible." She explains that when the learning has much recall of the old in it, the learner may stop at partial mastery and fall back on the old when he can "make do" with it. This is due in part to discomfort in his greater proneness to focus on himself rather than on the new learning. The greater consciousness of self is engendered in part by a sense of loss of something in himself. He may struggle to regain the old competence and thus not give himself freely and fully to the acquisition of the new.

All learning, however, engenders some self-consciousness, because the new is sensed as dangerous until proved otherwise. When one is in danger, attention automatically is focused on the self with, as Miss Reynolds depicts, the concerns, "What will it do to me? Will this hurt me?" and with readiness to defend self through fight or flight. Miss Reynolds' delineation of some of the educational implications of each of five stages in the use of conscious attention related to the safety of the person as well as to the goal of mastery of the

11. Dr. Charlotte G. Babcock in an unpublished communication to the author.

experience is well known to social work educators. Many have been guided in their practices by the understanding imparted.[12]

Because often in social work education learning must be put to use immediately, when conscious attention and groping trial-and-error experimentation obtain, social work learning may involve a particularly troublesome stage of acute self-consciousness. Although this subsides as the individual loses and finds himself in his work, it must be regained in the form of sensitive awareness of self and sustained readiness to face his feelings, attitudes, and conduct for their import in specific professional services. The behavior pattern of responsibly looking to the self desirably should become automatic and effortless. That it ever becomes completely effortless is doubtful. Through repetition for mastery, this pattern may become relatively automatic by proving to be useful. Often insight will be painful, so that seeing one's self realistically in order to regulate emotional responses which distort one's thinking and doing will not always be possible. Sometimes the threat implied may interfere with habitual tendencies to self-inquiry or make the process useless, even though one goes through its motions. The responsible professional worker cannot permit himself the comfort of becoming deeply unconscious of self. He must always be consciously attentive to the import of his activity. The educable student in the course of his professional training will have shown capacity for the gradual attainment of considerable self-discipline. Through readiness to assume this responsibility without marked anxiety, he will have shown that he has accepted the concept that self-mastery can never be an accomplished feat but must be a lifelong endeavor, part and parcel of the work which he has undertaken.

With reference to the interrelatedness of the two principles of learning, Alexander points out that the principle of economy serves and supports the principle of stability: "The organism tends to perform the functions necessary for maintenance of constant conditions with minimum expenditure of energy." For equilibrium when more change is occurring than the organism can integrate, the principle

12. Reynolds, *op. cit.*, chap. vii, pp. 69–85. The five stages are: (1) acute consciousness of self, (2) sink or swim adaptation, (3) understanding the situation without power to control one's own activity in it, (4) relative mastery in which one can both understand and control one's own activity, and (5) learning to teach what one has mastered.

of inertia may impel it to cling to outworn automatic behavior or to revert to it when learning becomes difficult or threatening. Thus the normal individual's learning responses under stress may approximate the "repetition compulsion" of the psychoneurotic.[13] Fixations and regressions in social work learning are well-recognized manifestations. They cause great discomfort and anxiety responses which are at times difficult to differentiate from true neurotic anxiety. This difference shows up as they subside with time or in response to modifications in the educational program, in response to certain educational measures, or in response to assistance focused on helping the student recognize and understand his learning problem.

For sound conduct of the educational situation, it is important to differentiate a profound regression from the plateaus and slumps in learning which are essential for integration. These occur as the new situation, with its multiple demands for attention and psychic energy, brings a temporary reversion to automatic behavior or former ways of doing rather than new and appropriate responses. Regressive manifestations and the help implicit in the educational process will be elaborated in subsequent chapters. The incidence and the occasional persistence of stereotyped responses in social work learning constitute a commentary on many factors, some of which will be discussed later. In each instance the response is noteworthy as behavior to be understood individually in the context of such factors as, first, timing, that is, stage of learning as well as timing in relation to demands of the total educational situation and pressures in the individual's life-situation; second, duration and extent of the response with reference to the nature of the student's relationship with classroom and field instruction; third, with reference to the educational measures used to help him resume learning; and, finally, his response to these measures as well as his capacities shown throughout the several areas of his program.

SURPLUS ENERGY FOR PROGRESSION IN LEARNING
AND FOR CREATIVE ACTIVITY

A third principle highly significant in lifework learning is that of surplus energy. There is evidence in human behavior that, in contrast to the tendency toward economy of effort, adherence to auto-

13. Alexander, *op. cit.*, p. 38.

matic learning, and regression to earlier useful responses, there is also a strong and inevitable impulse toward progression. There is movement into new experience; giving of self to creative activity; giving of energy to work that serves a purpose beyond the "in order to survive" objective; giving of self in relationships which contribute to and gratify others, as well as serve the purpose of self-gratification. Just as the physical organism, when it reaches its limits of growth, tends to reproduce itself, so the human personality, in the process of maturing, begins to reach out beyond itself. Alexander considers the impulse to expand beyond the limits of self a very basic one. It is his impression that this occurs when "a point of saturation is reached." He comments:

> Sexuality proper is the expression of the surplus energy of the mature organism as a whole. As a container filled with water overflows so the mature organism cannot any longer add to its own completion, and the tendency toward personal growth gives place to reproduction, which is nothing but growth beyond the limits of the individual person.

He states further:

> Sexual desire and love and the desire to care for children are not the only indications of maturity. The creative tendencies of other sorts contributing to the interests of society at large are parallel expressions of this surplus energy. The whole range from totem poles to modern sculpture, music, and painting, as well as the discoveries of science, are products of this creative activity. Most economic activities are similarly motivated—though utilitarian factors cooperate—as can be seen in the peasant's attitude toward the soil or the artisan's toward his handicraft, or the industrialist toward his plant.[14]

The limitation of an educational process in which the integrative task continuously approximates and intermittently exceeds the individual's integrative capacity is the lack of surplus energy either for creativity or to invest in learning beyond a marginal level.[15]

Social work, by its very nature, needs workers who have considerable capacity to live beyond absorption in self and who are potentially creative. This potentiality the student is prone to bring to social work education in the measure that his physical, mental, and emotional needs have been met adequately during the early years of life

14. Franz Alexander, M.D., *Our Age of Unreason* (New York: J. B. Lippincott Co., 1942), p. 207.

15. This is discussed in chap. 4, and the educational implications are noted repeatedly throughout Part II.

and sometimes also when his strivings to compensate for lacks have brought nurturing relationships and opportunities. In the last analysis this capacity is contingent on hope and confidence out of past success in achievement and in relationships. The capacity is revealed in the educational process through a liking and concern for people as individuals, which holds when they, in the midst of disadvantageous circumstances, are often least likable. It is revealed in readiness, as knowledge and understanding is attained, to assume responsibility, to give understanding as well as services, to endure the denial and frustration of unresponsive or hostile clients—in short, to give both mind and heart to the learning experience.

Inability to live beyond absorption in self is shown in excessive need to be given to, a need which may have compelled the student to pursue work with people for purposes of self-gratification. Out of past failures and deprivation, these individuals are more wishful than hopeful. These students may need to be served by the people whom presumably they are there to serve, and they may use the client as an outlet for their hostile impulses or for their frustrated wishes. Sometimes, giving their minds but not their hearts to learning, they are peculiarly defensive about criticism. To grade high is to be loved, and to subject one's self to criticism is to incur punishment. The resultant hostility may inhibit creative activity and beget stereotyped learning responses. Or the stereotyped learning responses may relate to the individual's adherence to the old and resistance to the new which requires a new investment of energy, more giving of self.

FEELINGS, EMOTIONS, AND ATTITUDES AS FACTORS
IN THE OUTCOME OF LEARNING

The important part played in learning by the individual's affective life, his feelings, emotions, and emotional attitudes, has been both implied and stated throughout this discussion. The place of these factors as helping or hindering forces in relation to the principles of stability, of economy, and of surplus energy or progression have long concerned educators and, as stated previously, have been an area of experimental research.[16]

16. Hilgard, *op. cit.*, and Prescott, *op. cit.*

POSITIVE AND NEGATIVE FEELINGS AS FACTORS
IN THE MOTIVATION OF LEARNING

It is generally agreed that feelings are the indicators of how well the basic equilibrium of the organism is being maintained. They range from unpleasant to pleasant as the aims of behavior are blocked or attained. They vary with the quality and intensity of sensory stimulation; they grow out of organic conditions in the viscera; and they are influenced by value-concepts which relate to the situation. Hendrick states: "The most fundamental of Freud's laws of instinctual activity is that the psychological (and social) activities are determined by a constant need to reduce emotional tension. These tensions are the locomotive factor in human life, and the production of the tensions is the function of the instincts. They are consciously perceived as painful or disagreeable feelings; activity is initiated by the need to perform some specific function which will reduce this tension; and the fulfilment of this tension reducing function thereby evokes the experience of pleasure. Freud therefore termed this fundamental law of instinct the 'Pleasure Principle.'" Hendricks comments that this induction from psychoanalytic observation coincides with the conclusions of scientists in other fields, notably Cannon,[17] the physiologist, in his theory of "homeostasis." He states: "Their investigations have been in separate realms yet their final conclusions in regard to the fundamental processes of life are the same: the psychoanalyst, that psychological processes are initiated by the need to restore an emotional equilibrium which is experienced as pleasure; the physiologist, that all organic processes are initiated by the need to restore a physio-chemical equilibrium which is experienced as health."[18]

Thus need and desire produce disequilibrium. This makes itself felt in terms of tension. This discomfort sets in operation activity aimed toward something which will meet need and thus gratify, through easing the discomfort produced by the disequilibrium. Therefore, the question arises, How long will the activity gratify without the meeting of the need which motivated it? The question of whether gratification begins in the activity itself or not until the

17. Cannon, *op. cit.*
18. Ives Hendrick, M.D., *Facts and Theories of Psychoanalysis* (New York: A. A. Knopf, 1938; 2d ed. enl. and rev., 1948), pp. 92–93.

goal is attained, whether motivation in learning is related to performance or to acquisition, has not been agreed upon among educational psychologists.[19] From the Freudian standpoint this would seem to depend on the nature of the need and what is at stake for the individual in fulfilment. It would also depend upon his expectancy, as determined by the past experience of the individual in the attainment of aims; hence age and success become important factors. Children out of inexperience have less ability than mature adults to tolerate unmet need, to postpone gratification, and to sustain activity toward a remote objective. It would seem, therefore, that whether the learning process is pleasurable or fraught largely with anxiety would depend on whether, through circumstance, it is accompanied by feelings of hope or grave doubt as to outcome. In professional education it has been observed that twofold feelings tend to accompany the learning process, hope and doubts alternating in dominance as the reality is experienced.

THE NATURE AND INTENSITY OF EMOTIONS AS FACTORS IN THE OUTCOME OF LEARNING

Feelings give rise to emotion, as the aims of behavior are blocked or facilitated. Thus we may have fear, anger, hate, disgust, disappointment, grief, love, joy, surprise, yearning—emotions varying both in nature and in intensity. They vary in nature, in stemming from feelings of pleasure or pain. It has been stated that "all emotional phenomena are adjustive reactions of the body alternating to adapt the body economy as a whole to the demands of the situation. The adjustive reactions vary with the intensity of the emotion more significantly than they do from category to category of emotion."[20] The relationship between the nature of emotion, the intensity of emotion, and learning has long concerned educators. Prescott reports that the conclusion from a number of experiments designed to study affective factors was that "both pleasant and unpleasant affect at the level of mild emotion facilitates learning, while unpleasant affect at the more intense level of strong emotion may inhibit recall for the sake of protecting the personality." He observes further that "under a maximum intensity or undue prolongation of emotion a more or less complete

19. Hilgard, *op. cit.*, pp. 148–53.
20. Prescott, *op. cit.*

disorganization of physical and mental functions may occur."[21] Among the many experiments concerned to determine the relationship between content of educational experience Hilgard refers to Lewin's observations on his theory of valence that learning is motivated through attractiveness of goals. With reference to the use of repetition in relation to the emotional values of the activity, Hilgard observed:

> When tasks are graded as pleasant, unpleasant, or indifferent and then repeated excessively, the unpleasant tasks, as might be expected, are first satiated. But it is the pleasant tasks which next become impossible to repeat, and the indifferent tasks are consistently last. Because of less ego-involvement in the indifferent tasks, their endless repetition does not develop the resistance found for either pleasant or unpleasant activities. Psychological satiation is not to be confused with fatigue, even though fatigue symptoms are prominently present.[22]

In social work education it has been observed that students have small tolerance for certain kinds of repetition. For mastery of learning, a degree of precision must be introduced early. Repetition is implied, but stereotyped repetition is to be avoided. Perhaps because there are few indifferent tasks in professional education, perhaps because of the high degree of ego involvement in professional learning, and perhaps also because of the intellectual level of the learners, repetition without progression engenders resistance. The educator's task, therefore, is that of determining what bears repetition as well as that of sustaining movement in the process of repeating what must be deeply ingrained, a subject which will be considered in the subsequent discussion of progression in learning experiences.

Furthermore, in social work education we have been intensely aware that affect may interfere with learning or make it very difficult. The stress of learning has been attributed to the fact that social work engages the emotions deeply. We have not been sufficiently cognizant of emotional investment as an essential factor in learning, one which facilitates it. Learning which effects change in behavior, as professional learning must do, will not occur unless the individual is emotionally engaged in it. It would seem that we have not been sufficiently oriented to the significance of the degree of the emotion. We have stressed the nature of affect more than its degree. Thus we have

21. *Ibid.*, p. 172.
22. Hilgard, *op. cit.*, p. 224.

seen pleasant affect as a facilitating factor, without awareness of its potentials for inducing stress. We have seen negative affect as a deterrent, without due recognition of its potentials as a motivating force. These finer differentiations are essential for understanding learning responses and for planning and conducting learning experiences. They are also important so that the educator may appraise emotion for its usefulness in learning rather than react to it automatically as a deterrent.

The situations in which the many experiments on nature and intensity of emotion have been conducted are not comparable to the learning situation in professional education, in that they have been more simple and artificial and have not deeply engaged the total personality. The complexity of adult learning, as well as the emotional demand implicit in professional education, points up the need for research in studying the influence of gradations of emotion on professional learning. Important also is the appraisal of educational means to absorb and channel emotions for the integration of learning.

The social work educator has observed emotions in learning from the point of view that identical experiences will have different emotional values for different students. Certain subject matters will provoke intense emotion in one; mild emotion in another. Likewise, the variation obtains in relation to examinations, educational methods, and all aspects of the experience. Furthermore, it has seemed that, within certain limits, the decisive variable has been the individual's capacity to deal with emotion. It has been seen that when emotional pressures are heavy, the student may be so immersed in defending himself that he is not free to learn. The general impression is not only that there is no one threshold of affect but that there is great variation in capacity to cope with it and variation in ways of dealing with it, some of which are more obstructive in learning than others. Students who seemingly have given evidence of mild emotion have been productive learners, apparently because they brought feelings, emotions, and attitudes to social work which needed to undergo little change. Others with like response either showed little emotion because they did not learn or did not learn because they were involved insufficiently. They skimmed the surface, staying on the periphery, so well defended that they adapted superficially without changing.

Many students who have evidenced strong emotion have been most deeply engaged in learning, and, while the going has been rough, they have been productive learners in the long run. Other social workers with strong emotion and motivation characterized by deep personal need have experienced more fragmentation than integration in the learning process. Probably every school has known the student who experienced a disintegrating degree of emotion, resulting in physical and mental breakdown.

Since social work educators' orientation is in the ego psychology of Freud, which has imparted understanding of the purposes served by the defenses in adapting the body-mind economy as a whole to the demands of the situation, it is the social worker's opinion that the threshold of affect is determined by the stage of growth and personality organization of the student. In this connection the motivation is significant, and the nature and organization of the adaptive mechanisms and defenses are significant. Strong drives and deep personal needs often lead to more frustration, hostility, guilt, and anxiety than the student can integrate without developing defenses of an extent and nature which interfere with learning. In many students, including those whose motivation has seemingly been sound, social work educators have seen evidence of marked anxiety, particularly in the initial stage of learning. This has been so universal as to be regarded as normal. Often it has interrupted learning and presented a dubious outlook with sufficient frequency that educators have been led to question methods. What can be done to diminish this so-called "normal anxiety" in the interests of more comfortable and more productive learning is a common concern today. It is our attitude that the student's emotional response is something to be understood, when it is both interrupting and facilitating learning. His response must always be viewed in the context of the situation in which it is evidenced, with close reference to stage of learning, subject matter, instructor's activity and relationship to the learner, and also to the over-all demands of the educational situation at the time. With reference to the whole matter of emotions in professional learning, there is general agreement that social work educators have the problem of reducing anxiety for integration rather than stimulating it.

PROFESSIONAL EDUCATION AS AN ACCULTURATION PROCESS—SOME
MEANS FOR CHANGING ATTITUDES

A profession has an ideology, an ethic system, by which its members are inspired and governed. A student entering a profession has both the need and the wish for a set of values to give direction and limits to his striving. What I am to think and feel in order to act as I should is a prominent anxiety of a neophyte in a profession.

Without guiding attitudes, the individual is confused and baffled. Allport describes attitudes as "a precondition to behavior." Attitudes prepare the individual to make a satisfactory observation and pass a suitable judgment. They determine for each individual what he will see and hear, what he will think and do.[23] The attitudes which the student brings to professional learning have decisive importance from the standpoint both of their rigidity or flexibility and of the extent of change involved. Attitudes toward study, toward responsibility, toward dependence, toward authority, toward problem-solving, toward giving, toward taking, toward human behavior, toward certain social groupings, determined by race, religion, nationality, and class—all these and many others have a bearing on the educability of the student for social work. It is essential not only that students acquire new attitudes but that they also often relinquish or modify old ones. Allport refers to the view supported by experiment that "attitudes are specific momentary integrations."[24] This implies that they have been intellectually and emotionally accepted as useful and they may or may not be readily subject to change, depending on many factors to be presented later in the discussion of the integrative task.

The process through which attitudes are acquired is essentially the same throughout life. The child out of his limited experience learns largely through identification. Out of trust in parents or for security through their approval, he incorporates parental attitudes as preparation for the coming events of his life. This is repeated as the individual finds himself in new situations. The primary attitudes are modified as they prove useless, and so are successive ones. In the child's search for self-dependence, parental attitudes are often

23. Gordon W. Allport, "Attitudes," in *Handbook of Social Psychology*, ed. Carl Murchinson (Worcester, Mass.: Clark University Press, 1935).
24. Allport, *op. cit.*

reacted against through converse attitudes. Primary attitudes may be clung to as a defense when sudden and drastic change makes the integrative task too heavy. They are relinquished or disguised under social pressure. They give way to the new in the context of valued relationships, individual and group, as these replace old relationships. Thus it is seen that, throughout life, attitudes, normal and abnormal from the standpoint of society, are formed to meet need and to serve a purpose in the individual's struggle for satisfying and comfortable survival. For this, human relationships continue to be a necessity. Man's concept of himself among men is determined by the attitudes and responses of others to him. For security in the group, he identifies with its prevailing sentiments. The processes through which attitudes, favorable or unfavorable, are acquired are fundamentally alike. As the larger social group replaces the family and as the individual strives for a place in it, the attitudes of the group become the individual's reality, to which he adapts readily or with which he struggles to come to terms. This occurs as the individual moves from family life into the life of the community and as he moves from one culture to another. The Freudian concept of family life as the prototype of the individual's life in the larger social group has implied that, throughout life, the individual tends to search for some repetition of the family group, that is, belongingness to some configuration of individuals in which he will feel at home. He will experience change in primary attitudes and much difference from the original experience, in so far as he experiences corrective relationships which contribute to his growth.

In relation to this, Lewin holds that "the re-educative process has to fulfill a task which is essentially equivalent to a change in culture." Since the individual's attitudes have been formed through relationships within the family and other organized groups, one of the outstanding means to bring about acceptance in re-education is the establishment of what is called an "in-group" in which the individuals feel belongingness. The individual accepts the new system of values and beliefs out of his need for belongingness to a group.[25] Lewin states further that the re-educative process affects the indi-

25. Kurt Lewin, *Resolving Social Conflicts: Selected Papers on Group Dynamics* (New York: Harper & Bros., 1948), see paper on "Conduct of Knowledge and Acceptance of New Values" (1945), pp. 55–68.

vidual in three ways. It changes his cognitive structure, the way he sees the physical and social worlds, including all his facts, concepts, beliefs, and expectations. It modifies his valences and values, which embrace both his attractions and aversions to groups and group standards, his feelings in regard to status differences, and his reactions to sources of approval or disapproval. And it affects motoric action, involving the degree of the individual's control over his physical and social movements.

The observations recorded in the literature on social work education confirm Lewin's concept that new intellectual orientation or even extensive firsthand experience does not automatically create correct concepts (knowledge); that social action that is professional doing is steered by perception of facts and values, which, if false, will not necessarily be rectified by correct knowledge; that changes in sentiments do not necessarily follow changes in cognitive structure (for example, new knowledge may not change an individual's feelings toward a minority group or toward unacceptable social behavior); that the individual's sentiments or feelings are determined not only by knowledge but also by the sentiments prevalent in the social atmosphere which surrounds him; that knowledge may produce tension through producing a bad conscience when the learner discerns that he should feel and think differently but cannot respond otherwise, and thus it may lead to defenses against change. These observations in social work education pertain to those instances where extensive and basic re-education is necessary. Often, however, the student entering a profession brings limited needs for re-education as well as strong motivation for it, in that he has voluntarily chosen to undergo this learning. Because of its importance, we repeat that new knowledge may therefore bring changes in feeling; in fact, new knowledge may ease anxiety, for often it is the lack of adequate knowledge for the task at hand which engenders realistic fear; firsthand experience may rectify erroneous concepts, particularly in the context of the group experience afforded in the professional school. A profession is an "in-group" as defined by Lewin, a group to which the new members are motivated to belong and where common knowledge, sentiments, attitudes, convictions, and practices prevail. The student in a very real sense enters a new culture in which he can put forth his roots through identification with mentors and colleagues, as they learn together. It is a social situation in which a strong "we feeling" can be created. As has been indicated, this means to the end of effecting re-education presents a problem. The problem is that the student may be patterned for inbredness in the long run of his professional life, unless he experiences in these formative years a sense of belonging to a group which highly values its relationship with other groups and which communicates and collaborates effectively with other disciplines and the community.

Social work educators have come to know attitudes as bits of integrated experience which may or may not serve as the foci for integration of new learning, depending on whether or not they are appropriate to the profession. We have seen them also as broad generalizations of specific meaningful experiences—generalizations which again may be sound or unsound. We have learned that they may have superficial or deep values for the learner. Sometimes they have been donned in the interests of a specific social adaptation and may be readily put aside if not needed in another social situation. When clung to, it is known that they are serving some purpose in the economy of the personality and for psychological equilibrium. Thus they often tell the educator something of the individual's motivation, his set of values, and the meaning of certain experiences to him. When discrepant, they may reveal areas of emotional conflict. Often they cannot be taken at face value, for they may be a defense. Their purpose may be to conceal rather than to reveal. One may find an attitude of courage in one who has many fears, an attitude of cheer in one who is depressed, or an attitude of submission to authority in one who is inwardly rebellious. When inappropriate attitudes not useful in the profession are adhered to, they are something to be understood. As with emotional responses which have not crystallized into an attitude, they must always be viewed in the context of the learning situation in which they are demonstrated, with reference to subject matter, stage of learning, instructor's activity, and the over-all demands of the current educational situation.

Change in feeling and in emotional need and response will be essential for the incorporation of new thinking for use. While professional students have sought this experience and have a generalized attitude of readiness to learn, they may not have an emotional set toward all its elements. A professional school may individualize the student to some extent as he learns, but it cannot individualize the learning demands. Hence there will be demands for change imposed from without with which the student must come to grips. His learning must be oriented to the reality principle of this new culture. Not only must his intellectual capacity be adequate for the work, but motivation must be sufficiently strong and the student sufficiently mature that he derives greater satisfaction and more comfort from meeting the demands of this life-venture than from escaping them or from struggling to ward them off. Whether or not he can integrate the change to which he will be subjected will depend upon the extent of re-education involved and his capacity for remotivation and reintegration as he experiences the impact of the educational process. In so far as professional education is functionally similar to a change in culture, it will depend on his readiness to emancipate himself from the old culture. In his observations on loyalty to the old and hostility to the new values, Lewin states that resistance to the new will be more pronounced when the individual is made subject to re-education against his will; also that hostility is more marked, the greater the loyalty of the individual to the old system of values. Hence he concludes that persons who are more socially inclined, therefore less self-centered, can be expected to offer stronger resistances to education, for the very reason that they are more firmly anchored in the old system.

If "socially inclined" is not equated with emotional maturity, perhaps this is so. Self-centered individuals may be gregarious or isolated. It has been the social work educator's observation that social inclinations which connote capacity for relationships, as differentiated from a needful striving for human contact, make for readiness to change. The factor of being submitted to re-education against the will does not obtain in professional education except in part as unanticipated demands are made. Strong loyalties to the old do not necessarily imply more marked hostility to the new when the old culture has been made the individual's own, to do with freely as he wills. Ties to the old which interfere with the acceptance of the new relate to personality development, in terms of immaturity and persistent dependence on past authorities, a response which will be discussed more fully in the next chapter. It will depend, therefore, upon his personality development and his potentiality for growth.

From the standpoint of the principles of stability, of economy, and of progression in learning, the demands of professional education at times threaten the intactness of the self or ego, present heavy reliance on automatic learning for mastery, and deplete energy. As a result, intense feelings and intense emotions at times stretch the integrative capacity to the utmost. To maintain stability of the personality, in the interest of its economy and in order that energy may be available for more than marginal learning, the student will need the help afforded through an educational process in which his need to learn in certain ways is met. Educational principles and measures which have the purpose of helping the student learn are presented in chapter 5 in Part I, and their application is developed throughout Part II on teaching social casework.

It is recognized that the student's learning responses, that is, his ways of economically maintaining emotional equilibrium for gratification of needs, have been patterned. It is possible to use his potentialities so that they are strengthened or to inhibit them at this decisive point when he is undergoing considerable change in feeling and thinking. The social casework educator, in his concern to help the student maintain an emotional equilibrium so that defenses and the struggle for adjustment may not devitalize learning, has used his basic understanding of the ego, its needs, its defenses, its adaptive mechanisms, to know the student as a learner. This orientation not only has given meaning to the learning responses and learning problems of individual students but often has also enabled the teacher to evaluate his own work, as well as the effects of the total educational system in terms of the student's professional maturation. In its presentation of the need basis of behavior and in its concepts of personality development, psychoanalytic psychiatry has made a significant contribution to the understanding of the emotions in learning in social casework. It has confirmed, extended, deepened, and provided a formulation for many of the observations of the social casework educator. We turn to a brief consideration of this theoretical framework.

CHAPTER 3

Personality Development

For the integration of learning, many social work educators have attempted to orient the educational process to the learning process in the light of the psychodynamics of behavior and the concepts of personality formation developed by Freud and his followers. It seems necessary, therefore, to present these basic assumptions. In doing so, we emphasize that there are clear distinctions between the use of these concepts in professional education and the use of them in psychoanalytic therapy or in the psychosocial treatment of the individual which occurs in social casework. The recountal of the development of the ego which follows does not imply that the educator must know the life-history of the student or that it is appropriate for him to engage in treatment. The educator's understanding of the learner is based on observations of his responses in the application and educational processes. These responses become significant to the educator and at times also to the student in the light of their knowledge of ego development and the purposes served by adaptive and defensive behavior in the current educational situation. Hence we share this orientation with the reader. Some of the distinctions between educational help and therapy will be presented in subsequent chapters.

Freud in 1921 generalized and classified all psychological data, conscious and unconscious, by assuming three functional systems which comprise the total personality. The use of this formulation over the years has brought changes in his original elaborations of each entity. Naturally, the trichotomous classification has increasingly become a continuum. Dynamic behavior can be described as interaction between these three continuously related functional aspects of the personality, namely, the id, the superego, and the ego.[1] The id is the fundamental mass of life-tendencies out of which the ego and libido tendencies develop, to converge as the ego which becomes the governing head of the organism, the integrated self. The id represents the elemental and largely unconscious urges and drives which operate under the pleasure principle to achieve satisfaction for needs of the impulses. The id is the source of instinctual drive and aim, of emotion, of tension. It is the primitive in man, which, in so far as he remains infantile—that is, in so far as his ego fails to develop or fails to function—impels him to have or to do what he wants when he wants it, regardless of, or without close reference to, reality factors. Hendrick states that "it comprises those features of human psychology which are most like the impulses observed in animals, a fact that is reflected by our need to refer to it ordinarily in the passive voice." The id is literally the It and the term implies—it wants me to, it makes me. "We feel as though the primal impulses were not truly part of our own personality, but rather something acting upon us."[2]

THE EGO

Immediately for survival the life-tendencies which comprise the id begin to be modified through the development of the ego. The ego grows as the individual's physical, intellectual, and emotional needs are consciously or unconsciously experienced and met, and notably as the libidinal needs and tendencies are recognized, expressed, and find adequate fulfilment. In the course of the individual's development from infancy to maturity, it is the ego that transmutes the primitive libidinal strivings of the id into social modes of expression. Thus, as the need and wish for the varied human relationships essential for survival and for growth are ex-

1. Among many presentations note particularly Franz Alexander, M.D., *Fundamentals of Psychoanalysis* (New York: W. W. Norton & Co., 1948); Ives Hendrick, M.D., *Facts and Theories of Psychoanalysis* (New York: A. A. Knopf, 1938; 2d ed. enl. and rev., 1948); Anna Freud, *The Ego and the Mechanisms of Defense* (London: Hogarth Press, 1937); Franz Alexander, M.D., Thomas M. French, M.D., *et al.*, *Psychoanalytic Theory: Principles and Application* (New York: Ronald Press Co., 1946); Franz Alexander, M.D., and Helen Ross, *Dynamic Psychiatry* (Chicago: University of Chicago Press, 1952), Preface and chap. i.

2. *Op. cit.*, p. 144.

pressed, recognized, and met, the ego grows in its own strength and increasingly determines the nature of the continuing relationships and the individual's use of them. Thus the individual's life-relationships become a continuum, for the nature of the relationship experiences and his use of them will determine the nature of those he seeks and his progressive or regressive response.

The ego represents those propensities, those innate and acquired capacities, and those cultivated qualities through which the individual adapts himself to the outside world. The ego accomplishes this through selecting the opportunity to express fundamental drives so as to meet important needs. These selections come about through perception, the ego's twofold capacity to perceive outer realities and inner needs and resourcefully to find ways of meeting needs which will be satisfying and not destructive to the self and to others. Thus, through the ego, the individual perceives the logical social outcome of means and ends and develops a scale of values.

Through the ego the individual becomes aware of gradations of feeling, so that he is able to connect them with their inner as well as their outer sources. It is the function of the ego to deal with feelings of discomfort through action which copes with their source or through the development of protective and defensive resources. In this connection it is the ego's task to find as much comfort and safety as possible and to protect the individual from both outer and inner danger in socially acceptable ways which do not produce the discomfort of guilt, in order that fear and anxiety may not increase, to serve as disintegrating forces.

It is through the ego that the individual learns from experience to weigh the advantages and disadvantages of his behavior, to force the outcome of prospective action, and to suppress and repress needs, desires, and impulses which endanger himself and others. It is through the ego that the individual learns by trial and error so that he is prone to repeat experience in order to rectify the past. Thus he is capable of repetition for mastery, hence inclined toward progression in learning, as differentiated from the uncorrected repetitive activity implicit in regression. He thereby becomes increasingly aware of the import of his needs, desires, and impulses. As this occurs, the degree of his ego strength determines whether or not he can deal with the discomfort produced by insight to attain mastery of them through conscious use of suppression as differentiated from repression, which is unconscious. As this mastery is achieved, he gains freedom to act selectively upon his needs, desires, and impulses and to use them creatively.

Thus, finally, it is through the ego that the individual overcomes his natural fear of and resistance to change, differentiating the change which threatens his self-identity from that which affords him self-maximation. This, again, implies perception, the attainment of capacity to understand difference and to relate the new to the old, without subordinating it to the old. The individual whose ego has not developed fully often keeps the past alive in the present, whereas the mature ego permits the past to give its life to the present.

From the standpoint of Whitehead's concept of stages of mental growth and of the process of mental development, in an educational philosophy which has influenced the practices described later in this book, a well-developed ego implies an individual in whom the rhythm of growth, the compelling search for difference in a framework of repetition, has not been arrested, as in the adult with an undeveloped ego, who adheres to the status quo through an insistent need for repetitive sameness. A well-developed ego implies also the three continuously interrelated propensities essential for productive learning, delineated by Whitehead, namely, readiness for imaginative consideration, readiness to subordinate this to precise thinking, and, finally, readiness to synthesize and generalize learning through imaginative reconsideration.[3] In so far as professional education is an acculturation process, as envisaged by Lewin, the individual with mature ego development moves more readily from the old culture into the new.[4] The integrative, protective, and executive functions of the ego aim at the preservation of the organism, physically and psychologically, for its intact survival. For equilibrium, this preservation psychologically implies the maintenance of self-identity and of self-determination within social limits and with reference to social change.

3. A. N. Whitehead, *The Aims of Education and Other Essays* (New York: Macmillan Co., 1929), chap. ii, pp. 24–44.

4. Kurt Lewin, *Resolving Social Conflicts: Selected Papers on Group Dynamics* (New York: Harper & Bros., 1948), see paper on "Conduct of Knowledge and Acceptance of New Values" (1945), pp. 55–68.

THE SUPEREGO AND EGO-SUPEREGO INTEGRATION

The fate of the ego, that is, whether or not it develops to attain personality integration, is contingent on the fate of its predecessor and lifelong colleague, the superego. For survival at the start of life, the child has great need for help in learning the rules of life which will insure his welfare. Throughout life the individual has need for a set of values, an ideology to give direction and limits to his strivings. As suggested in the term, the superego is the higher ego, in the sense of "given or imposed from on high."[5] Hendrick describes the superego as "a specialized portion of the ego, representing one aspect of the total personality function, much as, in the social organization, the courts of law dictate what shall and shall not be allowed, while the executive branches of the government make their mandates effective." Learning starts immediately with birth. The child learns in part through his own trial-and-error experience, but parents, in his interest and their own, intervene with influential feeling responses and attitudes. They impose guidance and exert control and discipline through regulations and rewards. Thus, in so far as parental activity expresses love, concern, and protection in the process of developing a superego, the child's ego is nurtured for growth. Alexander states that "the superego develops through the child's identification with its parents' attitudes, opinions, and judgments which is one of the most important factors in the learning process. The ego learns correct behavior through identification with others who have mastered it. By repetition this behavior becomes automatic and habitual. . . . This identification with the parents and *incorporation* of their images conditions adjustment to the social environment. One part of the personality *accepts* the code and becomes its internal representative."[6] The superego, then, is the conscience, the inner disciplinary force, the rules of life, the ideals of the group culture *taken in* by the individual first through the parents and progressively through others. It includes the individual's ego ideal, that is, his concept of himself among men.

A decisive factor for learning and growth is the extent to which the ego of the parents and the ideals of the culture have been internalized, that is, integrated by the ego so that the individual has

5. Hendrick, *op. cit.*, p. 148.   6. *Op. cit.*

truly made his heritage his own. When this occurs, it would seem that the superego would be subject to change as the individual develops. Acceptance implies taking something in and making it one's own. What is one's own, one can use freely. Hence in the normal growth process one would expect some conflict between the maturing ego and the superego on a realistic basis, in so far as children grow beyond their parents and adapt to and incorporate social change. As the maturing individual finds the outworn past useless and irrational, this conflict will be more or less readily resolved. It is probable that all individuals fail to integrate the superego completely. Alexander states: "There is continuous conflict even in normal persons between the earlier unadjusted instinctual tendencies and the restrictive influence of the superego."[7] The extent and degree to which the superego has been integrated is decisive for emancipation or enslavement, for growth or regression in the learning process as the individual encounters life's demands. For an understanding attitude toward and objective response to individual differences in the tempo of learning, as determined by defenses against learning or marked readiness for it, it is essential that the educator know that learning occurs at both the conscious and the unconscious level. Hence when he teaches something new, whether contrary to or reinforced by something learned in identification now unconscious, the student's response will be conditioned by the unconscious import of the new for him. The student's resistance or receptivity, therefore, is not wholly to the current teacher, his methods, or the immediate subject matter, but in part to the past in the present. When the teacher realizes that everything is not contingent on his doing, the amount of feeling which he brings to the situation may be lightened, so that he may be more free objectively to understand and to individualize the student's response.

A misconception has prevailed that a *strong* superego may interfere with learning and growth. It is often said that the "superego is too severe" or that in the neurotic "the culture has taken all too well." We have all known the individual whose life is lived by others, dominated by what other people think, carrying a parent on the shoulder to whose dictates he ambivalently submits or revolts. His discomfort may be expressed in reproach and self-reproach. It

7. *Ibid.*, p. 90.

is probable that the first learning of such an individual was done in the context of a relationship which was more frustrating than nurturing. The nature of the parental feelings and attitudes obstructed the child's inner acceptance of guidance and regulations. Consequently, the values of the parents and the culture were submitted to, rather than accepted and integrated. Submission implies dependency, hostility, guilt, more submission, and often more revolt. It implies, also, devious solutions, a corruptible conscience, compromises, and explosive reactions rather than socially constructive sublimations. Some of the most tenacious attachments to parents and to the past occur in those individuals who have not integrated the superego. They go through life clinging to and dominated by an external set of values, a false conscience, in that it is not fully their own. Their adjustment is precarious because they continuously enact a part projected onto them. They are not free to live their own lives, but, instead, they react in accordance with or in revolt against an imposed pattern.[8] *The problem would seem to be one of weak ego more than strong superego.* These individuals are ambivalently motivated by the pleasure principle and the reality principle. They have not renounced the dominance of the former through integrating the two so as to be motivated by "the improved pleasure principle" described by Alexander.[9] This personality development has limitations for social work. The reader is asked to reflect at this point on its implications—that the social worker must be strongly identified with the conscience rather than with the fears of the community; that he must contend for the profession's values in a world which frequently contests them; that he must prove not only his own worth but his profession's worth! This organization of the personality, wherein the ego is undeveloped through not having incorporated learning by means of satisfying identifications, has great significance in a pronounced tendency to resist change. Of the ego's normal resistance to change out of the deep tendency toward self-determination, it has been said:

This principle for which every name is misleading, call it will, ego or self is fundamentally *resistive to change* from without and is even

8. Charlotte Towle, "The Individual and Social Change," *Social Service Review*, Vol. XIII (March, 1939).

9. *Op. cit.*, p. 90.

slow to recognize as its own and accept responsibility for any process of change from within. Its fear of loss of its own identity and control may inhibit even its normal growth process. It seeks its own likeness in the world outside, selecting elements here and there that can adhere to it without changing the unique organization which sustains it as a separate self unlike every other self in the universe.[10]

Granted that growth is gradual for the organism's incorporation of change, still it might be expected that the well-developed adult ego, through the very fact that it has experienced and survived much change, would not be predominantly compelled toward its own likeness in its selective learning process. One might expect a well-intrenched tendency toward progression and sufficient inner security to seek new experience, to live beyond self, and temporarily to endure some tension and disequilibrium. Out of past experience, the individual would have foreknowledge that the efforts to learn would soon bring order and gratification. A well-developed ego implies capacity to endure denial, to postpone gratification, to enter into the unknown with minimum anxiety, to learn by experience, and to make learning a conscious process. Nonetheless, social work educators have noted profound resistance to change and heavy reliance on identification in learning. This observation raises several questions to which this discussion will return shortly.

THE PLEASURE PRINCIPLE IN RELATION
TO THE REALITY PRINCIPLE

With reference to the ego's basic function, that of maintaining constant conditions in the organism, one of its tasks is to ward off excess external stimuli and to relieve the pressure of needs, impulses, and wishes. One of its many ways of accomplishing this is through selection, which implies alertness to cues that indicate the significant and the insignificant. Educators have long noted that we learn selectively. It is often necessary to endure pain or to engage in unpleasant and exhausting tasks to insure the gratification of certain important needs. A scale of values must be developed by the ego and important desires subordinated or relinquished if they are in conflict with more important ones. A well-adjusted ego implies freedom to develop a *scale* of values, as differentiated from a *rigid*

10. Virginia P. Robinson, *Supervision in Social Case Work* (Chapel Hill: University of North Carolina Press, 1936).

set of values, for flexible use with nice reference to time, place, and person. A well-integrated ego implies a capacity for purposive functioning, as differentiated from scattered or constricted activity. Learning throughout life is selective, and in the educable adult it is oriented to reality. An integration of the pleasure principle and the reality principle occurs as the individual matures. "It becomes more satisfying to meet the demands of life than to escape them or to be continuously engaged in a struggle to ward them off. Stated differently, the pleasures of the adult are different from those of the infant."[11] It follows that there is greater satisfaction in independence than in dependence. There is satisfaction in giving as well as in receiving. The lifelong urge toward self-determination operates freely within social limits, and the individual finds security in those limits. They have been incorporated and serve as the basis of the scale of values and hence as a determinant in selective learning. This integration of the pleasure principle and the reality principle is never complete. There are vestiges of childhood in all of us. Hence when unrealistic demands—demands beyond our integrative capacity—are encountered, there may be some reversion to the infantile pleasure principle and the individual's capacity to select on the basis of mature, reality-oriented value-judgments may be lowered, partially and temporarily or more wholly and enduringly. The extent of external stress in relation to the degree of personality integration (ego-superego integration) attained will be the decisive factor. In a new experience this is chosen, that is repeated, something is taken on superficially, only to be sloughed off, a little of the total to which the learner is exposed is taken in and incorporated for use. The adult has well-established patterns of selection and ways of learning that vary widely among individuals.

SOME IMPLICATIONS OF EDUCATION IN
EGO-SUPEREGO INTEGRATION

Professional education exerts a pressure on learning for immediate use. The profession has a scale of values and a hierarchy of goals as to what must be known, what must be deeply incorporated, what is most important, and what is less important. The student in social work, however, in that he begins practice at once before

11. Alexander, *op. cit.*, p. 90.

he knows the what, the how, and the why of the profession's realistic demands, may feel that the many parts of the total learning to which he is being exposed are equally important. As a result, his usual selective habits may be disturbed and his habitual unconscious protective measures enhanced. In academic learning he was safe in warding off some things for others, provided that he "took on" enough of all to pass examinations at some future date. Time permitted him to find himself and to use his habitual ways, or gradually to form new ways for survival. But is he safe here? He must "take in" for use at once, and increasingly he gets the sense, as time goes on, that this is a situation in which one cannot survive adequately through giving only a part of one's self to the experience, that is, through peripheral learning.

Much school learning of many students up to now has not been individualized. Often it has not occurred in the context of teacher-pupil relationships which have contributed to the learner's development, through affording an opportunity both for identification and for experiencing the worth of his difference. Thus the ego-superego development and integration begun within the family have not been fostered or corrected. Opportunity for learning has consisted of a pressure system in which much has been imposed at a rapid tempo, requiring intellectual grasp and retention to meet certain tests at prescribed times. Many students have endured and survived the system through erecting defenses rather than through participation in an educational process. Certain attitudes and ineptitudes in the present generation of adults cannot be attributed specifically to their educational experience; but often we wonder about the part it has played in the gamut of their human relationships in creating or in not modifying such attitudes as resistance to authority, abject worship of and dependence on the printed word, fear of new contents of knowledge, with resultant indifference or submissive acquisition rather than assimilation, anxious evasion of truths, a preference for half-truths, and an inclination for myths rather than realities. We ponder also upon such responses as contentment with seeming to be rather than satisfaction in being; self-aggrandizing striving for prestige, evidencing a need to grade well in life with less concern for doing well; worship of certain walks of life rather than appreciation of all forms of occupational endeavor; unwillingness to participate in action for the common good; resignation to things as they are, with disinclination to initiate change or to tolerate it.[12]

This is the state of many educated individuals in our society today, even of those who have had opportunity for higher education. One wonders to what extent American educational systems have operated as a repressive, regimenting force, thereby strengthening man's dependence on imposed patterns, rather than as a vitalizing force through which he has been helped to develop his potentialities for continuous growth. In this connection it has been said:

> Only as the individual and his social group are caught in situations that stir fundamental moral ideas can character be changed. Failure to take account of this fact is one of the weakest aspects of the prevailing educational program. The preoccupation of this program with facts and objectivity, information and erudition, renders current practice impotent in the modification of basic beliefs and ideas and leaves untouched the character which the individual imbibes from his culture. It succeeds only in covering the old character structure with a veneer of words and facts. The individual talks better, he is better informed; but he is essentially what he would have been without the influence of the school.[13]

This seemingly has been the plight of some students who have had a meager capacity for social work—a plight which makes it clear that the objectives of professional education, delineated in chapter 1, should be the objectives of education at all levels. Perhaps it might be said that education concerned to develop the good neighbor, the good parent, the good citizen, is essential preparation for the professions. The educable student has survived the past system, perhaps because he has been able to slough off a great deal. We surmise that he has had resilient strength and superior selective capacity—in short, a well-functioning ego, derived through other life-experiences in which his needs have been met and in which he has learned how to learn. It is clear that the aims of professional education imply a system which does not repeat the limitations of prior educational experiences—in terms of regimentation and perpetuation of the old.

12. Towle, *op. cit.*

13. Othanel Smith, "Social Perspective as the Basic Orientation of the Curriculum," in Virgil E. Herrick and Ralph W. Tyler (eds.), *Toward Improved Curriculum Theory* ("Supplementary Educational Monographs," No. 71 [Chicago: University of Chicago Press, 1950]), p. 13.

The development of the ego-superego has great importance in professional education. To what extent are its perceptive, executive, and integrative functions well developed? Or have its protective functions been overdeveloped at the expense of its other resources for maintaining equilibrium? In the educable student one would expect the protective function to operate in the interest of integration and execution. Because of the special stresses in social work learning, the protective function may at times be a prominent response. The student momentarily shuts out some demands in order to meet others; he relies heavily on repetition for the mastery of fundamentals, before he can make creative use of them. He may regress fragmentarily, to ease anxiety or to work through old disturbed feelings and conflicts. He may repress feelings in order to carry on responsibly, while at the same time he will be experiencing release from other feelings which have inhibited psychological insight and understanding. He may handle feelings of inadequacy due to realistic incompetence with overcompensated strivings, that is, he must overdo in order to do, in order to learn. In the interest of assimilation, he may react strongly against new thinking and doing as a last assertion against too precipitous acceptance. He may seek the support of close identification with teachers, supervisors, colleagues, clients. Sometimes only through a phase of overidentification with clients can he bridge the gap created by experience which is beyond his and become accepting and understanding of individual differences. *These normal protective responses,* as differentiated from defenses which impede learning, which are implicit in learning with a deep emotional import, are sufficiently pronounced at times to arouse anxiety and grave question in both learner and educator. We refer again to the observation of social work educators who have noted seemingly profound resistance to the change implied in learning and heavy reliance on the first mode of learning, identification. Among the questions which they frequently voice are the following: To what extent are these responses due to conditions unfavorable for learning in our educational systems? Are we needlessly arousing defenses against learning? To what extent are these responses defenses signifying that learning is interrupted? Are they implicit in the nature of social work learning? Does this learning involve so much change that the integrative function of the normal adult ego functions below par in the process?[14] To what extent do these responses signify the gravitation of people with heavily protective ego defenses into social work? This matter of differentiating the defense-encrusted "protective ego" from one which realistically and flexibly protects in the interest of integration and execution is an important problem in the professional school's selection process and in the subsequent response to professional education. In order to appraise our educational systems, we must understand the needs which students normally bring to them. Freud's theory of the structure and function of the mind has been tested largely through attempts to cure individuals whose behavior has been abnormal, hence persons whose learning was not proceeding normally.[15] As a result, we have more understanding of the ego's protective function in instances wherein it constricts or impedes learning than where it supports the integrative and co-ordinative functions for productive learning. In order to understand the purposes which adaptive and defensive behavior serves in the learning process of adults who are relatively normal in a situation in which they are not seeking a cure but are instead seeking help in learning to help others, it is necessary to consider briefly the development of the ego.[16]

THE DEVELOPMENT OF THE EGO

The individual comes into an unknown world, a helpless infant whose manifold needs must be met by others. He early connects gratification and frustration with those who minister to his needs. The infant's first satisfaction comes with eating, his first displeasure with hunger, and his first human relationship with the person who feeds him, ordinarily the mother. He early reaches out to have his need met and learns that, just as his mother can give, so she also

14. Charlotte Towle, "Emotional Elements in Professional Learning," in pamphlet entitled *Professional Education* (New York: American Association of Schools of Social Work [1 Park Ave.], 1948); and "The Contribution of Education for Social Casework to Practice," *Social Casework*, October, 1950; also in *Principles and Techniques in Social Casework: Selected Papers, 1940–50*, ed. Cora Kasius (New York: Family Service Association of America, 1950).

15. Alexander, *op. cit.*

16. This consideration aims to make known the significance of ego development in professional learning. It does not imply that educators should attempt to know the student's developmental history.

can withhold. In short, she controls the gratification of his need. Soon he values her as a source of security and develops anxiety about her. He wants her near, her embrace is comforting, her very presence reassuring that he will be given to again. He early learns to make known his need and gets a sense of control as his ways bring satisfaction. In so far as he is given regular care, is cuddled, and is able to elicit a positive response from a relaxed mother, he gets a sense of well-being (love) and of mastery of self in relation to his world. In so far as feeding is not timed to his need and is conducted in ways which convey tension and irritation, the infant feels discomfort (lack of love) but if, when he expresses his rage, food and the mother finally arrive, he gets a sense of power in having enforced care. With small feeling of security, he develops imperative ways of connecting with and controlling the mother.

When the mother is anxious and a meticulous adherent to a rigid feeding schedule, the infant may experience hunger and frustration and a greater sense of the mother as a controlling person than as a giving person. If feeding is not timed with his need, he may be driven to great lengths in expressing his rage, but in so far as his assertive demands do not bring results in saving himself a period of denial, he may get a feeling of himself as powerless. Restless activity and demanding ways may be developed, or his response may be a pattern of passive dependence, of waiting apathetically to be fed. Perhaps the factor of energy in relation to the mother's feeling toward him operates to determine the infant's unconscious choice. But here in this first relationship primary learning patterns are being formed. Learning throughout life is a nurturing process, in which the individual seeks, participates, contends, aggressively demands, or passively expects. These primary patterns will, of course, be reinforced, modified, and ramified by other experiences and relationships. There is wide variation in the extent to which the primary patterns are changed through extra-familial experience. In toilet training he generally meets the first well-defined demand of the mother that he give up his impulse to do what he wants to do when he wants to do it. In addition to exerting self-control, he must give up certain ministrations which may have been gratifying. In learning these new socially acceptable ways, he may be motivated by the reward of an affectionate response or by fear of hurt and loss of love, conveyed through disapproval and punishment.

As the child has been developing through the nursing and toilet-training periods, he has been exploring his environment and learning much on his own through trial and error. Much of this has been rewarding and has aided his self-delineation, but mishaps have occurred to cause hurts and fears. In the interest of his survival and for their own comfort, parents have intervened. They have offered protection and guidance. They have exerted forcible control, they have disciplined, they have eased the hurts derived through his own trials and errors, they have recognized and acclaimed his small but momentous successes. During the ups and downs of his days he has revealed his strong feelings, his uncontrollable emotions, his powerful drives of possessive love for his mother, of rage at frustration, and persistence in defying obstacles to his gratification. He has revealed heartfelt wishes and engaged in fantasy to bridge the gap between his needs and their fulfilment. He has revealed deep fears and compelling curiosity. These have motivated repetitive activity, verbal and physical. Doing, doing, doing, experimentally, the same thing over and over again to the repetitive refrain of What? How? Why? Toward brothers, sisters, and father he has shown plurality of emotions, loving, hating, fearing these rivals for the mother's love.

During the first months and earliest years the child patterns his ways of satisfying needs and of controlling them. He also is patterning his ways of reacting to the need and demand of other persons, and, during this early life-period, most prominently to the mother. In the process his ways of learning through relationships, that is, his ways of getting and of giving in order to get, may have become as gratifying as the ends attained. To change his ways is disturbing, because interference with them threatens the attainment of the satisfactions he seeks. They are his source of security. They have eased anxiety, engendered by need and desire, anxiety which derives from the reality experience that one's needs and desires are not always met.

The nature of the parent-child relationship and most notably that with the mother is decisive for the first patterns formed and for their resilience or rigidity as he proceeds through subsequent stages of growth.[17] The manner in which direction has been given and limits have been set to the child's activity, to the enactment of his feelings, or to his needs and demands in various family relationships may be decisive. Has he predominantly been supportively helped to meet reality demands or coerced into submitting to them? Has intervention, conveyed through the feeling accompanying it, been loving concern to protect the child from harm because the parent cares or deprivation of privileges for the parents' own comfort and convenience? As gratifications have been postponed or withheld, has there usually been sympathetic understanding of the child's want and frustration or irritation at and condemnation of his display of negative feeling? For the most part, have new achievements demanded of him been recognized in ways that convey that he would be loved, had he failed, or that, instead, he is loved only conditionally? These factors are decisive because they determine whether or not an individual's learning is motivated largely through love and hope or through fear, hostility, and anxiety. Here we encounter an important learning principle: Motivation is an important determinant of the values of the learning, that is, what the individual derives therefrom. For example, a child who in toilet training gradually and patiently is helped to accept this reality demand, in ways which engage his participation rather than his angry submission, is compensated for renunciation. He has experienced

17. See David M. Levy, M.D., *Maternal Overprotection* (New York: Columbia University Press, 1943), for discussion of the part played by the mother-child relationship in the child's learning in general, as well as in school learning. In the latter, attitudes toward school, special aptitudes, and learning problems in special subjects are considered in relation to mother's attitudes and needs and their import for the child (note pp. 77, 91, 183 for observations on school learning). See Anna Freud and Dorothy T. Burlingham, *Infants without Families* (New York: International Universities Press, 1944), for discussion of differences in learning between those children in contact with their mothers and those deprived of this relationship in the early years.
Biographies of artists, scientists, statesmen, writers, and educators show repeatedly the influence of early parental relationships on the creative work and the art form of the individual. Among many, the following are notable: Joseph Wood Krutch, *Edgar Allan Poe* (New York: Alfred Knopf and W. W. Norton & Co., 1937); James M. Barrie, *Margaret Ogilvy* (a portrayal of his mother and her influence on his life and on his work); August Forel, *Out of My Life and Work* (autobiography), trans. Bernard Miall (New York: W. W. Norton & Co., 1937); Cecil Woodham Smith, *Florence Nightingale* (New York: McGraw-Hill Book Co., 1951); John Middleton Murry, *Between Two Worlds* (autobiography) (London: Julian Messner, 1936); Clara G. Stillman, *Samuel Butler, a Mid-Victorian Modern* (New York: Viking Press, 1932).

denial, he has modified or given up the gratification of an impulse, the gratification of the assertion of his will; but in return he has received love, social approval, a sense of greater adequacy through identification with his parents, and a sense of self-mastery. He has done it; it has not been done *wholly* to him. In contrast, a child who has submitted to this reality demand largely out of fear of loss of love and fear of punishment has experienced the same denials of gratification. In return, he has received an avoidance of pain but little substantial pleasure. Renunciation has brought deprivation and conditional safety. There is little sense of greater adequacy through his achievement, for often this child's identification with parents has been tenuous or shallow. And, most important, there probably has been little sense of self-mastery, a feeling of retreat rather than a sense of progression.

And so in the succession of experiences in which the individual encounters reality demands, the child who achieves socially acceptable behavior with a deep feeling that he will be loved, regardless, is free to fail, though not without discomfort. This freedom is not absolutely essential to learning, but it facilitates it. Furthermore, the discomfort over failure will not be handled predominantly through inordinate wishes and fantasy. Having repeatedly experienced loss without losing, he grows progressively less fearful of the strange and the new and less anxious and resistive to the change implied in learning. Actually, there will be less necessity for change in him in the learning process, for the primary ways of relating which he has developed will continue to be constructively useful. They will need only to wax strong. His intense desires will be accompanied by minimum anxiety, because he anticipates gratification and does not greatly dread denial. His relationships with those from whom he learns will be infused with more positive than negative affect, so that hostility, guilt, and anxiety will not loom large, to confuse and complicate his learning. A child who has had this positive constructive experience in his first learning in the primary relationships in the family will be emotionally set to create a repetitive situation for himself as he moves out to school and into other social groups but will also be emotionally prepared to tolerate some difference if it is not too great. Unless traumatic events occur, that is, stresses beyond the integrative capacity of his years, his development stands a chance of proceeding smoothly. There will be ups and downs, but ordinary reverses which all children must meet will be adapted to and incorporated for use.

On the other hand, the child who achieves socially acceptable behavior largely through submission and fear will be bent to learn the hard way. He will not be free to fail; in fact, his learning is motivated largely through fear of loss of love and by failure to survive on satisfying terms. Having repeatedly experienced inadequate compensation for the denials which he has endured, he will be fearful of the strange and the new and will be intensely anxious and resistive to the change involved in learning. The demand for change in his patterns will be heavy, for his ways of relating frequently will be unacceptable and not useful in learning. There will be discomfort and conflict between risking change and adhering to the past which he will handle through erecting defenses against change. His intense desires will be accompanied by great anxiety, because he anticipates denial. As a result, he may defeat his aims through exaggerated unsustained strivings which are characterized by hostile aggression. Or he may not dare desire much for fear of disappointment, in which event spasmodic, uncertain effort will operate against productive learning. Or he may cushion his dread of frustration with wishful gratification through fantasy in which the kernel of reality is small. Feeling hopeless, his hopes are inordinate and soon fail of their purpose, that of reassuring him that he is safe. Instead, they often doom him to another hurt. His relationships with those from whom he learns will be infused with more negative than positive affect, so that hostility, guilt, and anxiety will loom large to confuse and complicate his learning. Hence he may be more free to fail than to succeed. A child who has had this negative destructive experience in his first learning within the family will tend to create a repetitive situation for himself in school and in other social groups. He will behave in such a way that almost inevitably he will evoke a response from teachers and playmates which will approximate the negative elements in his parental and sibling relationships. If in his early years teachers and other adults outside the home understand his need and meet it in some measure, the corrective experience implied may modify his ways of relating, so that learning may proceed more productively.

As traumatic events occur, he will have little inner resource to cope with them. The usual ups and downs, the ordinary reverses which children at his age meet, will be traumatic events beyond his integrative capacity, so that he will survive them only in so far as his defenses prove socially useful.

It is not unreasonable to assume a continuum experience for these two children, as they move from infancy through the oedipal period, through the latency period and adolescence, into adulthood. This will occur in so far as the parental handling and the family relationships in which the primary learning patterns and responses were formed remain essentially the same. It will occur, in part, through the child's own making. As stated before, the individual's life-relationships are often repetitive in nature, because the primary relationships experienced and his use of them determine the nature of those he seeks and his progressive or regressive use of them. In the light of this assumption, what will be the essential differences in personality structure and functioning of these two individuals as they reach adulthood?

THE IMPORT OF EGO DEVELOPMENT FOR PROFESSIONAL EDUCATION

The adult who was the child with the predominantly positive experience and who now is motivated largely through love and hope will have a well-developed ego. This implies that he will have evolved from the normal emotional state of infancy, in which he loved the world as part of himself, to loving himself as part of the world. Loving self now is self-regard, in so far as he lives beyond himself and contributes to others individually and collectively. Thus *he will have developed capacity to love and to be loved* without marked conflict and anxiety over the implied dependency and demands. He is motivated through his love of others, his obligation to others, and his self-regard, his obligation to himself. He will have developed also a capacity to live and let live. Thus he will be free to be aggressive for survival, but, because there is minimum hostility in his aggression, he will let others do likewise, for he has little fear of retaliation or loss. He will have developed *a capacity to renounce many things* in order to possess other things more securely and fully. Thus his strivings for gratification are *oriented to reality*. His conscience is a true one, in that it is his own, that is, an integral part of his personality, so that following its demands is an affirmation of the whole self. His intelligence can be used to the utmost, and his aspirations will tend to be commensurate with his intellectual abilities. He will have attained an inner equilibrium, a moral, spiritual stability, which stands him in good stead against confusion and disaster. Without anxiety, he will accept responsibility commensurate with his capacity. When the responsibility is so great as to produce anxiety, it will motivate him to seek solutions rather than drive him to purposeless activity or into inertia. He will accept the stresses of life with equanimity, even with a kind of eagerness sprung from the sure knowledge that somehow or other he will have what it takes to carry through. If the stress is excessive for his capacities and escapable, he will protect or defend himself satisfactorily. Guilt not being great, he will be able to compensate. Furthermore, he will have the wherewithal for compensation, and because his need is not excessive, his compensatory drives will not be extreme. His projections will be fragmentary, his regressions and his fantasies temporary and self-healing. His primitive urges unacceptable to the ego will be handled more through sublimation than through regression, particularly if the circumstances of his life permit sports, hobbies, intellectual pursuits, and creative activities. Identification as a means to learning will not be so deeply involving as to obliterate self-identity. Under traumatic conditions, when used as a defense, the ambivalence created by negative affect will not be so great as to create a problem in learning. He will not be deeply tied and submissive through hostility or driven to extreme expressions of negative affect. This matter of identification, both as a means to learning and as a defense in professional education, will be discussed more fully later. In relation to unattainable goals he can give up, without loss of face. In short, his experience has been such as to develop highly the integrative and executive functions of the ego. The protective function will have served him freely and flexibly in the interests of integration and discriminative action; but his defenses will not be highly organized and rigid to serve as a bulwark to an undeveloped ego.

The young adult with a well-developed ego approximates these specifications. He has these potentialities. As he assumes and carries responsibility, as he masters a progressively demanding reality, as he survives stresses, they will become full-fledged capacities and well-intrenched ways of life. Professional education appropriately chosen will afford an opportunity for this fulfilment of self. In this portrayal of an individual with a well-developed ego, it must be noted that this development is conceived of as occurring through circumstances in which needs were *largely,* but not wholly, met, in ways which were *predominantly* satisfying and conducive to growth. It is the assumption that when conditions prevail which make for the intact survival of the organism for growth and when those conditions are sufficiently well sustained to permit learning to proceed, with quick retrieval of any interruptions, considerable deprivation and frustration can be absorbed or handled by defenses which in mitigating the trauma permit a corrective experience, so that they do not long interfere with integration. It is probable that within every such well-developed personality there are the scars of old hurts, certain latent conflicts, some encapsulated vestiges of childhood, to constitute neurotic tendencies. As reported by Dr. Grinker and Dr. Spiegel in their observations of men in combat, acute neurotic states may occur in persons whose egos have functioned well in the past. When anyone is inescapably exposed to difficulties beyond his powers of adaptation, latent neurotic tendencies may be called into action, and an acute neurotic state may develop.[18] Or, in the words of Dr. French: "A neurosis is the result of an interrupted learning process."[19] And so with the young adult with the well-developed ego, it might be war, it might be a series of social disasters, or it might be professional education inappropriate to his capacities or education conducted without reference to his integrative capacity which would interrupt learning and produce marked emotional disturbance.

As for the adult who as a child had a predominantly negative experience, so that learning has been motivated largely through fear, it is to be expected that he will have inadequate ego development. His ego may or may not be strongly defended; this would depend on varying factors not brought out in the shadowy and oversimplified psychogram above. In the framework given, one could sketch many configurations, in which factors of constitutional endowment, social

18. Roy R. Grinker, M.D., and John Spiegel, M.D., *Men under Stress* (Philadelphia: Blakiston Co., 1945), p. 74.

19. Alexander, *et al., op. cit.*

circumstance, and timing of actual life-events, combining with infinite variation, would serve as a springboard to the whole gamut of psychopathology and to a wide range of social adjustments of a sort. Only a few possibilities are sketched to suggest the range of ego development, focusing largely on those personality constellations, encountered in professional education, which are problematic for it but which may be educable. At least, for better or for worse, they have in the past survived professional education, sometimes with seeming "success," and often with growth, even though the process is more painful than in the well-integrated person.

If early learning has occurred in relationships which have been extremely depriving and punitive and a continuum of this experience has obtained, with no corrective relationships of decisive import, the personality organization may be characterized by strong id, weak unincorporated superego, and underdeveloped ego. Never having been loved appreciably, the individual has not developed the capacity to love others sufficiently to be willing to give up his own desires for the wishes or welfare of others. He is "impulse-ridden," highly wishful, and without conscience. He is motivated to conform only through fear of consequences and has a "guilt" reaction only as he is caught. Such a narcissistic character, whether or not he is involved in social or asocial acting out, is basically unsocial. For obvious reasons he is probably seldom attracted to professional life, so he may not be encountered in professional schools—at least, he is seldom seen in schools of social work.

In infancy and early childhood the relationships may have conveyed enough positive affect to motivate the child to respond to the demands of the parents but aroused sufficient negative affect that he is deeply fearful. In such instances enough attachment to parents has developed that the child values their love. He makes more than a tenuous connection with their sense of values and the reality demands which they have attempted to impose, and strives to inhibit his impulses. Parental responses, however, have not given love commensurate with his need, and often only conditional love has been given. When parental methods have also made the child feel helpless, so that his ways of satisfying needs and of controlling them are not successful and his patterns for reacting to the need and demand of other persons are ineffectual, then the personality organization may be characterized by a strong id and by a prominent superego which remains relatively unincorporated. In such instances, when the demands of life are heavy, the ego may partially or wholly give up its function of estimating the external world and of adapting to it. Instead of repressing, it projects, thus distorting reality and allowing instinctual impulses to find expression in deep regression and in marked aggression, either or both manifested directly, symbolically, or in fantasy. As might be expected, when the groundwork for a psychosis has been laid, the break often occurs in professional school, where the individual must truly meet the demands of adult life or make a comprehensive adaptation of which he is incapable. That the break did not occur in adolescence may mean that the young person was sustained by a less demanding social situation in which high intellectual capacity may have served as a defense. In social work the relationship demands of field practice and the import of material conveyed in casework and in psychiatric courses constitute an emotional demand so far beyond the integrative capacity of the weak ego that defenses break down. Relatively few individuals who become psychotic are encountered in schools of social work, but those few who have chosen social work come with varied motivation. Sometimes the choice has seemed purely an erratic response to chance circumstance. Notable, however, in some instances has been the malnourished ego's last struggle for emotional gratification through intimate relationships which the individual cannot establish spontaneously in his personal life and which he hopes will occur through the enforced contact with people. Quite often these individuals have left their first vocational field because they felt they had mistakenly chosen work which isolated them or did not afford intimate relationship. Notable also in their motivation has been the prominent but dangling superego, a perpetuation of the old struggle to make more complete the identity with the parental and cultural ego, through playing the parent role. This identification as a defense proves fatal. "The introject remains a foreign body within the ego and is reacted to with the same ambivalence as prevailed toward the original love object."[20] The resultant conflicts have a disintegrating effect.

It commonly occurs that learning, that is, adjustment to reality,

20. Alexander, *Fundamentals of Psychoanalysis*, p. 117.

is interrupted during the oedipal period when the child is brought into intense conflict with others in the development of the superego. In the earlier months of infancy and childhood he has received enough positive affect that parents have come to have considerable value for him—in fact, there may be depth of attachment. He has received enough love that he is not deeply fearful. His primary ways of satisfying needs and controlling them, as well as his primary patterns for reacting to the need and demands of others, have been sufficiently effectual to give him some feeling of adequacy and power. His ego strengths are sufficient that he enters the negativistic stage of childhood with normal capacity to assert "I will" and "I won't." The defiance pertains to all areas of the child's life and often the issue is "I will have my mother or father, I won't give him or her up to the other parent." At this decisive point, when fear of his own aggression arises, guilt over his own love and hostility emerges by very reason of his attachment to his parents. If the parents handle his behavior in ways which intensify fear, hostility, and guilt, a complicating dependency may be engendered. Also the interparental relationship may be such as to involve the child with one more than the other, so that the oedipal conflict is not resolved and guilt and anxiety persist. When development is arrested at this point, the individual continues throughout life to struggle ambivalently to fulfil or to overpower his emotional needs and ambivalently to strive for or inhibit his unrealistic wishes. The personality structure is characterized by conflict between the ego and the superego in the domination of the id. The individual keeps the parental sense of values and reality demands alive in the present, even when outworn, to combat the ego, which often is "id"-dominated, as it was at the childhood period of negativism when the interference with learning occurred. The ego-superego relationship is much the same as at this period. A neurosis develops in any area of life whenever a person cannot satisfy his needs in a given situation without internal conflict. The impulse at such a time is to regress to an earlier lifeperiod or situation when needs were satisfied. Usually there is a struggle before recourse is taken to infantile or childlike gratifications. If the defenses developed in the struggle do not solve the conflict, regression occurs. As the individual does regress, the primary conflicts are reactivated. Neurotic symptoms of substitutive gratifications and self-punishment represent the individual's futile attempt to resolve the primary conflict.[21] As the neurotic's behavior is noted by an observer, it seems to say "my ego must appear strong because it isn't, and my superego must appear weak because it exerts a strong pressure."

Thus the strong impulses to dependency must be repressed or denied or, if expressed, disguised. Hence the dependency may be repressed and denied through pretensive independence, in which the individual overcompensates for his inadequacy in such a way that he outreaches himself, overdoes, etc. He thereby creates a situation in which his dependency is expressed in disguise, as through falling ill. Thus dependency need may be concealed through illness, through the overuse of a minor handicap, or through getting into complex situations in which he is justifiably helpless. It may be disguised through choice of work, which enforces dependency, like the army or other regimented situations. Or one may prolong dependency if economic circumstances permit and if one is competent intellectually, through remaining a student. By being indefinitely in the position of learner, one with a front of adequacy and prestige is fed the substance of life without needing to meet its full demands.

Another aspect of the dilemma is that the superego presses the individual toward authority. He seeks the support of authority as represented in parent-persons, employers, teachers, and/or knowledge, only to react against them as the ego asserts itself as though they were the family figures or experiences of childhood. In this traumatic situation, identification may be his defense. He will become the authority—a parent, a teacher, an employer, a learned one. Not having accepted authority himself, he will not exert authority in a mature way, but, instead, he will probably use his position as an outlet through which to express his feelings about authority. Accordingly, all that he has suffered may be projected onto his subordinates. He will be authoritative, perhaps ruthlessly so, perhaps uncertainly, as evidenced in indecision prompted by insecurity and guilt. History is rich in records of this kind of leadership, and every profession has suffered these child-adults in its fold.

The problem of the neurotic individual in the profession is now

21. *Ibid.*, pp. 208–14.

a concern of schools in all professions engaged in educating, healing, or helping people. From this oversimplified description of the bare bones of the structure of the neurotic personality, it is logical that any one of these professions, with its great responsibilities, its humanitarian aims, and its position of prestige, would attract these personalities for several reasons. The responsibilities give promise of meeting the need of such persons to repress, deny, and disguise their strong dependency impulses, their ,need to strive to identify with authority, their need for social approval. In a culture where learning is loved, the learner gets a sense of being loved through the acquisition of higher learning. Their need to repress, deny, react against—that is, compensate their hostile impulses through humanitarian work—their need to ease guilt through demanding work or through devotion to a cause may seem to bring satisfaction. An adequate consideration of neurotic motivation would involve specifying the greater and lesser attraction of the profession and of certain other professions to various types of neurosis. On this there is a growing body of impressions but little published data based on research. With reference to the idea that certain professions attract specific neurotic personalities, one is reminded of the impression afloat that many "compulsive types" seek the professions and notably social work. Dr. Alexander states: "The typical compulsive is usually a highly intellectual person who has learned to detach his emotions from his reason. He is inclined toward abstract thinking, believes often fanatically in abstract causes and principles, and is apt to neglect the practical aspects of life. He is loyal to causes rather than to persons, is a theoretical lover of mankind but somewhat detached from immediate associates. . . . The letter of the law dominates his sense."[22] The aim of social work is a better-ordered world and better-ordered individual lives. It is not surprising if compulsive personalities go astray into its fold. Consider their dilemma when they come up against the means to that end—the need to feel with people, the need to care deeply for people as individuals, the need to be concerned with the practical aspects of life and with practical measures for dealing with them, and, above all, a sense of the spirit of the law.

There is quite a push to eliminate the neurotic personality in

22. *Ibid.,* p. 231.

schools' admission procedures. But this is not readily done, except to screen out the grossly pathological and the acutely ill. Here we encounter the reality that all human beings have limits to their integrative capacity and that the threshold varies widely. All persons carry within their personalities some vestiges of childhood, some unresolved conflicts to serve as vulnerable spots, some latent neurotic tendencies. We are confronted, then, with the degree of neurosis, the type and configuration of defenses, how well they work and what they do to the individual's way of functioning in relation to the demands made on the personality by the particular profession. Since neurotic character disorders are so frequent in the general population, the question of selection hinges much more upon the flexibility of the neurosis than on whether or not it is absent. There is recognition of the need for systematic observation of students' learning responses in relation to personality factors. These studies will demand careful appraisal of educational systems with reference to the factor of traumatic neuroses, of which it has been said that anyone may develop this illness if the stress is severe enough or attacks an individual where he is vulnerable or when he is overloaded with mastering other problems.[23] As research is done in this area, criteria may be established for use as evaluation measures at admissions.[24] Research may also contribute to educational planning, so that systems will be designed to foster growth wherever there is flexibility, as well as to avoid stresses which traumatize students needlessly.

Whether the adult who as a child has had a negative experience is qualified to engage in educating, helping, and healing people when he reaches adulthood would depend on the extent, the nature, and the timing of his deprivations. It would depend also on the ex-

23. Grinker and Spiegel, *op. cit.*

24. For statements concerning research to determine personality qualifications for medicine and for social work see the following: Henry N. Brosin, M.D., "Psychiatry Experiments with Selection," *Social Service Review,* Vol. XXII, No. 4 (December, 1948); Sidney Berengarten, "A Pilot Study To Establish Criteria for Selection of Students in Social Work," *Social Work as Human Relations: Anniversary Papers of the New York School of Social Work and the Community Service Society of New York* (New York: Columbia University Press, 1949), pp. 170–94; Gordon Hamilton, "The Interaction of School and Agency," *Social Work Journal,* Vol. XXX, No. 2 (April, 1949); R. W. Waggoner and T. W. Ziegler, "Psychiatric Factors in Students Who Fail," *American Journal of Psychiatry,* C, No. 3 (November, 1946), 369–76.

tent, the nature, and the timing of the negative parental handling. Decisive factors will be: How much capacity has he developed to love and be loved? How great are his anxieties and hostilities in relationships? Has guilt been so great that he has been unable to permit himself to compensate? If not, have compensatory relationships beyond the primary ones offered opportunity for growth and for the resolution of conflicts? How great is his need still to be dependent? Has he so much anxiety about it as to obstruct his acceptance of dependency in others? How much hostility has he toward persons upon whom he must depend? How much denial can he tolerate for eventual gain and for freedom of choice? To what extent has the superego been incorporated? These questions are decisively important for professional education. When the parents and the culture have been submitted to, rather than accepted and integrated, the individual in this educational process tends either to combat new ways of feeling, thinking, and doing because he is not free to depart from the old, or, if he uses the school as a new superego, it will be with an urgency to repeat the submission, dependency, hostility, guilt, and ambivalent submission of the earlier life-situation. In the two-way feelings lie the seeds of revolt which often make him more resistive to the content imparted than accepting of it. In large measure this is because he is more against than with those from whom he learns.

Social work by its nature, in that it rather literally is taken to represent the conscience of the community, in that it is literally thought of as playing a parental role in the lives of people, draws some individuals who need, through identification, to support their own superimposed consciences. Social work educators know the limitations of these students and the stresses of the educational experience, if they come to grips with the change implied. Many have survived, because it has been possible to sustain a pretensive role in which submission has passed for acceptance. The nature of the ego's defenses will be a decisive factor in the outcome of learning—for instance, whether the ego has developed in such a way and to an extent that its defenses augment rather than impoverish it, as when compensations have been possible or as when repression has not operated to such an extent that energy has not been available for sublimation, and the need to distort reality has not been so great that projections are extensive and rigid.

REFLECTIONS ON THE SOCIAL IMPORT OF EARLY
EXPERIENCE FOR PROFESSIONAL EDUCATION

In this consideration of the development of the ego, its needs, its adaptive capacity, its defenses and their relationship to learning, it is hoped that it is clear that there is a vital relationship between the satisfaction of dependency need, the nourishment of the ego for growth, and the learning process. The ethic of love is the basis for all learning through which the individual becomes a social being. This implies motivation to work for the common good rather than solely to strive for self-maximation, in short, the capacity to live beyond narrow absorption in self and in those in close relationship who are an extension of self.

In making this statement, we are not unmindful of the human proclivity to sublimate unsocial impulses and to resolve conflicts through good works and creative activity. Again the lives of many artists, scientists, statesmen, and writers proclaim lifelong efforts to compensate for, to sublimate in diverse ways, the lacks, hurts, and conflicts of early experience. In these life-experiences, if known precisely, one suspects that beneath the capacity for compensation and sublimation there may well have been sufficient satisfaction in relationships to provide the security and hence the hope essential for creative effort, which always implies some degree of departure from the established order. The part played by great gifts of mind and high energy also cannot be discounted as means for the nurture of the ego. The extent to which repressed unsocial impulses can be sublimated and deprivation and trauma compensated for the common good merits investigation. It seems probable that compensation and sublimation can occur to better advantage through some forms of creative activity than through others. To what extent *educable* social workers have been misunderstood children who, out of persistent need for understanding, now strive to understand others is not known. To what extent they have been lonely individuals who in this work vicariously seek intimate relationship is not known. Nor is it known to what degree educable social workers have been hurt children who, out of their persistent need for pity, now are sensitive rather than susceptible to the sufferings of others. It seems probable that such needs and wishes have been modified so that there is greater remembrance of need than persistence of it, as well as hope which is not merely wishful. It is well known, however, that many uneducable individuals have been burdened with the past. This inclines one to the point of view that the deprived, traumatized individual whose needs persist relatively unmodified may better contrive an invention, formulate a mathematical theory, paint a picture, compose a symphony, write of human suffering, or deal in sociological abstractions than try to help troubled people solve their problems. This is a moot question, because selfless goal-directed endeavor is valued highly in the pursuit both of science and of the arts. It does seem, however, that a work of art to inspire mankind can be subject to, and hence bear the imprint of, the doer's personality and capacity to an extent not possible in healing, helping, or teaching people. In the professions we cannot create people in accordance with our inner lights. We cannot overpass the established order of the personality being served. Our creativity in helping, healing, or teaching is contingent on the individual's readiness and capacity to respond. His potentialities cannot be bent, shaped, or used to the utmost in the realization of our aims.

With reference to this delineation of the import of early life-experience for personality organization and hence for educability in social work, the question frequently is raised as to whether individuals from a predominantly satisfying and constructive life-experience often enter social work. Do these individuals have the need and the wish to help troubled people or to right social wrongs? Or if they do enter social work, out of their inexperience with adversity can they feel with individuals who are having difficulty in the mastery of circumstance or themselves? Are they sensitive to social ills and perceptive of human suffering? Decisive here is the difference between "largely" and "wholly" and the fact that no individual's experience has been wholly positive or wholly negative. Decisive also is the wide variation in the meaning of seemingly identical experience to different individuals. In the context of conditions and relationships most favorable for growth, it is probable that all individuals have known deprivation, defeat, and frustration in some measure. Fragmentary sufferings may have been incorporated through not having been overwhelming rather than defensively sloughed off, as often is the case in gross, repetitive hardship. Because he is not inured to disaster or calloused by it, the small and subtle sufferings of the relatively advantaged individual may foster imaginative consideration and a degree of identification with the human sufferer. His hurts, through their very limits, leave him free to understand, to relate, and to help more effectively than if his experience had been more completely "at one" with those of the individuals and groups to be served. In summary, it might be said, by and large, that the social worker brings from life's gratifications and from the self-realization which has been his lot the strength and the capacity to help. Also through his deprivations and his frustrations, provided that they have not been too great, he is attuned to feel with the disadvantaged, and almost inevitably there will be times or instances when he will feel like them and, therefore, at times more against them than with them. In these instances his effectiveness as a helping person will be undermined.

When a child's dependency needs have been met adequately through positive constructive relationships with parents and teachers, learning is a process of accretion, one which occurs naturally, gradually, and with a minimum of pain and disorganization. It is conducive to repetitive reorganization of the personality as he moves from one developmental period to another. His learning is a process of reorganization and integration rather than of disorganization. In so far as these relationships have permitted resolution of normal conflicts, increasingly as he matures he will have been positively conditioned to the pleasures of learning. The momentary pain implied in change will be eased through the certainty of eventual pleasure.

It is an unfortunate commentary on family life and on our educational systems that more individuals do not reach professional school constituted for smooth and ready learning. Today in adult education we are teaching those who came up in the depression and war years, when family life was maintained under stress and when school systems were not at their best, when the world was a hostile place. It is not surprising, then, to find many who learn the hard way and for whom school learning, like living, is an anxious, precarious process. For the child, one of the strongest deterrents to learning is derived from a negative relationship between learner and teacher. Many children become completely blocked in learning under these circumstances. Recent studies of reading and arithmetic disabilities show repeatedly the dual incidence of unsatisfactory parental relationships and a teacher who repeats the parent. Therapeutic tutoring in these instances emphasizes as a first step the establishment between tutor and pupil of a strong positive relationship—in short, a corrective relationship. It has been noted that some children early establish the pattern of struggling against this deterrent, negative relationship between child and parent, teacher and pupil. It is as though they learn not merely in spite of the lacks in the relationship but to compensate for it or even to retaliate against the parent-person. It is a conflict of wills, in which they refuse to be deprived and in which they are bent toward outwitting, outdoing, and, in the long run, mastering the opponent. Clinicians over the years have come to know the limitations of this learning pattern, which frequently does not culminate happily for the learner or for society. The hostile aggressions which permeate the educational strivings of these learners are familiar to many of us. When the guilt over the hostility mounts, we have seen this motivation result in a neurotic need to fail at a decisive point in life, as, for example, on the verge of long-sought success. Repeatedly also, among other results, we have seen these people use their learning in self-aggrandizing rather than in social ways. In social work we have seen them use their professional orientation against the client's welfare rather than for it; or we have seen them develop marked fears of hurting or failing people, as a reaction against the impulse to do so.

This does not mean that the individual who has experienced hurt and frustration in his early life-relationships inevitably will be uneducable for social work. Out of negative experience, provided that it has not been too great and that hurts have been compensated and conflicts resolved, some individuals are attuned to feel with the disadvantaged and have depth of understanding. A great need in our profession today, however, is that of weeding out those individuals whose professional strivings are permeated to the saturation point with hostile aggression and with self-centered aims and whose basic anxiety has produced rigid defenses of a nature which limits social work learning.

These concepts have been stated as pertaining to learning in the early years of life, when patterns are formed. We should like to consider them as they obtain in adult education, where systems will be geared to the educable adult rather than to the child. By "educable adult," we mean, in this context, individuals whose personality growth has not been seriously obstructed by the deprivations and unresolved conflicts of the early years; those persons who have a well-developed ego-superego structure so that their emotional needs are unlike those of the child, in that there is greater capacity for self-dependence, while interdependence has replaced in considerable measure the dependency of the early years. Their inner conflicts, in so far as they have been basically unresolved, are being quite adequately handled through constructive ego defenses.

Presumably, if these are the essential differences between the adult and the child, then in an adult education system one would expect the following: the basic dependency needs having been met, the individual is free to learn and will learn readily, provided that he has intellectual capacity and aptitude for the content taught and also provided that knowledge and skill are timed to his assimilative powers—not given at too rapid or too slow a tempo; provided that the value system of the new culture involved in learning is not so totally different that complete re-education is essential. However, the individual with a well-developed ego, which implies an incorporated superego, would accept considerable change in attitudes, habits, and values through the fact that he no longer depends largely upon external superego controls for the maintenance of equilibrium. In the adult education situation we would expect the learner to be able to handle more competently than the child the concomitant emotional stresses of his personal life, so that they do not interfere to the same extent with learning. Likewise, he may have certain conflicts, but learning may proceed in spite of them, or even because of them. Reference is made here to the resolution of conflict through creative activity. In adult education one would expect the learner to be less dependent upon the nature of the relationship with the teacher. It is the conviction of some social work educators that he will still learn more readily through a positive relationship but that he will be much less put to rout than a child by a negative relationship.

And, finally, we anticipate that the well-developed adult will have energy for life, beyond absorption in himself, for expenditure in professional education and in professional service. This implies energy to work with and for others, so that the individual is free to meet the needs of others rather than enslaved by his own need. Obviously, the extent to which these several responses obtain in the adult situation will depend on many variables which will determine not only the learner's integrative capacity but also the size of the integrative task.

In closing this discussion we repeat that this recountal of the development of the ego has not been to indicate that educators must know the life-history of the student or that it is appropriate for schools to make clinical studies of prospective students. The educator's understanding of the learner is based largely on observations of him in the application process and the educational process. His responses become significant to the educator in the light of his knowledge of ego development and the purposes served by adaptive and defensive behavior in learning.[25] We turn now to a consideration of personality development and the integration of learning.

25. For further discussion of this see chap. 4.

CHAPTER 4

Personality Development and the Integration of Learning

The outcome of learning hinges on three sets of factors which are continuously interrelated—the individual's motivation, his capacity, and the opportunity afforded him to attain his aims. While this chapter focuses on motivation and capacity as part and parcel of personality development, it is not possible to consider these aspects completely out of context of the educational opportunity.

I. ESSENTIAL ADAPTATION TO THE EDUCATOR'S POINT OF VIEW

Social work educators, in their concern with education as a means to growth, have drawn heavily on basic learning principles as formulated by those who have been concerned with psychoanalysis and psychotherapy as means to learning. This has inevitably occurred as social work practitioners have brought to their educational practice knowledge, insight, and skill derived through their work in helping people who have been referred for, or who have sought, help of a psychotherapeutic nature. Actually, this orientation has not led them wholly astray in understanding the learning process. There has long been agreement among specialists in behavior that normal and abnormal behavior constitute a continuum rather than a dichotomy. Deepened and extended study to test the assumption that "the integrative process in rational behavior, in neuroses and in dreams can be analyzed into component factors that are in part common to all three"[1] is now in progress. Findings of the near future may well have import for educational practice at all levels and in all professions directly concerned with human welfare. Of

1. Thomas M. French, M.D., *The Integration of Behavior*, Vol. I: *Basic Postulates* (Chicago: University of Chicago Press, 1952). Among other works concerned essentially with this problem see John Dollard and Neale E. Miller, *Personality and Psychotherapy: An Analysis in Terms of Learning, Thinking, and Culture* (New York: McGraw-Hill Book Co., 1950).

decisive importance will be the delineation of differences in the integrative process in relation to personality organization of normal, irrational, and neurotic individuals. This will be important for social work education, because in our educational practices some individuals have tended to operate on the assumption either of sameness or of complete difference. This is suggested in inappropriate use of psychiatric and casework learnings in the educational process, or failure to use them, seemingly out of an attitude that they are irrelevant to education. Others, aware of essential differences between education and therapy, have sought to modify their use of these insights in the educational situation. Roughly defined, the essential differences between client and student which have guided social work's attempt to adapt insights gained elsewhere in education have been, first, that the client does not recognize social casework treatment as a learning process, even though, when skilfully conducted, it is one.

The client comes not expecting to learn something, but with difficulties or symptoms from which he hopes to be relieved. The client who seeks help generally has not totally despaired of solving his problem, but hope may be at low ebb, and he may be greatly discouraged. He often neither trusts nor has much confidence in the helping person. He is as prone to anticipate an unhappy outcome to his efforts as a successful one. "I came as a last resort" is a common presenting attitude, and often he sees and feels himself unimportant in the eyes of the helper. Often the learning task implied in his current experience has become traumatic, sometimes even to the extent that goal-striving has broken down. In these instances the initial charge on the social worker is that of helping the client find new goals, adapt old goals, or resume pursuit of abandoned goals. He may need help in taking hold, in order to regain confidence to strive anew. In contrast, with the educable student goal-striving is high. He enters the situation with a set of goals for himself. The hierarchy of goals structured for him may or may not prove to be compatible, but, until found incompatible, he has an expectancy of a happy outcome. He brings an admixture of self-doubt and self-confidence characteristic of the realistic adult embarking on a new experience. Fortunately, he is not predisposed to blind trust in his mentors so much as to a conditional confidence in their competence to teach him. He rightly expects to be regarded and treated as competent unless proved incompetent, and he relates himself similarly to those in charge of the educational situation.

The second important difference between the client and the student is one which makes for decisive differences in the helping process as differentiated from the educational process. This centers about the marked difference between the status of a problem and that of a goal in an achievement-worshiping culture. The needs and wishes which drive, that is, motivate, a client to seek help are seen and felt as "a problem." Something has been too much for him to do alone. He therefore seeks help, with some predisposition to depend on the helping person, but with complicated feelings about it, because, after all, he should be able to cope with his own difficulties. The bigger his problems, the more problematic he feels, that is, the more helpless, inadequate, and humiliated. The services which people seek from social work commonly represent a failure in their expectancy of themselves and in the community's expectation of them. Consequently, the "give" of social work is taken with more humiliation, fear of social consequences, resentment, and resistance than ordinarily occurs in other helping relationships.

In contrast to a problem, the needs and wants which motivate the student are seen, felt, and regarded by others as a goal. He has faced the fact that it is a goal which he cannot attain unaided. He therefore seeks education with a predisposition to depend on and to accept the authority of teaching helping persons. There most probably will be authority-dependency conflicts in this for the adult learner, but their social import in relation to his concept of himself among men is normally quite different. The threat differs markedly in nature and kind. Goals are respectable and beget feelings of self-respect until or unless the individual finds them unrealistic or has set them for himself largely as a defense against feelings of inadequacy. Furthermore, he does not expect himself, nor does society expect him, to educate himself for a profession; hence the dependency of the student role is a respectable, even a prestige-bearing, dependency. It will be reacted to as such unless the student, having an inordinate need to keep the past alive in the present, responds to professional demands as though they are parental demands, or unless the educator regarding the normal dependency implicit in learning as pathological dependency enacts the parent through treating the student like a child. It is to be remembered that, in a culture where learning is loved, social approval accrues to the individual who lends himself to being taught at any stage of life. Educators can well be slow to react to the student's submission to learning as a problematic response, lest they needlessly inject a feeling of stigma not implicit in the situation.

When one considers the very real differences which ordinarily would obtain in the import of these two kinds of experience for the individuals involved, it is not surprising that students need and want a different relationship with their mentors from the helping relationship of social casework or psychotherapy. This has been amply demonstrated in their responses to being "caseworked" or "treated" in the educational situation.

A student's normal adaptive response to the difficulties that he must overcome in the learning process should not be confused with a neurotic patient's defense against conflicts that he cannot face frankly. Even when a student becomes emotionally disturbed and develops defenses which interfere with his learning, we should regard his emotional disturbance and his defenses against it rather as a complication in the learning process than as a primary object of our concern. Our task is education, not therapy; and these two aims cannot profitably be mixed or performed at the same time by the same person. We should deal with the student's emotional difficulties only in so far as they are interfering with his learning. If he needs more therapeutic help, then we should refer him elsewhere for therapy. In those instances where students have entered the profession primarily to solve their own personality problems, help advisedly focuses on directing them elsewhere for therapy or on accepting a change in occupational goal. By and large, the educational measures of a professional school will be oriented toward the aims which students commonly have when pursuing the goal of training for a profession and to the common import of the experience for educable adults, whose personality development approximates the portrayal in the preceding chapter.

In considering the integration of learning in professional education, we envisage a goal-striving situation in which a hierarchy of goals has been structured and in which the student has a set of

goals for himself, which at the onset of training he anticipates
will be at one with those of the profession. This may or may not
prove to be the case. We assume, also, students, by and large, who
have considerable, though varied, capacity to sustain their pursuit
of goals and to integrate learning. In social work education the
literature attests a long-standing concern with the import of personality development for the integration of learning. It sets forth,
furthermore, many observations of characteristic goal-directed behavior which suggest much regarding the integrative task involved.
Pending systematic research, such observations lend themselves to
dubious inferences. At the present writing the best that we can do
is to attempt to appraise our observations in the light of current
theories of behavior and to formulate as best we can the thinking
which has not only guided our educational practices but also roughly tested our assumptions.

II. THE INTEGRATIVE PROCESS IN GOAL-DIRECTED BEHAVIOR

In this chapter we draw on Dr. French's formulation of the integrative process in goal-directed behavior as a frame of reference,
because it is compatible with the point of view which has long
guided our educational practice. It is compatible specifically in that
he focuses sharply on how the individual integrates his experience
for equilibrium and intact personality survival; he gives prominence
to the concept of behavior as a continuum from the normal to the
abnormal rather than as a dichotomy of normal and abnormal; he
affirms the long-standing psychoanalytic assumption, one sometimes
overlooked by those applying psychoanalytic concepts in helping
and in teaching processes, that adaptive and defensive responses
may be used successfully or unsuccessfully, depending upon the
nature and source of the anxiety and importantly upon the individual's capacity to develop and integrate guiding insight as he strives
to attain his goals.

Dr. French summarizes his postulates regarding the integration
of behavior for application in the goal-directed behavior of professional learning as follows:

Goal-directed behavior is motivated by needs and hopes. A person's
needs and unsatisfied desires put him under pressure which spurs him
on to activity; but unless he has hope of being able to achieve a desired

goal, it will be difficult for him to subordinate his activity to any consistent purpose. In order to achieve a goal it is not enough just to do something. One must also know what to do. Purposive behavior must be guided by insight into how to achieve one's goal; and even if he knows how to achieve his goal, he must also be able to subordinate his activity to plan. Too intensive desires or anxieties may interfere with this subordination of behavior to purpose; if a person's unsatisfied desires or anxieties are too great, he may be thrown into a panic and become quite incapable of concentrating his effort on a sustained purpose. In order to subordinate his activity to purpose he must have an "integrative capacity" adequate to absorb and channel the pressure of his unsatisfied needs and anxieties which constitute his integrative task. "Integrative capacity" we define as the capacity of the ego to withstand and master pressure and, in particular, to channel the pressure of unsatisfied desire into effective goal-directed effort. This "integrative capacity" has its chief source in a person's confidence in being able to execute his plan and achieve his goal. Such hope is based in past successes and in opportunities perceived in the present. And from this it follows: (1) that those students who have a background of past success to give them confidence in their ability to master new tasks will be the ones who will be best able to overcome the difficulties inherent in the educational process; and (2) that the difficulties in the educational program should he judiciously dosed so as to make it possible for the student to build up his confidence progressively by ever new achievement and to protect himself from the disintegrating influence of disillusioning or repeated failures.[2]

In the preceding chapter we attempted to portray the nature of ego development and ego-superego integration characteristic of maturity. The significance of this development for the integration of learning in the goal-striving of professional education, though manifest in general, merits some specification.

First, the needs and desires which motivate the relatively mature student, as previously envisaged, tend to be appropriate, in that they can be met for the good of all concerned through the work of the profession. Furthermore, not given to wishful thinking as a defense against inadequate ego development, he has tended to pursue a goal within his intellectual, physical, and socioeconomic scope. In accordance with the American tradition, however, he may be stretching himself considerably from the socioeconomic angle, a stress which is eased in part through the culture's support of his striving. When he has become involved in unrealistic striving through a misconception of the demands of the profession in relation to his needs and wants, he can relinquish this pursuit and make

2. Dr. Thomas M. French, in an unpublished communication to the author.

a substitution without frustration of a disintegrating degree. This is not to say that he "gives up" impulsively or is not emotionally disturbed by his misdirected expenditure of time and effort or that there is not some sense of failure. Depending in part on his reality situation in terms of time and money invested in relation to his age, prior experience, and his economic situation, he may be greatly inconvenienced and very disturbed. The nature of the student's ego development and very notably the ego-superego formation is often dramatically manifest in his ways of dealing with his discomfort in the process of goal termination, as he is "counseled out" of the school or initiates this action himself. Noteworthy responses of the relatively mature student at such a time are: readiness to appraise himself in this situation somewhat realistically, hence with relatively little wishful thinking and rationalization, though this may occur to some extent for intact personality survival. There is, however, relatively little projection of blame or motivation to make the school a rejecting parent. This does not preclude valid criticism of wherein the school realistically has failed him in some measure. Notable also as movement within this stressful experience is the act of reaching out to consider the next course of action and to appraise what this experience has shown regarding his aptitudes and limitations as a guide to the future. Notable movement also is his receptivity to guidance and a sense of relief and renewed hope at having extricated himself from a self-defeating pursuit. Obviously, even the mature student's capacity to come through this stress with responses of this character is contingent in large part on the conduct of the advisory sessions in which he is helped to clarify his aims and come to grips with adversity. This implies knowledge, understanding, and skill on the part of faculty advisers in giving individualized help. In this connection it is important that the adviser realize that the student conceivably can have a healthy personality, even though he cannot do social work. When an adviser erroneously conceives of a misfit student as a misfit in general, he is prone to conduct the terminating session in ways which weaken rather than support the ego, thus needlessly fostering rationalization and projection, to the exclusion of the self-appraisal of which the individual is capable. Through giving his life very largely to his profession, a member of a profession may come to feel that his profession is the world. He thus totalizes the student's failure and anticipates a greater trauma for him in termination than may occur.

Second, it is recalled that ego-superego integration implies emancipation from old authority-dependency ties, hence freedom on the individual's part to make new experience his own and thus to depart from the established order within social limits. There is implied a marked reduction in fear of change and resistance to it. It follows that, with relative freedom from fear, he has sufficient hope and confidence that his energy is made available to his fantasy. He is free to engage in imaginative consideration because he has both the energy and the daring to act. Rather than being enslaved by fantasy, which substitutes for doing, he is free to put fantasy to use. Hence out of capacity for imaginative consideration his goal-strivings give rise to adaptive responses. He learns through trial and error and even avoids error through quick perception, which makes selection possible either as a realistic choice or as a needed defense. This sensitivity to cues and perception of connections, a capacity for width of relationship in the sense of readiness to apprehend the whole in its broad generality, bespeaks a capacity for imaginative consideration, through which, in part, identification as a means to learning comes about and guiding insight essential for the integration of learning is acquired.

It is characteristic of this stage of development that the student out of his self-dependence seeks knowledge of what to feel and think and how to act. In orienting himself as to how to get along, he reaches out for a scale of values, as to what is of primary importance, what is less important, or unimportant. He reaches out to master obstacles with an expectancy of success which stems from a feeling of adequacy in past endeavors. In grappling with obstacles he is not prone to let them become an end in themselves through repetitive but futile attempts at mastery. He does not readily accept neurotic substitutions, subgoals for primary ones, fantasy for reality, and thus go astray in his goal-striving. Out of an integration of the pleasure and reality principles, he can contain considerable tension because he can accept postponement of gratification; the tension of postponement is lowered through his perception of connections between immediate and remote goals.

This brief summarization delineates roughly the major implications of adequate ego development, in which ego-superego integration is a prominent feature, for the integration of learning in the goal-striving of professional education. It is to be remembered that the relatively mature student brings these potentials for productive learning to the educational experience. There is wide variation in the size of the integrative task for the individual student, however, as well as considerable variation in integrative capacity among students who could be characterized as having adequate ego development. Some of the variables which make for ease and difficulty in this integration of learning are now presented.

III. THE INTEGRATIVE TASK

We return to the concept, on which there is general agreement among educators, that the integrative task is heavier where the intensity of affect is heavy. Dr. French states that the integrative task is heavy or light, depending on the depth and strength of the needs and wishes which motivate the individual's goal-striving and the extent to which they give rise to fear or hope. It follows that it will be heavy or light also in terms of the emotional import which the experience of striving has for him, that is, whether or not his needs and wants are met, the frustrations and gratifications encountered in the process of goal attainment as he attains subsidiary goals and masters obstacles, as well as the tempo of the process of goal attainment. It will be heavy or light, therefore, in terms of the total affect load, and notably heavy in relation to the predominance of negative affect over positive affect. The size of the integrative task will vary from individual to individual in relation to his motivation and the degree of hope which sustains him, thus enabling him to absorb anxiety and discomfort, and in relation to the nature of the educational opportunity and the concomitant social circumstances. It is difficult to envisage the integrative task apart from capacity and opportunity, because the three are continuously interrelated. In spite of this fact, we attempt to consider each separately but find it not quite possible.

As the individual strives to attain his goals, his needs and desires beget fears. Of this Dr. French says: "I want something very much— wish strong. I fear greatly the consequences—fear strong. The educational task becomes traumatic when the integrative task of absorbing anxiety is greater than the individual's capacity for this. When anxiety mounts beyond bounds, considerable disorganization can occur unless the individual is successful in defending himself against it." The decisive point is that defenses arise as anxiety is pushing the individual beyond his capacity to contain it. Depending on their nature and extent, the defenses may or may not greatly obstruct the integration of learning. Earlier we portrayed the mature student as being relatively free from fear and as having resources in terms of his ego development for containing negative affect and for dealing with it constructively. What are some of the specific fears and major sources of anxiety which commonly heighten the integrative task to the point that defenses may be erected which impede learning?

1. *The Fear of Helplessness Due to Lack of Knowledge and Skill*

We place first and foremost a realistic fear which bedevils the mature student by reason of his maturity if, as in social work education, he begins practice at once before he knows the what, the why, and the how of the profession's ways of working. He lacks knowledge, understanding, and skill to help clients in the solution of multiple problems. Out of a mature sense of responsibility, out of a well-developed conscience, out of concern not to fail those who need his help, as well as out of his high expectancy of himself in terms of performing well in order to grade well—in short, out of a well-developed ego—he is sometimes acutely fearful as specific case situations are beyond either his realistic competence or his feelings of competence to function. The social work student has a supervisor at hand to help him think what to do and why or even to tell him "the whats and the whys." But overnight she cannot help him ingrain the "hows." Hence it is not only the lack of knowledge, at times, but the gap between newly acquired knowledge and skill, at other times, which produce more anxiety than he can contain. In these instances this anxiety, if not overwhelming, creates an urgency to learn which motivates him to close the gaps in his knowledge and to expand his understanding and skill. Inevitably there will be times when, in spite of high intelligence and emotional readiness to learn, the tempo of learning cannot keep pace with the demands of practice. At such times anxiety will mount, and learning will normally be impeded or temporarily interrupted. The defenses which signal an impasse vary widely, but emotional constriction and stereotyped behavior are an often encountered defense against disorganization resorted to by the relatively mature student in his attempts at mastering himself and the situation. He becomes inhibited and task-centered. Whether or not he gets involved in repetitive futile activity which seriously interrupts learning is contingent in part on the nature of the educational help given him. The repetition for mastery implicit in these task-centered, constricted phases is not to be confused with obsessive-compulsive behavior. His response to competent teaching at such stages throws light on the problem.

With reference to realistic lack of competence, it is well to recall that earlier we specified the mature student's hope and confidence arising out of previous success in goal-striving as being an inner resource for the integration of learning. This very expectancy of success now frequently brings disappointment. A commonplace occurrence is the advisory session sought by the student who always graded "A" in college and who is dismayed at the "come down" in his grades in professional school. In social work education, this occurs more often in field work than in classroom work but may occur in both areas. Advisers may be irritated by what they feel to be "childish" concern with grades. Actually, it is not just the lower grade, but the grade as confirmation of the feelings of incompetence he has experienced which leads him realistically to appraise himself in this situation. Why am I not doing well in learning this profession I have chosen? Will I be able to become a social worker, a doctor, a teacher, a nurse? He is struggling with the important questions. Is the goal worth striving for? Can it be achieved?

He may find reassurance in the advisory session through an orientation to the normalcy of his inability to measure up to his expectancy of himself. But he probably will also become aware of himself in a new light, conscious of himself in a relationship of a different nature with people than he has experienced before, one in which he finds that he has unanticipated shortcomings. This normally produces considerable anxiety, often more than he can contain, and commonly he responds in one of two ways in relation to instructors and notably to supervision. He may struggle against his feelings of inadequacy through reacting against his need for help. He measures himself against his instructor or supervisor who has been able to become a member of his profession. They have attained what he wants but may not be able to attain. These persons have the power to prevent him from attaining his goal through grading him. There follows a phase of resistance to his dependency on his instructors. He must feel adequate in their eyes. There is resistance also to their authority. Normally, adult students feel some rivalry with adults, often near in age, from whom they must learn. Because the acid test of his learning occurs in the doing of practice and in social work education because of the closer relationship with field supervisor than with classroom instructors, the authority-dependency conflicts of this stage tend to get focused and worked through, largely in this relationship. The decisive point is that the anxiety produced by realistic incompetence gets reinforced by the fear-hostility-guilt feelings evoked in the relationship with those upon whom he must depend in order to attain his goal.

Or, instead of denying himself help when he feels incompetent, the student may seek it urgently. Since he realistically needs it, this is a reality-oriented response and often a less problematic one than the denial of dependency. If the supervisor or instructor sees mounting dependency at this stage as a potentially constructive means to ease anxiety, she will meet the student's needs for help freely and in ways which help him become competent, thus easing the anxiety through solving the dependency problem. If, instead of regarding it as the normal dependency implicit in learning, she regards it as pathological regression, she will probably render help in ways which inject conflict over dependency and thus reinforce, rather than relieve, the anxiety which produced the defense. Social work educators and perhaps other educators vary in their responses to these two ways by which students adapt or defend themselves when their anxiety over incompetence is great. It is our impression that there is wide recognition of the import of these reactions and increasing skill in educational practice in meeting the student's need. It is our impression, however, that social work educators have traditionally been more accepting of the student who denies his dependency and resists help than of the one who accepts it and seeks help. Perhaps they have tended to respect this defense because they have regarded it as an adult one, bespeaking ego strength. Consequently, they have been more ready to help the student work through resistance to dependency than to give to the one who does not resist it. They have felt safer, perhaps, in giving to the student who has some fear of taking than to the one who reaches out confidently to take. They have failed to see the ego-superego integration import of the absence of fear of dependency. Ironically, then, they have created resistance and needlessly produced a problem to solve. Perhaps out of their social work practice they have felt more at home in dealing with resistance than in giving freely to the nonresistive individual. Perhaps also their practice has inclined them to regard lack of resistance to taking help, in a relationship which ordinarily stigmatizes the recipient, as pathological regression, because this often has been the case.[3]

We summarize our discussion of one common fear experienced by the relatively mature student by reason of his adequate ego-superego integration as follows: Lack of knowledge, understanding, and skill, as well as the gap between knowledge and skill, operates in an educational regime where the student begins practice at once to produce more anxiety than he can contain. At such times adaptations and defenses, only a few of which have been presented, occur which have the purpose of aiding integration, even though some of them may temporarily impede learning. Whether or not they seriously obstruct learning depends in part on the response which the student encounters in the educational situation. Traditionally in social work education too little importance has been given to this source of anxiety. Much greater emphasis has been placed on the sources which follow.

2. Fear of the New by Reason of Its Nature and Meaning

Fear of the new is widely recognized as a universal lifelong reaction, one which operates to produce tension in learning and to heighten the integrative task. One may expect this fear to be more prominent in the early and late years of life than in adulthood. The relatively mature young adult has experienced the new without trauma of a degree that has interrupted growth. He has integrated change in himself and in his external world. As a result, he ap-

3. See this chapter, pp. 88–89, on differentiation of social import in taking help in client-worker relationship as compared with student-instructor relationship.

proaches the new with expectancy of capacity to master it. Normally he craves new experience and is restive with unmodified repetition of the past. Normally at this stage the individual wants to see the world and experience its variety in peoples and places. It, therefore, is not newness itself which frightens the young adult but, instead, the nature of the newness in relation to needs, wants, and capacities brought from his previous experience. Social work educators have emphasized, sometimes to the exclusion of other factors, that the nature of social work knowledge and experience produces anxiety, first, because it exerts a demand for much change in the learner and, second, because it is prone to ignite and reinforce the latent and active psychosexual and psychosocial conflicts of the young adult. While the principle of resistance to marked change persists throughout life, it could be said that at this stage the individual with adequate ego-superego development and integration can accommodate himself to marked change with greater ease than he can earlier or later. In delineating the general objectives of professional education and of education for social work in chapter 1, we have implied many of the changes which the educational process aims to effect in the learner. These obviously impose a larger demand for change in some individuals than in others; hence the size of the integrative task, in terms of anxiety over change, varies among educable individuals. It can be said, also, that while these individuals will be subject to conflicts, as specified, the conflicts will not be of an extent that the anxiety will be overwhelming.

a) Experiences which threaten self-dependence.—There is variation among individuals entering a profession as to which new elements arouse fear. Certain ones, however, have seemed to induce anxiety more commonly than others. As one reflects upon them, they suggest that the young adult is peculiarly vulnerable to those new demands which threaten his self-dependence, his sense of adequacy as an adult. A few years earlier he could more daringly risk new experience which might render him helpless, not only because protective parent-persons were at hand to put things right but also because it felt right to be helpless in disaster. He could more comfortably expect others to rescue him as well as to pick up the pieces. The young adult in a world which expects of him something different from this has a different expectation of himself. Normally he is consciously and unconsciously committed to have what it takes in whatever he undertakes. This implies that the outcome depends on him and that he must suffer the consequences. Not yet inured to this much self-dependence, he may strive to attain it unrealistically through denial of dependence, as described earlier. It is only, therefore, as he has more inner assurance of his adequacy than frequently obtains at this age, that he is not defensive about his realistic dependency. We turn to the new elements in social work education which prominently threaten his commitment to responsible adulthood. Other professions may have noted comparable elements.

Social workers continuously are engaged, directly and indirectly, in helping people to help themselves and in helping them whether or not they can come to help themselves. Up to now the student often has taken more help than he has given. Out of what he has been given he has developed considerable capacity for self-help and a sense of obligation to others. Consequently, more often than not, he has given help, as necessity and conscience have pushed him to do so and as his own needs and desires have motivated him to meet the needs and wants of others in a relationship valued for one reason or another. The decisive point is that helping others probably has been a minor refrain in his total experience. He has not made a lifework of it. While his nuclear experience in self-help and in giving and taking help will have considerable carry-over into professional helping, he suddenly finds that he is no longer just a person helping people in accordance with his own necessity and predilection. He is no longer an independent giver, but, instead, he is the representative of an agency specifically committed to help certain people in well-defined and measured ways. He senses the agency as something bigger, more knowing, but less free than he had conceived of himself as being. Later, when he has become an integral part of the agency, he will find greater security than if he operated alone. At the start, however, this feeling of not being able to be himself in his efforts to help others arouses anxiety. In this there is the dual fear of helplessness and of being controlled. His sense that unless he masters the use of the agency it may master him motivates him to identify with others, depend on them, and learn from them. The stress of this demand varies widely with individuals in relation to feelings about dependency and authority and in relation also to the nature of the help given the novice in his first agency experience.

As he struggles to make the social agency his means to helping people, the student early perceives that it is accountable to a community of persons who not only have pronounced convictions and cherished feelings about the recipients of social work help but also feel competent and entitled to dictate on matters calling for professional knowledge and competence. He is subject to the pressure of these attitudes, for they are imbedded in agency policies and in statutory regulations which govern his activity. The student who in entering social work has been motivated by a need and desire to effect social change is deeply frustrated when he experiences his profession's dependence on others for the attainment of its aims and its inability to control more completely the conditions which affect its practice. Anxiety stems not only from frustration implicit in postponed gratification but also from self-doubt, as he questions whether he can find satisfaction in working for tomorrow's uncertain and at times seemingly improbable gains.

The demand that the student subordinate remote goals to immediate ones, that he identify with and relate to those who impose demands, comes at a stage when, recently emancipated from parental controls, he often seeks through his work opportunity for self-expression, for individual creativity, and for the independent acting-out of his own urges in the interest of self-realization. Commonly he experiences frustration as he finds that he cannot be either a free-lance worker or a free agent within the agency, the profession, and the community. The young adult, viewed from the standpoint of Alexander's concept of surplus energy or Erikson's concept of the nuclear conflict of generativity versus stagnation, is bent toward progression, the giving of self to creative activity, the giving of energy to work which serves a purpose beyond the "in-order-to-survive" objective.[4] He therefore is restive at playing safe and at working within limits. The educational system now, in contrast

4. Franz Alexander, M.D., *Our Age of Unreason* (New York: J. B. Lippincott Co., 1942), pp. 144–48; Eric H. Erikson, *Childhood and Society* (New York: W. W. Norton & Co., 1950), p. 231.

to many college regimes, holds him more strictly accountable through closer supervision. This, until he has experienced the adult demands of the work which make the system anxiety-relieving, gives a feeling of regression which often provokes anger, resistance, and anxiety. Complaints of the school's childish procedures and an outcry for adult freedom are commonplace at the start. This fear of regression heightens the initial integrative task. It poses a problem for the professional school, that of helping students accept rather than submit to the discipline of professional education, in order that, in giving up certain freedoms, they may not have their inclination for independent and creative thinking inhibited. Among other developments, this implies the attainment of primary concern for those whom the profession serves. For the welfare of the client one makes the ways of the profession one's own. It implies also the development of a relationship between mentors and students in which the student has conditional confidence in those from whom he learns as differentiated from blind trust in them.

b) The demand for understanding experience beyond one's own. —Another fear to which the student is ordinarily subject in social work and perhaps also in certain other professions stems from the fact that he is called upon to understand and to help people whose experience is beyond his experience. As has been delineated, the student at this stage has a certain readiness to go beyond his own experience, so that vicarious experience interests and excites him. At the same time, it is demanded that he think objectively in situations which involve him emotionally. In helping people in time of trouble he encounters them when they are emotionally disturbed. He must feel *with* them in order to relate to them with sympathy and understanding. He risks coming to feel like them. When this occurs, he experiences, in addition to their disturbed feelings, the frustration which comes from being helpless rather than helpful. In such instances anxiety may stem from feelings of helplessness and anger at himself and at the individual who induced his discomfort. Or, as he reaches out to see and to feel situations from the standpoint of the troubled person, he may feel quite out of touch, uncomprehending when he should comprehend, unmoved and judgmatic, instead of compassionate and understanding. He may solve the problem of his distance from the client by overreacting emotionally in one way or another, through denial of the feelings provoked, or through an exaggerated emotional response of pretensive identification. All this requires that he make learning a conscious process so that he may understand in order to regulate his own emotional responses. Making learning conscious immediately brings the student up against the unconscious, which looms large to produce a complex of fears.

c) The responsibility to sustain consciousness of self and to use the concept of the unconscious.—The concept of the unconscious ordinarily is not new as the student enters professional school. For many, however, it has been an abstraction which may or may not have caused discomfort. That it has been provocative of feeling is suggested because it has been something fascinating to talk about, to laugh off, or to use haphazardly and dubiously against one's self and others. Now in social work education and perhaps elsewhere, the student must purposively attempt, seriously, to use formulations regarding the unconscious, reliably, in his appraisals of the motives and behavior of clients, colleagues, and himself. Dr. Charlotte Babcock, in her association with social workers as case consultant and as therapist, identifies this new element as one which ordinarily mobilizes considerable anxiety to heighten the integrative task. Occasionally it precipitates profound anxiety, making known unapparent personality needs and conflicts. Marked anxiety also may bespeak an attack upon the scale of values, the mores of the student's culture. This new orientation, put to use, attacks much that the student has valued highly—for instance, his concept of man as rational and responsible and in full control of his thinking and action. As he works with the concept that man unwittingly and unwillingly is prompted and pushed by unconscious needs and wants, the student's measuring stick goes awry. Mistrust and self-doubt encompass him. What to believe of what the client says, what to make of what he does, absorb him. Whom to praise and whom to blame bedevil him. Students have been known to protest that there is no virtue in good deeds or no lack of it in bad behavior, in so far as the unconscious takes over. The student may swing from judgmatic attitudes to unrealistically permissive ones, his rationale being that one cannot hold the individual accountable for what he unknowingly does.

Furthermore, this new orientation attacks the student's security in an intellectualized approach in which direct inquiry, reassurance, and persuasion have been prominent. He feels helpless when he gets the full impact of why he has been unable to, or should not have tried to, reason an individual out of his ills into new ways of feeling, thinking, and doing. He may go through a phase of seeing man as more irrational than he is, until he can encompass the duality—of man operating consciously and unconsciously, rationally and irrationally. This occurs as he experiences the values of understanding the rationale of the seemingly irrational, unconscious needs and strivings if one is to engage the individual's conscious, rational self in productive problem-solving. In order to participate as a professional helper in problem-solving, the need to take into account our own unconscious needs and responses ordinarily induces discomfort. What to make of what he thought he felt and what he thought he knew of the whys of his own doing involves a degree of self-questioning which the student resists in the interests of his own integration. He necessarily and advisedly moves slowly into self-analysis and in lending himself to penetrating appraisal because insight at rapid tempo may be disorienting. Frequently it is the student with well-developed ego and adequate ego-superego integration who does not precipitously get deeply absorbed with his own unconscious. This is partially because he has some insight and also because his unconscious serves him well, so that disasters in his conduct of his work do not occur to reveal needs and strivings which are markedly unacceptable. Consequently, his gradual insight gains are not traumatizing, even though they provoke some anxiety.

The concept of the unconscious also attacks the student's deeply cherished feeling about and conviction of man's right to privacy. If the individual's unconscious needs and acts make sense and thus lend themselves to appraisal, he unwittingly betrays himself. Others can see through him. As the student participates in looking beneath the surface of those who seek his help, he feels and knows that what he is doing to others will be done to him. Those who are teaching him "how" have the "know how" to use against him. He feels exposed and defenseless, and at such times his defenses may mount. It is normal to resist intrusion. It is probable that certain immature individuals who take pleasure in exhibiting themselves can tolerate feeling transparent when others find it intolerable. In so far as the student has been shocked, repelled, and harsh in his judgments as he has glimpsed the deeper import of the client's behavior, his anxiety about being seen through by his mentors will be more profound and his defenses greater unless, being overwhelmed, he is impelled to ease tension through revealing himself in order to know where he stands. This is because he will have ambivalently feared and hoped, on the one hand, harsh judgment comparable to his own of the client and, on the other, understanding and tolerance of the needs he has provocatively or searchingly revealed.

Commonly, the student deals with his discomfort through combating the new ideas and practices verbally and through being slow to infer anything but the obvious.[5] He may cling to the old as a defense against the new by emphasizing the rational, reality-based explanation of his own behavior as well as that of the client's. Unless his fears are profound, as in instances where the defenses hold the fort against the emergence of pathology, this sensitivity to exposure will gradually subside as the student finds that depth of understanding is used to help people rather than employed against them. It will subside also as he finds that insight helps the individual to become more resourceful in coping with his problematic reality. It will diminish also as he finds that he himself functions more adequately in helping as he tentatively and experimentally uses his deepened understanding of the client to help him. Concurrently and sequentially, he gains confidence to move into seeing himself with a new eye.

Among other means to handle discomfort induced by having to take the unconscious into account is a headlong approach, in which the student daringly attacks that which threatens him and attempts to master or to obliterate it through swallowing it whole. In these instances one sees an almost obsessional absorption, characterized by indiscriminate use of the new orientation. This phase normally bespeaks experiment for mastery, and in such instances misuse will taper off with time. When overuse persists, however, we may suspect

5. An example of this is given in chap. 10: the two students who resisted the idea that the client's behavior reactions were subject to appraisal.

that the student's zeal for seeing through others does not include himself. In these instances he fails to test his inferences through putting them to use in rendering help. He may even be inept in establishing and in sustaining a helping relationship. As time goes on, his inferences do not become more individualized with nice reference to reality. Instead, as though lifted out of context, they take on a stereotyped character. A few examples follow: Late appointment means resistance to help; a gracious smile or appreciative comment is an indicator of veiled hostility; when someone falls and incurs injury, the student ignores the ice on the stairs or the concealed banana peel to infer "accident-prone out of self-punitive impulses." Thus one sees a superficial orientation being used as an intellectual defense against the threatening implications of that which he seemingly embraces, comparable to pseudo-intimacy as a defense against relationships.

3. *Dual Intellectual Process and Multiple Demand*

Finally, the integrative task in professional education is large because of a pervasive duality in intellectual processes. Compassionate attitudes must coexist with dispassionate thinking. Intuitive judgments must precede and accompany well-considered ones. Imaginative consideration, to the point of speculative thinking, must go hand in hand with precise thinking supported by evidence, especially in social work education. All these qualities of mind are valued and become educational goals. The attempt to set in operation, that is, to pattern, this disciplined, but unconstricted and flexible, intellectual functioning occurs within an educational scheme which is characterized by high pressure rather than by any degree of leisure. Many courses, much library work, many written assignments, course examinations, comprehensive examinations, thesis requirements, field work, often at a time-consuming distance, constitute an incessant barrage of demands which he must meet within rigid time limits. Physically the social work educational scheme is designed to heighten tension and anxiety rather than to guard against it.

4. *Summary of the Integrative Task*

All this adds up to several significant conclusions. The student is having to undergo change in his feeling and thinking at rapid tempo against heavy reality demands, frequently at a vulnerable age. Often he is in the early years of adulthood when regression to the dependency of earlier years is more readily precipitated by the demands of the adult world than when he is a little older. At this time, also, anxiety over his adequacy as an adult in the workaday world may be at a peak. This is the lifework he has chosen, and ordinarily there will be a great deal at stake in making good. Because of its decisive importance, we state again that the individual's professional endeavor involves his concept of himself as an adequate adult, a concept which is a composite of his needs and wishes, bearing also the imprint of deeply influential relationships. The extent to which the individual is committed to this course of action will determine the degree of anxiety to which he is subject as obstacles arise, as well as the degree of frustration which he experiences as his purpose is thwarted. With a compelling need to attain the standards of near-perfection implicit in professional adequacy, there will be anxiety about normal dependencies. This conflict over dependency serves to mobilize him against the return to childhood often symbolized in seeking and taking the help which realistically he needs. It can be a healthy assertion of his strong impulse toward self-dependence. Dissatisfaction with shortcomings, the sense of unrealized possibilities which push for realization, and a kind of petulance with incapacity may serve to motivate learning, provided that the conflict over that dependency implicit in learning is resolved. This matter of the relationship as a corrective element and a means to integration will be elaborated later.

The content of the educational experiences may serve to activate only partially resolved conflicts and to shake and sometimes even to break down ego defenses which had seemingly been well intrenched. Consequently, one finds that learning involves the growth process. It may demand personality change at rapid tempo. This means that there will be a larger element of disorganization than in many other learning situations, and hence reorganization—that is, reintegration—will occur at a slower tempo. There may also be some lag in integration of the various components in learning. Educators in the professions frequently note and commonly decry the slowness with which integration occurs. In social work education perhaps we are making an unrealistic demand when we expect students to achieve a nice integration of content within the two-year period, at least under our present educational schemes.[6]

In short, the demands for integration at times are sufficiently beyond the student's capacity that seemingly his normal capacity for integration is lowered. While the ego structure has not broken down, its protective function at times is operating at the expense of its integrative function. When the learning situation provokes more anxiety than the student can contain, one may expect regressive responses and marked resistance to learning and the formation of defenses against it. One capital defense may be "I cannot learn because you are not teaching me properly." Projection of responsibility for learning can be expected. Blocked in thinking, the social work student may fall back on the many stereotypes in which the field abounds. Fragments of theoretical formulas, such as "maternal rejection," "castration complex," "oedipal conflict," "acceptance," "supportive," "insight therapy," etc., become the basis of easy generalizations, which connote pretensive adequacy when there is not an adequate intellectual or emotional grasp of concepts. Swamped by too much, the student's defense may take the form of creating or adhering to dichotomies—this is black *or* white; the problem was caused by this *or* that. Pending the gradual development of insight which normally will occur, frustration and confusion will be evidenced when the student must consider gradations or multiple causation. The grays and the "ands" will be reacted against vehemently. This fragmentation can be regarded as a normal phase of breaking the whole into parts for assimilation, unless it persists overlong, when it signals a learning problem. Temporary adherence to generalizations which fitted certain facts in one situation for inappropriate application in other situations where there are common and different elements may be regarded as normal in view of the principles of stability and economy. "The natural tendency is to adhere to what has already been achieved. Revision requires effort; old formulas can be repeated without a fresh investment of energy."[7] When such a response persists, its meaning must be

6. Charlotte Towle, "Emotional Elements in Professional Learning," in pamphlet entitled *Professional Education* (New York: American Association of Schools of Social Work, 1948).

7. Franz Alexander, M.D., *Fundamentals of Psychoanalysis* (New York: W. W. Norton & Co., 1948), p. 41.

understood. It may indicate a generalized resistance to the learning progression, or the formulations, old or new, may have specific disturbing import which prevent the development of insight. The nature of social work education being what it is, an experience demanding growth from within, we can expect normally that growth will be gradual; there will be phases of resistance to change expressed in various ways, notably through ambivalence, which must be given time to be resolved for productive learning. There will be fragmentary regressions expressed in many forms, with plateaus and slumps in learning which are significant of the size of the student's integrative task and capacity. There will be considerable partialization of learning because synthesis is difficult to achieve and partial insight is gained usually before it becomes total. The human mind in a complex learning situation tends to become somewhat obsessive and to seek generalizations and dichotomies and thereby to center on one aspect of a situation to the exclusion of others. What social casework teacher has not struggled with the problem of conveying multiple causation, multiple motivation, the this and this and this of the situation, only to have students blot out totality for a comfortable "this or that" factor? This atomistic tendency not only has been the student's means to deal with complexity, but often it also has been the instructor's easy adaptation.

IV. INTEGRATIVE CAPACITY

Integration of learning implies perception of relatedness. It requires the ability to relate one thing to another, the readiness to put the parts of the whole together and to see the significance of the whole. In so far as the learner is able to see the whole as something more than the sum of the parts, he is potentially creative, with the possibility not merely of attaining his goal but of moving beyond the established order of his mentor's thinking in some way or in some degree. Beyond native intellectual ability, perception of relatedness is contingent on the extent to which realistic hope absorbs some of the anxiety and tension implicit in learning, so that they serve to motivate rather than to impede learning. It is recalled that anxiety and tension arise from the needs and wants which have motivated the individual to pursue a goal. Pending the release of anxiety and tension through the gratification or reward which goal attainment brings, the accretion of anxiety and tension will depend on the course of events in the goal pursuit. Integrative capacity is this hope-engendered power to bear anxiety and tension so that goals may be attained or abandoned when unrealistic, without excessive cost or damage to the personality. Since in education at all levels in all fields of endeavor educators are concerned to strengthen and develop the integrative capacity of the learner, it is essential that we identify the several major elements which combine and interact to operate for hope and confidence in learning.

1. *Personality Characterized by Adequate Ego Development*

As indicated earlier, integrative capacity in professional education which makes a heavy emotional demand is conditioned prominently by the individual's emotional development, his readiness to come to grips with reality, to struggle with and face interrelationships, and to think and act for himself apart from others. It depends heavily, therefore, on his personality development, in terms of the nature and organization of defenses and adaptive mechanisms. Decisive for or against educability is the way these function to make for large, adequate, or meager capacity to deal with emotion in himself and others, so that constructive helping relationships and effective working relationships can be established, sustained, and terminated with clients and colleagues. This implies capacity to deal with emotions to an extent that learning can become a conscious process and the learner develop insight for depth of understanding of others. These specific capabilities are contingent on the nature and extent of the individual's ego development and ego-superego integration, as delineated earlier in this chapter and in chapter 3.

It is well to recall, however, certain specific features in adequate ego development which operate in the individual's capacity to contain and absorb certain anxieties, peculiarly prominent in learning social work, so that there is a minimum accretion of tension in the educational porcess. First, implicit in emancipation is the important fact that authority-dependency conflicts are minimal; hence there is freedom to meet dependency and to use authority constructively without an increase of anxiety; minimum hostility, guilt, and anxiety in relationships which demand subordination of one's own needs and desires; freedom to relate to different people differently rather than largely in terms of one's own compelling needs and wants; energy to invest in the educational experience and in the concerns of others; a well-developed and integrated conscience as differentiated from repressive, poorly integrated superego formation as a nucleus for the development of social consciousness and social conscience. Second, out of integration of the pleasure and reality principles there is a wide span for postponement of gratification. Operating here are hope and confidence stemming from past success and the integration of former failures; receptivity to remotivation which implies readiness to let socially learned needs and desires (professionally acquired drives) compete with and replace the primary ones, which brought the individual into social work.

2. *Native and Acquired Intellectual Ability*

Personality organization characterized by a well-developed ego and adequate ego-superego integration is basic in integrative capacity. Such an individual's capacity to contain and absorb anxiety depends on other factors and obviously on his native and acquired intellectual ability. The intellectual capacity which the young adult brings to professional education is comprised of his native mental endowment and his educational preparation in terms of ways of studying and habits of mind, as well as in terms of essential basic knowledge. The integrative task—that 'is, the amount of affect to contain—will be much heavier in those instances where the student has not acquired disciplined study habits or learned an orderly way of thinking so that he is ready to engage in problem-solving. In chapter 1 we indicated that an objective of professional education is to strengthen this ability; but if it has not been acquired by adult years, it is doubtful that it can be attained in professional education. Social work educators decry the necessity to teach what should have been taught earlier to every well-educated citizen.[8] To what extent an adult's ineptitude in orderly thinking stems from lack in his educational background or has significance in

8. Helen R. Wright, "The Professional Curriculum of the Future," *Social Service Review,* Vol. XXV, No. 4 (December, 1951).

terms of native intelligence and personality development poses a question which one can attempt to answer only in individual instances.

Likewise, the integrative task in professional education will be greatly lowered and the integrative capacity enhanced when essential preprofessional content is delineated and required, so that the student has the basic knowledge to use immediately in the acquisition of professional knowledge, understanding, and skill.[9] There is more involved in adequate preprofessional training than the possession of knowledge, namely, the important fact that some of the changes in the learner in terms of feelings and attitudes which professional education undertakes to effect in a short time can have been set in operation earlier. The current uneven educational preparation of students makes it difficult to establish performance norms. Inadequate preparation in individual instances makes it difficult also to gauge integrative capacity, because the relatively mature student, out of his orientation to reality and his readiness to engage deeply in learning, will develop more anxiety over being ill prepared than will an immature student, who may be more inclined to be superficial and hence content with marginal learning.

As for native mental endowment, an essential element in integrative capacity, professional educators traditionally have valued intellectual ability. The first specification in the selection of students will be a statement to the effect that above average intelligence is required and superior intelligence highly desired. In spite of the fact that high intelligence may enhance integrative capacity, the degree of correlation between the two varies widely. Social work educators, like all educators in fields where intellectual competence is a "must" for the mastery of their teachings, have been prone to overevaluate the high intelligence quotient per se or seeming evidence of it in "high-grade" transcripts. It is very difficult to make ourselves look beyond this for evidence of other qualifications, notably personality qualifications or qualities of mind which constitute special aptitudes for social work. We have to remind ourselves repeatedly that intellectual ability may serve

9. See *ibid.* for statements concerning the content of preprofessional education.

as a defense against integration when the individual is still in the conflicts of immaturity and when he is still without ego strength to resolve the conflicts of maturity.

To those engaged in child-guidance work there early came the realization that the higher the intelligence quotient, the greater the integrative task was for the child in many life-situations, and notably outside the schoolroom. This is a decisive point for subsequent professional education, in that it is not solely academic learning. When markedly high, the child's intelligence could operate against the development of integrative capacity, that is, confidence in self essential for the ability to absorb anxiety and tension in learning. This is in part because the intellectually superior child exposes himself to experience beyond his years. He perceives so much, and, sensing many of the implications, he reacts to and becomes involved in learning which makes an emotional demand beyond his stage of personality growth. In such instances his intellectual capacity may be employed as a defense against learning. When these children as adults enter the professions, as frequently they do, the nature and extent of their anxiety as well as their capacity to contain it will depend on the nature and extent of the trauma of these early years. It will depend on what high intelligence has done to their personalities; on whether or not it has constricted and distorted their relationships with people; on whether or not it has been exploited by others as well as by themselves; in short, on whether or not it has made for width and depth of relationship or for narcissism. We give one example which illustrates, roughly, what has been known to occur in certain instances.

Among many factors which may have operated to distort the personality development of the highly intelligent child is the inordinately high value placed on intellectual precocity by some parents, teachers, and total communities. This is peculiarly prone to occur in frustrated parents who have much narcissistic need to meet through the child's achievement. When the child meets their urgent need, they unwittingly exploit him through pushing and exhibiting him. He gets approval or disapproval in accordance with his performance. They act as though they value solely his intellectual prowess, which does them proud. In such instances the child has early felt loved conditionally and hence loved uncertainly. He early develops the anxiety that, unless he achieves intellectually, he will be worthless and rejected. Conditional love begets, among other responses, hostility toward those who love him reservedly and who he feels drive him. Inordinate strivings result which enact both his search for love and his hostile aggression. Learning becomes a precarious quest fraught with hostility, guilt, and anxiety. With so much at stake in his goal-striving he is often unable to contain the anxiety and tension, so that defenses are erected which interrupt learning. These children experience much failure in social situations, and sometimes they fail in school, and notably they are prone to do so at the stage of adolescent revolt against parents. Often, however, they become constricted, task-centered achievers, who shut out experiences which would contribute to their emotional development, and their relationships notably become constricted and distorted. As education proceeds, deprived and frustrated, they do not feel successful, nor do they anticipate success. When seen in social work education and perhaps also in other professions, they are not hopeful, confident students. A kind of narcissistic need to excel, to win in competition with others and not to be found wanting in intellectual competence, results in intolerance of criticism, impatience with limitations in others, a need to exhibit their powers, and often a ruthless disrespect for lesser minds. An individual who approximates this alienates his colleagues and even some parents and mentors who in time love him less than they did as a child. He thus elicits hostile rivalry instead of affection and begrudging recognition in lieu of wholehearted respect. He is destined to become progressively deprived and limited in his capacity for give-and-take relationships. While the outcome in adulthood of this kind of experience varies widely among intellectually precocious individuals who have been set apart through their superiority and exploited, the obvious implications as preparation for most professions and for social work especially need not be specified.

We have presented this gross but not unknown situation because it typifies what happens in our society, and in some segments more than others, to many children to a lesser degree and with less extreme consequences. In a highly competitive achievement-worshiping society and particularly in those cultures where academic learning is loved, the precocious child tends to be a marked child. Apart from the burden imposed by community attitudes toward him and expectations of him, his abilities set him apart so that often he is thrown out of close relationship with contemporaries and into competition with older children whose psychophysical development is beyond his. He is drawn into experiences beyond his physical competence and stage of emotional growth. Among them it may be difficult for him to be anything but a fledgling. The resultant hopeless feelings, which beget fear, hostility, and anxiety, may get compensated constructively through intellectual achievement, or they may motivate destructive or problematic use of his prowess.

When parents, teachers, and others overevaluate and reinforce this adjustment through failing to perceive the unmet needs and wishes and the social import of the heightened striving, they do not help him solve some very real social and emotional problems as they arise. Fortunately, there is growing recognition today among parents and educators of some of the developmental discrepancies to which such children are heir. While the problems are not simple of solution, much is being done to afford experiences which will help them attain maturity with fewer conflicts and less personality deviation than in the past. The decisive point in the current scene is that superior intellect may or may not operate to lower the integrative task or to enhance the individual's integrative capacity. Whether it does or not depends on the values the individual's endowment has had for him in his social situation; how he has had to use it for psychological survival; and whether or not the use has nurtured or impoverished the ego.

3. *Physical Condition and Energy Endowment*

Integrative capacity stemming from self-confidence is often contingent also upon the general state of health of the student. We refer here to his energy endowment, as well as to the presence or absence of physical disability. Illness and some handicaps not only produce fatigue, which discourages the individual and lowers his power to absorb anxiety, but they tend to engender anxiety in proportion to the seriousness of the condition, the extent to which it is a life-threat or a more limited ego threat, and the extent to which the individual is habituated to illness so that he has learned to live with it. In a goal-striving situation where the individual is deeply committed to attain his aims, illness or a handicap which interferes with his efficiency brings loss of hope, frustration, and anxiety over the outcome of his strivings in relation to his needs and wants. Hence the individual who ordinarily takes illness for granted because he is habituated to it may develop anxiety if realistically it impedes his progress.

When the educational experience exerts a demand beyond the individual's intellectual ability and/or his ego strength, so that, being discouraged, more tension and anxiety is marshaled than the individual can contain, he may fall ill. Hence illness, fatigue, and inertia may be defenses against learning, a flight from it, a symptom that the integrative task exceeds the individual's integrative capacity. Sometimes these flights into illness are used in the interests of integration, a respite in which the individual recovers from acute anxiety and tension and gets himself together to try again, with a subsequent favorable outcome. This will occur only when there is not marked intellectual and personality incapacity for the work. Otherwise, one can expect repeated flights and a final exit through illness. Unconsciously determined functional and psychosomatic illness may occur both as a defense against learning, which by its nature at a given time engenders fear, and as an ego defense against failure to learn. It is less deflating to the ego to be ill than to lack ability or to expose one's self as ill prepared.

The individual may be realistically well endowed or poorly endowed physically for the attainment of the goal which he has undertaken. Anxiety in learning, accordingly, may be lowered or heightened by his physical resources or lack of them. When poorly endowed, there is great variation among individuals in their basis for hope and in their capacity to contain the resultant anxiety, as with anxiety from other sources. There is variation in the extent to which integrative capacity will be lowered by recurrent illness or persistent fatigue. Strength of motivation, intellectual ability, and the nature of the organization of the personality combine to enable some individuals to surmount physical limitations better than others. Finally, it is to be remembered that the individual's physical endowment, like his intellectual endowment, is part and parcel of a personality and accordingly operates characteristically in the total economy of the personality under stress. Accordingly, it will be used as a resource of the ego in the interests of the integration of learning, or as a defense against anxiety, at which times it may or may not seriously interfere with learning.

4. Concurrent Social Circumstances

The student's extracurricular social situation is another element which operates for or against his integrative capacity, through supporting or lowering his power to contain and absorb anxiety. The load of anxiety mounts when the stress of learning is added to and reinforced by concomitant stresses in the form of family disasters or momentous occurrences which bring marked change into the life of the individual or into the lives of others in close relation-

ship to him. For example, a social work student who had been unusually able showed acute anxiety at the close of her first year.
Anticipating failure when realistically she could expect success in the
comprehensive examinations, she came through them below par for
her. Acute anxiety had been evidenced at this same time in her field
work, notably in her efforts on one case which involved helping an
elderly man decide to enter an institution. In this situation she was
caught in the ambivalence of the client. Though she had actually
slowed up the client's decision, she became acutely fearful that
she had pushed him too hard and too fast. This case had activated
conflict over the institutionalization of her father, which had occurred during the year and which was made necessary by her sister's
marriage and her own decision to remain in school, rather than
return to her former work, which might have made it possible for
her to manage to keep her father at home. The timing of events
fraught with emotion with eventful stages of learning is decisively
important in whether or not the student's integrative task stays well
within his integrative capacity, strains, or exceeds it.

In professional education we encounter young adults at a stage
of life which normally teems with emotionally charged events. They
are growing into the assumption of heavy adult responsibilities other
than that of learning to become responsible professional persons.
Engagement, marriage, parenthood, assumption of responsibility for
aging or widowed parents, are all incidents potentially fraught
with growing pains. Some students in social work undertake a massive integrative task when they concurrently, within two years, embark upon professional education, marriage, and psychoanalysis. To
faculty advisers it sometimes seems that it is in the nature of social
work learning that it not only activates the past but gives new
significance to the present, with the cumulative effect of an urge to
live and love at heightened tempo. We have to remind ourselves
that it is in the nature of life at this age in these times, that they
are young and resilient, and that the growth attained in other
newly assumed adult responsibilities may well reinforce social work
learning. At such philosophical moments, however, reality dictates
that we not generalize the beneficent effects of the impact of life
on the concurrent learning experience. There is great variation in
growth tempo among individuals who could be characterized as

having adequate ego development and good potentials for social work. Students in any profession vary in the number of vital experiences which they can encompass at once. Individuals differ in whether or not concomitant events which have a growth push in them widen or narrow the ego's integrative span for use in the immediate situation.

Significant of individual difference is the fact that some students at this age, while engaged in professional education, become so absorbed in it that they seemingly withdraw from involvement elsewhere. This may bespeak adequate ego development and integration rather than meager energy or constricted personality. As noted previously, the relatively mature student tends to strive within his scope. In these instances the discomfort produced by untoward, unsought stresses may impede, but not disintegrate, the learner. Other students can learn productively while seemingly engaged deeply in other affairs. Still other students seem widely engaged out of extensive need and inability to focus their drives. It is as though they want everything here and now as a defense against deprivation. They compete in every arena in order to feel adequate. In such instances the wide scatter carries them beyond their integrative capacity, so that learning is impeded or breaks down.

The acculturation task is another social factor which affects the integrative capacity of the individual student. We recall an earlier statement to the effect that a profession's traditions, its rationale, its ethical system, its body of knowledge, its vocabulary, its special function, tend to make it a culture with'n a culture. The means to becoming part of a new culture is through relationship with its members. This implies that, instead of identifying as a defense in order to survive in a foreign realm, the individual forms influential relationships, through which his identity, modified but not obliterated, goes native without loss of that individuality essential for creative work. Identification as a defense dooms the new member to remain a foreigner, striving to act like a native but reverting to his old ways of feeling, thinking, and doing, particularly at times of stress. The integrative capacity in professional education may be heightened to the extent that the value system of the student's culture is not completely foreign to and incompatible with that of the profession. While all students will bring some unsuitable feelings and attitudes, in the form of bias and prejudice, to professional education, it has been clear in social work that there have been great differences in the extent of them. Some students have been reared in a milieu where attitudes compatible with those of the profession prevail; others have not. Dr. Charlotte Babcock states that the culture will aid the learning process at those points where the value attitudes of two cultures overlap to give security. Learning is impeded or facilitated by value-attitudes only in relation to whether they give ego security. When incompatible, learning will take longer. How great the demand will be on the individual's integrative capacity will depend on the timing of relationship demands, since anxiety in acculturation is always related to an interpersonal relationship, past or present. The tempo of learning, therefore, will depend on the amount of anxiety evoked by new relationships. Dr. Babcock states further with reference to the implications of acculturation studies for professional education: "Because value attitude systems tend to be defenses, in admissions work, we must evaluate basic ego structure rather than merely know the culturally determined attitude systems which may be the same in a range of personality types. The value attitude systems may be expressed alike by the psychopath, the neurotic character, and others."[10] The observations of social work educators confirm this. It has long been held that rigidity or flexibility of attitudes stems from the student's relationship experiences, hence to his emotional development, and prominently to his capacity for deep and meaningful relationships. Currently as part and parcel of a long social work tradition, we do not focus sharply on culturally determined attitudes and behavior but, instead, on trying to gauge whether or not the individual is rigidly defended against change.[11] We, however, take cultural factors into account in appraising the stress of learning.

10. In discussion with the author of the findings in William Caudill, *Japanese American Personality and Acculturation* ("Department of Anthropology, University of Chicago, Genetic Psychology Monographs," No. 45 [Provincetown, Mass., 1952]), pp. 3–102.

11. Since this chapter was written the author has noted the same opinion as to the weight to be given to culture factors in social work education in England (see Margaret Ashdown and S. Clement Brown, *Social Service and Mental Health* [London: Routledge & Kegan Paul, 1953], p. 61).

5. *Summary of Integrative Capacity*

In conclusion it can be said that marked variation in concurrent social circumstances and in concurrent goal-striving among students makes it difficult at times to gauge educability. The demands of the educational situation are fairly well defined and, in the long run, inflexible, that is, the student is expected to give evidence of having attained certain knowledge, understanding, and skill in order to qualify for a degree. As students are evaluated along the way, the difficulty lies in determining how much to take stress into account in evaluating the student's potentials for development in the long run, particularly if, as in social work, the time span is a short two years. This period does not allow much leeway for individual variation in tempo of learning. Such questions as follow do not always lend themselves to a ready answer: In a given instance, has learning proceeded unusually well in the light of the student's social circumstances? In that his tempo has been slowed by a massive integrative task, has he shown remarkable integrative capacity? Should he be encouraged to continue, and what help and allowance can be given him without subordinating the needs and demands of the profession for competence to the immediate comfort of the individual, thus performing a disservice to both individual and profession?

In specifying the elements which lower or heighten integrative capacity we have indicated the individual's sources of security and of anxiety as he engages in learning. Intellectual capacity, emotional development, physical capacity, and social circumstances may interplay to nurture and support the ego or to impoverish and threaten it. The foregoing grouping embodies not only source but also, by implication, the extent and degree of stress, as well as the capacity or incapacity of the individual to deal with anxiety. For example, knowing the demands of social work, if an individual's anxiety in learning stems from a combination of intellectual incapacity for social work and immature personality development, we have some measure of his stress and of his lack of resources to deal with the anxiety which will inevitably mount if he continues in training. The source of difficulty in relation to needs, wishes, and personality organization will determine not only the quality and quantity of anxiety but also whether in the educational situation it should be taken for granted or dealt with through modification of the educational situation, through educational measures, through psychotherapeutic help secured elsewhere, or through the learner's withdrawal from pursuit of this occupational goal.

V. EDUCATIONAL DIAGNOSIS

While for educational diagnosis and prognosis the source of the anxiety is an important clue, it cannot be isolated as an indicator of educability. Educational diagnosis and prognosis therefore must weigh a complex of factors. Responses which bespeak anxiety are more readily identifiable today than in the past. To one who would understand the part played by anxiety in learning, each *recurrent* response is noteworthy. One must consider the timing of anxiety in relation not only to the age of the learner and his stage of learning but also to the progression of intellectual and emotional demands in the total educational situation and the pressures in the individual's current life elsewhere. One must also be alert to the source and extent of the response and its focalization or pervasiveness with reference to the nature of the learner's relationship with classroom and field instructors, to the educational measures used to help him sustain or resume learning, and to his abilities in the several areas of his program. This implies observation and evaluation of the individual learner, with an attempt to answer such questions as follow. Having identified the precipitant or precipitants of the anxiety, one considers whether this student has experienced more or less anxiety than other individuals of appreciably the same age at the same stage of learning. When this is the case, one considers other circumstances which differentiate this individual from the "norm." One considers also whether this individual is reacting with greater or lesser dependency, aggression, or retreat and whether any one of these responses is prominent, persistent, and interfering with his capacity to put learning to use.

With reference to the source of the anxiety, it is to be noted that educational diagnosis focuses largely on the individual in the current educational experience. The educator does not attempt to know the basic causes of the anxiety. He does attempt to know the precipitants in the educational situation. The clues to the basic difficulty lie in precipitating factors as the specific content within total subject matter, the particular relationships, the specific demands of learning which disturb the student. The nature and timing of the learning problems and the issues which arise bear close scrutiny. When anxiety is pervasive and when the defenses are rigid, that is, when they do not give way to teaching helping measures, which ordinarily allay anxiety and permit learning to proceed, one infers a basic difficulty. Because educational measures cannot help the individual in these instances, one assumes that the demands of learning have activated an earlier traumatic experience so disturbing that learning in this situation is permanently interrupted.

It is not the educator's responsibility, nor is it appropriate for her, to help through other measures, even though she may have the requisite knowledge and skill. Since therapy is not her province in this situation, the educator does not attempt to know the earlier traumatic experience through exploring it. Often she may have some idea of its nature through the clues provided in the precipitating factors; and this may serve to guide her in her teaching efforts, in her evaluation with the student of his learning problem, and in her prediction as to the outcome of her efforts to help him define his problem. It is in response to evaluation of his work and to efforts to define the problem that the social work student's ability or inability to progress in learning is revealed. Often when crises arise as learning activates earlier trauma, the student precipitously recalls the past. The educator then helps him define the problem and his need for help, which often must be obtained elsewhere, through therapy and/or through pursuit of some other goal. The educator does not encourage further unburdening and makes known why she cannot help him.

When, on the other hand, anxiety is narrowly focalized, and when the defenses permit the individual to confront his learning problem and achieve mastery of it, he will find the educational experience a corrective one. In these instances education is therapeutic.

For example, a student may reveal marked anxiety in trying to help a client who rejects her child. His hostility toward this mother causes him to swing back and forth between the expression of punitive attitudes and the withholding of help, to opposite behavior in which he must correct his professional "misdemeanors" through permissive attitudes and giving excessive help. From all this student says and does, the instructor is reasonably certain that the student is undergoing a repetitive experience which is painful and confusing. She does not explore the student's early experience in his relationship with his own mother. She focuses instead on eliciting and on understanding the student's feelings about *this* mother. She directs him to consider how this woman came to feel and act as she does, and she holds the student accountable to try to understand and to meet this woman's need for help, regardless of whether or not he feels kindly toward her. She refers the student to classroom teaching and to readings which throw light on the client's behavior. She grants that the woman's behavior is unacceptable, but holds that the woman herself is to be accepted and understood and helped. As the student sees and feels that this mother fails her child out of having been failed in her own relationships, the student becomes less aligned with the child against the mother. He begins to feel with the mother, and as the mother responds positively, making more productive use of help, the student is able to fulfil his professional responsibility.

As the student's own hostility and guilt are lowered, he frequently gains insight. In these instances the past may be touched on only briefly through the student's acknowledgment of the import which the client had for him. When the student does not repeat this response in comparable situations, one assumes insight gains. When he does repeat it, his problematic response to certain kinds of behavior must be identified and the student directed to consider its import for social work. His readiness to gain insight for the mastery of obstacles to the attainment of goals is tested at this point. The decisive feature is that the educator should concentrate on helping the student learn rather than on treating the student. Help focused on learning difficulties, which often involve factors precipitating anxiety, is help focused on personality conflicts in the current reality. In so far as those reflect basic personality conflicts, the educational experience affords an opportunity to resolve them or to regulate them which the student may or may not be able to use. Decisively important, therefore, is close observation and evaluation of the student's use of any and all individualized teaching and helping measures which ordinarily facilitate the learning process. As this has been done, out of the very fact that educable students as well as uneducable ones have anxiety, the social work educator has been able to formulate some criteria of educability, to identify initial responses which raise grave questions, and to delineate some criteria of noneducability. We are slow to put the latter to use until ample time and repeated helping efforts have tested the pervasiveness and persistence of certain responses.

It is not a simple matter to predict educability and to eliminate those students who cannot make productive use of education, either prior to admission or early in the learning process. Significant responses are often identified early, but their outcome is often not reliably predicted at the start. In social work education this is due in part to our lack of diagnostic skill in a situation which calls for a high degree of discrimination, in' that reality pressures obscure the import of the learner's responses. As we have become increasingly aware that our educational systems lack much and are not nicely geared to facilitate rather than impede learning, we have been more prone than formerly to blame the learner's ineptitude or his seeming pathology on the defects in the educational situation. In this connection, professional bias may well operate. The social worker is committed to focus on social stress and to postulate "situational neurosis" until clearly proved otherwise. Hence the benefit of the doubt accrues to the learner rather than to the situation.

In the field of social work we are slow to eliminate the uneducable also because we have not yet well-established learning norms for social work education as a whole, though considerable headway is now being made in developing them. We lack confidence in our criteria of educability because, based largely on individual formulations out of individual educators' experience, they vary from educator to educator particularly with reference to specific social work functions. We have tended to think of educability for social casework, for social work research, for social work administration, for social group work, rather than for social work as an entity. As individual educators, we have not been clear, and in any one branch of social work we have been conveniently unclear as to the personality qualifications essential in areas of social work other than the one in which we teach. Thus there have been easy assumptions that this obsessive-compulsive learner, though unsuited to social casework, will do nicely in social work research. Or this student whose absorption in routines and whose need to control and to dominate is regarded as weakness in social casework will be appraised erroneously as having strengths for administration. We have observed that this practice has not been peculiar to social work education. Whether or not it is as inappropriate elsewhere is not known to us. Recently, it has become clear that social work is all of one piece in its demands that workers apply ideas and principles to new situations and that they synthesize and formulate their experiences for the advancement of their own learning as well as that of the profession. It has also become clear that essentially the same demand obtains for complex problem-solving and for establishing and sustaining productive working relationships which require taking and giving help freely. The obvious import of all this is that the intellectual capacities and personality qualifications required do not vary widely from one social work function to another or from the one operating level to another.[12] We have wondered whether or not this would be true in other professions. Hence the student who binds his hostile aggression through obsessional absorption in routines as an end in themselves, whose rigidities permit him to acquire knowledge but operate against the use of it in new fact situations, whose hostile rivalry in competition with others results in concern with self and the minutiae of situations, can be afforded no niche in social work from which he will be enabled to make a contribution.

VI. SOME PROBLEMS IN UNDERSTANDING THE SIGNIFICANCE OF THE LEARNER'S RESPONSES

The need for research in the learning process is obvious. Equally obvious is the necessity to study the place of anxiety in the development of the productive learner. In the learning process of adults who are relatively normal in a situation in which they are not seeking therapy but are, instead, seeking help in learning to help others, it is important that we come to recognize and to correlate the outcome of learning with behavior patterns, adaptations, and the purposes served by defenses. Social work educators have begun to identify behavior configurations which seemingly are more or less productive or unproductive. Unfortunately, as with the psychiatrist and as with the social caseworker, social work educators are better able to delineate problematic learning patterns than productive ones. This is because the defenses and adaptations implicit in the uneducable student's responses appear in more exaggerated form and in greater isolation than in productive learning patterns. Occasionally, the

12. For further discussion of this see Charlotte Towle, "The Distinctive Attributes of Education for Social Work," *Social Work Journal*, Vol. XXXIII, No. 2 (April, 1952).

primary patterns established in early life stand forth in bold relief, notable for their simplicity. Having been little modified or ramified through extra-familial experience, but instead reinforced, their import is obvious. Problematic learning responses are more intelligible also because they have presented the educator with a problem to solve, so that, out of the necessity to understand in order to help, he has observed them more intently. He consequently has been more analytical both of the learner's response and of his own teaching or helping measures. Having identified certain configurations, he is alert to their recurrence in others, so that he is aware of them repetitively. Hence individual social work educators have made tentative rudimentary formulations of some problematic learning responses frequently encountered, whereas they have formulated less about the normal or superior learning responses. As might be anticipated, marked similarity in specific ways of responding but marked difference in totality and rigidity of response may be noted in productive and unproductive learners. Some aspects of these roughly defined formulations which approximate clinical impressions might serve as assumptions to be tested through research.

In a complex learning situation it is not a simple task to study learning patterns which, though they lend themselves to grouping, have individual elements decisive for the outcome of learning. Complexity has served as one of several deterrents to the small beginnings which might otherwise have been made. Communication with those studying learning in other professions or at other educational levels is indicated. Of the complexity of the research problem in studying learning at the college level, Benjamin Bloom states: "One of the great hopes for research in the relation between personality and learning is the possibility that only a small number of personality characteristics are really significant for school learning as distinguished from the much larger number of characteristics or variables which may have significance for individual therapy and diagnosis."[13] Professional education is a re-education process more akin to therapy than to academic teaching as practiced at the col-

13. Benjamin S. Bloom, "Personality Variables and Classroom Performance," *Journal of the National Association of Deans of Women*, Vol. XVI, No. 4 (June, 1953); also Eugene S. Gaier, "Selected Personality Variables and the Learning Process," *Psychological Monographs, General and Applied*, LXVI, No. 17 (1952), 349.

lege level. As has been shown, a large number of variables are significant for diagnosis and for the outcome of learning. The social work learning process may not lend itself to the kind of study of personality characteristics reported by Bloom and by Gaier. The findings in the studies which these authors report are intelligible, however, to the social work educator because they affirm some of our observations. Such studies as these may not serve as patterns for our research, but they may have certain values for us, in that they may make our own observations more meaningful and thus may sharpen our diagnostic skills. They may give us ideas for the breaking of our complex problem into researchable questions and units.

Social work knowledge operates both for and against understanding the learning process in the normal adult whose goal is learning to help others rather than getting help. Derived in part through the study of problematic or pathological behavior, it presents the liability of inducing a propensity to regard negative responses to learning and normal adaptive responses as failures of the ego. There is considerable confusion in the literature and in discussions of behavior between the members of professions, a confusion not peculiar to social work. There is a growing tendency to think of normal adaptive responses as defenses against instinctual urges and normal learning efforts. One hears such expressions as "flight into reality" and "flight into health." Humorously, one entertains the idea that we may get so bogged down in defense systems out of context of reality that we may think of health as a defense against illness, of breathing as a defense against dying, and of all learning as a defense against not knowing.

Against this tendency to regard all behavior as a negative means to uncertain survival, instead of seeing much of it as a positive expression of man's urge to live confidently and even dangerously, it is essential to define "defense" more narrowly. In an unpublished communication to the author, Dr. French defines defense as "an attempt to master emotional conflicts which are in excess of the individual's integrative capacity and which threaten to overwhelm the ego so that learning and adaptation are no longer possible." He states further that defense mechanisms are sometimes successful. They are able to prevent such paralyzing conflicts from being more than minimally activated, and, by shifting to a problem that is less difficult, the individual may find it possible to continue the learning process and even after a period of reassuring and enlightening experience be able to return with a new readiness to master the original problem. In some cases, however, the defensive mechanism may succeed only in maintaining precarious control over a disturbing conflict that has already been activated, but only at the cost of utilizing all available energy to ward off the danger.

In the process of assimilating new knowledge for use in meeting new demands, the learner normally takes hold, then lets go, only to take hold again. He is working in characteristic ways, at his tempo, in accordance with his learning patterns. For equilibrium and economy of effort he is momentarily attacking-withdrawing, embracing-resisting, accepting-rejecting, pushing forward–pausing, repeating-progressing, incorporating-excluding, adopting-renouncing, with the purpose of attaining his aims. This implies meeting the demand of the situation, the mastery of the learning task. The rhythm of learning, the fact that he moves in and out, now ahead and now retreating, represents normal ego functioning. It does not necessarily imply that the integrative task at any point is beyond an individual's integrative capacity. Throughout the ins and outs, the ups and downs, he may be learning. Consequently, certain behavior responses, notably the negative responses among those specified which we frequently term "defenses," may not have been defenses.[14] The decisive point is that the protective function of the ego operates for the integration of learning. When it fails of its aim, the defense system operates against the disintegration of the learner.

Significant here is the fact that we have been prone to think of all anxiety as neurotic anxiety and therefore of anxiety as a deterrent to learning. Actually, when it is not excessive, so that the individual can hope to attain his goal, it does not heighten the integrative task beyond the individual's integrative capacity. In these instances it

14. Earlier it was said that in an educational process it is essential that regression as a phenomenon of pathology be differentiated from regression as a mechanism operating against disintegration and as a means to integration. For sound conduct of the educational situation it is important to distinguish regression from the plateaus and slumps in learning which are essential for integration. These occur as the new situation, with its multiple demands for attention and psychic energy, brings a temporary reversion to automatic behavior rather than new and appropriate responses (see chap. 2, pp. 28–29, 38).

can serve as a motivating force. When we characterize the individual's efforts to survive as "defenses," aggression essential to master learning may be referred to as a defense against feeling inadequate rather than as an aspect of the individual's characteristic learning pattern. Or when an individual accepts the new with some reservation, questioning it, analyzing it, breaking it down into bits to reflect upon, we characterize his behavior as resistive and think of it as a defense against change, when actually he is busily engaged in incorporating change. Or, again, when an individual intrusts himself rather freely to the learning experience, we may see his adaptation as abject submission and characterize his amenable response as a defense against hostility. He thus gets lumped with those individuals who truly are defending themselves against activity in learning out of their fear of their hostile aggressions.[15]

It is therefore indicated that *whenever possible* we accept the individual's way of learning until we get some idea of its import and probable outcome. This implies that we do not react to negative responses as necessarily problematic. If they operate for the integration of learning, they will subside. It is not always possible to do this, however, because in learning the hard way some students make it hard for clients and colleagues. When this occurs, the student's learning pattern constitutes a problem with which he must be confronted as the problematic situations which it provokes arise. When he cannot modify his behavior in the interests of the client or for productive work relationships, we may have a learner whose personality is unsuited to the work he has undertaken. He may be characterized as not having aptitude for the profession, in that his learning patterns imply inappropriate behavior. The student's response to the educational experience and notably to evaluation and to help is a major diagnostic means in the educational situation.

The social work educator's tendency to regard many responses as defenses, when, strictly speaking, they are not, has had an unfortunate effect upon the educational practices of many individuals. It frequently has led them to postulate a problem in learning, when learning has actually been proceeding normally. Since social

---

15. Earlier it was stated that it is important to differentiate the defense-incrusted "protective ego" from one which realistically and flexibly protects in the interest of integration and execution (see chap. 3, pp. 63–64).

workers are problem-defining and problem-solving people, remedial measures often have been instituted prematurely and inappropriately to produce problems in relationships between teachers and learners. These, in turn, have often obstructed learning. For example, when the learner, as commonly is the case, finds himself engulfed by too much all at once, the protective function of the ego operates to enable him to select a little at a time. This ability to resist stimulation, to handle it internally without need for immediate response, makes it possible for him to sort stimuli and to group them into manageable integrative tasks. It may make it possible also for him to mobilize his resources for self-activity in learning and thus operate against undue dependency on those from whom he is learning or on the authority of the written word. In such instances he questions, explores, weighs, and assimilates rather than submits passively.

In educational psychology this selective process has been regarded as a capacity of the organism for differentiating and integrating rather than as a symptom of the failure of the integrative function of the organism. This also is in accord with psychoanalytic thinking, which holds that selection is part and parcel of the integrative process, a function of the ego. "As mastery of a part is attained, selection may perform a synthesizing function which permits focus, depth, assimilation of the knowledge with insight, thus allowing energy to be freed for the next task."[16] Because in social casework and therapy we deal with individuals at a time when life is too much for them, we are prone to identify selection as a defense against overwhelming reality. As a carry-over in the educational situation we are often prone erroneously to view the demands of learning as overwhelming and the student's response as resistance to learning. While, in dealing with psychopathology, we have learned not to crash defenses, we are not prone to support them unless or until we have tested them and determined the individual's incapacity to relinquish them. Likewise, in the educational situation we may find the student's selective tendency, his inclination to focus on this to the exclusion of that, provocative when we regard it as a defense to be tested, we may unwittingly be quick to test his capacity to encompass more than he is ready to assimilate, thus

16. Dr. Charlotte G. Babcock in an unpublished communication to the author.

engulfing him needlessly. Thus to regard selective learning as a symptom of the ego's failure is a tendency to be overcome, if possible. Actually, measures which attempt to cope with this proclivity as a problem are indicated only if selection amounts to constriction or to an escape which is resulting in fragmentation rather than in integration of learning. For example, when the learner deals with his anxiety by selecting the old and familiar and by clinging to it rigidly as a defense against the new, one recognizes a problem in learning. When the learner consistently absorbs himself in trivia and minutiae to the exclusion of the significant and the general, it is clear that fragmentation rather than integration will result. This may be the problematic learner who becomes task-centered to a degree that activity has become an end in itself rather than a means to learning. When the individual in classroom or field, in attacking learning, centers upon people, the instructor, or colleagues more than upon subject matter, when he is intent upon outwitting others rather than upon putting ideas to use, hostile rivalry may well be leading him astray into the irrelevant and the trivial.

When exclusion is initially regarded as a capacity of the organism for differentiation and integration rather than as a defense, this behavior is accepted as the way individuals learn throughout an educational process. Educational measures are shaped accordingly, with recognition of the importance of an orderly progression in learning and of emphasis and focus. Some of these general methods which we believe have import beyond social work education will be presented shortly and applied in subsequent chapters. The essential point is that in professional learning the protective function of the ego *normally* may operate in the interests of integration. The import in education, therefore, is that the educational regime should, *first*, strengthen the integrative function of the ego by supporting essential adaptations and, *second*, lessen the need for defenses. This is not to discount the importance to the professional educator of psychoanalytic principles, even though they have been derived largely from the study of psychopathology. Because of the fact that human behavior is a continuum from normal to abnormal and because individuals vary widely in the extent to which they can cope with threatening situations before resorting to behavior which is maladaptive, psychoanalytic insights have contributed much to education and will do so increasingly as they are put to use in understanding a wide range of learners at all educational levels. It is essential, however, that our acceptance of the concept that behavior is a continuum from normal to abnormal should not operate against precision in diagnosis.

In summary, the distinctive characteristic of the productive learner is not that he is defenseless but that his defenses, by and large, in mitigating the conflicts activated by learning permit him to confront them and to have an educative and often also a corrective experience. Another characteristic of the productive learner is that he often seems more "defensive" than he actually is. In schools of social work we are concerned primarily with conducting an educational program to facilitate learning for the educable student. We are concerned that our educational process shall not overburden him and thus impede learning. In the educational situation, as in learning throughout life, we want the individual's integrative capacity to exceed the task by a margin which permits something more than an anxious struggle for the equilibrium essential for psychological survival. It is as this occurs that he becomes more social and more creative in his strivings. Aware of the narrow margin for this which often obtains in professional education and aware of the possibility that the task may intermittently exceed the individual's capacity, the question uppermost in the educator's mind is: When and under what circumstances does the learning task prove to be traumatic? At what stage and to what extent is affect tolerable for integration? On the whole, this is a highly individual matter. In social work it has been noted that the initial stage of learning is characterized by much anxiety, by repetitive effort, and by other responses that suggest fragmentation and stereotyping. Close scrutiny will often show slow but progressive development. The individual is experimenting variously; he is learning by his mistakes; thus learning is not interrupted. It seems that there is no fixed time when the demands of learning become traumatic, nor is there one traumatic threshold. There are wide variations in the degree and nature of change which social work education will imply for individual students. There is diversity not only in the time of occurrence and the degree of discomfort, anxiety, and resistance but also in the individual's capacity for integration.

The implications of all this may be stated as follows: First, educational measures to help the student deal with learning problems will have to be individualized, even though the content of learning and the demands of professional education cannot be individualized. Second, it is essential to evaluate defenses in relation to the educational source of the learner's anxiety and in relation to their timing, notably the age of the learner and his stage of learning. For example, it is important to differentiate repetition for mastery from stereotyped responses in the early stage of learning. Third, it is essential that educational measures widen the ego span through their positive nature, oriented to instil realistic hope and to engender self-confidence whenever possible. We turn now to the educational approach and to certain elements in the educational regime which have special import in the integration of learning.

CHAPTER 5

Educational Principles and Process

Traditionally, educators have been concerned to motivate the learner. For productive outcomes in learning, they have sought to stimulate active interest in a field of study through appeal to associated interests and by other special devices. This responsibility to foster interest is appropriately assumed at the lower educational levels where students are required to attend school. In professional education the educator does not have the same responsibility to incite interest. If the field of study does not progressively engage the learner, it may well be that he belongs elsewhere. It is possible, however, for an educational regime to obstruct learning. Through needlessly creating stress, it may lead to automatic rather than creative effort, fragmentation rather than integration, and hence to a breakdown in drives originally appropriate and strong.

The professional educator's concern with educational principles and measures does not have the objective of motivating the learner so much as that of safeguarding his motivation. It has the aim of strengthening the integrative, executive, and regulative functions of the ego and of lowering the ego's need to operate protectively. This is in order that the individual may absorb and deal with anxiety and tension through adaptations which promote learning rather than through defenses which impede it. As the educational process attains this aim, it can be expected that the individual's motivation, if appropriate, will be strengthened and modified so that his behavior will be useful to the profession. The general import of the following educational principles and measures for ego development as delineated in the earlier chapters is manifest. Discussion of their specific import calls for individualization. For these reasons, therefore, we do not attempt to relate each measure to the specifics of ego functioning.

We review the several resources which facilitate learning. Of primary importance, of course, is what the learner brings to the experience. The part played by intellectual capacity, augmented and moti-

134

vated by the personality development and organization of the individual learner in the integration of learning, has been delineated. Also, since professional education is education for use, there is a body of knowledge, understanding, and skill to be imparted. While the impact of this arouses anxiety, pending mastery, there is increasing recognition of the fact that knowing eases anxiety over not knowing. Lack of requisite knowledge and skill is a source of tension in professional learning, not to be lost sight of in the current emphasis on other sources, most notably the threat of change implicit in learning. Another resource is the selection and arrangement of learning experiences for continuity, sequence, and integration. The faculty's responsibility to graduate the integrative task so that it is realistically attainable through structuring a hierarchy of experiences is now being assumed to a greater extent than formerly. As we increasingly recognize that the skilled professional practitioner is not necessarily a skilled educator, we may well seek the help of the educational expert. Finally, an important integrative and corrective means to facilitate learning is the relationship which obtains between the learner and his mentors. Great prominence has been given to this factor in social work education, for notable reasons.

I. EDUCATIONAL RELATIONSHIPS, A MEANS TO PATTERN THE
CONDUCT OF PROFESSIONAL RELATIONSHIPS AND A
DETERMINANT IN THE OUTCOME OF LEARNING

Throughout the life of a helping relationship, it is demanded of a social worker and his agency program that the recipient of help be offered adequate essential services in the context of a relationship which is flexibly oriented to his changing needs, capacities, resources, motivations, and behavior responses. Experience has made indisputable the fact that the relationship afforded the client is a decisive component in his use of help. In social work, therefore, to a greater degree perhaps than in some other professions, the relationship is regarded as an integral part of the helping process. We have been peculiarly concerned with what is done to people as we do for them. We have been peculiarly aware that the recipient's response embodies something of himself and something of the worker and of community attitudes embodied in the agency's regulations, policies, and procedures. The conduct of the helping relationship has been a major, rather than an incidental, responsibility. Other professions have more recently become concerned with the part played by the relationship in the recipient's use of their services. Perhaps it was in social work's significance to those who support it, administer it, and use it that we early identified this dynamic element. Perhaps, moreover, owing to the very nature of our profession, there will probably continue to be greater concern with the relationship as an integral part of the helping process than may be found in other fields.[1]

Professional educators are becoming aware that the individual and collective teaching, helping, and administering relationship with the student is the core of his preparation for professional relationship, in that it patterns his conduct of his relationships with those whom he helps and with whom he works. A peculiar attribute of social work is that we have long been conscious of the relationship between learner and teacher as a means to help the learner to work purposefully with people in ways appropriate to social work. The importance of the relationship as an integral part of social work's helping process gives the educational relationship its prominent place as an integral part of the learning process. We turn now to a consideration of the nature of the educational relationship and to this relationship's place as an educational measure in relation to the other important elements specified—knowledge and skills, the arrangement of learning experiences, and the personality organization of the learner.

1. *The Relationship a Means To Effect Change in the Learner*

Having the emotions uppermost in mind as important in learning, we are fully aware that in an educational situation the means of effecting change in feeling is through the intellect. New ideas and new intellectual orientation in the context of an influential relationship may bring a change in feeling, in attitudes, in thinking, and in action. In classroom and field we bank heavily on the occurrence of this change. A teaching situation differs from a psychotherapeutic session, a class group from a group-therapy session, in its heavy reliance upon the students' capacity to experience change in feeling through an intellectual approach. In professional education, both in

---

1. For further discussion of this see Charlotte Towle, "The Distinctive Attributes of Education for Social Work," *Social Work Journal*, Vol. XXXIII, No. 2 (April, 1952).

classroom and in field work, the initial approach or attack is upon the intellect. Feelings are provoked, and, while these feelings are of primary importance in determining what the person learns and whether or not he is able to learn, they must have a secondary place. This is in contrast to the psychotherapeutic situation, where thinking is imparted as feelings are expressed, released, understood, and changed. Thinking nicely timed to the individual's psychological readiness cannot obtain in the classroom or in field instruction.

Hence an educable student in a professional school is one who can stand up to an intellectual approach, to content imparted without reference to his emotional need or psychological readiness of the moment. "Stand up to" implies that the feeling provoked will not be so great and so involving of the total personality and basic conflicts that he cannot deal with his feelings with the help of educational methods that give recognition to the place of the emotions in the learning process. These are methods based on understanding of common needs and responses and of what ordinarily is helpful. In social work education, conditions are favorable for intellectual concepts to bring a change in feeling because they are accompanied by field practice which affords opportunity for the immediate demonstration and use of the class content.[2] There are certain provisos, that is, certain conditions under which a new intellectual orientation may bring a change in feeling and attitudes and hence in thinking and action. Changes in attitude may occur under the following conditions:

a) Provided that the student does not have a deep need to think in the old ways because ideas have been *intensely* satisfying and still are *basically* useful.[3]

b) Provided that the student's convictions have not been derived through a relationship on which he *still* depends for gratification and

2. Charlotte Towle, "The Contribution of Education for Social Casework to Practice," *Social Casework*, October, 1950, also in *Principles and Techniques in Social Casework: Selected Papers, 1940–50,* ed. Cora Kasius (New York: Family Service Association of America, 1950).

3. Lillian Smith, *Killers of the Dream* (New York: W. W. Norton & Co., Inc., 1949). For a penetrating portrayal of how feeling fashions thinking, of how attitudes derived in early relationships become deeply ingrained through love and hate, gratification, guilt, and fear, and are clung to for the purposes they serve in the individual's struggle for a safe survival.

safety, or which he is unfree to leave because of fear, hostility, and guilt.

c) Provided that his old thinking has not been the tradition of his entire social group and he is still *closely* aligned with the group out of its deep emotional import for him, positive and negative. As indicated earlier, fear of the new, by reason of its nature, is prominent here, a fear often subject to gradual change as the unknown is slowly tested. While it is to be remembered that some of the most tenacious ties to individual and group stem from fear of separation engendered by hostility and guilt, this second factor must not be overweighted so that the first possibility is overlooked.

d) And, last, provided that the new orientation does not come from an individual or an authority whom the student mistrusts, toward whom he feels *deeply* hostile or resentful. When driven to identify as a defense, the student may pretend to assume new attitudes, but he will not incorporate them. Conversely, new concepts may be more quickly influential when they are imparted in a relationship which has *strong* positive values. Here we come to the factor of relationship between teacher and learner in which identification is an element of great import. There is a body of knowledge, of understanding, and of skill for the systematic conduct of this working relationship as a means to the re-education of the individual for the profession.

In order to assess the conditions under which new intellectual orientation will or will not readily bring changes, one must consider the intensity and nature of emotion attached to the old thinking, the extent to which the past persists or is useful in the present, and the nature of the relationship between the learner and his mentor.

2. The Co-ordination of the Relationships through Which the Student Learns

a) *The school as an organic whole.*—Within the total educational system, social casework learning, with its supervised field experience and discussion courses, becomes a core experience and major determinant of the student's development. The student's over-all learning experience might be described graphically as occurring within three concentric circles that revolve around him.

In the inner circle is the field-work instructor, closest to him by reason of regular individual contacts, contacts which help him put his new learning to use.[4] Since the demands of the field, from the very start, proceed at faster tempo than learning can be implanted in the classroom, the field-work supervisor is helping the student when he most needs support, through supplementing the classroom instruction. Throughout his training she will be most closely engaged with him, as he undergoes change, as he ambivalently resists and accepts the total learning. The nature of this relationship is decisively important for the student's initial orientation to and continued use of the school as a whole.

The next line of relationship, the middle circle, will be with the classroom teachers. There will be great variation in their import for a given student, depending upon the subject matter in relation to the student's interest and aptitude, as well as upon the personality factor and the methods used. It is common opinion that courses taught by the discussion method make for meaningful relationships between students and instructor. Personality factors and skills operate here, however. Strong connections may be established by students with a didactic teacher. Like Franklin Delano Roosevelt in his "fireside chats," some instructors have the capacity to talk *with* rather than *to* students, engaging them deeply for and against their thinking without their verbal participation. There is wide variation also in the nature, extent, and depth of relationship established by the discussion method, depending on the instructor's attitudes and skill in eliciting and sustaining responses.

The third, and often at the start the more remote, circle is the school as an institution, as represented in the administration. A positive relationship may develop between student and "the administration," a relationship which engenders security and freedom to participate in some management of his affairs. This circle may remain remote and threatening, the top authority to which the student finally is accountable. "They" may loom large in the student's mind as *those* people who set requirements, who are responsible for the whole beneficent or iniquitous system, and who finally pass judgment on him *in toto*. Fortunately, the organization of the school of social work, by and large, operates against this. The fact that in

4. For simplicity, the feminine pronoun is used for the supervisor and the masculine form for the student.

most schools administrative faculty teach, that they serve as advisers and as co-ordinators of field and classroom, that methods of orienting students at the start have the purpose of relating the student to the school as a whole, that social work faculty and students are "democratic process conscious"—all have tended to afford the student a relationship with his school at the administrative level. Today there is recognition that this experience constitutes essential professional preparation for a social worker's subsequent administrative ability at all operating levels of services from within an agency of which he must become an integral part.

It is clear that the student could well become dizzy at the center of three revolving circles if they were to operate separately. They must be interconnected; in fact, they must soon become a pattern, closely woven and of clear design, which supports rather than entangles. Because the relationship with the field supervisor is most meaningful and the field work most deeply engaging, it is easy for this component to become walled in within the whole. The field versus the school is an ever present problem, despite various co-ordinating procedures designed to prevent it. Decisively important is the field-work supervisor's respect for and acceptance of the student's total program and of the several other relationships that are being meaningful to him. She must be staunchly identified with the school as a whole, if the student is not to turn his back on the classroom when he reaches the field and if he is not to be resistive and in conflict in the classroom whenever inevitable discrepancies in practice and theory arise. The finest co-ordinating procedures will have negligible values if the supervisor is not aligned with the aims of the school and does not respect its demands beyond the field-work requirement.

The student, as he spins his connecting lines between classroom, field, and administration, needs to find the school an organic whole. There must be sufficient unity that he will get a sense of one relationship in which the specific relationships may vary in importance from time to time. This sense of oneness will be obtained to the extent that the student in all his contacts with faculty in school and field consistently finds the same attitudes toward people. This implies the same basic philosophy of social work, a like set of values, and fundamental purposes and aims that are identical. Differences in thinking as to specific means to ends are usable, provided that they do not violate the philosophy or defeat the aims. This implies a universal attempt to understand the student as a learner, in order to give help in the mastery of learning. It is essential that social work educators be conscious of the fact that their teaching, helping, administering relationship with the student determines in large measure his very capacity to work purposefully with people in ways appropriate to the profession, whether in the helping relationship between worker and client, in collaborative work with colleagues, or in his relationship with subordinates and persons in authority within the agency hierarchy.

b) Problematic aspects of the learner-mentor relationship.—Since the relationship between learner and mentor is a significant means to the development of professional competence and integrity, it is well to consider conditions essential for the attainment of its aims, as well as some of the problems which this corrective and integrative means presents.

A relationship implies some degree of identification between two separate identities. It is seen as a means to learning, through the opportunity it affords the learner to become like the mentor in some respects. This implies making what he takes his own and using it with a freedom which does not violate his professional identity. An educational relationship should develop the identity of the learner rather than obliterate it. Hence the maintenance of the learner's identity within the professional self is implicit in this means. Identification is a vital means to learning in professional education, for several reasons. It lends support to the learner under the stress of the demands of the experience. It facilitates the adoption of the ways of feeling, thinking, and doing of the profession. It makes way for the attainment of personality growth for the distinctive demands of the profession. Whereas the young child learns largely and comfortably through identification, the adult does not do so. In spite of his need to identify in this situation, he has a more ramified identity to defend. Some ambivalence about this element of inner and outer pressure for identification is inevitable. Dependence is implicit in professional learning. Again, the adult cannot be so comfortably dependent in a relationship as a child. Some discomfort about dependency is not only inevitable but desirable as motivation to professional self-dependence. It is to be remembered that while the relationship is a means to *lower* certain anxieties in order to aid integration, it produces other anxieties which may operate against integration. Aware of this, many social work educators have learned means to deal with the responses to the relationship in ways appropriate to an educational situation. This has occurred most prominently in field-work instruction.

An inordinate demand is made on the field-work instructor, however, when he carries this responsibility alone. When this factor is not recognized and dealt with elsewhere, students may bring excessive need for supportive identification and excessive dependency into this one relationship. Experience has shown how readily and ill-advisedly the supervisory relationship can crash the line between educational help and therapy. There is wide recognition of the fact that the field-work component may become walled off from the total educational experience. There is wide concern both in the school and in the field of practice with the overdependence on supervision which workers frequently take into casework practice and which this practice fosters through a system of prolonged supervision.[5] This implies, as previously stated, that students, as they experience all instruction as well as the administration, need to find the school an organic whole.

3. Knowledge, a Determinant of the Nature of the Relationship

It is clear that the relationship between learner and faculty—be it field supervisor or total faculty—cannot be relied on as the major means to integration. Inadequate knowledge, useless knowledge, knowledge poorly timed, or learning experiences arranged without careful reference to continuity, sequence, and integration create intellectual stress and thus engender feelings of helplessness, anxiety, resentment, and guilt, which exert an inappropriate demand for therapeutic relationship in the educational situation. Likewise, the unrealistic demand exerted by overcrowded programs creates stress which may lead to automatic rather than creative effort, frag-

5. Since this chapter was written the author has noted a perceptive discussion of this problem (see Charlotte G. Babcock, "Social Work as Work," *Social Casework*, Vol. XXXIV, No. 10 (December, 1953).

mentation rather than integration, hence dependency, resentment, and mistrust. When the educational task becomes too heavy, the learner can borrow strength from the teacher. Until identification can occur, the need for emotional support may mount so that the student may be driven to identify pretensively with his mentors as a conscious or unconscious defense. When this occurs, learning may not be incorporated. Instead, it will be submitted to, used ambivalently, and, unless supported by the mentor's understanding and acceptance of the defense as a necessary one, will later be reacted against. In these instances the relationship will have constituted poor preparation for alignment with the social conscience, for contributing to the profession's ideals, and for identifying without loss of identity—in short, for the development of professional integrity, that is, for professional self-dependence. It is frequently stated that our knowledge is conveyed in the context of a relationship which serves as a corrective element and as a means to integration. Emphatically, it is important to add that the knowledge conveyed—its nature, organization, and quantity, as well as the methods used to convey it—shapes the relationship—in fact, determines its very nature. Experience has shown that a working relationship has often been distorted and rendered unproductive through the impact of a program notable for its educational defects. It can be said, therefore, that the nature of the program as a whole determines whether the relationship element can fulfil its potentialities as an educational measure.

Furthermore, knowledge may effect change in the learner's feelings, thinking, and doing. Many a social worker has not taken a resolute stand and thereby has supported the unrealistic fears of his community out of deficiencies in knowledge rather than from lack of a well-incorporated identification with resolute mentors. With reference to this one distinctive demand of social work, learning of many kinds is required—knowledge of the nature of the profession's relationship to the community, with recognition of the import of certain well-known attitudes toward social work and the people it serves, as well as of attitudes which do not give way in response to educational measures; knowledge of group and intergroup dynamics; grasp of principles for understanding the import of behavior responses and attitudes and for effecting change in them, individual by individual and group by group; a well-developed sense of the importance of knowledge of issues and a sense of responsibility to seek, communicate, and interpret it intelligently. In short, a professional person does not deal with attitudes in a vacuum but brings facts and figures to bear on them. He uses his knowledge of the history of social work and awareness of its importance in problem-solving. In assessing the significance of events in terms of reaction or progression, as well as for perspective, he draws on his knowledge of trends, his sense of ebb and flow, for that hope which relieves frustration and renews courage.

4. The Student's Use of the Relationship an Indicator of Personality Development and Integrative Capacity or Incapacity

The nature of the relationship between student and mentors, individually and collectively, has been stressed as a vital element in the learning process. Earlier it was emphasized that, as the individual engages in social work learning, the relationship with those from whom he must learn tends to re-create the first learning experience and to activate the conflicts of the early years. It is important that this *not* be overemphasized. One must bear in mind the fact that the educable student, as specified here, will not be thrown back literally and completely to the first stage of individuation. One need not anticipate, therefore, deep regression, profound negativism, or an authority-dependency conflict of infantile character in which hostile aggression is pronounced. The educable student, however, may undergo considerable dependency on two levels: realistic dependency, created by lack of knowledge, understanding, and skill to meet freely and confidently the demands of the job; and emotional dependency, engendered by several factors—his realistic inadequacy, the psychological threat of enforced change in himself, the activation of the vestiges of authority-dependency conflict of the early years, and, finally, the meaning to him of those who are dependent upon him for help. Often the young adult will have conflict about giving way to his dependency needs. His total being may assert, "Of all times and places, I must not be dependent here and now." This is commonly seen in the student who does not seek the help he needs. One fact is well established: the stronger the wish to be dependent, the more anxiety there will be about it except in those students who have small reaction formation against their infantile impulses.

In spite of the universality of some responses in relation to the educational sequence which is the same for all, each student's use of the relationship will be individually patterned and timed. Learning will proceed in spite of the stresses because of several factors.

a) Not having a strong wish to be dependent, the student will have minimum anxiety and little, if any, guilt about his realistic dependency. He does not feel *basically* inadequate through not knowing. His past success in mastering knowledge, his foreknowledge that order will come out of confusion as he exerts an effort to learn on his own and through others, will give him hope. He is free to seek help and to take it because in early learning his relationships were predominantly positive and gratifying rather than negative and frustrating. Consequently, he brings little hostility toward those who help him and hence minimum guilt and anxiety. Not having been dominated by parent-persons, he has minimum fear also of the loss of self-mastery as he enters a relationship in which he must look to others for guidance.

b) The enforced change causes some discomfort, but the student is not put to rout by it because much that he brings will be useful. His ways of getting his needs met, of controlling his needs, and of meeting the needs of others will not be wholly unacceptable. There will be the task of modification, of different use of what he brings, rather than total basic change.

c) In so far as the superego has not been incorporated, there may be some areas of conflict, some reactivation of early dependency-authority tensions. In view of the fact that the student's heritage, the parental and cultural ego, has been made largely his own, it is his to use freely. Consequently, he will be free to change, and there will not be profound anxiety, as created by deep and entangling attachments to the past. The vestiges of childhood still present may be outgrown, and the fragmentary unresolved conflicts may be resolved, as the student accepts and uses the relationships in this educational experience.

d) The student's identification with those who are dependent upon him may cause discomfort and anxiety; but, because this alignment will not activate basic feelings of inadequacy and early conflicts, he will not have an insurmountable task in separating himself from others. His growth, his emancipation from parents, has involved other separations; in fact, he brings to social work considerable capacity to identify and to separate himself from others. And, finally, in so far as his needs in relationships with those upon whom he must depend and those who depend upon him become conscious, as they must if he is to assume responsibility for the conduct of professional relationship, he will not be confronted with such painful self-awareness that he finds it intolerable.

In contrast, the immature or neurotic student will present a different response throughout, so that the educational relationship will necessarily be modified and often will prove impossible to sustain. The adult whose social adjustment is being maintained through defenses will have difficulty in handling the affect which social work learning engenders. The ego-superego conflict of the individual who has not integrated the parental and cultural ego will be great. Often, having a strong wish to be dependent and feeling basically inadequate, he will have great anxiety and guilt about his realistic dependency. He feels inadequate through not knowing. As learning throughout life has been an anxious quest, the student is filled with more uncertainty than hope. He may not be free to seek help and take it because former helping relationships have been complicated by fear, hostility, and guilt. If he takes, he must be dominated or must dominate. If he replaces old authorities with new ones, his guilt makes him anxious. He wavers between submission and rebellion. He has a strong wish to succeed, but he may feel that he deserves to fail. He brings much hostility toward those who help him and consequently may mistrust those from whom he must learn. He feels that they are there to outwit him. He fears loss of self-mastery as he enters a relationship in which he must look to others for guidance.

a) The enforced change causes maximum anxiety because great modification is implied. This student's ways of getting his needs met, of controlling his needs, and of meeting the needs of others will be largely unacceptable. He may not be free to change because of deep and entangling attachments to the past. His heritage is not his to use freely in relation to the demands for change which he now encounters.

b) His regressive responses will re-create vividly the authority-dependency conflicts of the early years, because this student often acts toward instructors and supervisors as though literally they are the parent. His primary patterns of getting his need met will show up clearly, often in the form of a hostile, aggressive self-assertion in which he contests what he is given and takes as little of it as possible; sometimes such patterns will be revealed in an assertion of dependency in which excessive demands for help are made.

c) This student's identification with those who are dependent upon him will be intense, often so painful that he will have to reject, punish, deprive clients, or align with them subjectively against the agency. He will have great difficulty in identifying with and separating himself from others. He will tend to do either, but he cannot do both. And, finally, to the extent that his needs in relationships with those upon whom he must depend and those who depend upon him become conscious, as they must if he is to assume responsibility for the conduct of a professional relationship, he will be confronted by such painful self-awareness that he will find it intolerable. Repression, denial, projection, identification, and other defenses will operate against his being able to function responsibly. Commonly seen in such instances is the use of identification as a defense. What he is experiencing in the supervisory relationship gets passed on to the client. In so far as he is being given to in ways that are acceptable and in so far as he feels comfortable, he gives momentary understanding and acceptance to clients. When criticism is being given or when limits are being set on his own excessive demands, he may become unable to meet the clients' needs, instead depriving and punishing them as he feels deprived and punished or aligning with them against the agency.

The extremes of personality development have been drawn here. At any one time in a school of social work both extremes are encountered, the highly educable and the frankly uneducable. Many students fall between the two extremes; in fact, personality development is ordinarily more uneven than has been depicted. In such instances there is potential capacity for the attainment of maturity, even though such students carry more of an emotional burden from the past than was visualized in the description of the educable student. The highly educable student, as envisaged earlier, doubtless will learn in spite of heavy odds. The experience of social work in itself will contribute to his continuing growth. A learning relationship which obstructs will cause genuine discomfort and may prevent his attaining the full professional development of which he is capable. A learning relationship which facilitates growth is decisively important for the large group of students who have capacity for growth but who need help in outgrowing the past and in developing ways of feeling, thinking, and doing essential for social work. Some of these people develop certain strengths in social work without experiencing a relationship in which the educators have afforded an opportunity for growth. However, the warped professional personalities of some social workers, in whom limitations are obstructing the use of good potentialities, bespeak in many instances the failure of the professional schools. It is possible for a relationship between learner and teacher to be corrective of certain defects in the individual's use of his personality. It is impossible, however, in professional education to offer a relationship between learner and teacher sufficiently strong and influential enough to be basically corrective of the needs and strivings of the individual whose growth has been seriously obstructed.

A notable implication of this discussion of personality development is that the educator, despite the wide variation in the student's capacity to learn, by reason of his character structure, from his life-experience, can well refrain from the use of methods which perhaps are appropriate at lower educational levels. These are measures which aim to incite interest through stimulating sibling rivalry and status competition; measures which, in aiming to be "therapeutic," are unrealistic—for example, the acceptance of irresponsibility or immature "acting-out" behavior not appropriate in this situation. To be avoided also are the misconceived attempts at ego-building through evaluation of a nature which implies the student's inability to take criticism or to function as an adult in dealing with discomfort. "Childish" methods arouse anxiety and resistance in the educable student, because they constitute an ego assault and impose on him the emotional burden of having to react against the regression implicit in the situation. The immature or neurotic student often provocatively elicits the educator's use of such measures. In these instances the educational relationship proves impossible to sustain, because the measures only reinforce his childishness or his neurotic behavior, instead of inducing change in a growth direction. We test the educability of the adult student for the high demands of a profession in so far as we consistently convey our expectation of adult behavior through treating him as an adult.

5. *Essential Qualities of the Educational Relationship Which Facilitate Learning*

What are the qualities of the relationship that educators should afford students in order that desirable patterns for professional relationship may be formed and learning integrated? Only general principles for differential use are stated, with emphasis on the fact that the first principle is an unwavering intent to understand the student's need as evidenced in his attitudes and responses and in the learning problems that call for help. The underlying principle of the entire educational process is to help the student keep his ego intact so that there will be a minimum of personality disorganization, so that reorganization and reintegration may occur gradually and naturally. It is important to recall that the integrative task is heavy or light in terms of the affect associated with learning and that more negative affect than the student can handle, in terms of the resultant anxiety and guilt, obstructs learning. Since the effects of the total educational experience are being revealed in his field work and since the field-work supervisor has the closest and the most continuous relationship with him, the important elements in the student-supervisor relationship will be considered first.[6]

a) *Readiness to accept and to meet the student's realistic dependency freely and fully.*—At the very start and throughout the field experience the supervisor should meet the student's realistic dependency freely and fully, thus conveying that the student is not expected to know everything and that the supervisor is there to help. Permission to seek help will be implied in the matter-of-fact

6. Certain portions of this section have appeared elsewhere. Charlotte Towle, "Emotional Elements in Professional Learning," in pamphlet entitled *Professional Education* (New York: American Association of Schools of Social Work [1 Park Ave.], 1948); "The Contribution of Education for Social Casework to Practice," also in Kasius (ed.), *op. cit.*; and "The Classroom Teacher as Practitioner," *Social Service Review*, Vol. XXII, No. 3 (September, 1948); see also in *Social Work as Human Relations* (New York: Columbia University Press, 1949).

proffering of it, but the supervisor's helping function and the student's responsibility to seek help should be defined as implicit in their working relationship. Thus his realistic dependency is accepted, and the threat to his ego is eased because he feels adequate in taking help. Naturally, as training progresses, the student should be expected increasingly to assume this responsibility. Naturally also, as learning progresses, he shows a gradual decline in need for help and a growing tendency to learn on his own.

In spite of the clarification of the supervisory relationship as a teaching-helping process, as the student moves into experiencing help, he may reveal discomfort in many ways. His responses should be dealt with as they are manifested. In so far as the help given has enabled him to be competent, more than transitory feelings of inadequacy will not arise, unless help in and of itself activates underlying conflicts about dependency and authority. Developmental norms have an important place in orienting supervisors to realistic need for help as differentiated from psychological dependency. They enable her to determine how much help she realistically should be giving as training proceeds; thus they enable her to identify learning problems of students. Often norms are useful in reassuring students when they are discouraged and anxious about criticism. Learning should be a conscious process. This implies that the student should see the evaluation of his work in relation to norms for individuals at his stage of training.[7] Research is

7. Dr. Charlotte Babcock reports that as she listens to social work students in therapy, she gets the impression that they tend to sense these norms only in field work, not in the classroom. This suggests several possibilities: first, that classroom instructors may not commonly orient the student to the process in which he is engaged and to the sequence of expectations of him as a course proceeds. They also, beyond grading, may not evaluate the student's work with reference to norms. Second, the highly individualized relationship between supervisor and student gives it deeper emotional import than other teacher-pupil relationships, notably in terms of the authority-dependency conflicts implicit in learning. Consequently, work evaluations in the context of this relationship leave a deeper imprint and in so far as they heighten conflict, concern with norms and with criticism is taken to the therapist. Furthermore, in so far as a student is having difficulty making learning a conscious process, he may be unable to do it except in the context of the supportive relationship which individual supervision affords. Third, this response might well be attributed, in part, also to the fact that the professional student, intent upon putting learning to use, is prone to measure himself in terms of his ability to practice rather than in terms of academic doing. If so, he would be more alert to norms in field practice than in the classroom.

needed for improvement of educational method through which present tentative norms may be extended and validated.

It has been noted repeatedly that knowledge imparted freely, that is, timed to the demands that the field work makes, and help given freely will stimulate growth rather than regression. Students whose realistic need is met in this way do not establish a pattern of undue dependency on the supervisor, because helplessness and anxiety have been kept at a minimum. As a result, hostility and guilt, the well-known bases of demanding dependency, are not engendered. The conflicts of the student with marked neurotic tendencies, the student with a persistent ego-superego conflict, however, will be brought into bold relief by this approach. As certain limited help is extended in relation to his disturbed feelings about the reality demands of the working relationship, he may or may not be able to use the help. Thus help focused on his reality need and his complicated feelings about it will test his educability. As students experience ready acceptance of their realistic dependency, as they experience some help with their feelings about it, and as they sense the lack of anxiety and of condemnation in the supervisor, they are prepared with like attitude and response to meet the realistic dependency and disturbed feelings of the client.

b) *Readiness to value highly the student's individuality.*—Along with the easy acceptance of the student's need for help, there should be ready affirmation and use of what the student brings to the situation. His thinking, his feeling, and his doing, whenever appropriate, should be acknowledged as valid and used to the utmost. Feelings of helplessness, frustration, and rage are to be avoided as far as possible, because he must begin at once to help people who often are having such feelings. When he feels like the client, the pain of the situation either may inhibit a desirable degree of identification with him or may cause a too intense identification. When minimum help in rendering services and minimum support of his own resources are given the student at the start, so that he is left to function poorly rather than competently, he does not gain a deep acceptance of his own or of the client's feelings. Instead, his own disturbed feelings about asking for and taking help and his own disturbed feelings about his incompetence may block insight and understanding. It is a well-established fact that emotional involvement produces blind spots and insensitivity rather than understanding and sensitivity. It is reassuring to the student to know early that he cannot be expected to comprehend fully the feelings of clients whose experiences are beyond his own. He can, however, develop an attitude of readiness to understand and to help. It is this feeling rather than experiences and feelings like their own which clients need to find in a worker.

An additional danger precipitating helplessness and disturbed feelings about taking help may arise if the supervisor at an early point focuses on eliciting the expression of the student's feelings. The student may thus be driven to the expression of negative affect and to self-awareness at such a rapid tempo that he becomes painfully self-conscious and anxious about the hostility revealed. In such instances a fearful withdrawal from a too involving supervisory relationship may occur, or great dependency may be engendered out of the need to submit for safety. Social work educators agree with Allport, who says: "It is an axiom that people cannot be taught who feel that they are at the same time being attacked."[8] It is important that identification operate as a positive means to learning rather than that the student identify with the supervisor as a defense. When the latter occurs, learning may not be incorporated. It may be submitted to, used ambivalently, and later reacted against. It is desirable that the first help given a student be focused on the conduct of his work, which he has come to learn to do, rather than on his needs and responses in the helping relationship. His primary purpose in coming to a professional school was not to get help with disturbed feelings about his dependency-authority conflicts. As he gradually experiences help focused on his reality need in relation to work demands, these conflicts will emerge if they are there. They can be dealt with gradually in the context of a more secure relationship with the supervisor. The principle is that it is inadvisable to engender and to precipitate the expression of too much affect early in the learning experience. One trusts that the student will grow less defensive and increasingly free to express his feeling as the educational demands exert pressure and as progressively he has experienced the supervisor's in-

8. Gordon W. Allport, "Attitudes," in *Handbook of Social Psychology,* ed. Carl Murchinson (Worcester, Mass.: Clark University Press, 1935).

tent to understand in order to help. When a student's feelings, attitudes, and behavior are repeated in a client, he often becomes aware of his own difficulties and their import as he discusses the client with the supervisor. The supervisor's understanding of the client with whom the student is aligned defensively may reassure the student so that he gains insight through applying the understanding of another to himself. The student thus has an experience in which he is "done to" as he must do. He may then be able to affirm the clients' strengths, respect their defenses, and travel with them at their own tempo in eliciting and in dealing with their disturbed feelings.

c) *Readiness to hold the student responsible to meet realistic demands while taking into account the unrealistic ones.*—Throughout the student's training, the supervisor will avoid making unrealistic demands but will firmly insist that the student meet realistic demands. One of the continuous problems in field work is that of avoiding unrealistic demands. It is difficult and often impossible to assign cases that represent orderly progression from simple to complex. When a big step ahead confronts the student, the supervisor, rather than overlook or waive requirements, should give additional help so that he may meet the enlarged demands. Critical evaluation of a student should always acknowledge the factor of accelerated demand, particularly when such demand has operated against the student's doing as well as greater experience would have enabled him to do. Reassignment of cases naturally is indicated when their demands are beyond the student's ability to use help in meeting them. One of the important learning experiences is that the client's welfare comes first and that we do not in good conscience assume responsibility beyond our capacity or beyond our time limits.

This reintroduces the factor of the field supervisor's alignment with the student's program as a whole. She must not assign work beyond the field-work time limits. Learning is interrupted when pressures are too great. Fatigue may be a factor in interrupted learning. When demands are excessive, one may note anxiety and defenses, one of which may be temporary regression, as evidenced in projection of responsibility and increased dependency. Or one may note stereotyped production in which the student is giving only part of himself. In the interest of survival, the student may acquire ways of "getting by." He will have had an experience in submission, in pretense, in seeming to be rather than in being, which is not conducive to the development of professional integrity. In short, when the integrative function of the ego is overworked, its protective function is called upon for overuse. In such instances the defenses erected operate against integration. In so far as the student is treated with that consideration implied in making realistic demands and in understanding pressures and in helping him meet unavoidable stress, he has experienced a helping process during stress which should sensitize him to the need of others for supportive help under stress. We cannot expect social workers to be understanding of hardship if their own stresses have been excessive and have not been understood.

d) *Ability to engage the student's activity in learning, to demonstrate professional conduct, and to maintain a purposeful working relationship.*—It is clear that the intensity of the emotional demand can be diminished both through direct expression and through indirect expression, that is, through activity in learning. Anxiety in learning is best handled by the student himself as he experiences his own adequacy in participation in every area. Among classroom courses, those in casework have been a major means to growth and the integration of learning. The nature of the content as well as the case-discussion method has afforded the student (1) opportunity for active participation through discussion; (2) opportunity to learn through doing (while doing for the development of skill is taught predominantly in the field, there is much teaching through doing in the casework classroom); (3) opportunity to experience change in feelings and attitudes, through testing his old thinking against the new, as he defends the old and explores the new, to express feelings which obstruct the acceptance of knowledge, to share in the group's discovery of facts and their meaning, to move into learning through identification with others. In so far as a sense of belonging to a group facilitates acculturation, the case-discussion class can play a vital part in this process. The practitioner as a casework instructor in classroom and field is reassuring to students. In this decisive life-venture, students reach out to identify with those who have what they lack. The practitioner knows firsthand the what, the why, and the how. She has been in the same boat. She has survived threatening demands. What she has done can be done again. Decisive in the re-educative process, therefore, is the instructor's capacity to sustain a way of thinking, a way of feeling and of responding, that is truly professional. This must operate in relation to clients studied and being served, to students individually and collectively as they respond to learning in classroom or field, as well as to colleagues in agency and on the faculty.[9]

A classroom instructor may teach didactically the necessity for objective evaluation of cause-and-effect relationships, but if she shows condemning attitudes, she impedes her own purpose in trying to help the student become objective. Thus she may criticize freely, but she may not caricature individuals, whether they be clients, students, faculty in other disciplines, board members, or the unenlightened director of a welfare program. Caricature does not develop respect for the human individual. Furthermore, it distorts and weakens the intent to understand. If an instructor is sarcastic in her critical evaluation of the part played by a worker in a situation under discussion, or if she ridicules a student's thinking or responds subjectively to the student's response of differing with her, she undermines the student's inclination to become understanding. The will to understand is inculcated and strengthened in so far as the student experiences understanding in the classroom. Furthermore, in participating in the objective evaluation of his own or of someone else's work, the student frequently is enabled to take the first step in the development of self-criticism.

An instructor is responsible for the management to productive ends of her relationship to the class as a whole. It should be a working relationship, and hence the instructor must keep the relationship focused on the student's learning purpose in relation to the school's educational goals. It should not become one in which students are absorbed in the instructor per se or the instructor in the student's response to her. In other words, the instructor should not stand between the learning content and the receptive capacity of the student. Studied efforts which place method before content put the self-conscious instructor in the foreground, and no instructor, regardless of how intriguing her method, belongs in the foreground.

9. For discussion of the import of the instructor's activity in the classroom see Charlotte Towle, "The Classroom Teacher as Practitioner."

Likewise, the instructor whose personal need for recognition leads her in one way or another, whether it be putting on a good show or some other compelling device, to win a response to herself rather than to the subject matter interferes with learning. When this happens, the dependency-authority conflict implicit in adult learning may be intensified so that resistance is aroused. Or the instructor's need may entangle students so that they become identified to the extent of losing their identity. When this occurs, they may "take over" without "taking in." Followers rather than leaders are developed when the emotional pressure of the teacher engenders the dependency, the anxiety, and the confusion which in the long run result when a student's professional orientation merely reflects that of an influential person.

In conveying a way of feeling and responding appropriate to social work, one would expect the skilled practitioner to bring to the classroom discipline in the regulation of her own need to the end of a focus on professional purpose. Capacity for objective management of relationships derived through practice should serve her now. Until, however, she finds herself as a teacher and is secure in her role, she may need reassurance as a person and unconsciously fail to use her skills in this new situation.

Thus, throughout the student's educational experience, educators aim to afford him a relationship which affirms growth through strengthening the ego-superego integration. This implies a relationship which affords security without fostering dependency, one which energizes his emancipation from old authority-dependency ties, hence one which widens his relationship span and patterns him to individualize those whom he serves. Such a relationship eases the anxiety and tension implicit in learning to become a helping agent and lowers the need for defenses. As the student is enabled to contain anxiety or to deal with it in ways which do not complicate learning, his emotions become purposively engaged. He thus becomes increasingly perceptive, selective, self-aware, self-regulative, objective in his relationships, and realistic in his goal striving. The relationship with mentors thus serves as one means to widen the student's integrative capacity, so that it may equal and exceed the task. As this occurs, he gains increased confidence through competent performance and has some margin for creative effort.

Social work educators have become aware that they must be teachers as well as practitioners, that there is a content of knowledge and skill in educational practice which they must master if they are to help students integrate professional learning. In learning which imposes a heavy integrative task we have recognized the importance of the learner's equilibrium. We face the fact that we have a maximum need for measures which aid integration. We have become aware that educational principles are generic. Shaped by the distinctive attributes of social work, our educational means may have certain peculiarities, but they are not unique. Out of our experience in collaboration with other disciplines we know that educational experts to whom we turn for help cannot select our learnings for us or tell us specifically what to do. They can give us perspective and certain insights and principles for differential use. We know that sound application of these principles will be contingent on the social work educators' depth of understanding of the subject matter and of the distinctive demands which social work learning makes on the learner. Social work educators have had experience in the re-education of individuals, the basic knowledge and principles of which can be translated for use in professional education. As we now incorporate certain knowledge from the field of education, we may orient the student's integrative task more closely to his integrative capacity. One major means to integration, the conduct of the educational relationship, regarding which social work educators are peculiarly well oriented, has been presented fully.

1. The Arrangement of Learning Experiences for Orderly Progression in Demand on the Learner

If anxiety is to be kept low so that the ego will not be engrossed in a defensive struggle for survival, there is a marked need for an orderly progression in learning. With change occurring at rapid tempo and much that is new to master, this is attained not only through consistency of relationship but also through gradual change in demand on the student, as previously indicated. It is attained also through orderly movement from simple to complex in both the intellectual and the emotional demands implicit in the experiences and materials selected. Order can be maintained in the classroom to a far greater extent than in the field. In the classroom one can move from the old to the new, revive the old, and forecast the new in structuring the sequence of learning. Once it is decided what ordinarily is simple and what is complex for the student at a particular stage of learning, a somewhat orderly progression can be sustained through the nature of the case selection, the grouping of cases, the selective assignment of readings, the conduct of the class discussions, and the careful orientation of written assignments and examinations.

Criteria have been established by some social casework faculties to delineate progression in demand on the learner. Implied are principles which should be tested systematically throughout the curriculum, as well as in casework teaching. These will be presented fully in subsequent chapters, but a few examples are given now. Among other earmarks in a casework sequence, the beginning course would require less new knowledge with which to think. Furthermore, at the start, when knowledge is limited, cases should be selected which are rich in material for inductive thinking, in order that inferences which the instructor is able to make by reason of his knowledge may be convincingly supported by evidence when presented to students. Thus in evaluating behavior responses, we may not inculcate the tendency to infer too much from too little, thus causing an unrealistic demand to throw students back on stereotypes as a defense. Hence a distinguishing mark of advanced courses would be that the student, within limits, could be expected increasingly to infer soundly from small evidence, to recognize the need for more evidence, and to look beyond the manifest. This involves the selection of case material for the early courses in which feeling is shown in relatively pure form rather than disguised, or if there is disguise, the circumstances of the individual's life and his repeated responses to them should be recorded so as to support clearly the inference. For example, one would present situations where resentment over taking help is obvious rather than disguised by abject gratitude and submission, or where dependency would be acted out rather than belied through repetitive protests against becoming dependent.

For progression in teaching the use of community resources, an early course would afford acquaintance with certain resources and discussion of their use, whereas in an advanced course cases could well present complicated interplay of agencies to afford study of lines of responsibility and to solve problems in interagency relationships. For progression in the emotional impact of the human drama in the study, for instance, of mother-child relationships, obviously the equivalent of *I Remember Mama* should precede those which are the psychological equivalent of *Medea*. For progression in learning to understand and to conduct a worker-client relationship, the early courses would afford cases in which the management of the relationship would present no unusual problems, in terms of clients' excessive need, anxiety, or resistance. The students would be learning the relationship's confidential nature, its respectful nature, and its objective quality in situations where the client moves into taking help fairly readily. In the advanced courses, more disturbed and extreme responses in the use of the relationship would be presented. These would involve teaching a deeper understanding of the transference situation and skills in directing and controlling the relationship to therapeutic ends.

Finally, in this matter of progression from the simple to the complex, it is important to state that the simple is not the unimportant or the nonessential. The simple beginnings must be what the learner needs to know first in order to begin to help people in ways appropriate to social work. They must be what he needs to know first in order to cope with greater complexity later. They are not such easy beginnings that they fail to challenge the learner and thus give him at the start an atypical sample of social work learning. They make a high demand, in that they require him to feel and think about old things anew. Throughout life he has known people, appraised them, related to them, given and taken help, worked with them. Now he must know them in a different context, see them in a new light, serve them in a different relationship, communicate with them differently—in short, begin to be not just himself but a social worker. Thus reality dictates that the hardest task, that of doing old things in new ways, comes first. For this reason it is essential that there be a careful selection of the basic elements. In so far as they are mastered, more complex combinations of them will be comparatively simple.

It is important to acknowledge that absolute order will not prevail, with the utmost effort on the instructor's part. There is great variation in the implication which the students in a class see in a given case. In the class discussion the comments, questions, and issues introduced by certain students will cause the discussion to leap ahead from more simple considerations to the complex. In the light of the specific situation, instructors will deal with this variously. Often it is possible to hold to the level of learning which the case realistically demonstrates and to give the students a sense of ongoing movement, through the glimpse of tomorrow's greater intricacies toward which we are heading and for which we will be prepared by putting first things first. The teacher who has structured a course with an aim toward an orderly progression will be better prepared to bring a wide range of responses within bounds, so that for the class as a whole the *abc*'s are not shelved for the *xyz*'s. A glimpse of the latter can then motivate rather than impede learning. While it is possible to select materials for orderly progression in the classroom, it is not possible to individualize the tempo of learning to the extent that this is possible in field practice. As indicated earlier, in field work the difficulties presented by disorderly progression in the demands made by cases assigned can be dealt with through individual help.

2. Making Learning a Conscious Process

Because professional learning presents a continuum of new elements, conscious intelligence must operate continuously. Automatic responses are not sufficient. The student will be less confused and better able to keep the management of the learning experience in his own hands if he understands the process in which he is engaged. As he senses that there is order in the seeming chaos in which he finds himself through comprehending the purpose and import of specific learning experiences in relation to immediate and remote goals, he becomes more secure. Because this security frees him to engage in intelligent selection and creative effort instead of having to rely on intuitive hunches or stereotyped behavior as a means to adaptation, it is important that a progressive effort to make learning a conscious process be instituted early. Guiding insight increases the integrative capacity of the learner.[10] We repeat: "Insight into the processes of

10. Thomas M. French, M.D., *The Integration of Behavior*, Vol. I: *Basic Postulates* (Chicago: University of Chicago Press, 1952), p. 217.

invention can increase the efficiency of almost any developed and active intelligence."[11]

In relation to subject matter taught, this implies teaching not only the what and the how but also the why of professional thinking and doing. If one were to differentiate the educational method of the professional school from the learning on the job of apprentice training, a major difference would be this emphasis on the whys. Apprentice training in its predominant emphasis on what to do and how to do it may produce a certain technical competence. Professional education has aims beyond imparting rule-of-thumb procedure, the stereotypes of technical competence. It aims, instead, to develop the learner's capacity to think anew, so that eventually he may modify, or depart from, the thinking and doing of his mentors. For this he must be habituated to appraise his activity. A continuous focus on the whys of practice is one means to this end. A student often finds the knowledge and the rationale of procedure quite irrational until he understands why we have to feel, think, and do this way. As perception is heightened, confusion and hence anxiety and resistance in learning are lowered or eliminated.

If the educational experience is to be a conscious process in order to lower anxiety so that the ego's integrative, executive, and regulative functions may be free to operate for productive learning, the student needs some orientation to the aims of educational content and measures. He needs an awareness of the purpose of procedures and some knowledge of the norms of learning and the nature of learning. For example, he needs to know that intellectual grasp normally precedes facile use; that resistance to change operates to produce ambivalence and anxiety in learning; that the relationship with those from whom we learn is a vital determinant operating for or against learning. Since there is small place in professional education, concerned as it is with the growth of the learner, for childlike trust in mentors, the relationship is something to understand in order that we may regulate our use of it. Seeing or feeling immediate goals as steps toward remote objectives avoids the tension implied in postponed gratification, which may lower motivation. Understanding of the educational system and insight into one's own learning responses

11. Brewster Ghiselin, *The Creative Process: A Symposium* (Berkeley and Los Angeles: University of California Press, 1952), see Introd.

may initially produce the discomfort of self-consciousness, but in the long run it will make for less haphazard use of the experience and for the greater security wrought by a more successful outcome. The exception obviously will be the student whose personality involvement compels him to defend himself against understanding and insight.

A conscious process in learning is essential for transfer of learning from one subject area to another, hence is decisive for the integration of the profession's learning as a whole. Transfer of training is possible when (*a*) similar conditions exist in different fields; (*b*) methods of thinking and the content in one field are appropriate to those in another field; and (*c*) a learner recognizes that two or more situations have something in common. A distinctive attribute of social work is that highly specialized knowledge and skills are not required for each of its several aspects and that its major processes have much basic knowledge, understanding, and skill in common. Therefore, social work learning has a high potential for integration. Is the student engaged in a research project aware of the fact that what he learned in social casework and in psychiatry or elsewhere of method, of studying a problem, of psychological insight, of working relationship, of agency structure, and of interviewing skills, can be used adaptively here? Is the student engaged in the study of social welfare administration aware that the learnings of social casework and psychiatry have import in the making and remaking of policy both in services to clients and in staff administration? Does he see the import of the understanding gained through his study of that small-scale social system, the family, for staff relationships in the agency where the hierarchy of authority tends to re-create family life? Does he see that the problem-defining and -solving process of casework is useful in administration where problems in human relationship are solved through a comparable, though different, shared inquiry between people involved in the problem? Such perceptions as these to aid integration are contingent in large measure on whether or not educators themselves are cognizant of relatedness and do something about it by providing opportunities for the identification of common elements in subject areas and processes. Only as total faculties participate in curriculum study to define course objectives, to know learning experiences selected to attain objectives, and to organize the various areas of learning for cumulative effect, may they help students to become conscious of the generic import of their separate learnings.

Students entering a profession ordinarily reach out to understand and to become more fully aware of the educational experience in which they are engaged. It is to be remembered, however, that this propensity is part and parcel of the professional growth process and that such consciousness will evolve gradually. In fact, one of the measures of professional maturity is the extent to which learning has become conscious. There is a progression here. Interpretations of the learning process will be abstractions until experienced. While some interpretation prior to specific experiences may make them more meaningful as they occur, the whys and wherefores will need to be appraised retrospectively, bit by bit, as learning proceeds. It is noteworthy also that students will be more receptive to insight when the outcome of activity has been successful than when they have failed to learn. They are more prone to reject the rationale of an educational process when it has not worked for them. This is not always the case, however, for sometimes the individual who is having a learning problem is helped to solve it through awareness of the purpose of certain procedures and demands. This tends to occur when the learning problem is related to the student's reality disorientation, as differentiated from emotionally determined confusion. It tends to occur, also, when he is not so threatened by failure that he needs to project it onto the educational system. He is thus able to assume responsibility for the problem and to make better use of the educational procedure through understanding it. While strongly motivated to learn, the student may find that not all areas of professional learning are equally attractive. Motivation in certain areas may therefore be relatively low. When he sees the relatedness of the unattractive demand to his goal, he may become aware of the necessity to learn what formerly was regarded as nonessential. Consciousness of the import of the negative elements in the experience may widen the learner's motivation and help him cope with the total reality.

3. *Spontaneity and Discipline: Whitehead's Educational Principles*

In order that the student may become receptive to insight and thus come to think objectively in situations which involve him emotionally, he should have the opportunity throughout classroom and field experience to express and to understand his feelings, emotions, and attitudes as they affect his work. This implies the creation of an atmosphere of freedom and spontaneity. In individual supervisory sessions or classroom sessions, instructors should not focus, nor should students be encouraged to focus, on their feelings apart from the professional situation on which they bear. An orderly progression from low demand to gradually heightened demand is indicated in this matter of self-expression and helping the student to become conscious of himself. Activity in this area must be individualized and oriented to time, place, and person. The progression in the place given to the student's emotional response in learning and to helping him develop understanding of his professional activity has been depicted to some extent in the literature.[12] It will be discussed further in subsequent chapters as the content and organization of learning are presented in considerable detail.

For integration of learning essential for independent thinking, the student needs to have an effective way of studying, a disciplined way of thinking, a systematic intellectual procedure to help him not only master knowledge but develop his intellectual grasp and range. He will be helped to attain a method which both flexes and disciplines his mind as he consistently engages in a process which takes into account the stages of mental growth through which the individual normally proceeds in learning. As this occurs, anomalies in intellectual functioning may be corrected. As indicated earlier, there are limits to which the mental habits of the adult can be modified, since they tend to be deeply intrenched and related both to mental endowment and also to personality development.

We, along with some other social work educators, have found Whitehead's dynamic educational philosophy compatible with the basic concepts of dynamic psychiatry as we have attempted to put both to use in professional education.[13] In that Whitehead conceives

12. Charlotte Towle, "The Classroom Teacher as Practitioner"; see also in *Social Work as Human Relations;* Helen Harris Perlman, "Teaching Social Case Work by the Discussion Method," *Social Service Review,* September, 1950; and "The Lecture as a Method in Teaching Social Case Work," *ibid.,* March, 1951.

13. Alfred North Whitehead, *The Aims of Education and Other Essays* (New York: Macmillan Co., 1929).

of effective education as a process which must be oriented to the organic growth process of the total personality engaged in learning, his description of stages of mental growth and of the process of normal mental development delineates an educational procedure which should support and foster mental development. In so far as we have been cognizant of these stages of growth in normal mental functioning and able also to conduct the educational experience with reference to the implied laws of learning, we have found that the resultant educational process has not only tested but also affirmed the student's ego development. Accordingly, it has been our aim throughout the educational process to have the stages specified by Whitehead—namely, imaginative consideration, analysis, synthesis, generalization, and imaginative reconsideration—proceed repetitively but progressively in new fact situations. Professional education presses the student to put learning to use. When fired with new ideas, it is a natural tendency, therefore, for the student to leap from imaginative consideration to generalization. Or when engulfed by complexity in the analytic task, he is normally inclined to generalize prematurely without synthesis of multiple factors. Beyond flight from a difficult situation, this may occur in part because generalization is the means to transfer learning for use elsewhere. As teachers are conscious of these stages in the intellectual process and hold the students to them, disciplined thinking may be ingrained for use elsewhere as well as in a specific subject area. Since first steps in learning tend to be pattern-setting, it is essential that these independent but related phases obtain, if only in rudimentary form, from the start. It is to be noted that although these aspects of thinking are sequential to a degree, they also interplay as the process proceeds. They move ahead together in varied combinations and with emphasis contingent upon the demands of the changing fact situation in relation to the knowledge at hand. Thus intermittently as analysis, synthesis, and generalization take place, imaginative consideration recurs. Also, to move forward analytically, one synthesizes as one goes. Sequence obtains, however, in that at the beginning of a learning experience, be it course or case, imaginative consideration is prominent; at midstream, analysis and synthesis predominate; while, at the close, generalization and imaginative reconsideration are ascendant. Subsequent chapters which deal with progression in learning both in content and in method will be cast in this "point-counterpoint" context. The general import of this rhythm in learning is stated briefly now.

For comprehension from the start, it is essential in a new learning adventure to envisage the whole of which a given experience is a part or in relation to which it serves a purpose. For instance, one envisages the place of a given field of study in the profession, the aims of a particular course in a sequence, or the major learning concerns of a configuration of cases within a course. Interest is focused and apprehension heightened through presentation of some of the problems to be solved, some of the questions to be answered, some of the issues to be clarified. The use of this approach in the orientation of learners is based on recognition of the importance of its several elements. Sound use of this measure facilitates learning through partializing it, in terms of conscious purpose, focus, and emphasis. At the same time, fragmentation is guarded against and integration promoted through the context of the whole in which a configuration of parts is continuously viewed. Through this measure it is possible to engage the emotions purposively, to foster identification, to heighten perception, and to channel interest. Thus one lowers the tension implicit in learning where interest is high.[14] Again orderly progression must obtain in the use of this measure as throughout the educational process. If perception is to be heightened, it is important at the start not to envisage too much. Therefore, the whole must be presented in broad brush strokes rather than in too great detail. In so far as the history of a subject is drawn in at the start, there must be no sterile narrative of the past but, instead, a stirring account which focuses consideration on the present and toward the future. Early identification with the aims of the profession is fostered as students get a sense of onward movement in which they are to participate, a sense of the significance of the work which they are undertaking. In setting out to solve a problem, too many considerations and questions will heighten tension through confusing, rather than

14. See Charlotte Towle, *Common Human Needs* (New York: American Association of Social Workers, 1945), pp. 107-9, for use of this measure in orienting new staff or students to an agency program; see also Charlotte Towle, *Social Case Records from Psychiatric Clinics* (Chicago: University of Chicago Press, 1941), Introd. and "Teaching Notes," for an early presentation of the use of this approach in teaching social casework.

orienting, the learner; hence one must avoid a sense of a labyrinth to be explored. A few major questions and concerns will give a sense of direction and chart a path to pursue. As students proceed, they can be expected progressively to initiate imaginative consideration, whereas at the start the instructor will carry major responsibility for charting the adventure.

Finally, one of the qualities essential for helping people is imaginativeness, the ability to see in the mind's eye what another individual's experience is meaning to him, even though that experience is outside the range of the social worker's experience.[15] Although this may be an innate ability, it probably can be developed through contact with people who habitually reach out to encompass the possibilities in another's experience. Thus as the student is encouraged to stretch his imagination, sensibility may be developed, even though it cannot be engendered. The previous educational experience of many students has tended to curb this inclination prematurely; hence the systematic use of imaginative consideration has the purpose of widening the range of perception and of fostering reflection for the gradual attainment of wisdom.[16] Imaginative reconsideration with some of the same purposes recurs fragmentarily throughout and occurs again prominently as learners are led to reflect retrospectively upon the import of what they have learned or of what has been formulated, as generalizations for wider use have been attained.

It has been said that, for mastery of learning, a degree of precision must be introduced early.[17] Analysis and synthesis introduce precision. For precision in thinking, knowledge is essential. Hence precision implies the selection of what the learner needs to know in order to think reliably, that is, to see the import of the facts. This involves selection of first things first. The instructor must therefore have considered carefully what the learner needs to know now in this fact situation in order to think and to do competently. For pre-

15. In curriculum discussions Dean Helen R. Wright has remarked about the possible importance of the humanities at the college level for the development of this quality.

16. Since this chapter was written, the author has noted a comparable discussion of the "ability to imagine truthfully" as an essential quality of the social worker (see Margaret Ashdown and S. Clement Brown, *Social Service and Mental Health* [London: Routledge & Kegan Paul, 1953], pp. 60–61).

17. Whitehead, *op. cit.*

cision, repetition is essential. If the reality principle and the pleasure principle are to be integrated so that the student finds pleasure in precision, drill must sharpen, not dull, the learner's faculties. For precision in differential thinking and doing, it is important that stereotyped repetition be avoided. Perhaps because there are few indifferent tasks in professional education, perhaps because of the high degree of ego involvement in professional learning, and perhaps also because of the intellectual level of these learners, repetition without progression deadens interest and engenders resistance as a reaction against the breakdown of motivation.[18]

4. Repetition Which Progresses

Repetition with difference is a factor to be considered in all aspects of professional education, one vitally important in assignments and examinations, if they are to carry forward rather than deter learning. Major ideas, basic principles, and methods bear endless repetition in new fact situations. The learner, in part because his expectancy of success is based on past success, is reassured through finding these old elements in the new. Through this use of repetition, the rhythm which aids integration is attained. Tyler stresses the value of a number of learning experiences focused on the same outcome.[19] Repetition in this instance reassures the learner through giving him a sense of security, the confidence that comes with finding, for example, that, despite variables in a new fact situation, given certain circumstances, certain results will follow and that the use of certain methods will bring certain responses. Social casework instructors have ample opportunity for this use of repetition not only in the study of developmental histories of individuals but in the analysis of interviewing methods. It is through repetition also that learning is carried over from one field of study to another. Tyler maintains that the rhythm which facilitates learning is attained through organization of learning for cumulative effect and that the criteria by which to judge organization of learning are continuity, sequence, and integration. Repetition is the common element in these three

18. Ernest R. Hilgard, *Theories of Learning* (New York: Appleton-Century-Crofts, Inc., 1948), p. 224; see also discussion in chap. 2 of this book (pp. 23–27).

19. Ralph W. Tyler, "Basic Principles of Curriculum and Instruction," *Syllabus for Education* (Chicago: University of Chicago Press, 1950).

attributes. For example, in teaching the problem-solving method of social casework, continuity obtains in so far as this method appears and reappears throughout the casework sequence, so that its important steps are iterated and reiterated. Sequence would obtain as this method would be repeated in new fact situations which exert a new demand and thus involve progression in learning. Here one finds repetition with a difference. Integration obtains as this method recurs in subject areas other than social casework, thus providing opportunity for reinforcement of the elements to be learned from one field to another, as well as differentiation in the elements between fields, so that the learner is prepared to use them adaptively elsewhere.

To get the cumulative effect which facilitates and intrenches learning, it is essential that faculty engaged in curriculum construction note not only where they are teaching repetitively but to what extent they are helping students to identify common and distinctive elements. Often instead they leave the transfer of learning to the chance propensities of the learner, because they in their separate niches are not fully conscious of the repetitive elements and of the generic nature of major ideas, basic principles, and methods. This is not an argument for integrated courses in which faculty members assume major responsibility for bringing together in digest form two or more subject areas. Such attempts endanger the creativity of the learner, in that they tend to do his comparative thinking for him. In the last analysis, the learner must be patterned to do his own integration. If he is to go beyond his predecessors, he will do so in so far as he establishes new connections to serve as a basis for thinking anew.

5. *Focus and Emphasis*

For that equilibrium which safeguards ego integration, it is essential to avoid engulfing the student. The learning experience must be partialized through breaking it into bits that can be assimilated. Always, however, the part must be taught with reference to a whole. This is attained through focusing learning and through emphasis. A given case can be focused through the instructor's giving certain definite formulations around which the student may center his thinking, thus teaching a part rather than the ramifications of the whole

case. Or a case can be focused in terms of its purposes in the learning sequence and taught with an emphasis on major issues. Focus is
attained also through helping the student define the problem to be
solved, the questions to be answered—in short, through adherence to
a method of case study. Boredom and confusion result when knowledge is conveyed without emphasis. Out of all this, what matters
most here and now needs to be considered repetitively. The weighting of part of a whole in which there is selection for use, in which
first things are put first and the subordinate identified, is essential
if the student is not to flounder in the shallows or drown in the
depths. Emphasis is attained through using one case to reinforce
another, through assignments and readings which explicitly point up
or underscore decisive areas of learning. It is attained also as courses
are timed to reinforce one another. In this connection an over-all
curriculum committee within a professional school is essential.

6. *Synthesis and Generalization*

Since professional education is education for use, fragmentation is
to be avoided in a situation in which many pressures tend to produce
it. Building the parts into a whole must be done systematically
through repeated summarization. Tying the bits together as we proceed through a case; formulating interpretive statements; summarizing thinking at the close of a case; viewing a specific situation in the
light of general knowledge and common experience, to identify its
predictable and discrepant elements; summarizing learning at the
close of a course—all these systematic efforts enable the student to
make a process his own and thus to bring his learning to fruition.
Habituated to relating the parts to the whole, he has the means to
discover wherein his understanding is complete or incomplete and
to account for its shortcomings. Analytic process should be motivated from the start by the intent to discover what all this adds up
to for use in a specific situation. This, in turn, begets an intent to see
what needs to be known and to decide what can be done, in the light
of what is known. Security is attained through the sense of competence derived in knowing the boundaries of one's knowledge, as
well as in knowing its usefulness. Whitehead defines synthesis as the
fruition of the process of precise analysis.[20] Gratification in learning

20. Whitehead, *op. cit.*

occurs as synthesis occurs. Imaginative consideration and eagerness to move ahead are renewed as this end is attained.

Progression from synthesis to generalization is the natural tendency of the professional learner. In a given situation he urgently reaches out to learn something for use elsewhere. Frustration and rage emerge quickly when the student cannot see the relevance of what he is learning in the classroom to what he is doing or even anticipates doing in the field. The novice instructor may select the bizarre situation for classroom use. The student may be momentarily intrigued, but he soon becomes restive. "All this is very interesting, but what am I going to do with it," is expressed in many ways. The instructor learns through experience that useful material is that which lends itself to comparison. It is important from the very start to affirm the student's natural impulse to compare as a means to integration of learning. The student seeks precedents in a new fact situation. It is essential, therefore, that he become habituated to comparative thinking, case by case, and to periodic attempts at tentative generalization, as in course summaries. It is only as the student experiences careful comparative thinking that he will know the limits to which one can generalize from one case. This will occur as he invariably finds individuality in the midst of sameness, to emphasize the point that general inferences must always be used with close reference to individual differences. In other words, he learns that there will always be exceptions to what commonly obtains. Only thus will he begin to learn to formulate principles and to use them differentially. Without this help, precedents will be seized on fragmentarily for dubious use. Disciplined generalization is the means to the mastery of knowledge implicit in professional wisdom.

7. Learning by Doing

It has been both stated and implied that doing is a major means to the integration of professional learning. Opportunity to experience change in feeling and attitudes is afforded through planned doing. Competent performance, step by step, gives hope and confidence. Whitehead states: "Get your knowledge quickly, and then use it. If you can use it, you will retain it." Hence the learner's active participation is desirable throughout the educational experience. Putting knowledge to use intellectually in the classroom and through actual use in the field is an important means to integration. Educators are continuously concerned to convey what the individual needs to know in order to do. The instructor's task in classroom and field is to select first things first, in order that the student may use knowledge competently as he proceeds. It might be said that the classroom emphasizes the teaching of the philosophy and science of social work, whereas the field emphasizes the art of doing in the light of this orientation. In spite of this differentiation, there is considerable teaching of skill in the classroom. Beyond the vicarious doing afforded through the study of professional activity in individual cases selected from the field of practice, there is the doing involved in discussion. Assumption of this responsibility is preparation for participation in group discussion in practice. It is preparation also in putting knowledge to use. Reading assignments and written assignments afford much doing. In short, actual practice, classroom discussion, and assignments and examinations which demand that the student think, not merely know, have long been major means to integration in social work education.[21]

A distinctive feature of social work education is the use of actual practice in lieu of observation. The novice begins not with observation of an experienced practitioner but with actual practice in an agency, where he is held accountable to do before he knows the whats, hows, and whys of doing. His doing in terms of actual practice, therefore, cannot always be competent, and hence ease anxiety. This factor makes it highly important that an orderly progression be obtained in classroom study, in assignments, and in examinations. When he feels competent in intellectual doing, he can hope for the gradual attainment of competence in practice. This system brings a large helping component and dependency-authority elements into the student-supervisor relationship. It is the meeting of this realistic dependency through teaching and helping, as well as the help given the adult learner to enable him to accept and resolve conflicts about the dependency-authority implicit in professional learning, which gradually implants the peculiar characteristics of the social worker–client relationship. An important aspect of the doing in field practice

21. Towle, "The Classroom Teacher as Practitioner"; see also in *Social Work in Human Relations;* Helen Harris Perlman, "Teaching Case Work by the Discussion Method"; also "The Lecture as a Method in Teaching," *Social Service Review,* March, 1951; Whitehead, *op. cit.*

is that the learner, having experienced a helping process in which he has survived stresses, in large part because he sought and took help, gains deepened respect for the recipient of help and finds his own anxiety over dependency lessened. This is an essential development in those who are charged to help people help themselves.[22] As a means to integration, progression in doing implies a gradual heightening of demand from a start in which help is given freely, particularly when practice has exerted an unrealistic demand. In the classroom also the instructor takes more responsibility in leading and in focusing discussion and in case summarization early in a course sequence than later. This principle holds in all forms of doing. Since first experiences, however, are pattern-setting, it is essential that some self-activity in learning obtain from the start.

In summary, it can be said that the aims of professional education imply a system which does not repeat the limitations of prior educational experience, which, unfortunately, has often not been concerned with the development of the learner so much as with erudition.[23] Professional education must break with the past in several ways and notably through affording the student a corrective relationship, one in which he can have confidence and use to the utmost. This implies helping the student keep his selective powers and ways of learning intact until gradually, through further participation in learning, he may experience change. The major change may be to use his personality more freely in a disciplined rather than in a regimented way. This requires that social work educators put first things first; that they engage the student's participation; that they help him select through teaching which focalizes, synthesizes, and generalizes from the start. For responsible participation, it is essential that learning be made a conscious process. This may be done in varied ways, but essentially through sharing the purpose of contents conveyed and demands made. This facilitates learning through helping the student maintain his orientation to reality. Throughout the educational experience in relationship with the faculty individually and collectively, it is hoped that the student will consistently have had experience in

22. Charlotte Towle, "The Contribution of Education for Social Casework to Practice"; also in Cora Kasius (ed.), *op. cit.* See also Charlotte Towle, "The Distinctive Attributes of Education for Social Work."

23. See chap. 3, pp. 60–79.

being treated as he will be expected to treat others. It should follow that he will have grown in his intent to understand; in his capacity to identify sensitively and to separate himself from others; in his inclination for self-understanding, self-criticism, self-discipline; and in strength to stand up for his convictions. Having experienced a helping process in which he has survived stresses in large part because he sought and took help, it is hoped that his respect for the recipient of help will have deepened. Having experienced frustration through his own limitations and through the limitations of his profession in society, in the context of a relationship that has eased the trauma, it is hoped that he will go forth with increased capacity to lose without losing. In terms of his personality structure, his professional education should have instilled that hope which widens the ego span and strengthens its integrative capacity.[24]

We turn in Part II to the content and organization of social casework learning for a consideration of its contribution to the professional development of the social worker. Meanwhile, we present from these reflections on the learner in social work education some of the possible implications for the selection of students and for professional education in general.

24. Charlotte Towle, "The Contribution of Education for Social Casework to Practice"; also in Kasius (ed.), *op. cit.*

CHAPTER 6

The Selection of Students

If the professions are to play their part in society's efforts to humanize itself, they must serve individuals in ways which foster development and which avoid lowering personality integration. In fulfilling their responsibility, the professions have a shared purpose, that of orienting their services to the individual in the context of his social situation with perception of what the service is doing to the person in the process of educating, helping, or healing him. This not only implies the common obligation of imparting certain knowledge for understanding man interacting with environment but also makes it necessary that professional educational processes develop the student's capacity for empathy and insight. This is essential in order that he may be able to understand and relate to the needs, wants, and strivings of those whom he is to serve. We all have the task, therefore, of teaching in ways which help the student come to think objectively and to act rationally in situations which engage him emotionally. This demands that our educational systems strengthen the student's ego-superego integration, thus reinforcing his potentials for growth in order that learning may proceed rather than become constricted or break down.[1] These aims require that we select socially educable students, those who can become motivated to work for the common good rather than be driven largely to strive for self-maximation or for the maximation of those who, closely related in his life-situation, are an extension of himself.[2]

We earlier quoted Ralph W. Tyler's statement to the effect that education is a process for changing the behavior of students in a desired direction. We earlier asserted that in professional education a student is expected to acquire ideas, habits, attitudes, interests, and ways of feeling, thinking, and doing which he did not have before

1. See chaps. 3 and 4 for full development of this point.
2. See chaps. 1, 3, and 4 for what is meant by a "socially educable individual."

he entered a professional school. Educators have in common an acculturation task which makes it necessary that the demands for change be paced as far as possible to come within the integrative capacity of the student. This implies an orderly progression in teaching, oriented to developmental norms.[3] While the demands for change cannot be individualized, the student must be individualized as he engages in learning and as he at times defends himself against change.

We also have in common an initial charge to select individuals who have not merely a capacity to change their behavior but who, within the time allotted, can begin to behave in prescribed ways. This implies the selection of students who can learn in a situation in which others have a set of values for them and in which a hierarchy of goals has been structured. This requires capacity not only to identify with, but also to relate to, those who impose demands. It is through relationship with educators, as differentiated from identification with them, that the student is enabled to make the ways of others his own so as to use them freely rather than to submit to them abjectly. This means that, instead of identifying as a defense in order to survive in a foreign realm, the individual can form influential relationships through which his identity, modified but not obliterated, goes native without loss of that individuality essential for creative work. This implies an educational process which fosters identification with the profession rather than dependence on mentors, an educational experience which lays the groundwork for emancipation from mentors, in order that the profession's learnings may be advanced and its practices changed.

In that professional education imposes a hierarchy of goals, professional educators are concerned with the individual's integrative capacity in the pursuit of goals. Also in that the student is embarked upon the attainment of a goal to which he often is deeply committed through his needs and wishes, we have in common the opportunity to observe characteristic goal-directed behavior through which much may be learned of the integrative process and of the import of our educational systems for that process. We are all concerned to select

3. In chaps. 10, 11, and 12 we present an attempt at an orderly progression in teaching social casework. Social work educators other than casework teachers and educators in other professions may find some principles for use in structuring courses so that the demand for change is paced appropriately.

students whose needs and wants can realistically be met through our profession's service; students who in goal-striving can absorb and channel anxiety and tension sufficiently not to be rigidly or extensively defended against learning and who therefore can develop and integrate guiding insight; students who have ability for the work, so that, as obstacles in learning arise, they can deal with frustration through solving the problems. This implies that the student have not only the requisite ability as a basis for realistic hope but also sufficient expectancy of success that he is challenged rather than frightened by the threat of an integrative task which closely approximates his capacity. The significance of these capabilities in terms of adequate ego-superego integration as delineated earlier is manifest. It is important that the educational regime not make it necessary for the protective function of the ego to operate at the expense of its integrative function.

Professional educators in general, whether or not they think and speak in these terms, are concerned that the demands of the educational situation strike a balance between engulfing the student with demands beyond his integrative capacity and making the task sufficiently demanding that, in striving to attain goals, his ego is exercised and strengthened, while his readiness and his ability to master the difficult are tested. There is common agreement that professional education must test the individual's capacity to function under emotional stress, hence give evidence of his ability to contain and deal with discomfort and tension so that it does not interfere with learning. In this connection it is important to remember that the individual's integrative capacity should desirably exceed the integrative task by a margin sufficiently wide that he may be patterned for creative activity. If there is continuously a close approximation of capacity and task, the student, in keeping abreast of demands, may become task-centered and his behavior become stereotyped.

I. CHARACTERISTICS AND QUALITIES DESIRED

In any consideration of qualifications for admission to a professional school, there naturally is variation from profession to profession in what is valued and required in terms of knowledge, skill, and aptitude. There often is variation also among educators in a given profession as to the preparation they value in terms of course content. The marked differences of opinion in the matter of specialized preprofessional curriculum versus liberal arts curriculum are well known. Increasingly, however, there is very little, if any, discernible variation among educators from profession to profession and within professions as to the kind of people they want, in terms of personality development. Terminology varies from group to group, but in one vocabulary or another we plead for the selection of individuals with the following potentials:

Students who will have the capacity to think objectively in situations which involve them emotionally; individuals, therefore, who will be able to make learning a conscious process as a means to regulating their own need. We value also a wide range of perception and sensibility, as shown in the ability to bridge the gap between one's own experience and another's, through being able to consider the experience of others imaginatively but without distortion.

We want students who can subordinate immediate goals to remote goals, without becoming more than temporarily task-centered. We want individuals who are sufficiently confident that they can absorb discomfort and anxiety so that it motivates learning or at worst impedes it only temporarily.

We value those who can identify with and relate to those who impose demands, who also can relate to different people differently rather than so largely in terms of their own compelling needs that their responses are stereotyped and without nice reference to the needs of others.

We want to select students who can form influential relationships without loss of individuality and vitality. We consider this highly important if the profession is to have creative thinkers and leaders. For this the inclination to change must be deep and abiding, rather than transitory in the sense of a strategic adjustment to gain an immediate goal, a striving for status instead of for something in the accomplishment of which he is willing to invest himself. This implies readiness not merely to relinquish old authority-dependency ties but also readiness to form new relationships. Among these the professional helping relationship demands a sustained response to the needs of others, ability to give and to withhold, to assume responsibility and to delegate it, and to use authority without personal need to be authoritative.

And, finally, we want individuals who are ready to commit themselves rather totally to the profession, who can come to have a sense of vocation, in contrast to the individual who wants to give a measured part of himself and hence seeks an occupation to which he gives definite hours and assumes specified and limited duties.

Briefly, we are describing the individual who can use the educational process as a means to maturation. It is generally agreed that there are individuals with adequate intellect who cannot use the educational process of any profession as a means to growth. There probably are others who will develop in one profession better than in another. There are other individuals who might well have chosen any one of several professions. The problem confronting each profession is that of selecting those who can arrive at maturity through attaining its particular goals, that is, through learning to assume the profession's responsibilities.

The specification of characteristics desired may impress the reader as being a wishful delineation, an unrealistic search for a paragon of virtues. Out of frustration with some of our own limitations and out of our strong desire that our successors will go beyond us in carrying forward the aims of our profession, we could be prone, individually and collectively, to want the unattainable. And yet, as one appraises carefully the attributes and acquired characteristics specified and as one tests them from day to day in one's experience with colleagues in one's profession and in collaborating professions in the turmoil and pressure of workaday life, one will find that many individuals function essentially in these ways in the performance of their work. This does not mean that they function in this way in all respects, all of the time, but that, by and large, the behavior of the competent, respected professional person could be described in these terms. It approximates this picture.

It is a commonplace observation that as this behavior at times breaks down, the individual tends to correct it shortly. Having integrated the mores of his profession, his concept of himself makes him quickly perceptive of the import of the responses of others to professionally atypical behavior, so that he brings his behavior into line with what others expect of him and with his expectancy of himself. In so far as the behavior pattern of responsibly looking to the self has become habitual, the individual has a means to discover lapses in professional behavior. Or some individuals who consistently fall short in some respects make up for it in other respects, so that even though the development is uneven, the over-all personality functioning is sufficiently good from the standpoint of its effect on the persons served that it sustains certain anomalies. Careful appraisals of social work students show that many of them in the course of two years are beginning to function as described; in fact, they give promise of approximating this picture.[4] In making this statement it is recognized that the professional school may not always differentiate between strategic adjustment to gain an immediate goal and genuine growth. Our awareness of this possibility reflects our experience, however, and bespeaks the fact that we have some criteria of basic acceptance, as differentiated from submission or superficial adaptation.

II. THE ADMISSIONS PROCESS

The problem of the professional school in the selection of students is to know what evidence it has of certain potentials for development. Out of the profession's responsibility to those whom it serves, the educator increasingly has the conviction that its schools have both the right and the obligation to demand that the candidate make himself known to a greater extent than he has often been required to do in other application situations. At the same time, by the nature of the profession's function in society, its educators continuously are concerned to help rather than to hurt individuals. Therefore, consideration of what admissions procedures do to the individual in examining him must shape our practices. Bearing in mind that the individual's application for admission is the initial step in a goal pursuit in which ordinarily there is considerable ego investment and hence much at stake emotionally, social work educators think of admission procedures as an introduction to professional learning for the student who is accepted. They should be a first step in effecting the desired changes in feeling and thinking sought by the educational process. We see them also as a means to that earlier understanding of the student essential in individualizing his educational experience.

Out of our professional experience in seeking to understand individuals, we have learned that an investigatory process cannot be coercive. One cannot force an individual to be truly revealing. Pressure to see into people begets concealment as a defense against intrusion. When the individual is committed to the attainment of a goal, he may consciously and unconsciously meet our demand for information by talking or writing to attain his goal rather than to solve the problem of determining whether the profession can

4. See chap. 13, summary of indications of progress in learning.

meet his needs and wants or whether he can meet the profession's demands. For the individual who is refused admission it is our desire that our conduct of the procedures will not have implied rejection of him as a total person. Because we do not find him worth while in our profession, we do not want him to feel that he is not worth much in general. In admission procedures we hope to redirect individuals rather than to defeat them. Admissions practices which attain these aims pose the problem of engaging the applicant's participation in exploring and considering the nature of the profession's demands as embodied in its educational regime in relation to his needs, wants, and capabilities. This is difficult to do out of context of direct contact with the applicant. Increasingly, the interview is valued highly and is being used whenever possible to supplement correspondence with the applicant and other informants.

III. CRITERIA OF EDUCABILITY

There are great variations in admissions policies and practices among professional schools and among schools in any one profession. Probably all place considerable emphasis on the academic record, with a focus on an unusually competent record in curriculum areas relevant to the demands of the profession. In medical education the practice has been to place great importance on high grades in the natural and physical sciences. It has been said that this selects "individuals with interest and proficiency in things rather than in people."[5] Furthermore, it is stated that these students on the basis of high grades do well in the first two years. Many men with lower grades but good personality traits who do not do so well in the premedical years suddenly bloom in the third and fourth years and make better records than many of the students with marked mathematical and scientific aptitude who have been at the top of the class.[6] The consensus at the Ithaca Conference on Psychiatry and Medical Education was that admissions committees be encouraged to experiment by admitting small groups

5. *Psychiatry and Medical Education: Report of the 1951 Conference on Psychiatric Education, Ithaca, New York, 1951* (Washington: American Psychiatric Association, 1952), p. 14.

6. *Ibid.*, pp. 11–23.

of students with more preparation in the social sciences or liberal arts and carefully following their progress.[7]

In social work we require considerable preparation in the social sciences, and we tend to emphasize high grades in this area. The social sciences constitute relevant preparation in terms of knowledge essential for social work. It has been thought that grades in this area might also indicate the outcome of learning to think in social work, because the social sciences, like social work, are concerned with the study of relations between individuals, group and inter-group. College educators in the social sciences report that their subjects engender some of the same emotional responses encountered in the social work classroom. When the instructor uses concrete materials for problem-solving in discussion courses, there is an opportunity to deal with the emotions in the interest of integration. Such courses should test to a degree the individual's capacity to think objectively when engaged emotionally, as well as his readiness to experience changes in feeling, in thinking, and in the artificial doing of the classroom. In social work it has been observed that students may come to think objectively about individuals and society, however, without their capacity to sustain orderly thinking and objective doing in the fact situations of social work having been tested. The facts of social work are troubled people in helping relationships of varying complexity. Thinking about people and planning social action oriented to the needs of the individual and society in the hypothetical situations of the classroom make a different demand. The capacity to continue to think about human beings objectively while knowing them at first hand in a relationship in which one is responsible to serve them in one professional capacity or another cannot be tested in the preprofessional social science courses.

Perhaps three principles significant for professional education in general are implied here. First, it may well be indicated that professional educators increasingly look for unusual ability as evidenced in high grades, whether in some branches of the natural and physical sciences or in the social sciences and humanities, the idea being to get evidence of intellectual competence and vital interest in learning. We should be concerned that there are some

7. *Ibid.,* p. 14.

high grades rather than that the high grades should be heavily concentrated in a given area. This is not to say that low grades in areas of relevant knowledge would be ignored or that each profession will not need to require certain knowledge peculiarly essential to it.[8]

Second, that as the professions become increasingly concerned to select the socially educable student and to develop his social sensibility, there will be requirement of work in the social sciences, with emphasis on this area's being taught in ways which stand a chance of both testing and developing the student's social intelligence. Some social science courses, as taught traditionally to convey knowledge by the lecture method with reading assignments, have often failed either to test or to develop the student's aptitude for understanding and working with people. Instead, their effect, in fostering categorical thinking, sometimes has been to strengthen prejudices. This may occur as the student has failed to integrate knowledge which has an emotional impact, perhaps because the situation has provided no outlet to his feeling through affording an opportunity for discussion and for putting the knowledge to use in problem-solving. In many instances this has seemingly resulted in the acquisition of stereotypes which serve to defend the student against learning in the early stages of professional education. The informational course may well have a place in social science sequences, but the student must have experienced some instruction of a different nature in this area if the social sciences are to attain the aims specified.

Third, because there often will be a fundamental lack of carry-over of competence in scientific thinking and doing from abstract learning to professional service learning, it will be taken for granted that the student's potentials for professional performance cannot be tested in the preprofessional classroom. This work can test whether or not the student has been able to acquire certain knowledge and skill essential for professional performance, but it does not reveal his potentials for putting intellectual learning to use in professional services. Because a discrepancy sometimes occurs between intellectual competence or even brilliance in the classroom

8. See chap. 4, pp. 112–13, for discussion of the place of appropriate preparation in the integrative capacity of the learner.

and ability to use this competence in professional performance, high grades in the social sciences do not necessarily connote a socially educable student.

IV. MEASURES FOR DETERMINING EDUCABILITY

Various scholastic tests have been used by schools of social work to supplement and to test the student's academic record. The profession's experience as a whole with these has not been formulated and reported, nor has any one school, to the writer's knowledge, reported on the contribution of specific tests in the selection of social work students.[9] Social work educators have not used extensively certain personality tests. They have experimented briefly with several of these but have found it difficult administratively to give any one of these tests prior to admission. Used after the admission of the student, they all have in common the difficulty of being cumbersome, difficult, and expensive to score and to evaluate.[10]

In the difficult diagnostic and prognostic task entailed in determining the student's social educability, social work educators have used most prominently our own professional means for understanding the individual. We turned inevitably to the "case-history" method, in which our sources of understanding have been: the student's academic record, together with letters from the college or university, which increasingly are giving some picture of students in various aspects of college life; letters of reference from employers and others who have known the student personally; observation of the student's way of responding to the entire admission procedure as well as within an interview or series of interviews. This implies appraisal both of the content of information given and of his responses as he files application, meets requests for references, for supplementary information, for biographical statement, and for interviews. Throughout, we note the student's activity with close reference to its context.

In the admissions process we have an opportunity to observe

9. We refer here to such tests as (1) The ACE (American Council of Education Psychological Exam); (2) reading and writing exams, University of Chicago; (3) general education tests; (4) graduate record exam given by Educational Testing Service; (5) Michigan speeds of reading test.

10. Reference here is to (1) the Thematic Apperception Test, (2) group Rorschach, (3) individual Rorschach, (4) Szondi (pictorial).

the individual's response to requirements, to obstacles, to problems. His ways of surmounting obstacles, of solving problems, of adapting to or defending himself against requirements, all are noteworthy. It is important that we differentiate a healthy degree of adaptiveness from abject submission and that we know that a degree of self-protection does not connote defensiveness out of a weak ego but often the opposite. For example, as we require information of a biographical nature, the individual who talks or writes without restraint in submission to our request—"I'll do anything you tell me to do in order to get what I want"—the individual who meets all demands unquestioningly, may present us with a less desirable response than the one who gives with some restraint, who wants to know the whys, in short, who demands some reality orientation and relationship as a context for his giving.

In predicting whether the anxiety engendered in professional education will motivate, impede, or disintegrate learning, we have the individual in the first stage of his pursuit of a remote goal. Owing to the fact that the application process is fraught with some emotion in so far as he needs and wishes to attain his goal, his ways of behaving are doubtless characteristic of him in pursuit of a goal and, as such, are significant. The decisive lack, however, is the lack of opportunity to see the individual experiencing the profession's work. For instance, the admissions process has some social work elements in it, but it is not social work. The fact of the matter, therefore, is that there are decisively important reality limits to our understanding of the individual's capacity for social work.

Psychiatrists have emphasized that a patient's capacity to use treatment is best known through treatment. Social caseworkers have long stressed the fact that the helping process is their most reliable diagnostic means. We social work educators admit that while we can make many sound evaluations through careful admissions procedure, in many instances the individual's potentialities can be known only through his response to the learning situation. Here, as elsewhere, our knowledge and our means to understanding do not permit infallible prediction of human responses in prospective experiences. We encounter this verity. The meeting of need, the nurture afforded through a desired experience, may contribute to the individual's growth so that he changes beyond our powers to predict. Gauging growth potentials precisely in all instances calls for a depth and range of understanding which we do not have at hand for use in the limiting realities of this situation. Because an individual's capacity for a profession cannot always be known in advance of the educational experience, this does not mean that we should not continue to attempt to know him, in order to evaluate and to predict for as reliable selection as is possible. This is essential not only for selection today but for more reliable selection tomorrow. Problem-solving is learned through prolonged systematic attempts to solve problems.

As for the sources of understanding which have been specified, all are important. By reason of the time limitations and the fact that we cannot test the individual through affording him an opportunity to do the work for which we are appraising his potentialities, a number of "views" of the individual over a period of time may offset the limitations of any one evaluation.

School records naturally are viewed first and foremost with an eye to grades, and obviously in social work and perhaps increasing elsewhere, out of professional concern to develop social intelligence, we will tend to emphasize the importance of high grades in the social sciences. This is because the individual has had to think about the individual and the social order for determination of his interest in people in contrast to things. As indicated earlier, social work educators are not worshipful of high grades per se. We know the importance of looking beyond them and of weighing them in relation to other factors.

In seeking information from references which the applicant has given, we have learned the importance of a differential and focused inquiry, which takes into account the circumstances of the relationship. Some informants will need to be told something of the demands of the profession with specific inquiry as to whether or not the applicant has certain capabilities and qualities. Letters of reference from schools, as from agencies and individuals, need to be weighed. Naturally, we come to know certain informants and specific schools; but, until they are known, there is always an uncertain element in them. Evaluating an individual for a profession implies knowing some of the demands which the profession makes on the personality. For example, with reference to the compulsive individuals who find their way into social work, the task-centered school may value highly the very qualities which are problematic for social work. Also as a gauge of the individual's capacity for relationship and for leadership, the student with a record of many extracurricular activities, who has been a repeated office-holder, may or may not have qualities for the relationship demands of social work. This will depend on whether the social inclinations stem from capacity to give and take or from a needful striving for human contact which permits little depth of relationship. It will depend also on whether the drive for leadership has power and prestige as its motivation more than basic ability to represent a group and to speak and act in its behalf.

While we welcome the trend toward personality evaluation of students, the faculty member or school official with a smattering of psychiatry may unwittingly overuse it. Fortunately, his vocabulary often reveals his stage of learning and enables us to give the evaluation a guarded appraisal. We sometimes undervalue the impressions regarding personality traits conveyed by the lay person, in contrast to the professional reference. One instance is recalled where a student proved to be compulsive, rigidly defensive, shallow in affect, and quite unable to perform in the field, although she made good grades in the classroom. On reviewing the admissions material, we unearthed a statement from an employer, a businessman for whom she had worked as a secretary. After commenting on her competent work performance, his thumbnail sketch of her constricted, withdrawn personality tallied with the gist of her field-work supervisor's report. The significant points are: Had this letter been from a professor in the social sciences or from a social worker on a job, it would have carried weight. Actually, the unjaundiced eye of the lay person who is not focused on noting pathology seldom finds it when it is not there. Hence such observations from the lay person are not to be taken lightly.

School and employment records are important from the standpoint that we see the individual through the eyes of others who have beheld him in an achieving, goal-striving situation, even though it made different demands than social work will. We note in particular how successful the person was in the opinion of others, even when success in the former situation may not assure it in this one. This is because the capacity to survive the stress of learning often hinges on the elements of hope and confidence. We recall that the integrative task arises out of needs but that the integrative capacity is based on hope. Not only what one anticipates in a prospective adventure is determined in large measure by what one has experienced in similar undertakings, but also success in the initial stages of an educational experience tends to make for success in subsequent developmental phases. This is true, provided that the individual, while succeeding, has *felt* successful. If others have regarded him highly, the chances are he will bring to this new experience hope and confidence. But this is not necessarily so. It may not be true of the individual who has an expectancy of himself beyond what others expect of him. This can be derived only through his own appraisal of his past experience in a situation in which he is free to be self-revealing. We turn to a brief consideration of what he tells us of himself through the interview and in the way he presents his case as he applies for admission.

One frequently hears it said that out of our identification with students applying for admission to a school, we, in social work, do not use our knowledge and skills to the utmost in arriving at a prediction of educability, in short, we do not diagnose the prospective student as freely as we do the client. There probably are grounds for this statement. There are several factors which limit us, one of which has been discussed—the conditions under which we observe him do not approximate the educational situation closely enough to serve as a rigorous test of his capacity for the profession. Another prominent limiting factor in social work, as we use casework insights and skills in interviewing, is the difference in the applicant's goal from that of the client as he participates in the admissions interview or interviews. A client presents a problem the nature of which illuminates the information which he gives. Furthermore, he is seeking help in the solution of a problem, and he has a need to tell a story which reveals rather than conceals the incapacity which makes asking for help necessary. Once his anxiety over our opinion of him is eased, he may not need to be defensive and he may become revealing. The student applicant is not seeking help. To be sure, he is asking us to give him something that he needs and wants, but his feeling, realistically, in the light of our recruitment efforts is often that he is giving himself and his resources as much as that he is asking for something. His concept is that he is proffering a service and being evaluated for a remote job. In understanding the applicant as a person, we must relate to him in terms of this concept. The focus, therefore, must be on him as a potential social worker useful to the profession, rather than as a client or patient with a problem to solve.

Normally, therefore, the student will talk himself into the school rather than out of it. Normally he will be intent on selling himself. Accordingly, he will show us his interests, his aptitudes, and his strengths rather than reveal freely his ineptitudes and the negative factors which may operate against learning. It is indicated that we come to know the significance of different ways of doing this. The student who is ambivalent about his goal, who is troubled as to whether or not this is the course of study for him to pursue, may more readily express self-doubt and reach out to use the admissions interview for help in problem-solving. These situations often lend themselves to a more reliable evaluation of the applicant than those in which the applicant is definitely committed to his goal. The applicant who has made up his mind to this objective, who is deeply committed through his needs and desires, and who has hope and confidence out of past success in managing his affairs may not relate readily to a consideration of pros and cons and may be initially resistive to an inquiry which conveys that he is being weighed in the balance and that he is being asked to reconsider his decision. This demand, however, is one which can serve as a test of the depth of his commitment to his goal and of his capacity in the integrative task of regulating antagonistic striving toward the mastery of obstacles.

The decisive point is that the school's demand that the applicant lend himself to and participate in some exploration of his personality capacity for social work constitutes a reality pressure to which the student is prone to submit. The more deeply committed he is to his goal, the more pressure he will feel in the school's request in the outcome of which he has much at stake. Consequently, initial defenses may be strong, but they are prone to give way to an adaptive response. Quick perception and sensitivity to cues from the investigator as to how he should act and what he should say in order to pass muster is characteristic of the resourceful, adaptable student. It is characteristic also of some neurotic individuals who, challenged by an approach which makes uncertain the attainment of their goals, value highly the unattainable and will pay any price to avert defeat. In these instances submission to demands may pass for adaptation, when the interviewer is unaware of the import of many fine-point differences in the nature of the production, one notable one being that the individual with adequate ego-superego integration will retain certain reserves. The individual will give freely within the limits of the reality relationship, and the logic of the school's inquiry, but probably not precipitously beyond it. In so far as admissions interviewers have conducted extensive and penetrative inquiry, somewhat routinely, out of context of shared purpose and a relationship which supports the inquiry, they often have overvalued the submissive response and been unaware of the healthy import of resistance. Under these circumstances less educable students are selected to the exclusion of more educable ones.

On the whole, we get a picture of the applicant's adaptive capacity *at this stage of the game*. It often is not deeply revealing of his personality and therefore may not serve as a basis for reliable prediction of his capacity at a later stage when he meets the profession's demands which activate conflicts, against which he cannot so readily defend himself, or in relation to which defenses may interfere with learning. It is well to remember that the school's demand constitutes a pressure to which the applicant is vulnerable in proportion to the intensity of his needs and desires and the resoluteness of his aims. We should therefore guard against inquiry which is inappropriate or for which the individual has not been prepared through knowing its purpose.

We have said that the student applicant does not often come to the admissions interview with a problem to solve. Nevertheless, there is one to solve, that of mutually determining whether the need he brings will be met through becoming a member of the profession and whether he has the capacity and can make the contribution essential for his success and the profession's good. The admissions interviewer has the task of defining the interview as a mutual undertaking and of setting it on a problem-solving basis. This implies conveying to the applicant the importance to both of us that he appraise himself in relation to his aims. He should feel that he is not being asked merely to submit to appraisal but to participate in an evaluation of his prospective course of action. An interviewer in admissions work will need to use all he has learned of human behavior in his professional training and all that he has of self-understanding in order to understand the applicant. Knowledge and understanding of the needs and strivings of individuals engaged in pursuit of lifework goals and of the purposes served by defenses and adaptations will be essential, not only in order to help a given applicant make himself known, but also for the evaluation of the applicant's potentialities to perform the work which he wants or thinks he wants to undertake.

Whatever the focus or method, the admissions worker will need to use his knowledge of the relationship as the basis for interviewing and to use all he has learned about conducting problem-solving interviews. We know that if we engage an individual in solving his problem, we support his ego rather than attack it, so that he is driven to defend himself against the realities attendant upon the problem. An admissions interview should therefore have a positive focus rather than a negative one, in the sense of conveying the interviewer's intent to understand what the applicant brings to the profession rather than what he lacks for it. Hence as the applicant's past is explored, the inquiry will be focused not on problems and pathology as much as on what experiences have been meaningful for the profession, what he has derived from his experiences to motivate him and to carry over into its work. Interviewer and interviewee would set forth hand in hand to explore and to discover the import of the factors and forces which have determined his goal and something of their significance for the profession. This does not imply ignoring certain problematic attitudes or clues to situations which should be explored. Instead, these must be identified, explored, and considered for their professional significance.

Finally, we emphasize the importance of all our sources for understanding the individual applicant. We emphasize also that the individual's response in the current experience of applying for admission and of meeting, step by step, the requests for information to establish his educability is regarded not only as a major diagnostic means but as an introduction to professional learning.[11] First experiences not only reveal patterns of behavior but also set in operation responses to subsequent experiences. Therefore, not only the way he moves through the entire application and admission process, but also the way we conduct the process in terms of whether we make it a realistic evaluative task to test his integrative capacity are noteworthy.

The prominence given to one source of understanding over another varies among us. We vary in the emphasis we place on the importance of securing a longitudinal history as compared with a picture of the individual in the present. In the latter instance past history tends to be volunteered or sought, only to throw light on present circumstances and responses. We vary also in the extent to which we seek a comprehensive history or focus our inquiry more narrowly to that which the applicant will see as relevant to his goal. For example, we may lead him to tell us about his life in general, focusing gradually toward the circumstances and experiences which bring him into social work. Or we may focus at the start on how he happened to become interested in the profession, what persons, experiences, and the like influenced him. In so far as we point toward the past, it will be in terms of the present—for instance, in social work what experiences he has had in taking or giving help which in his opinion prepare him to help people. We vary also in our conduct of admissions interviews in the extent to which we structure them or let them be spontaneous and flexible.

Many of us do not minimize the importance of relevant past history. Among many values, for diagnosis and very importantly for prognosis it serves as a check on our own conduct of the admissions procedure. When the response given to the procedure is markedly inconsistent with the applicant's history as given by himself and by others, we can well question our part in inducing a seemingly atypical response. Thus the views of the applicant gained from several vantage points tend to confirm one another or challenge one another and to correct our own alignments and distortions or to make known the need for further exploration. Furthermore, the experience afforded the individual to try to know himself

11. For use of this source as a basis for evaluation of the applicant see Margaret E. Bishop, *The Selection and Admission of Students in a School of Social Work* (Philadelphia: University of Pennsylvania Press, 1948).

in relation to some of the demands in his prospective course of action has in it potentials for effecting certain desired changes, thus demonstrating his capacity to change. Today in contrast to yesterday, we take care in our work with students not to crash the line between educational help and therapy. It is highly important also that admissions interviews do not, through the nature of the exploration, create an expectancy of a kind of relationship which cannot be continued in the educational situation. Our admissions procedures can be structured to secure some evidence of the student's potentials for the profession. They can arrive, at times, at judgments in which we have confidence, but often, only at tentative appraisals, which need to be tested further through the educational experience.

It is clear that admissions procedures, in order to yield valid and useful findings, must be structured, conducted, and appraised in the light of our utmost knowledge and understanding of the common needs, wants, and behavior of intelligent young adults in a goal-striving situation. This implies, among other insights, understanding of the purposes served by work in the development of the personality and of the social significance of certain kinds of work for many individuals in a particular society. It also implies disciplined skill in individualizing this general orientation. Social work, in drawing on its professional learning, could well be expected to be in advance of many other professions in its knowledge and skill in the use of the "case-history method" in admissions work. We have had the problem of adapting a method continuously used in the helping processes of social casework to the educational situation, but there has been much that we have not had to learn completely anew. We might well have formulated a great deal more than we have for general use within social work and elsewhere, had certain deterrents not operated. Ironically, schools of social work have not always used, and only recently are beginning to use to a greater extent than formerly, skilled social caseworkers in admissions interviewing. The several known and speculative reasons for this will not be specified.

The reality factor of difficulty in conducting application interviews occasioned by wide geographical distribution of applicants made it impossible to make interviewing a habitual procedure. In seeking a universal means, we did not develop our **interviewing** procedures with the available students. At an early point many schools, instead, turned to the written autobiography and came to rely on it heavily in lieu of the interview, thus contributing greatly to the lag in the development of interviewing. These autobiographies have certain values, and possibly they can well be accorded a place as one means in the selection of students. The decisive point is that the autobiography is not an interview and cannot substitute for it.[12]

The individual's response in a written statement given out of context of a reality relationship has different import from a seemingly identical response in an interview. For example, writing without reservation to an unknown and hence fantasied person has a different significance from talking without reservation in the process of relating to a strange person who is physically present. Or, for instance, an individual who may be quite inarticulate in an interview and show meager capacity to relate to others may write beautifully and expansively of himself to a fantasy person. This may bespeak his need to be understood, his yearning for human contact, rather than his readiness to understand others or a capacity for relationship with others. Some social work administrators and educators have failed to perceive this difference and have tended to appraise the individual's written production as though it were a response in an interview. Here one finds an example of the human proclivity to transfer learning from one fact situation to another without adapting it. The autobiography must therefore be recognized as a different instrument from an interview, and its findings must be appraised in the light of this difference. It approximates the sociologist's questionnaire, an instrument with which the social caseworker is not at home and which she must learn to use intelligently, if it is to yield valid findings.

V. SOME DEVELOPMENTS IN ADMISSION PRACTICES
IN SOCIAL WORK EDUCATION

In spite of this distraction produced by reliance on the autobiography, some schools of social work, operating in their separate

12. See Charlotte Towle, "The Place of the Autobiography in the Selection of Students," paper read at National Workshop on Admissions Policies and Selection of Students, Council on Social Work Education, St. Louis, January, 1953 (publication pending).

niches, have given greater place to the interview than have others. Consequently, within the field of social work education considerable skill in the use of the interview in the time-limited, contact-limited, help-limited procedures of the selective process had been attained sporadically. No attempt to collect basic criteria of a fundamentally reliable sort or to formulate interviewing principles and methods had been made until recently, although as early as 1929 the problem of selection of students was acknowledged and action in studying and developing selection methods was urged.[13] The New York School, Columbia University, Pilot Study, instituted in 1947 and made possible by a grant in commemoration of Dr. Marion E. Kenworthy's twenty-five years of service to the school, marked a great step forward in admissions work in social work education, beyond the confines of the New York School.[14] The Pilot Study, now more than six years in operation and still continuing, has been reported on from time to time.[15] It has exerted a wide influence, in that its aims and its procedures have been shared from the start. Concurrently, interest in sharing thinking and experience on student selection had been mounting among the schools of social work, as attested by sessions on the subject at the annual conferences of the American Association of Schools of Social Work. The New York Pilot Study reports focused and gave impetus to this activity, leading to the appointment in February, 1950, of a Committee on Admissions Policies and Selection of Students within the associa-

13. Porter R. Lee and Marion E. Kenworthy, M.D., *Mental Hygiene and Social Work* (New York: Commonwealth Fund, 1929), pp. 257–63.

14. This project has been directed and manned by experienced social caseworkers with a psychiatrist, Dr. Marion E. Kenworthy, serving as consultant and as a member of the faculty advisory committee.

15. Sidney Berengarten, *Pilot Study: Criteria in Selection for Social Work* in *Social Work as Human Relations* (New York: Columbia University Press, 1949), pp. 170–94; also Sidney Berengarten, "A Pilot Study To Establish Criteria for Selection of Students in Social Work," paper read at annual meeting of the American Association of Schools of Social Work, Boston, Massachusetts, January 29, 1949; "The Pilot Study," *Alumni Newsletter* (New York School of Social Work, spring, 1950), pp. 8 f.; "A Pioneer Workshop in Student Selection," *Bulletin of the New York School of Social Work*, July, 1951; Irene H. Kerrigan (ed.), "Selection of Students for Training in Social Casework, with Emphasis on Essential Personality Criteria," *Institute Proceedings, American Association of Medical Social Workers, National Conference of Social Work*, Atlantic City, N.J., April 29, 1950.

tion, a committee which has continued its activity under the Council on Social Work Education.

This has been done by publication of papers read at professional conferences and through workshops. The workshops have been of two types, first, those conducted by the New York School with the purpose of training its experienced graduates throughout the country in preadmissions interviewing, as a means to overcoming geographical limitations to the school's universal use of the interview as an admissions procedure;[16] second, those conducted by the Committee on Admissions Policies and Selection of Students of the Council on Social Work Education, with the purpose of studying the total admissions process as well as the use of the interview in the assessment of students.[17] The work delineated is ongoing, and it is expected that reports may in time contribute to improved selection practices in social work education. The prospect is that individual schools will benefit both by staff participation in the deliberations described and through published formulations, conclusions, and recommendations. Each school faculty can be expected to put its learning, through these means, to use within its particular system. Despite greater uniformity in basic thinking and in the use of criteria of educability, variation in admissions practices will continue, as determined by size of school, financial

16. Under a special grant from the Field Foundation and the New York Foundation, the Pioneer Workshop in Selection, reported on by Sidney Berengarten (*op. cit.*) was held in New York City for two weeks in June, 1951. A comprehensive report is to be published, which will include teaching method and content, the process of the group's analytic thinking, as well as their specific formulations of working concepts, conclusions, and recommendations in admissions interviewing.

17. Committee meetings have been made possible by a grant from the Mental Health Division of the Public Health Service. The committee, in collaboration with the research department of the American Association of Social Workers, has undertaken a study of application material submitted by students who applied to more than one school, especially when the schools took different action, e.g., one or more accepted and one or more rejected some student. The committee has planned prepared materials for and conducted two workshops, made possible by grants from the Field Foundation and the New York Foundation. A five-day workshop on the total admissions process, held in St. Louis, January, 1953, was attended by 65 faculty members responsible for admissions work from 52 schools in the United States and Canada. A two weeks' workshop for the intensive study and application of the use of the interview, led by the New York School Pilot Study and held in New York City in June, 1953, was attended by 44 persons responsible for admissions interviewing in schools of social work.

circumstances, and the point of view of those responsible for the work.

It is to be expected also that, as the experience of social work education is shared with other professions, we may mutually learn and teach. It could well be expected that social work might have a peculiar contribution to make in the use of the case-history method in student selection, in that one of its highly developed professional skills needs only to be adapted for use in this work rather than acquired. This does not imply that social caseworkers should be employed to do the admissions work in other professions; but it does imply that they may have a contribution to make to those responsible for this work in other professions. It is our opinion that the members of a profession must do their own selection. There are several reasons for this, a notable one being that the admissions process should desirably be an introduction to professional learning, a first pattern-setting experience, in which the applicant begins to relate to, and is appraised by, his potential colleagues. Therefore, beyond the fact that social work had a cultivated aptitude for the work entailed in student selection, a sound precedent was set in the New York School Pilot Study, through the psychiatrist's wisdom in serving as consultant rather than in participating in the actual interviewing of applicants. This is noted because it frequently is recommended that other professions make direct use of psychiatrists and psychologists for personality evaluation in preadmissions interviewing. It is our opinion that they should be used instead to help the members of professions not versed in the case-history method, to structure procedures, to focus their inquiries, and to appraise the findings of the total admissions process. In all professions, the pychiatrist can well be used to appraise the special case where there is a question of pathology. It has been noted by social workers at home and abroad that the psychiatrist does not have special skill in appraising the individual of relatively normal personality for the demands of a profession other than his own.[18]

18. See discussion of the use of the psychiatrist in the selection of psychiatric social workers at the London School of Economics by Margaret Ashdown and S. Clement Brown in *Social Service and Mental Health* (London: Routledge & Kegan Paul, Ltd., 1953), pp. 83–85.

It is to be hoped that, in these times when applications for admission to professional schools are relatively low, there will not be a declining interest in those professions in carrying forward the start that has been made in studying and in improving admissions practices. The current low application rates afford an opportunity to learn who is best suited to our respective fields. In that we may be taking more nearly all who apply, of those who meet basic minimum grade and course requirements, we will have the chance to check on our appraisals in those days when we took an upper percentage. Were our uppers truly uppers, or have our values been awry? If we now investigate as carefully as before, if we also systematically record our appraisals, being quite specific as to the grounds for our opinions, we may get some measure of our former judgments and perhaps some correction of misconceptions. It is possible that educators have unconsciously valued highly characteristics and qualities akin to their own, even though they consciously have tried to measure individuals with reference to the demands of the profession. As we now take students on the basis of minimum requirements rather than on fine-point preconceptions, it is important that we check on the outcome of learning in a cross-section of preadmission ratings, with a sharp eye to high and low ones. The individual who causes the evaluators to be ambivalent about acceptance will be well worth scrutiny for a check on personal value-judgments.

In summary it might be said that the problem of selecting the socially educable student has not been solved. We believe that more reliable selections are being made as we have defined the demands of the profession on the learner; the specific aims of the educational process in terms of the changes to be effected in the learner; and as we have delineated some of the attributes and capabilities which characterize the educable student. These accomplishments have been helpful in so far as our knowledge and understanding have enabled us to identify and interrelate responses which are significant as the individual participates in all the admissions procedures. Some headway seemingly is being made on this.

Greater reliability in the selection of students awaits more extensive and sustained use, in the conduct of the educational process, of current insights on the behavior of intelligent young adults in the goal-striving of professional education. As our educational procedures facilitate the integration of learning, we will be able better to differentiate the problematic learner from the learner rendered problematic by unnecessary odds. Greater precision in selection awaits, also, systematic study of all learners as they engage in learning, for the formulation of criteria of movement in learning. We know more today about the problematic learner than we do about the normal or highly productive ones. Current thinking as to indications of movement probably varies considerably from educator to educator and the formulations of each are experience-derived tentative impressions unsupported by research.[19] For greater dependability in our admissions decisions and for appraisal of our educational efforts there is need for systematic study both of the outcome of learning in relation to preadmissions ratings and of the outcome of learning in subsequent practice.

Finally, it is our conviction that there are reality limits to great precision in the selection of students. This is due not only to the time-limited, contact-limited, relationship-limited nature of the situation but also to human inability to predict the responses in prospective experiences of the individual who is within the range of the normal, even when there is opportunity to know an individual intimately. Potentials for growth and change as the individual is nurtured through a desired experience are not readily known out of context of the experience. In spite of this, we favor the use of all that we know to appraise prospective students carefully, not only for as discriminative a selection as possible but also for early mutual understanding in those instances where the individual is admitted. When we conceive of the admissions process as a potential introduction both to learning and to teaching, we are committed to a heavy investment of time, knowledge, and skill in the work.

19. For an example see chap. 13, in which the author records her tentative formulations.

CHAPTER 7

The Social Component in Education
for the Professions

I. THE PURPOSES OF THE SOCIAL SCIENCES
IN PROFESSIONAL EDUCATION

As the professions in common see social intelligence as essential for professional competence, we are concerned with the social component in professional education. In accordance with our tradition as educators, we first think in terms of what knowledge must be imparted to help students become socially intelligent. In this connection we agree that, granted differences from profession to profession determined by needs peculiar to the function of each, we all want to impart some understanding of the individual in his social context, of society and of our profession's place in society. This leads us to the social sciences and to the behavioral sciences, notably, economics, sociology, political science, psychiatry, psychology, and social anthropology. To decide what of these can be made an integral part of a particular professional curriculum and how the areas selected may be taught to attain our aims is our common problem.[1]

We need to remind ourselves that to have knowledge of the individual and society and to become socially intelligent, which implies putting this knowledge to use, are two different matters. We could agree, however, that to be socially intelligent as we perform professional functions demands specific knowledge and a discipline in subjecting social data to orderly thinking. Earlier we stated one of the aims of professional education to be that of training individuals to think objectively in situations which involve them emotionally. We also indicated that this implies that our educational regimes must strengthen the student's ego and serve as a means to personality

1. For one blueprint for the future see Norman Cameron, Ph.D., M.D., "Human Ecology and Personality in the Training of Physicians in Psychiatry and Medical Education," in *Report of the Conference on Psychiatric Education, Ithaca, N.Y., 1951* (Baltimore: Lord Baltimore Press, 1952), pp. 63–96.

growth and integration. In this chapter we consider several guiding concepts for the attainment of these aims, as well as some of the problems presented. We indicate some essential knowledge and a few generic principles for curriculum revision. We also share something of what we have learned regarding the conduct of interprofessional teaching, an important procedure for helping the student use his professional orientation more intelligently in a widened and deepened social context. We comment briefly on tutorial instruction and advisory systems as essential instruments for individualizing the learner in the interest of his professional development.

II. DISCIPLINED USE OF SOCIAL DATA
AN ESSENTIAL AREA OF LEARNING

In the opening chapter we noted and discussed the observation of educators to the effect that the data of the natural sciences are more readily submitted to scientific discipline than are social data.[2] The need for specific knowledge for objective thinking is well illustrated by some members of the medical profession. Disciplined in their use of biological data, some physicians, without knowledge of the meaning of the patient's behavior as he responds to his illness and to medical care, categorize behavior in relation to social circumstance, as the poor, the rich, the middle classes, the age, the nationality, or the race of the individual. Smatterings of knowledge of human behavior and social conditions lead some to generalize invalidly. A wealth of medical knowledge and a well-ingrained scientific attitude enable them to individualize disease, to diagnose specifically, and to know when they cannot diagnose. A lack of knowledge of human behavior in relation to illness and to social conditions and stresses, as well as an attitude that social data do not lend themselves to a scientific approach, may prevent them from individualizing their treatment of the person whom they are treating medically. Their social psychiatric diagnoses are characterized by generalization and categorical assumptions, often more conclusive than tentative.

The need for discipline in the use of social data is shown in the following incidents.[3] At a professional meeting, a group of physicians

2. See chap. 1, p. 18.
3. Examples might have been given from a number of other professions. Medical practice is chosen for several reasons: (1) physicians are known to be

strongly approved cuts in Aid to Dependent Children grants. They joined with those who categorized the recipients as "lazy chiselers." No one questioned the validity of the accusation or asked for evidence that ADC recipients *are* a bunch of chiselers. No one of them considered the health implications. of income reductions below a minimum standard. In another instance a group of physicians signed a petition protesting Aid to Dependent Children grants to unmarried mothers. The petition argued that financial assistance is increasing sexual delinquency and illegitimacy. How many of these members of the medical profession would have impulsively diagnosed a physical ill and called for no evidence to support a contention that this factor caused that disease? Throughout the country, physicians have been among those opposing the new Permanent and Total Disability Provision (HR 6000). They fear its sinister implications for the neurotic, the hypochondriac, the chiseler, and these people are all lumped in the same category. In the social worker's opinion the administration of this provision presents many problems, but they are problems to be solved rather than to be shelved. The notable feature is the lack of carry-over of a principle ingrained in medical education that the remedy for an ill may produce problematic responses which constitute new problems to be solved. Remedies for social ills likewise bring problems in their wake, which challenge our best thinking for their solution, rather than an emotional response of rejection or indifference.

We repeat that we have chosen to establish our point through examples which show the physician's failure to subject social data to scientific discipline not because he offends any more grossly than the members of other professions but because he has known a

---

disciplined thinkers within their traditional biological orientation; therefore their response strongly argues the point that there is need for training in the use of social data if they are not to be subject to misuse; (2) medical education has recognized the problems delineated in this chapter, and changes in educational practice to solve these problems are taking place. The points made are therefore supported in the literature of medical education. The critical comments in this chapter, together with the examples given, were solicited by and have been published by the American Psychiatric Association and the Association of American Medical Colleges. See Helen R. Wright *et al., Reply to the Questionnaire on Community Needs* ("Preparatory Commission Documents," No. 087; 1951 Conference on Psychiatric Education, Ithaca, New York [Washington, D.C.: American Psychiatric Association, 1785 Massachusetts Avenue, N.W., 1952]). This document is among those designated as suitable for general public distribution.

rigorous scientific discipline. Without specific knowledge in the social and behavioral sciences and without discipline in the use of scientific method in other fact situations, his method often does not carry over.

A noteworthy characteristic of the incidents cited to show a breakdown in disciplined thinking is that the human situations had implications which might well involve the physician emotionally. At the meeting where Aid to Dependent Children grantees were characterized as chiselers, one young member exclaimed, "Let them work for their money." He spoke of how hard doctors work and recalled the poverty and hardship of their internship days. The concluding statement, "Let them pull in their belts like we did," won acclaim. The attitudes in these instances may represent a projection of the physician's own harsh educational experience. The rigors of medical education which tax him physically and emotionally, the sacrifice of normal life in the community for several years, the heavy financial expenditure, the period of work with small remuneration, the lifelong commitment to do considerable work whether or not one is paid—all may combine to create a feeling of having been exploited, which might make him peculiarly vulnerable to harsh feelings toward those who are financially dependent. He has permitted himself so little dependence. In so far as in his student days and in the early years of his practice he has had to give more than he was psychologically able to give, we could expect restrictive attitudes, need for a scapegoat, and overcompensated strivings until, with time, the balance is restored through gratification in professional service. The danger is that the heavy demands of medical practice may not be basically compensating, so that some come to regard prestige and economic gain as all too little reward for early sacrifice. In this event the unsocial attitudes may persist.[4]

4. The need for the social component in medical education and other problems in medical education implied by this discussion have long been recognized, as is attested in the literature of medical education for some years, in changes which are occurring in medical education, and in reports of committee work and conferences such as: "Education for Professional Responsibility," in *Report of the Interprofessional Conference on Education for Professional Responsibility* (Pittsburgh: Carnegie Press, 1948); "Widening Horizons in Medical Education," in *A Study of the Teaching of Social and Environmental Factors in Medicine: Report from the Joint Committee* (New York: Commonwealth Fund, 1948); "Psychiatry and Medical Education," in *Report of the 1951 Conference on Psychiatric Education held at Cornell University, Ithaca, New York, June 21-27,*

204 *The Learner in Education for the Professions*

For professional education in general we emphasize, first, that the lack of carry-over of orderly thinking for problem-solving from the natural and physical sciences to the social sciences is not peculiar to the medical student but that it can be expected to occur with any student whose discipline in thinking has occurred largely in another context. This is in part because disciplined thinking does not occur in a vacuum. It must be supported by knowledge with which to think. We repeat that it is in part also because there is greater complexity in the systematic study of the interaction of man with his human environment and of the individual personality and social trends resulting from this interaction than is involved in the study of the physical world, of man as an isolate, or of his parts per se. A basic factor in the complexity of the science of human relations, clearly, is that the learner brings to the consideration of social-psychological problems a greater degree of emotionally determined thinking.

For professional education in general, our second point is that these examples of physicians' attitudes illustrate that when the over-all integrative task of professional education intermittently exceeds or continuously approximates closely the student's integrative capacity, the educational experience as a whole may be sufficiently traumatic to leave some scars. In these instances, learning may proceed to an extent that knowledge and skills are acquired, sometimes at the expense of the personality. When this occurs, the developmental lags often are shown in unsocial attitudes, in which the individual's frustration is expressed through negative attitudes. In relation to individuals, these may take the form of constricted giving and restrictive professional practices. Toward the world at large, conservatism may bespeak his need to maintain the status quo, a need which says that the precarious struggle for equilibrium, ingrained perhaps by his educational experiences, persists. It is in relation to such consequences as these that professional educators have in common a concern to improve their educational practices so that the integrative task may not be needlessly increased. It is to this problem that this book is addressed.

1951 (organized and conducted by the American Psychiatric Association and the Association of American Medical Colleges) (Baltimore: Lord Baltimore Press, 1952).

III. PROBLEMS OF SELECTION AND TIMING
IN PREPROFESSIONAL EDUCATION

Having agreed that there should be an integration of the biological, social, and psychological sciences for all professional students who are going into direct work with people, to educate, to heal, and to help them, individually or collectively, as practitioner, teacher, or administrator, each profession has the problem of what to do and how to do it. A common problem in professional education is that of adding anything more to an already overcrowded curriculum. If the social component is lacking, the act of tacking on a social science course or two may fail of its aims. When we approach this curriculum-construction problem with an additive, rather than an integrative, point of view, we tend to do two things which defeat our purpose. First, we are prone to add the new on late. It is as though we say to ourselves, "The student must have this before he leaves; but we must put first things first, and our old things are most important." And so, on the last breathless lap, we give him a minimum and emergent dosage of that thing it is now being said he ought to take. Second, with this attitude we do not carefully select what we give. If the educators in a professional school regard the current emphasis on the importance of the social and behavioral sciences in professional education as a passing fad, the attitude that any harmless medicine will do for a psychogenic ill will lead them to annex what is most readily available and least vital on the shelves of one department or another. Instead, coming to grips with the questions— Why do we want this additional learning experience? What do we want it to do, to and for our students?—leads to careful selection and appropriate timing. *Selection for the use of the particular profession and timing for maximum integration* are major means to the solution of our problem.

Careful appraisal of the curriculum in any professional school may lead its educators to raise the question, recently propounded by one social work educator—Why are we having to teach all this now? Certainly this and this and that objective of social work education is unrealistic if we have to teach it wholly now. A great deal of what is taught in several areas of learning should be taught at the college level.[5] Repeatedly one hears at curriculum conferences that the shortcomings of any one level of education can be charged in part to the shortcomings of an earlier level, and thence one repetitively travels right back to the nursery school and the family circle. Certainly, we start with the family circle as marking the beginnings of the socially educable student, the beginnings of a learning process which will operate for or against that degree of ego development and personality integration which disposes the individual to use extra-family experience as a means to growth. We have noted the conditions of family life, the kind of relationships which lay the groundwork for the attainment of the aims of professional education.[6]

We have noted also certain well-known deficiencies in early education. Often it has been too little concerned with the personality growth and moral development of the learner. Sometimes it has been too little inclined to teach individuals to think rather than merely to know. And, finally, in recent years it frequently has been so committed to develop self-dependence and creativity in students that overstimulation results because freedom of choice is imposed beyond their years in a range of experiences beyond their integrative span. In such instances spasmodic rather than sustained effort operates against learning to think systematically. In the resultant fragmentation of learning, the student may become task-centered in the constricted sense or a distracted thinker. It is essential that humanity's efforts to humanize itself be focused on the early years of life through promoting family welfare and through providing educational experience to pattern the individual to become socially intelligent.

Actually, the secondary schools have the learner at a decisive age for this. Adolescence is a transitional stage, an acculturation phase in the sense that the individual is moving from the cultural demands of childhood to those of adulthood. His concept of himself as an adult is forming, he is easing his anxiety over growth and change through looking to and planning for the future. For support he is reaching out for a system of values and ideals to guide him, so that he is highly receptive to relationships with mentors, which afford

5. Helen R. Wright, "The Professional Curriculum of the Future," *Social Service Review*, Vol. XXV, No. 4 (December, 1951).
6. See chaps. 2, 3, and 4, but most notably chap. 3.

him an opportunity to identify with the attitudes and ways of the adult world. This is a time of personality reorganization when ego-superego integration may be facilitated through relationships corrective of the past. It is a period, therefore, when the rudiments of the social sciences, if taught in ways that engage the learner, may leave a deep imprint. One deplores overcrowded schools, staff shortages, *depleted* teachers, and a failure to individualize the learner. The opportunity to develop socially minded citizens and the inclination for a life of service such as the professions afford may well be lost. All the professions out of self-interest should be concerned with what happens at this educational level. It is the time to build for the recruitment of teachers.

As professional educators solving curriculum problems today, there is not much that we can do about those early beginnings for the current student body, except to do our utmost in the light of our current insights to work as effectively as possible within reality limits. Actually, our present knowledge of sound professional education exceeds our current use of it. For a better immediate tomorrow we can do two things today.

First, we can work individually and in collaboration to improve our educational practices, so that we will send forth students better prepared to serve the individual in society, both as citizens and in a professional capacity. With the increased interprofessional teaching and collaboration which characterize today's education, health, and welfare scene, it is conceivable that the professions concerned will soon not be defeating one another and hence themselves, as they often have in the immediate past. With the changes that are occurring right now in medical education, it is conceivable that physicians, confronted with a social legislation issue, may in time not unwittingly sabotage social work's basic achievements through impulsive judgments. It can be expected that they will have a different orientation to the provisions and import of the Social Security Act and that, with awareness of a need for knowledge, they will turn to the profession that can be expected to have an expert opinion on the specific issue. Hence in social issues they will be turning increasingly to social scientists and social workers, when in doubt of the reliability of their own knowledge. With the changes that are occurring now in the education of teachers and of school administrators, it could be expected that in the near future current beginnings in remedying the afore-mentioned defects in early education would be expanded if conditions were to make possible the use of the modern educator's orientation. Teacher shortages, inadequate school facilities, low salaries, all of which deter recruitment of teachers, as well as reactionary trends against federal support to education, comprise an obstacle to the attainment of education's goals. If the social intelligence of the profession of education were to be implemented by community support, we could have hope that in the near future students would be better prepared for the professions. The professions are among society's important instruments for making the benefits of civilization available to mankind. As we administer those benefits increasingly in ways which promote family welfare and individual growth, we will be building toward a social order which will better sustain the aims of professional service and toward students who will be better able to make constructive use of professional education than we have been in the past.

Second, for a better immediate tomorrow, the educators in the professions can make every effort to be less cut off from college education than perhaps some have been within universities. It is the responsibility of the administrator of the professional school not only to make known what educational preparation its students need but also to participate in the work of committees in solving curriculum problems at the college and preprofessional level. This implies at the professional level a careful factoring out of what is appropriately taught there and of what is being taught which should and could be taught earlier.[7] Stratification and the problem of communication between levels in the hierarchy of education have long been recognized and are gradually being tackled. Do we in professional education make known that we want all students to have certain courses or certain areas of learning and kinds of discipline which might be taught variously in terms of courses? Do we also make known the need that they be taught in ways which begin to effect some of the changes in the learner delineated earlier?

This is not to say that it is important that only those students entering a profession should have a deeply meaningful educational

7. See Wright, *op. cit.*; in this article the author, in identifying what should be taught earlier, indicates important generic preprofessional content.

experience in their study of the social sciences. If society is to sustain adequately the aims of the professions, it is important that all students be taught in ways which foster integration of this learning, so that they may think with this knowledge rather than merely possess it. It is peculiarly essential, however, if we are to solve the problem of the overcrowded professional school curriculum, that those entering professions have been patterned to use this knowledge in problem-solving. In professional education we have the responsibility, when it is indicated, to make known the values of certain educational methods over others for the adequate preparation of students. Through the fact that professional education has a long tradition of teaching students to put knowledge to use, its educators know the limitations of teaching which fosters the annexation of knowledge as differentiated from the integration of it. Teaching the application of theory rather than imparting theory per se permeates professional education. The professional educator is therefore more experienced in teaching intellectual doing in the classroom, in addition to teaching professional practice, than is many a college instructor. It is recognized that great headway has been made in recent years in solving this problem at the college level, so that it may not exist in the social science instruction of some institutions. But that many students still have not been taught to subject social data to orderly thinking for problem-solving is evident.

In making this statement the author is taking into account the breakdown in orderly thinking which may occur as the individual who has integrated social science learning begins to put it to use in professional services, a response to which there is repeated reference throughout this work. This factor makes it difficult at times to differentiate the teaching problem from the learning problem. In social work education, a basic lack of integration characteristic of poor preparation may be distinguished in the early sessions of the first casework course, in the student's inability to tackle problems, in his distracted use of stereotypes, and in his fragmented use of information. When such a response is checked with descriptive data on the student's previous educational experience, one's suspicion of educational problems is frequently confirmed. If continuity, sequence, and integration are to obtain for the maximum outcome of education in effecting changes in the learner, there must be communication between the levels in the educational hierarchy, on method as well as on content.

There is growing agreement among professional educators that the student is best prepared for the professions through a general education at the college level. One university chancellor describes general education as follows: "An education that gives its students a general view of the important intellectual achievements of man. . . . It is concerned in imparting an understanding of both the interrelations among these achievements and their differences in materials and methods. Its aim is to produce men and women who know that nothing is alien to them that is of fundamental importance to humanity."[8] Chancellor Kimpton, addressing the alumni of the University of Chicago, states further that, beyond a wide view of human achievements, general education gives, in addition, "a special grasp of some field of human endeavor in which you move with confidence and purpose, adding to it contributions of your own . . . the combination of an understanding of the achievements of others and at least a start toward self-achievement." While there is wide agreement on this concept, there is not agreement as to the means to attain these aims. Considerable controversy centers around the definition of what comprises a start toward self-achievement and how much specialization is necessary for a special grasp of some field of human endeavor.

For preprofessional students in those professions engaged in direct work with people, there is a growing conviction that there should be an integration of the biological and social sciences rather than the study very largely or wholly of one or the other. The literature on professional education increasingly urges that a start be made in teaching the human behavior sciences. Thus the student may take to professional education not only essential knowledge but a bent toward the psychological and social components which permeate all professional practice. Educators widely hold that at the college level all students, whether or not they enter the professions, should get a concept of themselves as citizens with a responsibility for intelligent leadership. Social work educators, by reason of the place of their profession in society, emphatically indorse this and

8. Lawrence A. Kimpton, "Growth through Change, Alumni Day Address, University of Chicago," *Tower Topics*, Vol. XX, No. 1 (July, 1953).

hold that for this there should be study of democracy as a way of life, of the interdependence implicit in a democracy, and of the social and economic measures essential for the attainment of its aims. In the light of the concept that nothing is alien that is of fundamental importance to humanity, the Social Security Act should be studied not as social workers study it for specific use but as a major development in economics and government to meet the needs of people. In the professional school the student who comes with a knowledge which every well-educated citizen should have of the philosophy of social security should find it quite easy to carry over this philosophy to other types of service.[9] In social work education, as we have delineated essential preprofessional preparation, we have been loath to crowd out the humanities. Traditionally in humanitarian work the humanities have been regarded as an important means to enlarge the student's capacity for imaginative consideration, to foster sensitive feeling with people, in short, to give stretch and range to the mind for perception in human relationships.[10] This learning would seem to be equally relevant in other professions serving people.

The problem of the overcrowded curriculum at the college level is heightened as we delineate what the student should bring to professional education. The problem is not easy of solution, but doubtless there are several means, and we can anticipate varied patterns for attaining the aims defined. It is clear that an additive approach is not the answer but that, instead, an integrative approach is indicated. Again selection and timing are important. For selection, the professions individually need to define specific areas of learning and disciplines which are basic minimum essentials for students entering the particular professions. It is important also that they indicate desirable learning beyond minimum essentials. The professions collectively, through interlocking committees and curriculum-study groups, need to appraise these to identify both specific and generic learning. Having determined what should be taught, consideration should be given to its context, its repetition, and the general method of instruction.

9. Wright, *op. cit.*

10. See chap. 5 for discussion of the place of imaginative consideration in social work learning.

The matter of context and repetition will be determined by both the nature and the importance of a particular area of learning. For example, it is anticipated that orderly thinking for problem-solving will be identified as a basic generic learning. It is, in fact, a basic process which can be learned in several contexts.[11] Some educators hold that when taught in one context it can be expected to carry over into another context. Hence social sciences and behavioral science courses given students who have experienced the discipline of orderly thinking in the biological sciences would not need to be taught in the more time-consuming way which subjects them to the discipline of orderly thinking for problem-solving in these materials. Other educators would contend that, because of the basic importance of this learning and because of its nature, in that it must be deeply integrated for use, it should be taught repetitively. Certainly, the experience of social work education, as indicated earlier in the discussion of the physician's dilemma in relation to social data, argues for teaching the social sciences by a method which affords opportunity for systematic thinking for problem-solving. This is for cumulative effect for integration. The biological and social sciences will be integrated by the learner in so far as he finds the basic methodology in both essentially the same.[12]

In contrast, grasp of the philosophy of the Social Security Act, appreciation of its import as a major development in economics and government, a milestone in "humanity's efforts to humanize itself," might be taught in any one of several courses in the humanities or social sciences and would not necessarily need repetition. As with all courses, however, consideration could well be given to its timing. Hence it could desirably accompany or follow immediately the work in the behavior sciences in which the student is acquainted with the growth and development of the individual and the common human

11. Alfred E. Emerson, "Dynamic Homeostasis: A Unifying Principle in Organic, Social, and Ethical Evolution," *Scientific Monthly*, Vol. LXXVIII, No. 2 (February, 1954). This in an expansion and revision of chap. x in *Goals of Economic Life* (New York: Harper & Bros., 1953). Dr. Emerson presents the theory that the methods and principles of natural science can be applied in the study of ethics or to any of the subdivisions of the humanities and the social sciences.

12. For discussion of areas of learning which require repetition see chap. 10, pp. 303–4.

needs which must be met for personality growth. In solving this problem of the integration of the biological and social sciences at the college level, it can be expected that variation will occur from institution to institution, in relation to the aims of students and varying circumstances, such as the availability of faculty, their special qualifications, points of view, and convictions. Doubtless many patterns will emerge for the attainment of the aims delineated. Success or failure will be contingent in large measure on the extent to which we have a realistic grasp of students' integrative capacity at this stage of life. We will fail to help them become more intelligent socially to the extent that we construct an unrealistic integrative task.

IV. THE PROBLEMS OF SELECTION AND TIMING
IN PROFESSIONAL EDUCATION

We return to the matter of teaching the common core of the human sciences at the professional level—biology, ecology, and personality. It is recognized that this core will vary in content from profession to profession in terms of its function. We indicated earlier in this chapter the importance of selection and of timing in this common core at the professional level. What part of a considerable body of knowledge to teach, and how and when to teach it so that it may be put to use are the questions now being answered as we experiment with curriculum revision. Assuming that the profession wants this new content not only as essential knowledge but also as a means to effect the changes in the learner specified earlier, then it must be introduced early and proceed in an orderly sequence. At an interprofessional conference one medical educator in a university where psychiatry was being taught at the extern-intern levels protested both expansion and time extension of this content, claiming that the bit given already had become "the tail that wags the dog." He described obsessional absorption in psychiatry and a dichotomy between physical and psychological, with an inclination to focus on the psychological (the new) to the exclusion of the physical (the old). It was clear that psychiatry had been added too late for ready integration. Certainly, we could agree with the medical educator that it would not be well to pile on more now. The psyche, however, would not have become a new attraction divorced from the soma, had the two been wedded at the start.[13]

Likewise in the education of teachers, concentration on subject matter and on teaching techniques, without orienting them closely to the human learner from the start, has been known to produce a comparable outcome.[14] We state a general principle. If understanding of human behavior and of the social conditions and forces which condition the individual's growth and our professional practices are to become an integral part of the backbone of professional education, rather than an appendage, they should be taught bit by bit in the classroom and put to use early. As for orderly progression, these contents should be relatively simple at the start and grow in the demand they make on the learner. The content of a given course should be selected to support learning in other areas and to be supported by it, as far as is possible.[15]

In the selection of content in professional education, the focus is always insistently on what the student must know in order to administer the profession's services. This same principle applies in drawing on related fields of learning. Since these areas are frequently taught by the members of other professions or disciplines, the task of differentiating what to teach in the context of this recipient profession from what one taught the members of one's own group is the initial charge on the educators in both professions or disciplines. What can be put to use as an integral part of the profession's function without distorting or changing that function is the test question to which all content must be rigorously subjected. We aim to improve the profession's services through the change which it will effect in its practitioners' ways of feeling, thinking, and doing.

13. Among other references which might be given which show medical educators' recognition of this principle and use of it in educational practices see J. H. Means, M.D., "The Clinical Teaching of Social Medicine," *Bulletin of the Johns Hopkins Hospital,* LXXVIII, No. 2 (February, 1946), 96–111; Lester J. Evans, M.D., "Medical Education for Insight," *American Journal of Orthopsychiatry,* Vol XIV, No. 4 (October, 1949); see also *Psychiatry and Medical Education.*

14. For discussion of a comparable phase in social casework teaching see chap. 10, section on traditional patterns and new patterns.

15. For delineation of criteria of simple and complex demand on the learner and for progression in teaching, which may or may not be useful in situations other than social work teaching, see chaps. 10, 11, 12, and 13 and particularly chap. 10.

We do not, however, aim to change the basic function. Hence, as we teach the social sciences, it is not with the purpose that the student in a profession may become a social scientist. As we teach the behavioral sciences, it is not with the purpose that the physician, nurse, social worker, teacher, lawyer, or clergyman may become a psychiatrist, however much he feels compelled to drift in that direction at a certain stage of learning. Selection, therefore, in focusing on what the student needs in order to put it to use in his profession implies teaching with a continuous focus on professional function.[16]

To illustrate this, we delineate our conception of the teaching of human behavior focused to function in the medical school. We could have selected any other professional school. The reader might well substitute teacher or lawyer or nurse for physician and imaginatively reword the context for full realization of its generic import. The physician encounters the emotional responses which *stem from* the illness as determined by its meaning to the individual and to those in close relationship to him. He encounters also those emotional needs and strivings which produce illness. It is important that the physician individualize the patient. This implies that he understand the meaning of illness, handicaps, hospitalization, and medical care to the individual concerned. It is clear that the physician needs sufficient knowledge and understanding of human behavior to enable him to deal with the patient's feelings and attitudes directly related to and stemming from the illness and medical care, emotional needs which, by very reason of the patient's feelings for him as "the doctor," he is better able to deal with than anyone else. This implies an orientation which could lead him either to refer many individuals whose basic emotional difficulties or whose social stresses are producing illness or interfering with recovery, to psychiatry or to social service, or to consult with these specialists in his own work with the patient.

There is need also for knowledge and understanding of human behavior directed not only to understanding patients but also toward insight and toward perceiving the interplay of personality

16. For two good statements on the integration of related learning in professional education see Grace L. Coyle, "The Role of the Teacher in the Creation of an Integrated Curriculum," *Social Work Journal*, Vol. XXXIII, No. 2 (April, 1952), and "New Insights Available to the Social Worker from the Social Sciences," *ibid.*, Vol. XXVI, No. 3 (September, 1952).

which occurs in any "working-together" relationship and notably in the medical helping relationship. There has long been recognition of the need for the doctor to feel with but not like the patient. This implies knowledge for enlightened awareness of the two-way relationship in which verbally expressed or enacted feelings and attitudes of the doctor or patient affect the other.[17] Important here as a means to learning professional conduct is the relationship between mentors and students and students and colleagues. Professional education is a re-educative process, with a task essentially equivalent to a change in culture. New members are motivated to belong and to incorporate sentiments, attitudes, and ways of doing through identification. The relationships within the educational situation pattern the service relationship of the profession.[18]

It has been both stated and implied that, for integration, the social component will have to be taught through systematic use. Of this Means states in medical education: "In the etiology of disease the entry of bacteria into the body may be no more important than marital unhappiness or fear of want. . . . The evidence upon which a truly complete diagnosis must rest may be biologic, psychologic or social. Often all three. . . . Social facts contribute to and sometimes indeed make the diagnosis. . . . Social hazards may thwart treatment. A diagnosis is not merely an answer to what has the patient got but how did he get it and why." It would follow that prognosis would take social factors into account. Without social data, how did he get it and why often cannot be answered, hence prognosis often cannot be made.[19] Comparably, in a school situation, the reason why a student learns with facility or has difficulty in learning may rest on biological, psychological, or social factors—often all three. Again social facts contribute to and often make the educational diagnosis. Social hazards may thwart learning. Sound educational planning

17. F. W. Peabody, *The Care of the Patient* (Cambridge: Harvard University Press, 1927); L. J. Henderson, "Physician and Patient as a Social System," *New England Journal of Medicine*, CCXII (1935), 819; Carl Binger, *The Doctor's Job* (New York: W. W. Norton & Co., 1945).

18. For further discussion of this generic principle in professional education see *Education for Professional Responsibility*; see also chap. 9, areas of learning in social casework.

19. Means, *op. cit.*

and prognosis of the outcome of learning would take social factors into account.

For teaching the use of the social and behavioral sciences, the team naturally replaces the individual instructor. This introduces complexity, and it is possible for a group of specialists in the several areas to operate against integration of the biological and social sciences rather than for it. This will occur if the profession is problem-oriented rather than person-oriented in its approach to those whom it serves. It will occur also if each specialty regards the other as having sole responsibility for the use of all the knowledge and skill in its area. An effective team implies that each discipline performs a different function but that learning is interchanged, for intelligent co-ordination of the parts and for common use of certain generic elements. It implies also that the professional person who is leader of the team must have a grasp and an acceptance both of the specific and the generic usefulness of each discipline. The leader of the team obviously would be a member of the profession in which the teaching occurs, for example, in hospital or clinic, a physician or psychiatrist; in a social agency, a social worker.

Through the very nature of social work, its professional schools have had almost a lifelong experience in drawing on other professional disciplines. Interprofessional collaboration in education has inevitably presented problems. In the attempt to solve them, certain principles have emerged which we believe are generally applicable. They are stated for whatever significance they may have for other professions.

Social work has drawn on related fields with a twofold purpose: first, for knowledge and insights for use in social work, and, second, for intelligent collaboration with other professions in program-planning and administration as well as in direct work with individuals and groups. We have therefore been concerned with the integration of learning at two levels. We have worked for thorough assimilation of certain knowledge and understanding from related disciplines, so that it might be made our own for use in our own ways. We have also sought that orientation to and grasp of the function and general methodology of related fields of endeavor essential for communication and collaboration through which each profession contributes to and facilitates the attainment of joint and individual aims.

Social work's necessity to learn from others and to work with others resulted at certain developmental periods in faulty collaboration. In certain instances social work has been more identified with, than related to, those from whom it has been learning while collaborating. Psychiatry has been a notable example, as has medicine. We have learned that annexed and inappropriate knowledge rather than integrated appropriate learning can produce confused identity and disoriented professional practices. It has become clear that the teaching to be eliminated is that wherein the members of one profession or academic discipline teach the members of another discipline certain knowledge and skills *unmodified* for use in the performance of their work. Essential knowledge is useful only in so far as it is deeply incorporated. The learner must do the integrating; but for economy of time and effort social work students need the help of social work educators in selecting and in applying learning from another field. This implies the following:

1. The selection of learning useful to social work. This dictates the selection, whenever possible, of instructors who have had consultative and collaborative experience with social work in the field of practice. When this is not possible, social work educators have the task of acquainting instructors with the nature of social work, the demands of the field which create a need for his particular contribution. Obviously, secondhand acquaintance is a makeshift measure. Prior collaboration with social workers is essential for the instructor's independent selection of what to teach.

2. Even when instructors have collaborated with social workers, it is essential that there be periodic curriculum-study conferences between the several instructors in another discipline and those social work educators who carry the heaviest responsibility for teaching the use of the subject matter. These conferences could well include consideration of the following: What part of the material which a particular physician or psychiatrist teaches is being considered elsewhere? Does the course gear in with elementary or advanced social work courses; hence at what stage of learning are his students in the social work sequence? It is essential that this be known in order that

content and method may be designed to make an appropriate intellectual and emotional demand. For example, the first course taught by a psychiatrist which accompanies the first course in social casework and the elementary courses in other social work fields of instruction should be less advanced in emotional and intellectual demand than the last course, both in nature of content and in methods of instruction.[20] It is the responsibility of social work educators to arrange the psychiatric sequence with this in mind.

3. It is essential that social work educators understand and accept the content of related discipline courses, in order that in their classes or field instruction they may help students see the import of its knowledge through using it in social work. Many of us recall the day when students in psychiatry classes were being oriented to this knowledge beyond the orientation of their instructors in social casework classes and in some field-work settings. Psychiatry not having been incorporated into basic casework courses in classroom and field or into setting courses other than psychiatric social work, the student, out of his urge to use the psychiatry imparted by the psychiatrist, was driven into psychiatric social work courses and field instruction, whether or not he wanted that specialization.[21] When he could not get this opportunity, his psychiatric theory dangled and served to confuse and confound him, so that it was subject to misuse or rejection. Psychiatry has a contribution to make to all areas of the social work curriculum as well as to the educational process. As has been stated, for integration into the total educational experience it is essential that all social work educators have a basic orientation, particularly in knowledge and understanding of normal behavior and desirably also in psychopathology.[22]

4. Where the members of a related discipline teaching in a school of social work do not have a close collaborative working relationship with social work in the field of practice, the measures for orienting the instructor to social work have had the limitation of placing the orientation burden on the social work educator. Conferences in which social work is talked about can accomplish less than if a

20. See chap. 9 for the full significance of this.

21. Here we had a situation comparable to that in the medical situation, where psychiatry was taught too late, cited earlier in this chapter.

22. For full import of this see chap. 8.

member of the instructing profession were to engage actively in knowing the recipient profession, in order to determine its specific and general needs from his field.

A significant project has been conducted at the School of Social Service Administration, University of Chicago, under a grant from the Russell Sage Foundation. A lawyer qualified to teach, in collaboration with the dean and faculty members of the School of Social Work, explored the rationale for teaching law in social work. The reason for doing so seemed self-evident, but the self-evident reasons had to be focused professionally to design a course which would "meet the need for a type of training in law which would have relevance and utility for the social worker and would, at the same time, impress upon her certain outstanding characteristics of legal problems to which no course short of complete legal training can do thorough justice."[23]

In attaining this aim Mrs. Rosenheim examined social work content to determine need, by conferring with faculty members, by attending social work classes, by reading social agency records, and by conferring with agency staff members.

The resultant course focuses on the legal process as a fundamental process in society for resolving conflicts between people. Legal case materials are presented for discussion which illustrate "fundamental areas of legal dispute and adjudication by cases which are pertinent and useful for the majority of social workers."[24] This undertaking illustrates the integration of learning at two levels delineated earlier, namely, drawing on a related field for knowledge and insight for use in social work and for more effective collaboration. The specific outcome of this project has been threefold: (1) A law course has been devised for experimental use with social work students; since its inception it has been undergoing change. (2) A syllabus has been structured for use by other law instructors. It is now being tested at several schools of social work.[25] (3) As a secondary gain, members of the social work faculty have been given a point of view which has

23. Margaret Keeney Rosenheim, "Readings in Law for Social Workers" (unpub. preliminary draft; University of Chicago School of Social Service Administration), Foreword, p. iii.

24. *Ibid.*, p. v.

25. *Ibid.*

helped them to deal more competently with legal issues in nonlaw courses.

Similar projects have been undertaken under grants from the Russell Sage Foundation in which there has been an effort to adapt principles and concepts of social anthropology and other social sciences for use in social work courses.[26]

Because of the close collaboration between psychiatrists and social workers in practice in clinics and in social agencies, where psychiatrists serve as consultants, because of the participation of psychiatrists in the training of students in field-work centers and in the education of social workers in agencies, such projects in psychiatry perhaps have not been undertaken. Thus the social worker's close affiliation with psychiatry in practice has operated against close collaboration in social work education. Often psychiatrists might have been helped to give more appropriately to professional education in schools of social work if there had been more working together on course content and method. Had this occurred, it is possible that the social worker's introduction to psychiatry might have been better oriented to social work than has been the case in many instances.

5. A major problem in interdisciplinary education is created by the factor of identification, which, as has been emphasized, plays a vital role in professional education. It is essential that learners in a given profession identify more closely with their own leaders than with the leaders of related professions. It is always possible that a mentor from another discipline may unconsciously and unwittingly foster identification with his own discipline. Or, the instructor being an "Auslander" whose authority of knowledge is imposed, the learners may identify as a defense. When this occurs, the learning may remain a foreign body within the ego, always to be reacted to with ambivalence and never to be deeply incorporated. Strong alignment with and reactions against other professions are prone to occur. This happens for various reasons.

a) The subject matter taught has great emotional import, in that its acceptance involves considerable change in feeling, thinking, and

26. See *Russell Sage Foundation Report, 1951–52,* pp. 18–19, for statement of work undertaken by Dr. Katherine Spencer, Professor Mary E. Hurlbutt, and Dr. Otto Klineberg at the New York School of Social Work, Columbia University.

doing. Thus as anxiety is provoked, resistance and rejection may be engendered, or in the struggle for mastery the individual loses his professional identity.

b) When the class is conducted so that feeling is elicited and worked on in the discussion process, the relationship with the instructor takes on deep import, often leading to strong identification. Because of the marked emotional import of psychiatric learning, many educators have advocated small classes and ample time for the expression of feeling and for the instructor to elicit and deal with these responses. Some educators, psychiatrists, and social workers are now of the opinion that these responses should be kept at a minimum and that they are best dealt with in the social work courses, particularly the basic process courses (social casework and social group work) as psychiatric learning is put to use. Thus not only is identification with the student's own professional mentors strengthened, but the tendency of any student to make the class session a therapeutic session can also be safeguarded very naturally when the focus is on his use of the psychiatric content in social work. When psychiatry is taught without reference to practice, the student tends to focus the content in relation to himself.

c) When the instructor in another profession teaches specific use of his discipline, the use taught will tend to be oriented to his field rather than to social work, thus fostering identification with the mentor or rejection of him. The latter will occur as the student finds the application useless. Professional students, however, are in anxious quest of the what and the how of doing. They therefore are vulnerable to strong alignments with expert doers whose authority of knowledge and skill they and their own mentors respect highly. The psychiatrist for many reasons is highly esteemed in social work, not the least of which is the fact that, realistically, psychiatry over the years has made a vital contribution to social work thinking and practice. It breathed the breath of human life into social work process.

d) When social work instructors in field practice are aligned with another profession and dependent upon it to an extent that they give over certain areas of their own teaching responsibility to other disciplines, they give their students unto those disciplines. The part the field-work instructor plays in the collaborative team, in terms of whether he maintains his professional identity or loses it, is decisively important. It is essential that social work educators be aware that the nature of their collaborative relationships will be pattern-setting for students. This dependence of casework supervisors on psychiatrists is an unsolved problem in the current scene. Several factors have contributed to it. One of these is the hierarchy system in social work, through which social caseworkers, as they become proficient, give up practice for supervision. Insecure through not continuing to develop their own skills, they may become dependent on the psychiatrist, who continues to practice. Furthermore, they brought to practice a strong identification with the psychiatrist as a mentor through whom they learned much. This propensity often has been reinforced in those social casework educators who have experienced or are experiencing psychoanalytic treatment. Since social work will always need an educational and re-educational contribution from psychiatry, this problem will be solved only as the members of both professions recognize it and deal with it in the context of the teacher-pupil, doctor-patient relationships.

In summary, in interprofessional teaching within professional schools two notable principles have been established in social work education which perhaps have generic import. First, the importance of the learner's identification with mentors in his profession makes it essential that content taught by specialists in related fields be accepted for and incorporated into the recipient profession by its own educators. Second, when one profession teaches another, it should be with close reference to the learner's function and with an attempt to orient the content to the nature of the learner's work and to the nature of his helping relationship. This inevitably implies that the educator in the recipient profession must predominantly teach the use of related learning.

VI. THE PROBLEM OF CREATIVITY IN PROFESSIONAL EDUCATION

The professions directly concerned with serving people have characteristics in common, goals in common, and common problems. These have been delineated in earlier chapters and will not be recapitulated comprehensively. We have in common an integrative task of a size and nature which calls for high integrative capacity. It is recalled that this capacity, in the last analysis, is contingent on hope and confidence, which are predicated on good past experience. This implies relationships which have nurtured the ego for growth and on abilities and personality formation which not only have made it possible for the individual to surmount obstacles but also have permitted him to *feel* successful.[27] We are all concerned to afford the educable learner, the student whose professional choice is realistic in terms of his ability and disposition, an educational experience which will foster maximum development for competent performance of his professional function and for creative activity when there are these potentials.

To those engaged in professional education it sometimes seems that we have a more difficult charge in fostering creativity and in not breaking it down than obtains in the natural sciences or in academic education at the graduate and postgraduate levels. If this is true, it would seem to be due to the following combined factors. First, for the welfare of the individuals served, the professional learner must not merely adapt to the discipline of professional education, but he must be patterned to work within the profession's code of ethics and structured rules of practice. He cannot be a free-lance worker, experimenting at will and departing from the established order as inspiration prompts him. His freedoms will always be freedoms within rigid limits set by his responsibility for human beings immediately under his care or tutelage. Perhaps there is more scope for creativity when one works with things or ideas, even though they eventually will have human implications. Second, the integrative task in professional learning tends more continuously to approximate closely the individual's integrative capacity. There has been repetitive reference in earlier chapters to the effect of emotionally charged work with people on orderly thinking for problem-solving. We recall that the integrative task in learning is heavy or light in terms of the nature and size of the concomitant affect load. In professional education, therefore, we often seem to be hard put to it to help the student maintain equilibrium in order that learning may be integrated. We want, however, something more than that state of equilibrium which, in making for bare survival, makes possible only marginal learning. The following statement is significant for education:

27. See chaps. 3 and 4.

As we try to define the properties of an organism today, such as the capacity to use air, earth and everything in nature, to grow in mass and complexity, to propagate itself, we must add one more very important property—the capacity to receive stimulation, but to release thereby more energy than the stimulus brought to us. A state of equilibrium is not what we are seeking. It is the extra energy above that required to maintain equilibrium, that will be used for other purposes. That is the creative part, the energy over and beyond what we need for just so called stability. This is what Dr. Ralph Gerard, the noted physiologist, calls "adaptive amplification."[28]

It is to be remembered that hope and confidence at a given time are measured by the extent to which the integrative capacity exceeds the integrative task. Hope and confidence are essential not only for creativity but for the integration essential for competent service. They are essential also for the development of sensibility and social intelligence. In social work practice we have long contended, against great opposition, for that something beyond dire necessity which frees the individual to become less primitive in his strivings.[29] As we have transferred these learnings to social work education, we have been contending, again against some opposition, for that margin between integrative task and integrative capacity which makes possible the emergence of certain qualities essential for professional service. Prominent among these is empathy and a readiness to relate to others with a giving spirit in terms of their needs rather than in terms of one's own needful strivings.[30] Perhaps we must take the attitude that the educational period will inevitably be one of stress, in which one cannot hope for more than equilibrium and marginal integration, promising ourselves that tomorrow, with experience in practice, "adaptive amplification" will come. One does not readily accept this idea if one believes that the educational experience is pattern-setting and a time for becoming, in small but rounded measure, what one will later become. With this conviction, one con-

28. Helen Ross, "A Contemporary Concept of Family Welfare," *Marriage and Family Living*, Vol. XV, No. 3 (August, 1953).

29. Among many other social work publications this is a major refrain in Charlotte Towle, *Common Human Needs* ("Public Assistance Reports," No. 8 [Washington, D.C., 1945; republished, New York: American Association of Social Workers, 1952]).

30. For recognition of this principle in a discussion of science as a humanizing force, see George R. Harrison, "Faith and the Scientist," *Atlantic*, Vol. CXCII, No. 6 (December, 1953).

tends for an integrative task which is not continuously burdensome, even though the student may leave the school less knowledgeable. With hope and confidence and a readiness to give of himself, he will be set to acquire knowledge and to learn in order to meet demands. In so far as this has occurred, a learning process will have been set in operation which will endure unless the student encounters markedly adverse circumstances in the early days of practice. For this, professional educators are concerned to lower the anxiety in learning and to heighten the individual's integrative capacity through means which strengthen his confidence through helping him learn.[31]

For the attainment of this aim, out of our growing identity as educators, we have reached a point of defining problems and seeking help from those whose profession is education. The educational expert cannot select a profession's teachings or tell its members specifically what to do. He can give perspective on professional education, certain insights and principles for differential use. Obviously, sound application of them will be contingent on the depth of understanding of subject matter which a profession's educators have. It will be contingent also on their understanding of the distinctive demands which their professional learning makes on the learner.[32] This implies a grasp of basic learning principles, the significance of behavior in a learning situation, and an understanding of one's profession as a social system.

In the current scene one notes the professional educator's efforts to arrange learning experiences for continuity, sequence, and integration for cumulative effect.[33] One notes also the growing concern to conduct class sessions and structure assignments and examinations so that learning is facilitated rather than obstructed.[34] Recognition of evaluative measures as educational means rather than merely as

31. See chaps. 4 and 5.

32. Among other ways in which the educational expert can be helpful is in the appraisal of the outcome of learning: (1) through principles and methods for structuring assignments and examinations to test for specific attainments, (2) through ways of appraising the educational task through systematically gathering evidence as to what is normal expectancy of a student at certain stages.

33. See chap. 10 for one example of the efforts of social work education to apply the principles stated by Dr. Ralph Tyler.

34. See chap. 12.

procedures to test the student and a resultant effort to have them facilitate rather than impede learning are noteworthy developments.[35] Of interest also in certain professions, notably medicine and nursing, is the use of the social scientist (sociologist and social anthropologist), not only to teach certain courses, but to study the profession as a social system, in order to define the acculturation problem to which students are subjected.[36] This should contribute to a more comprehensive appraisal of the integrative task. Is the educational situation structured to facilitate or impede learning? What is it designed to do to students? Will it, by its very nature, effect desired changes in the learner or make them difficult to attain? These are important questions to be answered if educators are to orient the system to the needs and capacities of the learner. Social work education has not used the social scientist for this purpose because its faculty members, by reason of their insistent focus on environment as a means to growth and on environment as treatment, have pioneered in this area. Social work literature attests long-standing awareness of the educational system's effect on learning, an awareness which has influenced our practices to the extent of our educational "know-how." More recently, use of help from the field of education is enabling us to make more intelligent use of our insight.

VII. TUTORIAL INSTRUCTION AND ADVISORY SYSTEMS—MEANS

TO INDIVIDUALIZE THE LEARNER FOR HIS

PROFESSIONAL DEVELOPMENT

It was said earlier that the demands of professional education cannot be individualized but that the learner can and must be for the maximum development of his capacities and for an identity with the profession through which his individuality has not been impaired. This is seen as important not only for creativity but also in order that the student may become a socially intelligent professional person rather than a narrowly professional one. Defensive alignment or inbredness may occur when his identification with the profession is tenuous or when he has not found himself in his work, so that he is not free to look beyond its confines.

35. See chap. 12.

36. *Psychiatry and Medical Education;* Leo Simmons, M.D., "Manipulation of Human Resources in Nursing Care," *Journal of Nursing,* July, 1951.

For the individualization of the learner, one notes a growing emphasis on the importance of tutorial instruction. This brings concern with the qualifications of faculty members for this role, as well as awareness of the importance of this relationship as one which tends to leave the deepest imprint. Tutorial instruction is perhaps best suited to teaching which involves helping the student put his classroom learning to use, as in supervision of practice and research.[37] It is in practice that problems in the integration of knowledge and theory emerge, that conflicts and disturbed feelings about the demands of the profession show up. These responses call for individualized handling. Tutorial sessions are being used to some extent as an adjunct to the classroom sessions. Among many advantages, one encounters the danger that in sessions in which problems in learning cannot be focused immediately on correction through professional doing, these problems tend to get intellectualized rather than solved. The student's sense of mastery of the problem is attained through putting learning to use in actual practice; therefore anxiety may mount through discussion until he tests his learning in practice.

Advisory systems have the purpose, also, of individualizing the learner. In social work these systems vary from the procedure of every student's having a continuous advisor who counsels comprehensively, to the procedure whereby the student seeks counsel or is periodically scheduled for it, with different faculty members in the several areas of his work. At Chicago we prefer the second system for several reasons: First, the student sees the person most competent to counsel him when the adviser knows him at first hand in a given area of work. Second, the range of faculty members experienced individually is enlarged so that the student becomes known as an individual to a larger segment of the faculty. This is very important when problems in learning occur in more than one area. Also he becomes related to the school as a whole, rather than dependent on, or aligned with, a segment. This is an important preventive to undue dependency on one mentor. It also solves the problem of the student whose dilemma under the one-adviser system is that he draws a faculty member with whom he cannot get en rapport and whom he therefore cannot use productively. Third,

37. See chaps. 8 and 11 for full discussion of the import of the supervisory relationship in social work education.

the student is patterned through a wide range of consultants, to seek help freely but responsibly. He learns to relate purposively in brief, time-limited, relationship-limited contacts. This is essential preparation for subsequent professional life.

It is obvious that tutorial and advisory systems are decisively important means for helping the student solve problems in learning and for becoming a member of the profession. They therefore warrant careful structuring. The faculty members engaged in this work can well regard it as an important teaching assignment, in which attention must be given to methodology for productive conduct of the sessions.

There is growing consciousness that professional education can be a means to growth. In the ups and downs of learning and growing, learning problems which involve the personality are recognized, worked on, and often solved. This has disposed some educators to regard education as therapy. In the process of helping students learn, they may not differentiate the two and get involved in helping efforts which could be characterized as psychotherapy. This is particularly prone to occur in tutorial and advisory sessions when faculty members, formerly engaged in casework or therapy, have not extricated themselves from practice and found their feet as educators. It has been known to occur in class sessions where the discussion method gets pointed toward group therapy.[38] It might be said for use elsewhere that social work education has established the fact that one cannot be both professional mentor and psychotherapist.[39] With reference to the educational process as a whole, it has established the fact that education is not the equivalent of therapy, either in methods or in goals. It is convinced that education is neither primarily intellectual nor chiefly a process by which the emotions are matured. It is a process which aims to integrate the emotions and the intellect for professional use. Furthermore, social work educators believe that professional education must impart and instil moral and ethical values. These are taught explicitly through knowledge and implicitly through a relationship which conveys understanding, respect, and judgments which hold the learner

38. See chap. 12 on the conduct of class session.
39. See chap. 4 for more detailed discussion of this.

accountable to realistic demands and to the ethical demands of the profession. While it has found that values may regulate curiosity, they need not stifle it, unless they have been derived in a relationship in which the learner, identifying as a defense, submits rather than adapts to and incorporates the value-system of the profession.

Amid the many difficulties which beset us as we in professional education attempt to attain our aims, we can be fortified by the thought that we live in the first age in which people have dared to think it practicable to make the benefits of civilization available to the whole human race. In society the professions responsible for educating, healing, and helping people are peculiarly charged to make certain of these benefits which are decisive for the continuance of civilization available in ways which have a humanizing influence. Ours is a challenging responsibility, one which we will fulfil in better measure to the extent that we work together for the attainment of our individual and joint aims. For this basic understanding of one another is important and is best attained through working together in the re-formative period of the educational process. These times commit us to afford our students an experience which we did not have, in order that they may go forth with social sensibility beyond our own. Our perceptions and our convictions may be limited by our experience, but we can cultivate thinking beyond it. It has been said that "we feel as our ancestors thought; as we think, so will our descendants feel."[40] We recall also the Talmudic precept, "Limit not thy children to thine own idea. They were born in a different time." In this lies the hope of education.

40. Mary Boole, *Master Keys of the Science of Notation*, cited by Ethel S. Dummer in *Why I Think So: The Autobiography of an Hypothesis* (Chicago: Clarke-McClary Publishing Co., n.d.), p. xi.

PART II

Applications in Teaching Social Casework

CHAPTER 8

The Place of Social Casework in Education for Social Work

This chapter aims to show the part played by the social casework sequence of courses in the attainment of the objectives of social work education. This implies an attempt to envisage social casework teaching as one means in the context of other means, to effect the changes which social work education must bring about or at least set in operation in the learner. In other professions those courses which are concerned with the profession's practices in rendering its services to individuals may well play a similar part in the attainment of the profession's educational objectives.

Traditionally, social casework has had a prominent place in social work education. The many reasons for this are beyond the scope of this chapter. Today there is general agreement among social work educators that schools of social work should not be schools of social casework with a fringe of other learning. There is divergent thinking, however, as to the place of social casework in the curriculum in terms of whether it should be a specialized field of study or a basic process in which considerable work within classroom and field is required of all students in preparation for functions other than social casework. The school of social work trains students for the practice of social work at various operating levels, as social caseworker, social group worker, supervisor of casework or group work, administrator of a social casework agency, group-work agency, or other social welfare programs. It trains also for community organization and for social work research. The organization of curriculums among schools varies considerably, but, in general, courses are offered in the fields of (I) social treatment (social casework) (social group work); (II) organization and administration of welfare services (this would include community organization); (III) social research methods; (IV) contents from related fields, such as law, medicine, psychiatry, and cultural anthropology (these allied courses serve the total curriculum and therefore are applied in all subject areas); and (V) the history and philosophy of social work. These may be taught both in separate courses and/or within the other subject areas. As courses, they may be listed in one grouping or another. Because of differences in point of view among educators as to the degree of specialization desirable and possible in the two-year Master's degree program, greater variation obtains among schools in the programs of individual students than in the fields of study proffered. A growing trend toward education for social work rather than for any one aspect of the field has brought less variation than formerly occurred. Students commonly are required to take, at least in the first year, a cross-section of the several fields of study.

I. SOCIAL CASEWORK LEARNING A BASIC DISCIPLINE

This book is written from the point of view that social casework is a basic social work process with a vital contribution to make to supervision, to administration, to community organization, and to social work research. It has a contribution to make also to social group work; but, in that the latter is another social treatment process, the implications of these two processes for each other are somewhat different. Social group work has a relationship to administration, supervision, community organization, and research comparable to that of social casework to these fields. It is the author's contention also that the changes which social work education aims to effect in the learner can be attained in considerable measure, but not wholly, through social casework learning. It is well to recall the specific changes to be effected: (1) the attainment of orderly thinking which approximates scientific method; (2) the development of appropriate feelings and attitudes; (3) growth in capacity to establish and sustain purposeful working relationships; (4) the engendering of social consciousness and social conscience; (5) the development of a philosophy. In showing the cumulative effect of the curriculum in the several fields of study in effecting these changes, it would be well to delineate the interplay of other learning with social casework rather than to feature prominently the contribution of social casework to professional education. My subject dictates this focus, however, so that it is possible only to convey by implication and to mention briefly in passing the part played by the whole. Past experience has shown that social casework as a means to produce a social worker falls far short of its aims when taught out of context of the other fields of study. It is maintained, however, that social casework has generic importance for the reasons which follow.

Since all social work effort, in the last analysis, is concerned with the welfare of the individual, individual human welfare becomes the test of every program and of every service. For instance, from the standpoint of administration, individual human welfare is the purpose and test of social policy.[1] Likewise, it is the purpose of social work research that the individual may have a better social reality. Through the knowledge contributed by research, agencies, and groups of agencies, the profession may make better use of and adaptation to their reality for the welfare of the client. The generic nature of social casework learning can best be shown through presenting the significance of some of its learning for certain fields. Administration and social work research have been selected.

1. *Contribution to Social Welfare Administration and Community Organization*

Social welfare administration has been defined by John Kidneigh as "the process of transferring social policy into social services and the use of experience in evaluating and modifying social policy."[2] In relation to administration, social casework could be said to have a threefold place. First, the findings of social casework should be drawn on in the making of social policy as related to agency services. Social casework has the charge to know and to make known the import of the agency's services. Administration has the charge to seek counsel and to take into account the findings of casework. Second, the insights of social casework could well influence the managerial policies of administration for more effective

1. Since this was written, a fine statement has appeared in the literature; see Gordon Hamilton, "The Role of Social Casework in Social Policy," *Social Casework,* October, 1952.

2. John C. Kidneigh, "Social Work Administration," *Social Work Journal,* April, 1950.

performance of the agency as a whole. Third, the incorporation of certain principles and working concepts implicit in social casework for imparting and sharing feeling and thinking could well contribute to wisdom in communication at the administrative level.

In a situation where services are rendered by people, with people, and for them, to synchronize processes is to synchronize people. Obviously, the administrator must have knowledge of common human needs, and the dynamics of behavior, individual and group, for the administration of appropriate services in ways which help as well as for the conduct of a variety of working relationships. It is held by some that understanding of needs and the dynamics of individual behavior is best attained through classroom and field-work courses in social casework as well as through psychiatric courses. Others hold that, if the psychiatry courses are set up for all students, it should be possible for the prospective administrator to use the knowledge and insights derived through the psychiatric sequence in his own classroom courses and field work in administration. For example, in psychiatry, the patterning of the individual's behavior in the early relationships within the family is delineated. With the administrative supervisor's help, it might seem that this knowledge from psychiatry could well be carried over directly into the agency hierarchy, for understanding the authority-dependency relationships in administrative management. Similarly, it would be held that psychiatry could contribute directly to other areas of administrative activity. Against this, the proponent for the inclusion of social casework learning would advance, among others, several arguments:

Social casework focuses the insights of psychiatry on understanding the meaning of social stress, on observing the behavior produced by adversity, on perceiving the import of agency experience, and on knowing the conditions which bring people to social agencies as well as the conditions which must obtain in a social work helping process if it is to be constructive.

Social casework continuously is concerned with the individual in his situation to a greater extent than is psychiatry. It patterns its learners to take the situation into account. The administrator, as a social worker, must think first of behavior in relation to situation; he must not only think of clients in their social context but also understand employees in the context of job demands and job relationships, not just employees in and of themselves.

The knowledge of psychiatry may remain an abstraction until experienced and put to use. Unless the learner sees at first hand the problematic attitudes and behavior responses which emerge from specific kinds of family and community relationships, the formulations of psychiatry may strike him as bizarre. They may well be unconvincing when the learner draws only on his own personal experiences to confirm them. It is not possible to know staff workers as one knows the recipients of help. The nature of the work relationship makes for concealment rather than for revelation of basic needs and strivings. Behavior dynamics are learned through first studying behavior in relatively undisguised form. Learning to understand behavior, then, in administrative field-work experience exerts an advanced demand, in that one must infer much, as one attempts to use theory.

In summary, one can get a superficial, fleeting acquaintance with the needs, strivings, and responses of the recipients of social work through the eyes of others. Once the helping process has been experienced, it may leave the deep and lasting imprint essential for the administrator "to be ready to testify on what he knows about human behavior in social functioning for use in establishing policy and framing laws."[3]

To the administrator's need for grasp of group process, social casework can make a rudimentary contribution. There is a possibility that the social worker in administration, particularly if he were to follow the trend in the psychoanalytic literature, might attempt to apply the theory of individual psychology to the behavior of the group. Thus groups might be characterized in personality-structure terms. Significantly, this has not happened to any appreciable extent in social work practice—probably because the fallacy of dealing with a group as though it were an individual has been self-evident through being impossible. Social casework learning, traditionally, has afforded intensive study of the dynamics of family life. One social scientist recently has observed that the family is a small-scale social system. He adds that there has been little occasion to consider the total family as a social system, though

3. Hamilton, *op. cit.*

this might yield insights not derivable from the "atomistic" treatment of each relationship in turn. He continues that the evidence is strong that the same fundamental conceptual scheme, the social system, is applicable from the largest societies to groups of such small size as the family.[4] Early social casework might have been described as an applied social science to a greater extent than it is today. It cannot be known what the characteristics of social casework would be today, had we drawn heavily on the social sciences concurrently with drawing on psychiatry. In spite of this asymmetry in our development, which may mean that we have less to contribute to group process than we might otherwise have had, social casework has a great deal to contribute to understanding the individual in group situations which repeat the family.

There is long-standing recognition that employment situations, in which there is a hierarchy of authority, often re-create the family in some measure for many individuals and for some more than others. This seems to occur to a marked degree in social agencies, an impression doubtless due in part to our recognition of the problem. Administrative policies and practices which do not take this factor into account in dealing with both individuals and groups are more prone to create a repetitive experience of a troubled nature than when they are guided by this insight. The insecure staff member who is having an anxious struggle or the immature individual who has not become emancipated from his family will be particularly prone to assign family identity to the agency, as well as parental and sibling identity to administrators and colleagues. Hence depth of understanding of the dynamics of family life may orient administrators to the meaning of their practices, as well as to the import of behavior responses, so that the conduct of working relationships which foster staff development may be corrective rather than repetitive of the past.

Social work, at all operating levels, is concerned continuously with defining and solving problems. Hence in professional education from one field of study to another, as well as within any one sequence, the problem-defining and -solving processes are essentially the same. A case, as studied in social casework, is always a prob-

4. Talcott Parsons, "Psychoanalysis and the Social Structure," *Psychoanalytic Quarterly*, XIX, No. 3 (September, 1950), 371–83.

lem-defining and -solving situation of varying complexity. Imaginative consideration, analysis, synthesis, and generalization proceed repetitively, but progressively, in new fact situations, with the possibility of being ingrained as a method for use elsewhere. This learning is not attained solely through social casework. Taught elsewhere, from the standpoint of cumulative effect, it is strongly reinforced in social casework, with certain values peculiar to this means, notably the following: In case analysis one must deal with the complex interplay of client in social situation, of worker, of agency, and of community. This configuration of factors is ever present, though in a different focus, in problem-solving at the administrative level. This implies not merely thinking of these several elements separately but thinking of them together in their interrelatedness. For example, casework learning should give depth of meaning to the concept of confidentiality through the individual's having experienced its meaning to clients and struggled against odds to maintain it. Relief cuts could be expected to have greater meaning for administrators who have had firsthand observation of the client's poverty and of the futility of his efforts to spend planfully when he can spend only emergently. To know what it is to be a caseworker, to comprehend the demands made upon him, to feel with, rather than apart from, him should be invaluable in gauging whether or not the administration's standards for competent service are realistic. What administrative policies do to and for the community may be most clearly perceived when they are viewed through the lens of their meaning to clients and workers.

Furthermore, in social casework the method of orderly thinking delineated is seen and used as a treatment, as well as a diagnostic, measure. That the problem-solving process does something to those engaged in it is one of the teachings in preprofessional science courses. Social casework affirms and deepens this earlier learning, fashioning it to the profession, so that it has significance for administration and for social work research.[5] At the administrative level, problem-solving often engages the very people involved in the problem. The teachings of casework obtain here. The study process

5. For a detailed statement of this area of learning in social casework see chap. 9, pp. 248–50. It is recognized that individuals currently engaged in social work research may have attained this orientation through means other than social casework.

may set the pattern of staff activity in work relationships with the administrator, who thereby is not left as the sole doer, with staff dependent upon him and hostile toward him for being "done to." Definite educational benefits may accrue to all concerned through participation in the inquiry.

Finally, the responsibility implied for marshaling the conscience of the community rests heavily, though not wholly, on administration. In the making of uncompromising social policy and in transforming it into social services, the administrator must have a highly developed social conscience and social consciousness, the potentials for which he brings to the professional school, the growth of which is nurtured by the soil' and climate of his professional education and practice. He must feel with and for people individually, not just collectively. He must have depth of understanding of democracy as a way of life. There will be variations in the extent to which this philosophy will have been experienced, integrated, and lived. In innumerable ways, the helping process of social casework puts the democratic process to an acid test. It is more difficult to translate democratic concepts into professional conduct through field work or practice which affords working relationships largely with members of the learner's professional group, rather than with the persons who need help. The poor, the sick, the foreign, the handicapped, the offender, the unemployed, the dependent, can remain problem classifications in the mind and feeling of the student. They may be categories to be done to and for rather than persons to be worked with until the student has known them as individuals in a helping relationship, in which he has come to feel neither autocratic nor paternalistic in relation to the recipients of his services. It is a distinctive attribute of social work that its social policy must be oriented to man as man, rather than to man as "male, or white, or Nordic, or rich, or wise, and that nothing less than the well being of all men can be the goal of social change."[6] Man as man becomes important to the individual who has come to understand the human personality from a scientific point of view through the use of psychosocial learning in the helping relationships of social casework. Differentiation based on social and economic status, racial,

6. Harris Franklin Rall, *Social Change, Religion, and Public Affairs* (New York: Macmillan Co., 1937), p. 217.

national, or sex factors becomes less well defined or incidental to his identity as a person.

Some of the significance of social casework learnings for community organization has been stated and implied in this discussion of their relevance for administration, notably as a means toward knowing community resources and their interrelationships as they specifically serve individuals. Furthermore, to organize and to evaluate human programs for service to people demands understanding of both those who administer and those who receive the services. Likewise, in problem-solving, in establishing and sustaining purposeful working relationships, and also in developing social consciousness, social conscience, and a philosophy of social work, the learning of social casework should have much the same import as for administration.

2. Social Casework and Social Work Research

Social casework and social work research, as has been indicated, have a common aim in their concern for the welfare of people. The processes have something in common, in that both are problem-solving, although under different circumstances and for different immediate purposes.[7] In many social work studies the researcher is called upon to start, as does the caseworker, with a presenting problem which may or may not be either the real problem or the one that lends itself to solution. The "client" in such instances in research is not an individual but an agency or an organization, and consequently there is not the same kind of discomfort as with the troubled person who is the caseworker's client. Often, however, the individuals concerned in the problem-defining task are emotionally implicated, as in social casework and administration. There may be productive or nonproductive motivation in seeking a solution through research. For instance, those asking for this service may want the problem to be solved by others rather than to solve it themselves. Or, fearing its implications, they unconsciously may ease their discomfort through minimizing the problem, through focusing on irrelevant issues, or through becoming task-centered as an escape

7. In this discussion of the contribution of social casework to social work research, the author has consulted with members of the research faculty, Helen R. Wright, Lilian Ripple, and Mary E. Macdonald.

into activity which becomes an end rather than a means. Sometimes, also, in seeking research, the individuals concerned are postponing action which is clearly indicated without a study. As the researcher is called in, then, his initial charge with his client, be it agency, organization, or committee, is the task of defining the problem to be worked on and of determining whether or not there is a problem. Whether there is a need for a social study or whether the answers are already at hand constitutes an inquiry somewhat comparable to that of the caseworker, who must early clarify with the client whether or not he needs help. The initial problem-defining task, therefore, is a somewhat analogous situation. In both instances this is contingent upon understanding the people who present the problem in terms of its meaning to them and their purposes in seeking, or in seeming to seek, a solution.

As the social work researcher conducts a study, there are many points at which he can draw upon his learnings from social casework.[8] Both have in common the method of objective inquiry, while both also draw on knowledge of human behavior. Sound social work research, like social casework, operates in the context of social work's value-system and, accordingly, is concerned with what it does to man in doing for him. It draws on psychological insights in gauging an informant's deception or self-deception. The social work researcher draws on these insights also in appraising his own blind spots, as well as in interviewing skills. Social casework knowledge and method, particularly of working relationships, can make an important contribution, for instance, in the study of an agency program. The meaning of the study to agency people has many of the same dynamics as the process of social investigation in which the client participates. The study may be a threat to the agency staff, who may be anxious as to its intent. Using the basic concepts of social casework, the skilled social work research person will draw on agency personnel as participants in defining the purpose of the study; will afford opportunity for expression of fears; and, aware of the anxieties and resistance, will ease the obstructive feelings with appropriate reassurance and interpretation. When a

8. We note our recognition that the social worker engaged in research is not the only researcher who recognizes and takes steps to deal with the problems specified or who has the insights delineated. Increasingly, social scientists have these insights and are taking account of the same factors.

study comprises a realistic threat in varied ways, he may help agency staff face it, one measure being that of focusing on its social welfare purpose. Sensitivity to an informant's or to a staff participant's defenses in investigating interviews or in defining the research project, together with the use of tested ways of dealing with defenses, may enable informants and staff to participate freely. The importance of this for valid findings is a basic learning in social casework interviewing which can be adapted to the research situation.

3. *Social Casework Contributes to, but Does Not Substitute for, Other Processes*

To envisage the many values of social casework learning for the other processes and functions of social work is not to say that these can be taught primarily through social casework. Special knowledge and skill are requisite for each endeavor. Social casework will contribute as described only in so far as substantial learning experiences are afforded students in all areas. Definite efforts to aid integration will be necessary if the several processes are not to remain separate segments. This demands educational methods which make for continuity and sequence across the board, as well as vertically within each sequence. This implies greater effort to teach social casework in classroom and field, with continuous reference to the other processes in relation to which it operates. It also implies putting both the human social worker and the human recipient of services more prominently into the teaching of all subject areas. In policy-making and in providing services, there must be continuous reference to their import for the individuals served. One must ask, first, what this policy will do to clients in doing for them and, second, what it will do to the staff, who, in some degree, will inevitably pass on to the recipients of their services something of what is done to them.

II. CONTRIBUTION TO THE EDUCATIONAL PROCESS

Another vital aspect of social casework learning in social work education has been its contribution to the educational process itself. In the development of feelings and attitudes appropriate to the profession, it has played a vital, though not a solo, part. This has been because it has offered an opportunity to deal with feeling engendered by new knowledge and the total demand of professional learning. The discussion method has been developed to a higher degree in social casework classes than in some other areas, partly because this method has suited the subject matter but partly because of the special knowledge and skill of the casework instructor in talking with, rather than at, people. It is no longer widely accepted that this method should obtain in social casework classes exclusively, and, accordingly, other teaching is increasingly being done through the use of materials comparable to case materials which afford problem-solving discussion. Not only has the social casework field-work learning occurred in the context of a relationship which has afforded individualization, but also, along with the casework classroom, it has traditionally provided instructors who have had greater understanding of the dynamics of behavior and the learning process than have field supervisors and classroom instructors in other areas. Fortunately, as these insights are becoming more generic to social work as a whole, social casework educators are not an isolated group in understanding the student as a learner. This is fortunate, because when this responsibility is not shared, students bring excessive need for a supportive identification and excessive dependency into their relationship with one segment of the faculty. There has been criticism that the educational programs of our professional schools overemphasize social casework. It is important to recognize that if this situation is changed solely through changes in curriculum content, social casework may still seem to be overstressed through leaving a deeper imprint. This will occur in so far as casework faculty in classroom and field carry the full responsibility for helping students use knowledge of human behavior and for understanding and dealing with the students' responses to learning. Furthermore, the conscious conduct of the relationship as a corrective and integrative means falls far short of its potentialities when it is limited to only a segment of the faculty. The old story of the left hand versus the right hand places an unrealistic demand on the active hand for helping students experience a constructive relationship to learning. For integration of learning there arises in this connection the earlier-mentioned need for students to find the school an organic whole.

As one looks to the future, the place of social casework in the total educational experience remains to be seen. Certainly, it is currently clear that some of the concepts which have been exclusively casework concepts are now identified as generic social work concepts. Likewise, some of the insights exclusive to casework educators, as well as some of the resultant responsibilities which they have carried alone, are today coming to be regarded as the insights and responsibilities of all social work educators. It is a moot question among current educators whether or not that basic understanding of the individual essential in the administrative, organizational, and research processes and functions is best attained through social casework, through either one of the social treatment processes that is either social casework or social group work, or through the direct impact of such knowledge as psychology, psychiatry, and cultural anthropology offer. In the latter instance the major task of integration of these learnings would occur in the classroom and field work of other sequences than social casework or social group work. When social casework and social group work are regarded as specializations rather than as basic generic learnings, it follows that students might specialize in administration, organization, or social work research with only that intellectual orientation to social casework and social group work that often is considered essential for collaboration. When social casework and social group work are regarded as basic areas of learning, one or the other is relied on heavily, but not wholly, as a means for the integration of learning which bears on understanding the individual in society. One or the other is relied on also as a major means to effect the changes in the learner which have been specified. This implies that all students would have a substantial experience in social casework or social group work, including one year or more of field work in the area selected. Other educators, out of the philosophy that individual human welfare is the test of any program or service, regard social casework as the basic area of learning for understanding the individual in his social situation and for effecting the desired changes in the learner. This persistence of the past in the present may well obtain until the student's previous educational experience better prepares him for social work education. We refer here to the opinion stated earlier that social work education unfortunately has to break with the past rather than

carry it forward in an orderly progression.[9] Thus the changes which
the professional school undertakes to effect could well be instituted
in earlier education, notably, capacity for orderly thinking; feelings
and attitudes appropriate to social work which are essentially those
of the enlightened citizen; capacity for collaboration in the attainment of a common goal; and well-developed social consciousness
and social conscience.[10] Whatever the future may bring, the place
of social casework in social work education has been envisaged in
the current scene and will continue to be oriented to it. This is a
period of transition, in which social casework is growing out of
carrying an inordinate responsibility, one in which its educators'
concern to put the human social worker and the human recipient
of services into the teaching of social work is becoming the common concern of all social work educators.

In summary, there has been an attempt to depict in a general
way the contribution of social casework learning to social work
learning, as well as to effect the changes essential if the learner is
to meet the demands of the profession. It is believed that the social
casework curriculum can conribute in these ways, even though it
has not always done so. Whether or not it does will depend on the
orientation of the total faculty, and importantly the casework faculty. It will depend also on the content and organization of the curriculum as a whole. In educating students today for tomorrow, there
is an increasing trend to give them in the casework courses, as well
as throughout the curriculum, a broad social work philosophy
through which knowledge and depth of understanding of the individual in society, derived in part through social casework, will be
used to the utmost in social welfare evaluation, planning, and administration, as well as in leadership, to effect change in those institutions which are failing to fulfil their functions. The social caseworker must be primarily a social worker and hence as intent as
his colleagues in other areas of social work practice to create conditions of life which will make fewer casework services necessary.[11]

9. See chap. 3, p. 62.

10. See Helen R. Wright, "The Professional Curriculum of the Future," *Social
Service Review,* Vol. XXV, No. 4 (December, 1951).

11. Charlotte Towle, "Curriculum Development," *Social Work Journal,* Vol.
XXX, No. 2 (April, 1949).

CHAPTER 9

Areas of Learning in Social Casework

Social work educators attempt to attain the objectives of professional education in teaching social casework in classroom and field through definable areas of learning. These areas are (1) an orderly way of thinking, which approximates scientific method; (2) knowledge and understanding of normal human behavior and of psychopathology, with focus on developmental periods, cultural factors, and social stress; knowledge and understanding of health and disease, with focus on the social aspects of illness, handicaps, and preventive and remedial medical care; (3) knowledge and understanding of working relationships and their management; (4) knowledge and understanding of agency structure and function, the agency's place in the community, its co-ordination and collaboration with other agencies and institutions; (5) knowledge and understanding of the community in terms of how to use its educational, health, and welfare resources, its institutions, and its legal framework; and (6) knowledge of history and law and how to use it in the solution of social problems.

The reader is asked to bear in mind that these areas of learning are not taught in sequence but move forward together, expanding and deepening from course to course in the casework series. Thus the beginning course teaches in a rudimentary form something in all these areas and is a basic course, in that it is a microcosm of the whole. Subsequent casework courses continue to be comprehensive, but with certain greater emphais on one or more areas of learning, as will be shown in chapter 10. Since all this content imparts and inculcates the philosophy of social work, philosophy is not listed as a separate area. The potentials for cumulative effect implicit in social work learning will be seen, in that several of the areas of learning are taught predominantly elsewhere than in social casework, while none of them is taught solely in this sequence.

Each of the areas of learning delineated above will now be considered further, to show in interrelated fashion the contribution of social casework learning to the professional development of the learner.

I. THE DEVELOPMENT OF CAPACITY FOR ORDERLY THINKING

An orderly way of thinking is taught continuously in social casework and pre-eminently in the research sequence. This learning is reinforced repeatedly. In all courses of study there are problems to be solved in which instructors insistently teach that we work by a logical process through putting this method to use. This should not be a new orientation. In so far as students throughout their educational experience have been taught to think rather than merely to know, the groundwork has been laid in the natural, physical, and social sciences of the preprofessional years for the extension of this learning.[1] Orderly thinking in the fact situations of social work, however, is new, and there is variation in the ease with which students transfer its use to psychosocial problems which involve the emotions.[2] There is variation also in the extent to which this intellectual process has been comprehended for conscious use.

1. A Means To Attain Skills Essential in Problem-Solving

Through the case-discussion method the students analyze actual case records from social agencies, to learn study, diagnostic, and treatment process and their interrelatedness. This involves teaching didactically and through discussion the method of inquiry as a diagnostic tool, as a basis of action, as a treatment measure, and as a means for evaluation of the results of action. Always in social casework there is a problem to be defined and solved. The instructor insistently teaches orderly thinking, the steps in which are: observation and gathering of facts; scrutinizing the facts in the light of certain knowledge; formulation of a tentative hypothesis;

1. It is recognized that the preprofessional and professional years sometimes have the inordinately large task of teaching orderly thinking because of defects in grade-school and secondary education (see chaps. 3, pp. 61–62, and 4, p. 111, for discussion of this).

2. See chap. 7 for discussion of the breakdown in this ability which may occur early in professional education.

testing of the hypothesis through further inquiry and also often through emergent action guided by the initial tentative thinking; formulation of an interpretive or diagnostic statement; action taken on the basis of the diagnosis, which is tested further and revised in accordance with the results of action; a continuous self-evaluation by the worker to discount his own bias. In the classroom study of a case, this implies that the student evaluates his own bias as a reader and that he evaluates the bias or subjective involvement of the worker portrayed in the case.

And, finally, there should be a formulation out of each case situation of certain basic concepts and principles which might be applicable to other situations. This is done as cases are taught comparatively, with the purpose of helping students work by principle rather than by precedent, through generalizing soundly. As indicated previously, this final step is a basic means to the formulation of a philosophy of social casework practice.

In social casework the method of inquiry is seen and used as a treatment measure as well as a diagnostic measure. The student is taught that the study process must not disregard the client's welfare. He is not a passive object of study who is "done to," regardless of his feelings and inclinations. He must be as active a participant in the study process as he can be.[3] The student learns that objective inquiry is one of the major measures whereby the client may be enabled to use his own capacities and resources; that a selective study may enlighten the problem for both client and worker; that the study process may early set the pattern of self-activity in the client's relationship with the agency; that, in so far as both client and worker participate, a purposeful working relationship may be established; that definite therapeutic benefits may accrue to the client through his participation in the inquiry, such as change in feeling about the problem and about himself in relation to it, which may imply perspective, resolution of conflict, gain in understanding—in short, a general clarification of, or reorientation to, his problem; that some clients will find the inquiry disturbing and that their own active participation will be

3. In teaching social work research, this also is greatly emphasized in studies which involve contact with clients and in determining the import of control groups for the individuals who would be involved.

productive of anxiety; that such responses are to be expected, understood, and dealt with differentially in the light of the significance of the response.

Through this area of learning the educable student learns not only diagnostic skill but also much treatment skill. What he learns in other areas, such as knowledge of human behavior, knowledge of psychopathology, and collaborative relationship, is enlightened and affirmed through use in this process. Furthermore, as the educable student begins to master, that is, to incorporate, this orderly way of thinking, he becomes increasingly competent to think and to function creatively.[4] Knowing how to take hold of a case, how to proceed in understanding the import of a person's problem to him, how to put two and two together, and what belongs together—in short, knowing a systematic method—enables him to proceed more automatically, so that his conscious mind is freed to make differential use of the method, as he endlessly encounters new fact situations. He is freed also to make comparisons of common elements and of differences. Thus, through his own increased "know-how," order begins to come out of confusion, his dependency is lessened, his defenses lowered, and his resistance to learning decreased.

2. A Means To Effect Change in the Learner

In this intellectual discipline he has a means to self-understanding. An intellectual process is set in operation through which feeling may be objectified if the student is not too involved emotionally to be free to think. That is, as he sees the sequence of cause and effect, he feels differently. He sees that the mother who fails has been failed; that irrational behavior has a rationale; that the worker who gives restrictively may be restricted by agency policy, which, in turn, has been shaped by restrictive social attitudes, which also have a rationale. Thus he may become less condemning of the mother, of people with poor judgment, of workers and agen-

4. In the two years of social work education, marked movement in orderly thinking is observed, together with some of these effects. Integration and mastery occur with experience, when the conditions of learning in the field of practice intrench and carry forward the beginning made in the professional school. They do not always do this. For a statement of this problem in social work practice see Charlotte Towle, *The Learners* ("Social Work Education in the Post Master's Program Series," Vol. 1 [New York: Council on Social Work Education, 1953]).

cies and the public. His mind is not closed by conclusive judgments. When one no longer condemns, one is free to understand
and to think in terms of a realistic approach to effect change. In
short, prejudiced thinking gives way to rational thinking, the very
essence of ego development.

As the student directs these methods of study and diagnosis toward himself, he may become anxious or even quite disturbed.
This area of learning creates some of the problems implicit in the
learning process in social work to which reference has been made
previously. Undue anxiety from self-analysis will not long trouble
the student in whom basic conflicts have not been activated. The
student with a well-developed ego will turn self-analysis into
understanding of self, and he will be no more harsh toward himself than toward others. Not needing to condemn himself, he will
be free to attempt to measure his frailties. The immature student
may or may not engage in self-analysis. In some instances he does
not assume responsibility for more than fragmentary self-understanding, which he may quickly shed. He thus is limited in understanding others because he does not discount his own bias and
projections. If parental conflicts have not been reconciled, a student may become absorbed in self-analysis. In so far as his hostility
is turned against himself in the process, he may become self-con-
demning, and his great sense of inadequacy may interrupt learning. Learning in this area may become a stereotyped repetition of
going so far and no further. Projecting his hostility, this student
may become a keen analyzer of people in situations. He avidly
finds out what is wrong, he breaks a situation down into its finest
components, but he is not motivated to put the pieces together or
to right the wrong. He gets a sense of seeing through people but
fails to understand them, so that he is not strongly motivated to
help them. In so far as self-analysis threatens a student's self-love,
he may retreat from it, projecting responsibility as bits of insight
bring awareness of limitations, and he may continue to see people
in terms of his own projections.

The groundwork for orderly thinking should have been laid in
early education and notably in college in philosophy courses and
in the several sciences. It will have been laid also in the student's

general life-experience, in so far as this experience has contributed to his emotional growth so that he can come to grips with reality and see relatedness, that is, see things as they are and think for himself apart from others. In some fields of work a marked discrepancy between intellectual competence and emotional maturity may not influence action. In social work the discrepancy may not show up in the classroom; in fact, some of the seemingly most orderly thinkers may be obsessively so out of basic emotional difficulties. Repeatedly this discrepancy shows up in the field in various ways, as brought out earlier.

II. KNOWLEDGE AND UNDERSTANDING OF NORMAL BEHAVIOR, OF HEALTH AND DISEASE, AND OF PSYCHOPATHOLOGY

The several areas of normal behavior, of health and disease, and of psychopathology are taught by physicians and by psychiatrists. Frequently, medical and psychiatric social workers collaborate with members of the medical profession in the classroom teaching of these courses. The subject matter is retaught in social casework and applied continuously in social casework and to a more limited extent in other processes. Some groundwork has been laid for this learning in the psychology, physiology, child-development, and sociology courses of the preprofessional years. Because of the great variation in what the student brings to social work education, human development, behavior dynamics, and the nurture of man must be taught anew. They must be taught anew also because they must now be taught with a professional focus, which implies a selection of content for social work use and an emphasis on the import of this learning for the social services. The burden of the professional school in teaching these areas would be lightened, however, if preprofessional teaching were uniformly adequate. They would still need to be brought into focus for social work through being taught in some form or fashion at the professional level.

In that these areas of learning draw on two related disciplines, medicine and psychiatry, interprofessional collaboration in education is involved. Some of the problems presented have been indicated in our earlier discussion of interprofessional teaching.[5]

5. See chap. 7, pp. 217–23.

1. *The Focus and Emphasis in Medical and Psychiatric Teaching Essential for Social Work*

Social caseworkers deal with people who are expressing some breakdown in their capacity to cope unaided with their own affairs. This breakdown may be due primarily to social factors beyond the control of the individual, that is, circumstances such as unemployment, poverty, physical handicap, or illness. The breakdown may, however, be partially, largely, or wholly due to emotional disturbance, interpsychic conflicts, or mental ineptitude within the individual. He may himself have created his social dilemma, whether it be unemployment, poverty, physical illness, disturbed relationships, or infringements of the law. In any instance social workers deal with people who are in trouble, who are having to ask for and take help, and who, regardless of the source of the difficulty, are prone to have disturbed feelings about it and problematic responses to it.

Furthermore, each individual in his own particular struggle for mental and physical survival has developed characteristic ways of handling his discomfort, to the end of diminishing it so that he may live comfortably with it. We have learned that it is how the individual feels about his problem which will determine what he will do about it or what he will permit anyone to help him do about it. We have learned also that his way of handling his discomfort, his way of responding to his problem, will be a decisive factor in his use of help. We know, too, that, even in those instances in which the individual's problem stems primarily from within himself, the social circumstances of his life not only may have had a part in creating his difficulty but will now play a significant role in fashioning his response and in determining its present usefulness or futility. This leads us invariably to focus on understanding what purpose an individual's behavior is now serving him in relation to a combination of factors and forces in his current situation. We know that we often cannot help him deal more competently with his problem unless we render our service differentially in the light of its meaning to him and in relation to the emotional and practical values, in terms of the futility or the usefulness, of his own solution. This implies a basic understanding of the individual, that is, insight into the meaning of his behavior.

In spite of the fact that each individual situation is unique, this understanding is aided by knowledge of the meaning which certain social circumstances commonly have for people. In understanding the personality, the social caseworker considers types of experience in relation to common needs and common ways of responding. How may malnutrition affect personality development? What may be the effects of physical handicap? What may medical care mean at different age levels? What effects may specific types of family organization or national or racial customs have on personality formation? There is involved here a knowledge derived not only from psychiatry, psychology, social anthropology, and medicine but also from social work learning implicit in its study of the import for the individual of family life, of cultural backgrounds, of community life, and of the context of the times.

Social workers are concerned primarily with the nurture of man for maximum growth. Nurture must be oriented to nature, and hence social workers must understand the nature of man as a developing individual and the conditions of life essential for the growth of the total personality. Granted the existence of basic biological drives and variation in constitutional endowment, the social worker operates on the assumption that the individual is fashioned largely by the circumstances and interpersonal relationships of his environment and, in turn, fashions them. The social worker's primary focus is on environment, broadly conceived, as a means to development and on environment as treatment when development is obstructed.

Students become conscious of the orderly procedure by which one understands behavior and institutes treatment in so far as medical and psychiatric instructors both present it didactically and use it in case citations. Awareness of a systematic approach is gained also as students encounter it in readings where cases are recorded in the literature. The effects of orderly procedure delineated earlier in relation to social casework learning can thus be reinforced in the medical and psychiatric courses. Since this knowledge is put to use in essentially the same way in the discussion classes of social casework, integration of the method occurs in these courses.

There is considerable variation among schools of social work in their organization of courses in the medical and psychiatric sequence to convey this learning. There is difference of opinion among educators whether learning proceeds best in any one of four sequences enumerated below.

a) One may start with normal behavior and personality development from infancy into old age and move therefrom into behavior deviations of children and pathology of adults. This sequence has been most commonly used for a good many years.

b) One may teach chronologically from infancy to old age but cover concurrently normal and deviated behavior in each developmental period. The proponents of this method argue that it makes clear both the relatedness and the difference of normal and abnormal behavior, thus lessening the gap between the two, while differentiating them.

c) One may start with behavior deviation and pathology and move therefrom to normal development and behavior. The supporters of this sequence claim movement from the simple to the complex, in that there is less disguise of feeling and of motivation by the defenses and less identification on the part of the student with the patient to obscure understanding. Opponents of this method grant these elements of intellectual simplicity but insist that there is a greater demand for knowledge with which to think as well as a heavier emotional demand in other respects at the start.

d) Or, finally, one might begin with the normal adult and move into normal childhood and infancy thereafter. Deviation in childhood behavior and adult psychopathology would follow. This sequence is upheld on the grounds that adult students identify more readily with adults and have more comprehension of them than of children. Young adults, particularly, may be repressing their childhood and adolescent experiences. Furthermore, starting with the normal adult coincides with, and thus reinforces, the casework sequence in which the beginning casework courses deal largely with relatively normal adults. Opponents of this sequence argue that it involves repetition; that for depth of understanding of the adult, one must also know the child; that learning in this order will be more affect-laden at the start because students will find the insights immediately applicable to themselves. This latter factor has both positive and negative implications.

The writer will not argue the pros and cons of these several approaches. Probably the effectiveness of each depends on several factors, two of which are its consistency with the educational rationale of the particular school as a whole and the arrangement of other learning experiences. Cutting across these several sequences, two recent trends are discernible in educational practice: the tendency to integrate the medical-knowledge courses with the psychiatric courses; the tendency to impart more child-development, child-nurture and growth-process content than to focus as narrowly as formerly on personality formation and structure.

In the School of Social Service Administration at the University of Chicago we continue to convey this total area of learning through sequence *a*, partly because of the preference of the instructors and also because of its administrative simplicity. We have wanted to experiment with plan *b*, but for several reasons it would have been more difficult to administer. We do not favor plan *c*. Plan *d* does not fit in with our educational approach, in that we move slowly into implicating the student in focusing this learning on himself. We think it best to keep affect low at the start. We refer to Tyler's principle on organization of material for cumulative effect—logical relations of content do not necessarily make for effective organization which is based on the student's development.[6] Our courses are as follows: "Development of Personality," which is taken concurrently with the courses entitled "Health and Disease" and "Social Casework I." These are followed by courses entitled "Behavior Disorders of Children" and "Psychopathology for Social Workers." This entire content is usually covered in the first four quarters of the two-year Master's degree program; hence the student has this orientation for use as he proceeds into more advanced work. The courses have been structured in conferences between teaching physicians, psychiatrists, and social work faculty, with the understanding that the blueprints are to serve as a guide. While each instructor aims to select and to cover the content delineated, there

6. Ralph W. Tyler, "Basic Principles of Curriculum and Instruction," *Syllabus for Education 360* (Chicago: University of Chicago Press, 1950).

naturally and desirably is considerable variation in the individual instructor's style in handling the subject matter. In the social casework series the medical and psychiatric contents are taught and retaught case by case, didactically and through discussion, readings, and assignments. Understanding people and their common needs and responses is the core of social work. Understanding *this* person and his particular needs and the precise meaning of his responses is the core of social casework. Hence, while these contents are used throughout the curriculum, they are worked with most thoroughly in social casework in the classroom and in the field. The contribution of each of these courses to the learning process follows.

2. The Study of Health and Disease, an Integral Force in the Dynamics of the Personality

The evolution of this course typifies the change which is occurring in other areas of social work education and professional education in other fields of endeavor. We therefore trace its development for the reader. The course replaces a traditional one, "Medical Lectures for Social Workers," in which physicians had presented basic information regarding maternity, infant growth, and the major chronic and disabling illnesses of childhood and adult life. It gave information more useful to physicians than to social workers. This was followed by a second course in which the focus was on selecting what social workers need to know in this area for use in the performance of their function. This course was structured to teach the socioeconomic and psychological import to the patient and to his family of conditions which have common denominators of disability, as, for example, great or prolonged restriction of physical activity, requiring radical readjustment in the individual's usual way of life; permanent or prolonged dietary modifications; deterioration (rapid or gradual) with a hopeless prognosis. The course was intended to develop an understanding of the normal emotional and usual social needs arising from illness and of the social worker's responsibility for meeting such needs through the resources of her own agency and through intelligent co-operation with physicians and medical agencies. For facts regarding a given disease, students were referred to selected medical texts or preferably to literature accurately pre-

258 *The Learner in Education for the Professions*

pared for lay readers. The instructor, a medical social worker, assumed no responsibility for imparting medical knowledge.

This course has given way to a third revision, taught currently, one which deepens and sharpens the focus on the dynamics of psychosomatic behavior in its social context:

> It aims to develop an understanding of the concept of equilibrium, as it is manifested in health, in the balanced functioning of complex and inter-dependent physiological and psychological processes. It endeavors to show the various kinds of dysfunctioning resulting from the impairment of specific systems or the destruction of organs and the potentials of the organism, both physiological and psychological, for adaptations and defense to regain a state of equilibrium. Specific disease conditions are presented, not to give factual coverage as such, but to exemplify particular kinds of dysfunctioning and to clarify the biological capacity of the organism either to restore normal function, or to compensate for damage to, or loss of, vital organs through modifications of function. In assessing this capacity, consideration is given to the influence of emotional forces and social-economic factors on adaptive capacity, as well as to the physiological import of a specific physical impairment or loss.[7]

Conceived by a medical social worker, the course has been structured and taught collaboratively by a medical social worker and a physician. The latter opens the course with two introductory lectures on what constitutes health and on what constitutes disease. The medical social worker then presents, in two class sessions, the social worker's twofold responsibility: to appraise the adequacy of the individual as he functions, in the light of what the students will have learned of biological adequacy and dysfunction, and to try to understand the purposes served by illness. This involves presenting its major purposes, as well as the varied behavior manifestations through which the purposes are revealed. In this connection the students are introduced to a way of understanding the language which the individual's illness and his response to it speak, an area of learning which is carried forward in the social casework courses, both in classroom and in the field. The physician resumes teaching in the fifth session, presenting, during the remaining sessions, the major disease categories which illustrate his introductory theses. In consultation with the physician, the medical social worker carries administrative responsibility for the course, that is, she prepares the bibliographies, structures and reads the

7. Dora Goldstine in an unpublished communication to the author.

examinations, and confers with students who seek help at any point. The evolution of this course typifies the growth and change which are occurring in social work education. It reflects the gradual trend from imparting factual knowledge, with which to think dubiously, to considering facts in relation to basic concepts which give direction, scope, and depth to the learner's thinking. The development in this course has reflected trends in medical education, from a narrow focus on the diseases of mankind to a focus on individual man coping with disease, to a focus on health and disease as an integral force, operating both as cause and effect in the dynamics of the personality. For cumulative effect this course has continuity and integration, in that it repeats and reinforces the use of the concepts of stability and economy of effort basic in the psychiatric and social casework sequences, as well as in both the courses on professional education and the orientation given learners to the educational experience in which they are engaged.

3. *Study of the Development of Personality as (a) Essential Knowledge and (b) a Means To Effect Change in the Learner*

This basic course in the psychiatric sequence aims to convey knowledge and understanding of normal human behavior in the context of family and other group life, in relation to cultural factors, social stresses, and the changing social demands of each developmental period. It is focused on man's nature and the nurture essential for maximum development of his capacities. It has been planned that these sessions should give a streamlined picture of the normal growth of an individual from infancy to old age. There should be a systematic evaluation of his needs and strivings at each age level and of the growth which can be expected as physical, intellectual, and emotional needs are met. This involves consideration of common ways of responding to vital life-experience, to new reality demands, to social stresses, which, in turn, leads to the presentation of the structure of the personality at different developmental periods. Attention is given to the purposes served by behavior responses. This course is essentially a study of the development of the ego, its function in the integration of the personality, and its capacities for adaptation and defense.

These courses in normal behavior in individuals under stress and under conditions favorable for growth are placed first for several reasons. Social workers deal with many people who are situationally upset because of adverse circumstances rather than because of any basic personality maladjustment. The social worker's contribution lies in affirming and using the strengths, the inner resources, which the client has, more than in overcoming his weaknesses, even when they are present. Social workers are focused on nurture for the growth of the individual. They must therefore understand what man needs in order to grow and also the norms of development. Past experience has shown that when courses in psychopathology were given first, students, not necessarily knowing what constitutes normal behavior, were prone to distort the significance of normal reactions in themselves, in their colleagues, and in their clients. For example, realistic anxiety was equated with neurotic anxiety; normal responses in a six-year-old were given a pathological import which they might have had, had they been encountered in an older child. Furthermore, the study of normal behavior probably stimulates less affect than the study of pathological behavior. Hence the integrative task is kept lighter in the beginning stage of learning, when the student is undergoing a major adaptation to much that is new. Lastly, one of the initial demands on the student as he begins to relate to clients sympathetically and with understanding is that he identify with them in some measure. He identifies most readily with people who are least strange, least unlike himself, a factor which has been taken into account in planning the content of the social casework series; further thinking on this important point is presented in later chapters.

Because some of our deeper insights into human behavior were derived through knowledge and understanding of psychopathology, this course traditionally has been taught by psychiatrists, a practice which persists. Frequently and increasingly, however, this subject matter is being taught by social work educators, a development which can be upheld staunchly. The social worker's experience with individuals normally troubled by social stress is richer than that of the psychiatrist. It is important, therefore, that the social worker assume responsibility for an area of learning in which he should be able to speak with authority. If social workers in practice are to hold themselves professionally accountable for self-dependence in the understanding of normal behavior, it is essential that students, early in their professional learning, identify this as peculiarly the social worker's area of competence. They will be sure to do this only in so far as the administrators in schools of social work have done so through delegating this teaching responsibility to their own faculty. Identification, a vital means to professional learning, operates decisively in this first pattern-setting stage of the psychiatric sequence.

4. *The Study of "Behavior Disorders in Children" as (a) Essential Knowledge and (b) a Means To Effect Change in the Learner*

In this course the deviations are oriented to the unmet needs and frustrated strivings of the child at different age periods. There is study of the onset and development of the problem in relation to the interplay of constitutional, physical, intellectual, emotional, and social factors. It is essential that students see the behavior symptoms as serving in the economy of the individual personality in the context of social realities and group demands significant for him. Thus as an outgrowth of their study of the development of personality, there is opportunity for them to learn that abnormal behavior, like normal behavior, is serving the same purpose of meeting need and maintaining a state of equilibrium; of comprehending that there is a reason for disturbed behavior; of grasping that the response has a logic which is understandable. It is through this insight that students are enabled to extend their emotional acceptance of the normal individual to the one whose behavior violates their standards. This may make it possible for them, while still rejecting the behavior as unacceptable, to identify with, to understand, and not to reject the person. It is desirable that current formulations regarding different types of behavior also be presented with a focus on the personality structure obtaining in each. Differential treatment is discussed from the standpoint of its general nature in relation to age periods, nature and extent of problem, nature of parent-child relationships, and the social situation. The major differences in the treatment of the young child, the adolescent, and the adult might be envisaged. Throughout the treatment discussion it is important that there be emphasis on growth potentials and on meeting need through modification of the child's reality situation. There should be some attempt to define the diagnostic factors which determine a child's needs for psychiatric treatment or other specialized treatment. In this connection there is again, as in the "Development of Personality," consideration of ego development and of the ego's capacities for adaptation and defense.

5. *The Study of Psychopathology for Social Workers, as*
(*a*) *Essential Knowledge and* (*b*) *A Means*
To Effect Change in the Learner

As in the preceding courses, this course is focused on the dynamics of behavior in the light of the interplay of constitutional physical, psychological, and social factors. There is consideration of the personality structure and purposes of behavior in the neuroses, psychosomatic illness, and the psychoses, organic and functional.

The purposes of this course are several: (1) to enable the social worker to recognize mental and emotional illness not only in its gross forms but as it is developing; (2) to help the worker become aware of the causal factors in mental illness, so that they may be alert to preventive measures; (3) to acquaint the worker with the general nature of the treatment, its type, its duration and prognosis, in relation to the nature of the illness and the degree of the disorder (this is for use in helping people get the care or treatment indicated and as a guide to the social worker in his own helping efforts in those conditions where he collaborates in treatment); (4) to extend and deepen understanding conveyed elsewhere of personality structure, particularly of ego development. The student is now confronted with the dysfunction of the ego and the failure of its adaptations and defenses, when viewed from the standpoint of social norms.

The aims of this course, as in "Behavior Disorders of Children," have been well stated by Dr. Roy R. Grinker in his class lectures; that students may see

mental and emotional illness as a deviation from normal behavior in which individual difference obtains within disease categories. It is decisively important that they get the point of view that modern dynamic psychiatry does not deal with a process, a classification, a prognosis inherent in the description of the disease. In each condition there is an individual development to be understood. All areas of individual background and relationship must be explored. Therapy must be individualized.

It is the incorporation of this point of view, along with the attainment of knowledge of psychopathology, which enables students to relate to the needs of the mentally and emotionally ill with feelings which make it possible for them to understand and to be helpful. This content, by its very nature and by the problem which it presents in identification, often provokes strong or even disturbed feelings.

The student with basic conflicts who suffers through a sense of difference may withhold from identification because it provokes too much anxiety. Thus the mentally ill still may remain shelved as "those *other* people." The student with the well-developed ego may find it difficult to identify and to get a real sense of understanding, because the conditions described are too different. The understanding remains on the level of theoretical knowledge and is not quite comprehensible. Field work in a mental hospital, movies, and novels make the conditions more real. Marked emotional responses may be expected in all students when learning in this area becomes more than abstraction. For learning, there is much at stake, therefore, in the point of view from which these contents are conveyed and in the attitudes and feelings of faculty responsible for instruction in classroom and field.

6. Summary of the Values of Medical and Psychiatric Learning

There are no more important courses in the curriculum than the courses in medical and psychiatric learning. Students can attain here a content of knowledge, a point of view, and an attitude of mind and heart about human needs and behavior which, as they become incorporated through use in casework courses, in field work, and in other areas of the curriculum, become the very core of their professional performance at all operating levels. In the administration of social welfare programs, in supervision, in community organization, in social research, in group work, as well as in casework, the knowledge and insight gained in these courses are decisively important.

The responsibility of helping students integrate this content for social work use naturally rests with social work educators. It makes a world of difference to the latter, however, when the psychiatrist is oriented to the objectives of social work education through knowledge of the function of social work. Not all psychiatry has been helpful to social workers. Some of it has been more decorative than useful, more adjunctive than integral. The psychiatrist who presents a concept of the individual as little more than a bundle of sexual needs and strivings will leave the social work educator with the total burden of proving the importance of food, housing, play, social life, education, work, health, illness, hardships, separation, death, or disaster for personality development and also their import even for psychosexual conflicts. The psychiatrist who emphasizes pathology and the insistent strength of regressive impulses more than the resilience of the ego, the resourcefulness of its defenses, and the individual's potentials for growth as needs are met, makes it difficult for the social work educator. She will have a hard task to instil any hope in the student's heart or to help him find his feet as a helping person whose area of competence lies in affirming and using clients' strengths more than in overcoming their weaknesses. Such undesirable emphases are less a problem today than in the past. Fortunately, as an aid to the integration of social work and psychiatry, what can be done with the person as he is rather than always what needs to be undone is now a concern of the physician and the psychiatrist as well as the social worker. Increasingly, psychiatrists and some physicians are giving social workers a content of knowledge with a nice integration of the psychosomatic, the psychosexual, and the psychosocial.

With reference to the objectives of professional education, it is clear that these areas of learning in their study of the logic of human behavior give students essential knowledge with which to think analytically and critically and to synthesize. They also affirm the process of orderly thinking which students must use throughout the curriculum. Consideration of multiple causation and of multiple motivation, together with the demonstration of the selection of significant configurations for differential diagnosis and treatment, exemplifies for them what they must learn to do in social work. It should therefore give substance to the discipline in orderly thinking which is occurring elsewhere. These areas of learning likewise serve to set in operation changes in feeling. In these courses students may take a big step ahead in self-awareness and self-understanding. They may, in fact, be pushed precipitously into more self-awareness than they can tolerate, so that they are compelled to defend themselves against understanding. In such instances the knowledge may serve as a weapon of attack or defense. Steeped in psychiatry, some students may be enabled to see into people only to feel more so about them. We repeat that it is possible to see through people and still fail to understand them. New thinking about behavior, however, will often enable students to feel differently about people and about themselves. When they see the relationships between mental illness and social conditions; when they perceive the unmet needs and frustrated strivings which have produced breakdowns or failures in adaptation; when they comprehend the potential strengths in the personality's struggle for survival against odds; when, in short, they begin to grasp the factors and forces which have shaped people to these ends, then pity may give way to respect, superiority to humility, and condemnation or cool tolerance to warm understanding. This area of learning contributes also to the attainment of the educational objective of helping students develop a capacity for collaboration, that is, of establishing and maintaining a purposeful working relationship. It gives essential knowledge for use in the fourth area of learning, to which we now turn, as well as in all social work's helping efforts. In the light of this knowledge, casework activity becomes client-centered, rather than worker- or agency-centered, and it thereby becomes differential rather than routine.

III. KNOWLEDGE AND UNDERSTANDING OF WORKING RELATIONSHIPS AND THEIR MANAGEMENT

Knowledge and understanding of working relationships and their management, the element of working together to some purpose which pervades all social work, are taught repetitively throughout the curriculum. Worker-client relationship, supervisor-worker relationship, administrator-staff relationship, staff-to-staff or interagency relationship, social worker–community relationship, profession-to-profession relationship, which often is the team relationship, are all taught in the social casework sequence. While there is a more continuous emphasis on worker-client relationship, the other relationships occur and recur from time to time, as specific cases in class-

room or field demonstrate them. The relationships other than that of
worker and client are taught largely in administration, supervision,
community organization, and research courses. Understanding of the
basic dynamics in work relationships for use elsewhere have been
conveyed through social casework learning, where the use of insights into human behavior have been given great prominence.

1. *For Skill Essential in the Conduct of the Helping Process*

With reference to the worker-client relationship, there is a content
of knowledge and skills to be taught for differential use. It is taught
through case discussion from records in which the activity of both
client and worker has been quite fully revealed and where the
activity of collaterals and other agency workers *has been recorded
at least briefly*. It is conveyed also through theoretical discussion,
reading, and some didactic teaching. And, very important, as
brought out previously, it is bred through the teaching, helping, and
administrative relationships experienced by the student in the classroom and field. In this whole area of learning the student works at
being a social worker. The intellectual concept of a consciously controlled professional relationship as the context in which all services
are rendered is grasped and understood to some extent in the classroom. Depth of understanding and some skill in use are derived in
field work through supervised practice.

Gradually the student learns the nature of the relationship, its
confidential nature, its respectful nature, its dispassionate and compassionate qualities. Early he is directed to consider its likeness to,
and differences from, other life-relationships. This differentiation
focuses on its purpose and on the emotional demands validly
brought to the relationship by both parties, client and worker. Its
distinctive features are identified as follows: It has come into being
out of one person's need for help rather than out of the need of two
people for each other. One person has the responsibility for understanding the needs of the other and for rendering the services indicated. One person has the responsibility for directing the relationship toward productive ends. Thus the student learns that the relationship has a different reciprocity than other relationships. The
client may act the same here as elsewhere, that is, he may attempt to
use the relationship to meet his needs, realistic and unrealistic. The

worker, however, cannot be the same person, that is, use this relationship as he rightly uses other ones for some self-realization.
Hence, as he withholds his own need, it is probable that the worker
will seem to be unlike other people to the client. He will feel different to the client, for it is in the nature of ordinary life-
relationships that each participant has something emotionally at
stake, some need to be met, some values to defend, which lead him
to respond subjectively rather than objectively to the difficulties and
troubled feelings of the other.

This sense of difference may give the client freedom to express
what he cannot bring out elsewhere: his hopes, which others might
ridicule; his aspirations, which others might oppose; his unsocial
impulses, which others might condemn or reinforce; his hostile impulses, which others might affirm or forbid or against which they
might retaliate. As the student is able to be sympathetic, understanding, and dispassionate, he repetitively discovers a client whose
feelings about his problem and himself change and who begins to
think differently and act differently. Often he shows gains in insight
or readiness to receive it. As the client grows better able to deal
realistically with adverse social circumstance, the social work student learns the significance of modifiable or rigid environmental factors to intrench or to obstruct those gains. He learns also the decisive importance of the response of others in close relationship with
the client to the change in him. This understanding may give focus
to his work with the client and may be the basis for extending help
beyond the client to others in his situation.

2. As a Means To Effect Change in the Learner

Gradually the student learns that clients will react to the relationship realistically or unrealistically in accordance with their need. He
sees that to some extent the relationship repeats an old relationship,
that is, meets a need met by a former relationship, out of which the
individual's conflicts arise. With this comprehension, the student's
feelings often are objectified, as he realizes, for example, that the
client's dependency, hostility, and negativism arise from his own
need and would be directed toward any worker. As he realizes the
positive import of the client's freedom with him, the student's anxiety
over being personally liked or disliked may subside, because feelings

of failure are replaced by a sense of adequacy. As the student realizes that this helping relationship repeats the client's former relationships, with a difference which is decisive in providing the corrective element, his intent to understand and to meet the client's need is strengthened. He then consciously begins to regulate his attitudes and responses to the client's need for help. Thus a noncommital attitude may free the client to think and act on his own. Or a permissive one may ease guilt so that he can feel, think, and act differently. Or an authoritative judgment may strengthen the client's conscience and thus help him meet social demands more realistically. The aim of education in this area is that the student may develop an urgent concern to afford a client a relationship which he can use to some advantage. This implies a capacity for flexible meeting of his need at his particular level of personality organization. Beyond being sympathetic with, understanding of, and dispassionate toward the client as he is, the social worker who helps him change must learn how to meet dependency in ways which do not infantilize, how to use authority, impose demands, and convey moral judgments or social evaluations in a sustaining way, so that the individual may become more self-determining or, at least, less self-destructive in his behavior.

3. *The Interdependence of Knowledge and Skill in the Conduct of the Relationship and Other Areas of Learning*

Interviewing and recording, taught largely in field work but also in the classroom, are specific skills in this area of learning. All helping measures operate within the context of this "working-together" professional relationship; therefore, as the student is learning what measures to use and how to use them and the reason for these measures, his understanding of the relationship and its management extends and deepens. Concurrently, his interviewing becomes more focused and more productive. This is ordinarily reflected in greater clarity and better organization of his recording. Gradually, he comprehends the relationship as an outgrowth of all the helping measures and as a determinant both of the client's use of them and of their usefulness to the client. For example, the initial inquiry, which has a prominent diagnostic purpose, may establish a purposeful working relationship or deter it. The giving of advice and the timing and content of interpretation, as well as the extending of the opportunity to unburden, are frequently decided by the stage of development of the relationship. In addition, as has been brought out, the student learns that the professional relationship can be in and of itself a helping or a treatment measure.

4. *Summary—the Integrative Role Played by This Area of Learning in the Educational Process*

The student learns that he, the social worker, is responsible for conducting the helping process; that in exerting those controls implicit in a professional responsibility, the relationship need not be a controlling one; that it is essential for him to bring a positive attitude to the helping situation, for it is through acceptance and understanding that the client becomes self-understanding and self-directive. In this whole area of learning the student must use all that he has learned of orderly thinking. He must examine his feelings and struggle to align them with that which is professionally acceptable. Regardless of how he feels, he must try to express feelings which help rather than hinder the client. He must draw on all that he has learned of human behavior and psychopathology. He must keep the relationship within the bounds of clients' needs and capacities and within the bounds set by the nature of the service as determined by agency function. In social work education there is an impression that the student's headway in this area of knowledge and understanding of working relationship reflects his total learning. Accordingly, it is noted closely as one of the major tests of movement in learning. As stated earlier, the attainment of the high demands of this educational objective is contingent in part upon the nature of the relationship which the student experiences with his professional school as a whole and with his teachers individually. The educable student can begin to develop capacity for the kind of professional relationship described here, to the extent that he has experienced it in the learning process.

There are several purposive working relationships other than that between client and worker. Each has its peculiar characteristics as determined by the functions and the responsibilities of the persons participating and by the structure of the agency or the organizational structure of the interagency program. The knowledge and understanding, the way of thinking and feeling, a body of working principles and methods derived in several areas of learning are synthesized in this area of knowledge and understanding of worker-client relationship and its management to carry over to other working relationships. Some of the specific contributions are a method of approach to a problem, a disciplined intent to understand and to use what another person brings to its solution, a way of relating to people, with focus on the central purpose of the relationship, which is that of defining the basic problem, clarifying the issues, and seeking the knowledge and resources for its solution through those individuals best qualified or responsible to act. This learning carries over, in modified form, horizontally from colleague to colleague, and vertically from worker to supervisor, to administrator, to board. There is a helping component which pervades the working relationships of an agency. There is an authority-dependency element in all working relationships. The help given by administrator to supervisor and by supervisor to worker is different from the help to which a client is entitled; but it has long been noted that a worker whose valid need for help in learning has not been met may fail to meet the client's needs, not only through lack of competence in the administration of agency services but also through negative attitudes and responses to his needs and rights. It is commonplace knowledge that an administrator's relationship with his staff may be felt most by the client. The worker who fails the client is frequently the worker who has been failed by the administration and by his supervisor. The educable student who falls short of his potentialities is often being failed in the teaching-learning relationship in the educational situation. For explanation of the prominence given to this area of learning, it is important to recall that the basic functions of social workers are contingent on the art and science of effecting interpersonal and intergroup relationships.

IV. KNOWLEDGE AND UNDERSTANDING OF AGENCY
STRUCTURE AND FUNCTION

1. *For Effective Use of the Agency in the
Interest of Client and Community*

Social work as a profession is practiced almost wholly within social agencies and institutions with a human welfare purpose. Social workers are seldom private practitioners. They are representatives of agencies or social welfare programs established to administer certain services, the range being from multiple services to one or a few specific services. It is the aim of the social work educator to help students use the agency creatively in the interest of the individual, but with reference to its function in relation to other agencies in the community. This area of learning is taught in casework courses in both the classroom and the field and also, at the University of Chicago, in a final course devoted to the study of the relationship of agency setting to casework practice. This final course summarizes and formulates earlier case-by-case teaching on agency structure and function as a determinant of casework practice. In the casework classes the learning is conveyed through careful study of the agencies which appear in the cases under discussion. The contents of courses in other sequences are drawn on for use in the case discussions, as are readings. The repetitive focus in teaching this area of learning is fourfold.

a) It aims to convey knowledge of the provisions of a particular agency. This includes habituating the student to focus on what its regulations and policies permit its staff to do for people, as well as on what the limits of its services are. With this realistic frame of reference, there is careful consideration of whether or not the client's needs were met and whether or not the worker used the agency's policies to the utmost in meeting the client's need in ways that were helpful to him.

b) It affords consideration of the ways in which the agency, through its policies and regulations, fashioned the service, that is, determined not only what needs were and were not met, what services could and could not be rendered, and finally, what all this did to shape the nature of the worker-client relationship. There is focus on the special problems created by the agency's structure and function which were taken into account or which should have been considered. For example, in the instance of an authoritarian agency, did the factor of an imposed service condition the client's response and thus make activity necessary in the initial contacts, to help him work through his resistance so that he could make productive use of the service?

c) It provides a critical evaluation of the agency. In the light of its purpose, its community's expectations of it, wherein did this agency fulfil or fail to fulfil its function? Wherein do its procedures and routines facilitate or obstruct its aims? Students should get the feeling that, as caseworkers, they are in a position to test out and observe the ways in which the agency works or fails to work. They should be habituated to think and feel whether they, as professional social workers, can continue comfortably and in good conscience to abide by the procedures and practices of the agency. If not, what can they do about it? Certainly, they cannot individually depart from regulations and violate policies. There is consideration of their responsibility to make known lacks in the service and of the channels through which they can direct their observations upward and outward. In casework this area reinforces what is taught more comprehensively in other courses.

d) Finally, there is, in the summary course mentioned earlier, the study of types of agencies, in order that students may quickly know how to find their feet in any social agency or institution and begin at once to use it appropriately and creatively. "It is possible to clarify and study the phenomena which characterize special settings and to formulate principles for their use."[8] It is possible also to define the agency conditions under which social casework can operate and the conditions which will defeat its aims.[9] The educational aim of inculcating a constructively critical attitude toward the profession's instruments is attained in some measure through repeated evaluation of a worker's use of a range of social agencies encountered in the classroom; through evaluation of the agencies themselves as instruments of the profession; through conveying a content of knowledge as to how to know an agency and of working principles for its use; and through experiencing at least two agencies in casework field practice, where it is expected that the educational approach to agency function will repeat that of the classroom.

2. As a Means To Effect Change in the Learner

Coming to grips with the implications of agency structure and function provokes considerable feeling, in that it makes a new

8. Helen Harris Perlman, "Generic Aspects of Specific Case Work Settings," *Social Service Review*, Vol. XXIII (September, 1949), 293–301.

9. Charlotte Towle, "Social Case Work in Modern Society," *Social Service Review*, Vol. XX, No. 2 (June, 1946).

demand. At the start when the student begins to realize that he is no longer himself but also an agency, he may have some discomfort. He may feel like an overburdened peddler with an unwieldy pack on his back. When he incorporates this learning, he gains security, for he has both authority and experience beyond his own to help him make decisions so as not to get caught in his own subjective involvements in case situations. He truly incorporates this learning rather than submitting to it and annexing it when he is infused with a concept of an agency as a dynamic organism subject to change to which he can contribute. In so far as this happens, the groundwork will have been laid for competent administration of casework services at all operating levels.[10] It is the social work educator's aim that students should not go forth like turtles, forever shielded within the rigid structure of agency shell, which serves as a hard defense and as a comfortable abode to which to retreat. It has been demonstrated that students normally have some difficulty in the process of integration of this area of learning, the reasons for which are fairly clear in the light of our understanding of the dynamics of learning. Agencies are complex organizations. If used resourcefully for individualized service, there is much to learn which cannot readily become automatic. Part of the complexity rests on the many personalities involved and on the fact that an organization with a hierarchy and a body of regulations repeats the family and authority for the young adult. His most recent achievement may have been that of getting out on his own, where he can be himself, in terms of carrying out his own thinking and planning. The educable student will soon find his place. He will relate and align himself in such a way as to be comfortable through adult compromises with the authority-dependency elements. The immature student, particularly if the agency re-creates family conflicts, will have a difficult time, commensurate with the degree of his immaturity and the extent to which he is driven from within to repeat old relationships. For many students with some unresolved family conflicts but who are accessible to relationships on a new footing, the agency will afford an opportunity *for reliving correctively rather than merely repeating* the old in the new. Thus it can be a vital means to professional development through personality growth.

10. Charlotte Towle, "Professional Skill in Administration," *News Letter, American Association of Psychiatric Social Workers,* May, 1940.

V. THE COMMUNITY—KNOWLEDGE AND UNDERSTANDING OF ITS
RESOURCES AND LEGAL FRAMEWORK

1. *For Effective Interprofessional Collaboration in the
Interest of Client and Community*

The community as the profession's context is taught in the social
casework courses through consideration of the use of resources. A
good deal of content derived in other courses is drawn on, as, case
by case, the social worker's use of the community is repetitively
evaluated. It has been said that the social worker, in a variety of
functional roles at various operating levels, is continually focused
on the relationship of man to his environment with the purpose of
effecting a constructive interrelationship. Traditionally, knowledge
of the community and resourcefulness in its use for the individual
constituted a large part of social work activity. With deepened insight into the nature of man and his needs for personality growth,
this area of activity assumes even greater importance than formerly.
In teamwork with other professions it is often the area of competence unique to social work, certain other knowledges and skills
being shared.

In the last twenty years there has been fluctuating emphasis on
helping the individual use the environment. There have been periods
of overemphasis on helping the individual in the vacuum of the
social worker's office. A corrective trend today gives proper place to
the importance of environmental lacks and stresses and to reality
opportunities in the re-education and healing of individuals. Accordingly, renewed recognition is being given to the knowledge and
skill involved in discriminative use of community resources. The
educational focus is on helping the student become resourceful in
strengthening the client's resourcefulness. This implies teaching differential help and differential use of community resources in relation
to clients' needs, strivings, and capacity to participate in planning.
The aim is to convey the idea that community resources should be
used in such a way as to become an integral part of the study, diagnostic, and helping process. Teaching this area of learning has a
threefold focus.

a) The evaluation of the worker's use of the resources in relation
to the client's needs, inclinations, and capacities is considered

repetitively in case after case to appraise whether the worker conceivably used community resources to the utmost. The focus is on the relationship of the worker's activity in this area and the outcome. Were there glaring omissions? Did he attempt to extend his own function and his agency's bounds instead of referring the client elsewhere or drawing on adjunctive services? Were the reality pressures of the environment ignored and the use of external resources overlooked in giving priority to direct psychological treatment of the individual? If so, was this emphasis indicated diagnostically? There should be continuous appraisal of the part played in the helping process and in prognosis by the presence or absence of community resources or by the nature of their use. What losses and gains accrued for the individual and his family through this aspect of the worker's activity and helping emphasis? When resources were used, were they an integral part of treatment, that is, were they selected and used with the client's participation and with nice reference to his needs and capacities?

b) The evaluation of the worker's activity in relation to colleagues in other agencies, institutions, and professions is attempted. The use of the social service exchange is given careful consideration, and principles are formulated for its use, in relation to both the client's needs and rights and the social worker's obligation to the profession and to the community.[11] As to the worker's approach to other agencies, was it one to win co-operation, arouse antagonism, or produce confusion? Careful study of referring procedures from the standpoint both of the client and of the resource should be habitual.

c) There is evaluation also of the broad social import of interagency co-operative work as it shows up in specific cases. Was there a sound division of labor in this instance? Have roles of responsibility been defined and aligned to safeguard the client, or has he been lost in the shuffle? Is the plan of co-operation oriented primarily to the client's need and welfare or to the greater convenience or prestige values of the several agencies? As often as possible, there should be consideration of whether a particular plan would be sound general practice; for example, what would it mean to all the children

11. For point of view taught see Helen H. Perlman, "The Case Worker's Use of Collateral Information," *Social Casework*, XXXII (October, 1951), 325–32; see also Charlotte Towle, "The Client's Rights and the Use of the Social Service Exchange," *Social Service Review*, Vol. XXIII, No. 1 (March, 1949).

served by a school social work program if the workers undertook play therapy of individual children rather than using other measures or securing these services elsewhere? What will it mean in the long run for sound social service to families if private agencies supplement the services of public agencies through assuming a major casework responsibility, while the public agency limits itself to financial assistance? What community resources were needed but lacking in a given case to make effective the helping process of a specific agency?

In summary it might be said that in teaching "the community" the aim is threefold. First, to give the student essential knowledge and skill for differential use of resources in the light of the individual's needs and capacities; second, to make him aware of the interdependence of social casework, social welfare administration, group work, and community organization; third, to engender a sense of responsibility to make known findings in order that essential community resources may be developed and existing ones adequately co-ordinated.

2. *As a Means To Effect Change in the Learner*

Consideration of the community does not at the start make the emotional demand of certain other areas of learning although later it may arouse considerable feeling. The student again will use all that he is learning of orderly thinking and appropriate feeling, his newly gained understanding of human behavior, and notably what he is being able to incorporate of purposeful working relationships. As these faculties are directed toward the social order, he has an opportunity to give vent to feeling caused in other areas, through envisaging "making things right." Here are tangible things to be done, activity, initiative, and aggression possible toward organized people, who are not defenseless. Later, as students gradually get the sense of their helplessness as caseworkers in the administrative hierarchy and a sense of the slowness of social change, teachers in the casework classroom and the field will need to help them with their frustration. In the classroom it is possible to direct them to other course contents, for knowledge and understanding of means to effect change. Thus casework may inspire and give meaning and purpose to other contents in the curriculum. It has occurred at times, fortunately now past, that social work educators in fields other than casework have had just cause to resent the siren role played by their colleagues in casework. Students have been lured away from vital interest in anything else. Perhaps this has been due in part to the content and method in teaching which has prevailed elsewhere. As instructors in other sequences rely less on imparting information didactically and use concrete materials in order that the learners may participate in problem-solving; as they increasingly convey factual knowledge in a frame of reference of generic concepts; as they orient their teaching to a basic understanding of the learner and the learning process, as has occurred in social casework to a greater degree than elsewhere, the other sequences will engage learners more vitally than they have in the past. Within social casework teaching in classroom and field, repeated consideration of the import of other subject matter, for a consistent emphasis on the interdependence of the fields of activity within social work, should strengthen the student's identification with the profession as a whole and thus motivate learning in other areas of the curriculum than in social casework.

VI. KNOWLEDGE OF HISTORY AND UNDERSTANDING OF ITS USE

1. As a Means to Professional Wisdom

For the solution of social problems this area of learning is taught in social casework as well as in all other course sequences. The members of a profession have responsibility for the evolution of its practice. It is their charge to exert effort that history may not retrogressively repeat itself.[12]

This obligation is a difficult one to discharge in social work. Social work always is practiced under urgent conditions. Social workers must make emergency decisions under pressure of changing circumstances, timed by forces beyond their control. It is easy for social workers to cultivate immediacy and to assign recurrent shortsightedness to pressures of time and circumstance. Throughout the curriculum, history is taught both as a content of knowledge and as a method. It is important that students get a sense that the profession's wisdom has not been born of this generation nor need it die with it.

12. Charlotte Towle, "The Classroom Teacher as Practitioner," *Social Service Review*, Vol. XXII, No. 3 (September, 1948); see also in *Social Work as Human Relations* (New York: Columbia University Press, 1949).

Accordingly, it is desirable to teach trends in thinking and practice. The pressure of the current scene on the integrative capacity of the student makes it difficult to teach the evolution of social casework practice more than fragmentarily in the time allotted. The character of social casework literature does not facilitate teaching trends, in that it is not "cumulative and structured."[13] For historical perspective beyond the span of time of his own experience, the instructor must engage in laborious research and largely do his own synthesizing.

2. For Skill in Problem-solving

Students are habituated to a historical approach in their use of an orderly way of thinking which approximates scientific method. This occurs most often as students repetitively explore the onset and development of a client's problem, as they look to the past in his life-experience to explain his present strength and weakness and to predict his potentials in the use of help. It occurs also throughout the curriculum as they reflect upon social attitudes encountered in individuals and groups and deliberate upon the possibilities of and the means to effecting change in those attitudes. It is realistic for the social caseworker to be concerned to know not only the purpose attitudes serve people in the present but also how deeply rooted they are in the past. One of the first steps in understanding an agency, in order quickly to use it competently and creatively, is to know the evolution of its program. How it got this way has decisive import for where it may go from here. It has import also for what use one can make of it today. In social casework, as elsewhere in the curriculum, students must experience again and again from varying angles "history's power to evoke and to solve problems still unstated and unrecognized." This element, in that it is recurrent throughout the curriculum, can constitute an integrative force, if taught systematically and dynamically, that is, with the purpose of solving a present problem. The attainment of historical perspective in social casework is greatly facilitated when history courses are not of the narrative type, that is, a recounting of a series of events. Students in

13. For development of this point see Roger W. Little, "The Literature of Social Casework," *Social Casework*, XXXIII (July, 1952), 287–91; see also Dora Goldstine, "The Literature of Medical Social Work: Review and Evaluation," *Social Service Review*, XXVII (September, 1953), 316–28.

the School of Social Service Administration at the University of Chicago for many years were privileged to study with Edith Abbott and to benefit by her rare ability to make the past come alive in the present. As this ability has been possessed by her successors, the carry-over to the casework classroom has been obvious in the student's readiness imaginatively to consider current issues as not entirely new ones.

In summary it might be said that to attain the objectives of professional education for social work, the areas of learning must be taught so as to instil a philosophical frame of mind. It is vitally important that social work students get a sense of their profession as an ongoing venture, always oriented to social change and responsible participation in effecting that change. A positive attitude toward change may be developed as students find continuity in it. This will come about as educators throughout the curriculum emphasize working principles, help students formulate philosophical concepts, stimulate comparative thinking, and convey historical perspective. This will come about also as educators consistently establish an orderly progression in their teaching within a course and within a series of courses. It is essential that school curriculum committees give careful consideration to the organization of learning experiences. Dr. Tyler states:

> The third major task of curriculum construction is the organization of learning experiences so that the cumulative effect of the whole series of them will be as great as possible in attaining the objectives of the school. . . . Each learning experience is not likely to show any marked effect, but if they are combined in such a fashion as to reinforce each other, they produce increasingly significant cumulative effects, with the result that profound changes and developments in the student may take place.[14]

Dr. Tyler presents three criteria by which to judge the organization of learning experience—continuity, sequence, and integration. *Continuity* implies that major elements should appear and reappear, so that important objectives are iterated and reiterated. *Sequence* means not only reiteration of important elements but progression at a broader and deeper level. *Integration* implies that the relationships between activities in the school and out of school shall be such that many opportunities will be provided for reinforcement of elements

14. Tyler, *op. cit.*, chap v.

to be learned from one field to another, as well as between school and out-of-school activities—that is, from one course sequence to another, from classroom to field work, from total educational experience to life-experience in general.

We turn now to more specific considerations in the teaching of social casework. At the University of Chicago, in order that the integrative task may not exceed the student's integrative capacity, the courses which comprise the social casework series have been structured with regard for cumulative effect through the continuity, sequence, and integration of their areas of learning. In teaching students to know, to think, and to feel with an intent to understand in order to help, we necessarily are concerned with their development beyond intellectual endurance. We therefore have tried to have our methods express our understanding of the student's needs and responses in this learning process.

CHAPTER 10

Selection and Arrangement of Case Material and the Use of Readings

We present the educational rationale for the selection and arrangement of case material and the use of readings in a sequence of four out of five required classroom courses in social casework. These courses extend over the first two quarters of the first year and the first two quarters of the second year in the two-year program for the Master's degree in social work. The social treatment sequence, which consists of courses in social casework, psychiatry, and health and disease, is one part of a comprehensive program of study that includes sequences in organization and administration of welfare services and social research methods. More specifically, within the social treatment sequence, these four courses are given in a context of six quarters of supervised social casework practice and four closely related courses in psychiatry and health and disease. The latter are undertaken in the first year and, ordinarily, are completed in the fourth quarter. It is recalled that in this program social casework, beyond training for this practice, is regarded as one means to effect the changes that social work education aims at bringing about in the learner. Furthermore, it is regarded as a basic process with a vital contribution to make to other areas of study and practice.

As an integral part of professional education for social work, the basic aims of social work education are the aims of social casework training. As in sound education at all levels, the objectives of social work education throughout are determined by the changes which must be effected in the learner in order that he may meet the demands of his profession in society. For the cumulative effect necessary to produce these desired changes, the social work educator is concerned to arrange learning experiences in all parts of the curriculum so that an essential degree of continuity, sequence, and integration may be attained. This discussion attempts to show the effect of this concern on the educational practices in one school, in the selection of case materials for progression of learning in social casework.[1]

I. TRADITIONAL PATTERNS AND NEW PATTERNS

Since changes to be effected in the learner should be set in operation early, we regard the first social casework course as a basic course, an introduction to the whole, rather than as a presentation of a part. Not only should elementary knowledge in all areas have been imparted, but also in this first pattern-setting venture the student should have experienced from the start the orderly way of thinking which he will use throughout social work. Likewise, he should have undergone some change in feeling as he has gained intellectual awareness of feelings appropriate to social work. Furthermore, he should have learned the rudiments of doing, that is, of constructive helping. The basic social casework course should be so structured and so taught that, in the final summary in which the instructor helps the student envisage retrospectively where he has come and prospectively where he will go, the instructor will be able realistically to say: "You know something of all there is to social casework. From now on in new and more complex situations we will be extending and deepening what you now know."

This concept of beginning with the whole in teaching social casework represents a departure from traditional educational practices. Traditionally, the casework sequence has been structured like a string of beads, one aspect of learning after another. Agency procedures and community resources, the instruments of social casework, often composed the first bead in the strand. The last bead, that luminous one, knowledge and understanding of human behavior and psychopathology as applied in casework, often was awaited restively and longingly, only to be annexed too late to show, that is, too late for incorporation. Timed thus, it tended to create a dichotomy between agency procedures and casework,

1. Ralph W. Tyler, "Distinctive Attributes of Education for the Professions," *Social Work Journal*, XXX, No. 2 (April, 1952); see also Tyler, "Basic Principles of Curriculum and Instruction," *Syllabus for Education*, No. 360 (Chicago: University of Chicago Press, 1950).

between casework and psychotherapy. This bead-stringing procedure in structuring casework sequences has undergone modification throughout social work education, but vestiges of the practice remain.

The breakdown of the casework sequence into parts has been determined, variously, by such factors as the nature of the problem, agency settings, age periods of individuals, methods, and skills. For example, courses commonly are designed as follows: casework with delinquents, the handicapped, children, adolescents, the aged; casework in schools, courts, hospitals, and the like; courses in interviewing, in counseling, in recording, and in the worker-client relationship. An educational principle on which this method of presentation has been based has been a concern not to give too much all at once, in the interest of emotional equilibrium of the learner. Hence one teaches part by part, and thus gradually one builds up the whole. It is our opinion that fragmentation does not aid integration but, instead, that integration is facilitated through continuously teaching the parts in relation to the whole. We try to avoid the too much too fast, through an orderly progression which implies relating the new to the old. We partialize at the start through not presenting exhaustively any one part. For example, in the first casework course we teach the rudiments of the worker-client relationship, whereas in the second course this part of the whole is extended and deepened. In the fourth quarter this area of learning is emphasized and taught to the utmost of our knowledge and understanding. The same principle obtains in the teaching of each area of learning, such as understanding of human behavior, use of the agency, the community, and the like.

To facilitate integration, we consider it important also to establish the habit of generalizing from the start. We select cases which lend themselves to comparison and teach them in triads or pairs. We continue this practice throughout the casework series. As we leave each case, it is with the acknowledgment that we will never encounter just this situation again, but with the question, What have we learned here for use elsewhere? As we leave each course, there is an attempt to summarize comparatively the concepts and principles as they have emerged in the various cases discussed throughout the quarter. Traditionally, social casework teaching has emphasized the uniqueness of each case situation and intrenched an attitude of not daring to generalize. As students enter the first course, they seek precedents and react with anxiety to the high degree of differential thinking that obtains in social casework. Traditionally, a natural impulse toward integration has been broken down rather than schooled in the early stages of social casework learning. We consider it important, therefore, that, from the very start, students become habituated to comparative thinking, case by case, and to periodic attempts at generalization, as in course summaries.

We have undertaken to teach generic social casework progressively for four quarters rather than to devote the third and fourth quarters to social casework in a specialized setting, as medical social work, psychiatric social work, child-welfare casework, family social work, school social work, and the like. Our case selection therefore includes a range of settings from the first course through the fourth course. We attempt to teach students to know, to think, to feel, and to understand in order to do what is appropriate to social casework, in a variety of settings, through experiencing all areas of learning continuously.[2] A given course will emphasize certain areas more than others, and each course may be said to have a predominant emphasis. As will be shown, each course has the objective of extending and deepening the learning of the preceding course in order that the student may be taught what he needs to know for competent performance as a social caseworker. We have had several reasons for this educational practice. The first and foremost reason is our conviction that the principles and processes of casework are basically and essentially the same wherever casework is practiced. Furthermore, we have found that the generic method aids the integration of learning. In the traditional pattern, that of teaching setting courses as advanced courses, it is more difficult to sustain an orderly comprehensive progression in learning as a means to integration.

When one structures a course with reference to a particular setting, primary concern with the function of the agency, the scope of the problems, and the services leads one to select cases which typify

2. See chap. 9.

the service as comprehensively as possible. Hence one is prone to get a range from simple to complex casework situations, and so one might repeat in an advanced course cases sufficiently simple to be in the first or second casework course rather than in the third or fourth course. While repetition is an essential element in learning, it should be repetition which moves ahead, which extends and deepens. If an instructor's focus is on the advancement of learning from a lesser to a greater demand on the learner, then when she structures a psychiatric social work course or a medical social work course, it will be difficult to have it truly representative of the setting; she can only select the relatively more complex situations, which would have the weakness of conveying the erroneous impression that this selection is typical. In short, a setting course cannot be equated with an advanced course. When we make them advanced we give an atypical setting course.

The second factor operating against the use of the setting course as an advanced course, if learning is to progress comprehensively, is that one area of learning tends to become overweighted to the neglect of others. The factors peculiar to the setting are emphasized through repetition, if through no other means. For example, in a medical setting, illness and its meaning to people, working relationships with doctors and other hospital personnel, community resources determined by the nature of the problem, and the world of the sick as differentiated from the world of the well fill the whole horizon. Now it is true that the general principles in helping people and in working with people in this experience could well be carried over to any and every other setting, but integration is more difficult. A greater burden is placed on the instructor to help the students comprehend that much of what they are learning here is not peculiar to this setting but has general import. In several years of teaching courses in psychiatric social work in which the cases were largely from clinics and hospitals to an undifferentiated group of students for use elsewhere, the author was repeatedly frustrated on hearing them say, or on reading their regretful comments to the effect that: "This has been an interesting, inspiring course. I am sorry I am working in an agency where I won't have a chance to use any of it." This occurred in spite of the fact that, aware of the problem of transfer of learning, the instructor had insistently pointed out general import and had almost routinely closed every case with a class discussion and some formulation in the vein: We will never see this case again. What have we learned here which may apply elsewhere, in other cases, in other settings? Repeatedly, assignments also were designed to direct thinking beyond setting. For example, in the case of Thomas Corrigan, a youngster treated through play sessions in a pediatric child-guidance clinic, such assignments were given as the following:[3] "Assume that you encounter Thomas in a social agency in a community lacking psychiatric resources, so that play therapy sessions would not be possible—state specifically what you might do to help him. Give the reasons for your choice of helping efforts." It has been our experience that this problem of transfer of learning is greatly diminished when advanced learning occurs through cases selected from the gamut of social agencies. Students experience the common elements, the common demands, the universality of certain working principles, the general nature of the casework process. Through the communication which obtains between students, they are close to the experience of their colleagues, who go from the same class to a variety of field-work settings. This intrenches the realization that what they have learned in class should be useful in whatever setting they may eventually practice.

Owing to the fact that agency function and structure are studied case by case, continuously throughout the social casework sequence in terms of its effects on social casework practice, certain decisive differences in settings are not ignored.[4] For their future migrations all students have the opportunity to learn at least enough of the differences to establish the point that it is important always to take setting factors into account and to orient one's work to agency structure and function. It is a worker's responsibility, therefore, to know the agency's peculiarities and to identify the ways in which they fashion the service. It is important with this scheme, as with any other organization of social casework class content, that the field supervisor be conversant with what is being taught in the classroom and what is not being taught. In so far as she had relied on the classroom to teach heavily the problems, the characteristics, the

3. See case of Thomas Corrigan in Charlotte Towle, *Social Case Records from Psychiatric Clinics, with Discussion Notes* (Chicago: University of Chicago Press, 1941).

4. See chap. 9.

peculiarities of her particular agency, she might well assume greater responsibility for this area of learning.

It is our experience that this content is taught more reliably and effectively in the field. It involves an "area of doing" which is better taught in practice than theoretically. Furthermore, if in the past supervisors relied heavily on class instruction for this, we failed them in large measure. For example, at any one time our classroom case selection in psychiatric social work did not cover comprehensively the manifold variations in our psychiatric field centers. For a period of time psychiatric social work students were having field work in a social service department of a large state mental hospital, in the teaching-research centers of a medical school and a state hospital system, in a large public child-guidance clinic, in a small teaching-research psychiatric service in a pediatrics hospital, in a neuropsychiatric service in a large general hospital serving both adults and children, in a small private institution for emotionally disturbed children, in the psychopathic hospital and the convalescent center of a Veterans Administration Hospital, and the mental hygiene clinic of a regional office of the Veterans Administration. It is obvious that we would teach nothing but the trappings of setting if in a two-quarter psychiatric social work course we were to attempt to cover the peculiarities of structure and function and administrative authority which, to a significant extent, shape social service activity from intake to case termination in each center; if this is to be taught in the classroom so that order emerges from a great array of variable factors, there will have to be a comprehensive attempt to present the common denominators and the essential differences in a range of settings. Our solution of this problem has been a final fifth course in the casework series, which summarizes and formulates earlier case-by-case teaching on the effect of agency structure and function on casework practice. We proceed now to a consideration of the selection and arrangement of case material as one means to the educational aims which have been specified.

II. THE BEGINNING COURSE

1. *Case Selection for a Basic Learning Experience*

On what basis shall cases be selected for an orderly progression from lesser to greater demands on the learner? Shall selection be

made, as traditionally, on the basis of the nature of the problem, the
age or economic status of the client, the type of agency setting, or
the skill required of the worker? Certainly, in order to represent the
field of practice realistically, one must present a range of life-experiences decisive for social maladjustment or adjustment; a number
of problematic situations; a range in mental and emotional conditions, normal to pathological; a number of age, cultural, and economic levels; a variety of agency settings; and a comprehensive
range of services and kinds of help that characterize social casework treatment.

In considering the basis for selection of cases, our first question
was: Shall it be the nature of the problem? Our immediate answer
was: No, not simply that! Though we help people solve problems, we
do not have stock remedies for their solution. It is the person who
has the problem rather than the problem in itself which is continuously of primary concern to the social caseworker and to the
agency the services of which he administers. It is not the person's
problem which determines our way of doing, so much as the meaning of the problem to him. Perhaps, then, simplicity or complexity
is introduced in large part through the individual's relationship to
his problem in terms of its meaning for him, his way of responding
to it, the purpose served by his response, and his capacity for dealing with the problem and for changing his response. The latter
implies also the simplicity or complexity of social circumstances as
they affect the individual's reaction and capacities.

From this point of view, for the beginning course we have
selected from public and private agencies cases in which clients are
victims of circumstance. There is a simple and obvious connection
between their social problems, their disturbed feelings about their
problems, and their external circumstances. Furthermore, their feelings are commensurate with the extent of the stress. Their defenses
bespeak normal ego developmnt, in that they are not rigid and
persistent but serve the purpose of helping the individuals maintain
socially acceptable adaptations. Clients in these case situations are
all men and women seeking financial assistance in public or private
agencies.[5] The need for this assistance is occasioned by unemploy-

5. This is not to imply that financial assistance cases are in and of themselves
simple. It is desirable that this resource recur throughout the progression of

ment, low wages in a large family, illness, or death of the wage-earner. The children in some of the families are relatively undisturbed individuals for whose development preventive measures are indicated. In those instances in which behavior problems occur, the relationship between adverse circumstances and behavior is clear. The possibility of the development of pathology under continued social stress is shown clearly in a nine-year-old's predelinquent behavior, the onset of which followed the death of his father and his mother's absorption in grief, in work outside the home, and in her pregnancy. It is shown also in the reaction of one man to his previous Works Progress Administration experience.[6] This is a man who had shown unusual fortitude and resourcefulness through long years of precarious living and adverse experiences but who, as he seeks private employment, is obsessed with the idea that no employer will want him because he has worked for the WPA. While this attitude had a realistic basis at the time of its inception, it is persisting unrealistically in spite of social and economic change that has brought a change in employer attitudes. Thus the student can begin to see how deeper emotional involvements may develop gradually under prolonged social stress. He may also recognize the importance for the modification of self-defeating attitudes of the worker's supportive activity in helping the man secure a job. As preparation for the cases which follow in the second course, the final case in the beginning course is that of an unmarried mother applying for an Aid to Dependent Children grant. Her conflict with a repressive, hostile mother, upon whom she has been financially dependent but from whom she becomes ready to emancipate herself as she receives economic support, enables students to experience the deeper psychological import of financial assistance. Without having to become involved with all the ramifications of the girl's behavior, they see change in attitudes through the modification of social circumstances as well as through some help given through the interview in dealing with her feelings about the situation.

Why have we chosen these cases? What educational principles

---

courses in order that students may not infer that giving money involves less skill than do other services.

6. The case examples are not from those currently taught. The principles illustrated still obtain in our case selection, which, however, would reflect the present social and economic scene.

dictated these choices? One begins where the learner is. One does not make an unrealistic intellectual and emotional demand. The student is undertaking to learn to help people. A first essential is to understand the person needing help, to understand at least something of the meaning of his problem to him and the meaning of this experience of having to ask for and take help. This demands some feeling with the person. It implies putting one's self into his shoes and viewing his situation as far as possible through his eyes, while retaining one's own vision. To relate to a person, one must identify with him in some measure. With whom do we most readily identify? Obviously, with people who are most acceptable, least strange, least unlike ourselves, with those for whom we have some respect, whose responses are rational and understandable. As the student enters social work, where is he in his thinking and feeling about himself and about those "other people" who need help? There is variation here; but, since our educational approach must be geared to the usual rather than to the unusual, we are guided by what has commonly been encountered in the educable inexperienced student at this stage of the game. His conscious concept of himself is of an adequate, strong, resourceful, rational young adult who under ordinary circumstances would not need help. At least he is striving for this kind of selfhood, and hence he will identify more readily with rational people whose need for help is understandable and acceptable, in that it arises out of exceptional circumstances. We therefore select exceptional circumstances rather than exceptional people in the beginning course, in order that the student may identify without ambivalent feeling. It is well for him to be able to feel: "There but for the grace of God go I."

We select these cases also in order that the student's first pattern-setting vicarious experience in a helping relationship may be with individuals whom he can respect rather than pity or blame. This is decisively important in relation to the methods of social work as determined by its philosophy. The current sound methodology of social work has been designed with serious intent to express its deep conviction as to the individual worth of man; its high regard for the importance of individual differences and man's right to be self-determining within social limits; its faith in the inner resources of man for growth under conditions favorable for something more than survival; and, finally, its realistic awareness that growth comes from within and that the helping efforts of social work are best employed in using and affirming the individual's strengths rather than in overcoming his weaknesses and reforming his personality. The selection of clients whom the student can respect is important also in relation to the preconceptions he brings with him. Often the beginning student anticipates that as a social worker he will be dealing with weak, helpless, pathological, different people who need to have much done for them and who will need to be made over in some measure. The student's feelings about this are often ambivalent. Gratification, on the one hand, at the prospect of re-fashioning people alternates with fear, on the other, of not being equal to the task, at least not immediately. This selection of cases affords an opportunity for the student immediately to begin to change his feelings about people who seek help. It avoids the affirmation of his less desirable reform motivation at a time when he has not the safeguard of knowledge to understand weakness and pathology and thereby the wherewithal to respect the individual with his limitations. We say "less desirable" motivation in spite of the fact that we would not give much for the social worker who does not bring into the field some concern to reform the world and the people in it. However, until the student has knowledge to begin to understand and differentiate between helping people change and making them over, this motivation is best directed toward circumstances rather than toward individual clients. More suitable cases, therefore, are those in which the clients have considerable capacity for change as social stress is alleviated.

2. Criteria of "Simplicity" in Demand on the Learner

These cases not only avoid making an unrealistic intellectual and emotional demand upon the student but also, from the positive standpoint, affirm the capacities that he brings, through demanding performance of which he is capable. Criteria for "simplicity" in case selection may be summarized as follows:

First, the people present well-focalized problems. The services indicated are obvious and procurable in some measure. The student identifying with the worker in the case record can envisage himself performing these services.

Second, the services are rendered in ways which call for negative as well as positive comment about agency resources and policies and about worker's activity. The student increasingly can feel that there is much to be done to improve conditions and that he could do as well as, or better than, the worker in practice. This is reassuring at the start, when the student needs to feel that his training will be wanted in the field for the improvement of practice. It is reassuring, too, because he is fearing his own incompetence and has anxiety about not serving clients sufficiently well. At the same time, something helpful is done in all the cases, so that the student can identify with the helping process and with social work as a worth-while effort.

Third, ready identification with the client is possible because of his essential normalcy. Thus the clients do not bring excessive need to the relationship, so that feeling with, and even a bit like, the client does not make a demand beyond the student's capacity for the management of the relationship.

Fourth, the cause-and-effect relationships are clear. This includes the relationship between social circumstance and the problem with which the client seeks help as well as the relationship between the client's feelings and the agency services. The feeling shown by clients is manifested in relatively pure form rather than in disguise. The clients are concerned with present problems. Their pasts are not revealed to any extent as operating in the present. Hence one does not have to go to factors remote in time to explain difficulties. All this implies that the diagnostic thinking demanded of the student requires a minimum of knowledge of human behavior. The cases lend themselves to inductive reasoning. The inferences arrived at by the class, for the most part, are convincingly supported by the evidence at hand. There are, however, enough gaps in evidence and enough obscurities in the clients' responses to set in operation the practice of recognizing the need for more evidence as well as for attempting to see beneath appearances and for thinking tentatively rather than conclusively.

Finally, this selection of cases avoids making an unrealistic emotional demand on the learner. The clients considered do not manifest great dependency, unsocial attitudes, or the extremes of behavior that offend, shock, or provoke anxiety through activating

repressed feelings and conflicts. Such cases are introduced gradually as the student has acquired knowledge for understanding himself
and others.

This selection has been guided by continuous concern to have the
student's integrative capacity equal the integrative task in the interest of sustaining his emotional equilibrium. In keeping the intensity of affect as low as possible at the start, it has been our conviction that the student could, through feelings of competence, gain
a foothold for standing up to an increasing emotional demand as
learning proceeds. Furthermore, through not being engulfed at the
start, he should be free to use his energy and his intellect resourcefully and to begin to become better acquainted with, and less fearful of, his own feelings. In the beginning course, students learn that
a worker's feelings are expressed deviously, if not overtly, and that it
is better to understand and regulate them than to repress them. Self-
awareness develops largely because the material and the conduct
of this first learning experience elicit a small, rather than a large,
degree of negative affect. We can permit ourselves to know our
negative selves a little at a time in the context of a situation where
we can also freely enact our positive attitudes and impulses.

III. THE SECOND COURSE

1. *Selection of Cases for Progression in Learning*

As we turn to the case selection in the second course, it is well
to recall that our criterion of simplicity or complexity is the individual's relationship to his problem. We move forward from people
who are victims of circumstances to people who have had some
part in creating their problems or whose problems have activated
underlying personality conflicts. In contrast to those included in the
beginning course, these clients are more deeply upset emotionally
by their problems and more deeply implicated in them. The children in the family situations studied are those with adverse life-
circumstances that are impeding growth and creating behavior problems. Disturbed family relationships are prominent. Cases with gross
psychopathology have been included in this course when work with
relatives and supportive measures for the patient have not demanded
knowledge of the dynamics of the personality disorders.

As in the beginning course, the clients are people who are seeking help with social problems. They apply or are referred because they need specific services rather than help with troubled relationships or their own personality disturbance per se. To some extent they see and feel themselves as victims of circumstance; and to a considerable extent they are, for, despite their own part in creating the social problems, they now have realistic adversity with which they want and need help. For example, there are requests for financial assistance; for child placement in a case involving marital conflict and in another involving hospitalization of a mother for mental illness; for help in securing prenatal care and living arrangements for a sixteen-year-old girl whose forced marriage culminated in separation and who is unable to live in the home of either of her divorced parents because of marked conflict with step-parents and father; finally, for help in planning with the family of a child who is retarded in school and in her social relationships. Thus the case selection in the second course repeats the old in its focus on helping people through specific services, but it introduces the new. There are differences in the people themselves, as shown in their responses to their problems, their capacities for dealing with them, and their capacities for change. There is also much greater intricacy of the social circumstances. It is well to recall that the new element has been forecast in the beginning course through two cases in which the students felt the impact of the idea that social stress, particularly if prolonged, may be internalized to produce personality problems. The old has been repeated in the new also, in that here, too, a number of the people, in spite of their more marked emotional disturbance, have sufficient ego strength to make productive use of help. A few examples are given to show the nature of the progression in demands on the learner that occurs through this selection of cases.

The first case of this second quarter repeats the first case of the first quarter, in that it presents an individual, formerly in good economic circumstances, who is applying for financial assistance for the first time. In the first quarter, the man concerned showed discomfort about asking for and taking help and considerable humiliation over being unemployed. These disturbed feelings, which had interfered with realistic activity in securing a job, were readily allayed through interpretation of his right to assistance and through help given in a way that restored his confidence in himself. He quickly moved from acceptance of agency investigation procedures into taking a job with less prestige value than his former one and into adapting his expenditure to his income. In the second quarter, the woman concerned, whose husband had suffered a stroke, likewise showed discomfort over asking for help and humiliation over her plight. Interpretation of her right to assistance did not ease the social stigma. In spite of the fact that she had every justification in terms of her age, her long role as housewife, her husband's need for her services at home, and the forces beyond her control which had brought disaster, she manifested a rigid and unmodifiable resistance to taking help except on her own terms—that there be no investigation. Certain meager and uncertain contributions from relatives and friends made it possible for her to maintain her strong defenses against taking help from an agency. The interviews, however, show clearly that the presumed social stigma had a deeper emotional significance to this woman than to the man studied earlier. The case presents a new and more complex diagnostic task, greater difficulties in handling resistance in the application process, as well as the opportunity to engage in the controversial question surrounding agency policies—How rigid should they be? Does one ever waive them? What might have been the import in the continuing helping relationship had they been waived in this instance? The latter question calls into play thinking, as far as the evidence permits, on the significance of this woman's response.

In the second course the type of services sought, as determined by the nature of the problems and the personality needs of the individuals and their families, also extends and deepens the student's learning experience in the use of the agency, the handling of collaborative relationships, and the use of community resources. In the beginning course the settings were entirely family welfare agencies, public and private.[7] In this second course two cases are from private family agencies. Two are from social service depart-

7. The initial field-work assignment ordinarily is in a family agency, hence this selection. Other agencies could be included, but the decisive point is not to have a wide range in types of agency at the start.

ments in public school systems, and two are from child-placing agencies. One of the clients was referred for the placement of his children after considerable service in a public assistance agency. Thus, not only are new kinds of agencies introduced but also there is the new learning experience of social service within a "host" agency. The child-placing agency in its work with own parents, with foster-parents, and with children introduces new complexity.

Both these child-placement cases afford study of the worker's efforts to prepare children for separation from their own parents, through interpretation in advance and through engaging their participation in the process. One of these cases is particularly rich in presenting a summarization of work done with own parents prior to and following the child's placement. The student has the opportunity through the material recorded to experience two parents, neither one of whom wants or assumes a responsible parental role and both of whom resist being head of the family. The evidence permits understanding of their personality limitations and of their sheer inability to meet each other's or their children's needs constructively. In contrast, the same case affords opportunity for the study of the interplay of normal family life in the home-finding study and supervisory reports on the foster-home. The realignment of family interrelationships following the entrance of the foster-child is dramatically clear and enables the student to get the feel of a family as a dynamic whole in which equilibrium is maintained through the proper balance of its constantly changing parts. Introduce a new member, and reorganization must occur for the reintegration of the family as a stable group again. Through this case and several others there is deepened study of the interplay of family life and of the import of family relationships in the growth and social adjustment of the individual.

The nature of the problems in relation to the more complex settings moves learning ahead in affording study of collaborative relationships. The two cases in school systems provide opportunity for consideration not only of the function of social service but also of ways of co-operating with school officials and teachers in order that the function may be fulfilled. In addition, these and other cases afford study of collaborative relationships between school and

social service; between child-guidance clinics and public health nursing service; between school social service and a public assistance
agency; between child-placing agency and family agency; between
family agency and industrial nursing service; between family
agency and physician and clergyman. The referral sources in these
cases introduce a new element, in that three clients applied on
being referred by people who had authority values for them—
school, public assistance agency, and father—whereas all the clients
in the beginning course made direct application.

This factor introduces consideration of the matter of working
through certain resistances in the application process and also of
establishing and sustaining working relationships with referral
sources. In the beginning course, learning in this area of collaborative relationship and of use of agency resources consisted
largely of acquaintance with a few resources and discussion of a
few simple procedures for their use. The interagency situations,
with one exception, were not problematic. The second course
affords study of more agencies and of more complicated interplay
of agencies, as well as discussion of lines of responsibility and
methods for solving problems in interagency relationship as they
show up in the handling of an individual case.

The final case in this course repeats the final one in the preceding
course, in that both clients are adolescents who became pregnant
illegitimately. Both were able to make productive use of help, but
the process was much simpler in the first instance than in the
second. In the latter more actual help in practical matters was
sought and needed. Furthermore, the girl was being overtly rejected by both parents. More condemned socially than the first girl
and less well sustained in terms of a roof, financial support, and
continuity of relationship, she brought more mistrust and more
emotional need to the worker. In order to help her make productive
use of the services, in order to help her live through a traumatic
period, in order to help her look to and plan for the future, it was
essential that the worker know enough of her life-experiences to
understand the import of her responses within this helping relationship. In contrast to the earlier case, it was necessary to think
through the many ramifications of her experience and the implica-

tions of her behavior for determination both of the nature of her present need and of her capacity to use help. Thus study and diagnosis were extended and deepened.

There were more contacts with collaterals, in order to understand the client and to help her plan realistically. The referral circumstances were more complex, in that the first girl applied for assistance, whereas the second was referred by her hostile father, who turned her over to the agency with punitive threats. Thus, from the start and throughout the establishment and maintenance of a constructive working relationship, this case had certain complexities not implicit in the first situation. The case afforded an opportunity for the student to gain a comprehensive grasp of the nice balance between meeting dependency freely and affirming strengths; the establishment of a strong positive relationship in which the client's negative affect is understood and accepted but the enactment of her hostile impulses limited; the identity which the client assigns the worker in this instance as a needed parental substitute; and, finally, the specific ways in which the worker made this a corrective rather than a repetitive relationship in the light of the client's need and prior relationship experience. This final case, through the extended and deepened study of emotional development and personality structure which it affords, as well as through what it has to offer in the study of the conduct of the worker-client relationship, serves as a steppingstone to the second-year casework course.

We attempt to teach students to know, to think, to feel, to understand, in order to do competently through experiencing all areas of learning continuously. Emphasis, in itself essential for learning, comes about as certain cases are richer in one area of learning than another and as each course has a predominant emphasis as determined by the case selection and the student's stage of learning. By reason of the fact that we are working with individuals who have had some part in creating their problems or whose problems have activated underlying conflicts, the predominant focus in teaching the second course is logically on extended and deepened study of the interplay of family life and on exploration of the past to enlighten the present and to predict the future. Looking at the individual's past to explain his present reactions was touched on only fragmentarily in the first quarter. Systematic consideration of data on the individual's past with identification of gaps in our understanding due to gaps in the stream picture of his life-experience represents a new element. The use of the past in relation to the present, to build up a picture of the individual's personality needs and limitations and capacities, serves as a basis for tentative prognosis. Thus the attempt to predict what use the person might make of continued help, how he will get along without help, what will happen to this child or adult in terms of personality development or retrogression if stress continues—this looking to the future is another new learning experience. This attempt to predict may lead to the decision that we cannot venture a prediction. In order not to speculate wildly, we need certain evidence which is lacking. Thus gaps in the study process often are shown up by this systematic practice.

Focus on the interplay of family life and on the past of the individual extends and deepens learning from normal behavior to psychopathology. Prior to this course the student has had the first course in development of personality, and he is taking concurrently the second course in psychiatry—behavior disorders of children. It is necessary to draw heavily on his learning in these two courses and to direct him to certain readings which throw light on the behavior responses of the individuals in the cases. To a large extent, however, we depend upon the case analysis focused on family interplay and the past, to supplement and to make meaningful the learning in the psychiatry courses. There is continuously a two-way relationship between these two fields of study.

At this stage the student is thinking in terms of the needs, strivings, and defenses in the individual's struggle for equilibrium as groundwork for later, more systematic structuring of the personality, in terms of ego-superego integration and the mechanisms of defense. The start made in the beginning course in understanding the individual's ways of easing discomfort for equilibrium in the interest of keeping his powers intact is now extended and deepened. The ego's adaptations and the mechanisms of defense are identified and discussed in terms of their specific purposes in meeting need in relation to fear, guilt, and anxiety as well as for gratification which nurtures, for example, the need to escape, to deny, to minimize, to place responsibility elsewhere, as through projection, rationalization, or self-justication; the need to react against impulses, to compensate for lacks, to be self-punitive, to exploit others. The individual's need to come realistically to grips with a problem, through assumption of responsibility, through activity that solves the problem, or through endurance of denial and frustration, is repeatedly identified as a behavior response which has the same aim as the flight, reactive, or compensatory responses. It has the aim of maintaining the individual's equilibrium for survival on satisfying terms with himself and the world. The relatively constructive use of defenses and adaptations is stressed whenever possible throughout. This is in order that the student may build up early a respect for the individual's defenses and a habit of questioning—"What would he do, where would he be, without them? In the light of the purposes they are serving for him, can he change unless his situation changes? How can he use himself better in order to effect change in his situation which then may nurture him for growth?"

2. Criteria of Progression in Demand on the Learner

It is evident that learning leaps ahead in the second course. The emotional demand of learning mounts inevitably when we move from normal responses engendered by external stress to social and psychological stresses created by inner needs and tensions. Identification, the basic mechanism in learning, is complicated when most needed. This movement would constitute a big jump whenever taken, no matter how long postponed. And this learning cannot be postponed. It is evident in the beginning course that the student is feeling a strong push in this direction, through his own motivation in having chosen to do social work and through the pressure created by the demands in his field work. Already he has felt somewhat held back in the classroom as compared with the field. In spite of, or perhaps because of, the inner and outer pressures which prompt him to reach out for this learning experience, this second quarter in the casework classroom ordinarily is heavy going. The subject matter pushes the student around, now forward, now backward, and, hopefully, forward again. Here we encounter an integrative task, which is made heavier by the intense need and desire created by the tempo in the field. It is essential, therefore, that instructors support the learning process through carefully planned educational measures.

First, because the student's knowledge and grasp of essential subject matter is limited, cases should be selected which are rich in material for inductive reasoning, in order that inferences which the instructor is able to make by reason of his knowledge and experience when presented to the student may be convincingly supported by the case material at hand. Thus, in evaluating behavior responses, we may not inculcate the tendency to infer too much from too little and, through making an unrealistic demand, throw the student back on dichotomies and stereotypes as a defense against meager knowledge and limited understanding. As for stereotypes, we have in mind the facile use of such inferences as: "A broken appointment means resistance"; "Overprotection spells rejection"; "Gratitude means hostility"; "A client's struggle for self-dependence reveals a strong impulse toward, or wish for, dependence"; and the like. This involves selection of cases not only rich in cause-and-effect evidence for nonspeculative inferences but also lucid in showing feeling response in pure form rather than in disguise.

When there is disguise, the circumstances of the individual's life and his repeated response to them are recorded so as to support clearly the more remote inference; for example, material in which resentment over taking help is acted out in expressions of anger and obvious hostile self-assertion rather than that in which it is disguised by abject gratitude and submission, or material in which a client's verbal protests against dependency are repetitively belied by his dependency responses. We cannot be too emphatic in stating that this is not the stage of learning for the use of the subtle case or of the sketchy case rich in clues to several possibilities. The student is at the point of knowing just enough to seize on the clues and to press the instructor into developing the possibilities speculatively. In doing this, much didactic teaching is entailed in which the instructor may convey wide knowledge beyond the student's capacity to assimilate. When this occurs, frustration and anxiety result for the student on several counts. He feels helpless in knowing so little when obviously he should know so much. The inexperienced instructor needs to beware lest unconsciously she select such cases out of a need to demonstrate her competence far beyond that of the student. In such a case the student becomes a passive recipient rather than an active participant in the study process. Not having taken in the fine differentials and qualifying comments in the instructor's presentation, he is left to decry that "one guess is as good as another." This naturally promotes anxiety, for, after all, how can one be sure of guessing correctly or of learning to do so? Good guessers are born, not made.

Second, cases should be selected which support rather than disprove the fundamental concepts which the student is learning. For example, if one were teaching a course in nutrition, one would not early demonstrate a case in which, by all the laws of nutrition, the individual should have beriberi but instead is in a seemingly good state of health. Likewise in social work, one avoids a record in which a child's early life-experiences have been such as ordinarily to interfere with his growth, but instead one finds a child who is seemingly the exception. He has survived unusual adversity with rare capacity to get along well. Here one has either to postulate positive elements in his early life which were not made known or teach the subtleties of defense mechanisms beyond the student's stage of learning. Knowledge has not been assimilated sufficiently for him to make highly differential use of it. Integration is aided through some repetition of cases in which similar life-experiences produce the same outcome.[8]

Third, closely related to these first two points is the self-discipline which the instructor must exert in this course, where learning is widening and deepening at rapid tempo, not to give all she knows or not to dive to the depths when swimming in the shallows will suffice. The criterion often is what the student needs to know for the solution of the problem which the client presents or for competent rendering of the services which he seeks. Then again it may be desirable to use a case as a springboard to experience beyond its confines. Each case presents an individual problem in timing, as does each class. The placement of the case in the sequence also determines whether this is the time to hold back or to leap ahead a bit in preparation for what is coming next. It is in this connection that there is value in joint work by casework faculty members in structuring their casework courses as a whole and in defining broadly the use to be made of a

8. Tyler, "Basic Principles."

given case at any particular stage. The timing of the use of didactic instruction and the assignment of specific readings is important. Criteria for the differential use of didactic instruction have been dealt with elsewhere.[9] At this stage, for assimilation of much that is new, full opportunty for active participation in discussion is essential.

Fourth, in this course it is essential that an instructor consistently use the same method in studying each case, so that the student becomes habituated to a way of doing. Through repetition of method he will make it his own and feel that he knows his way into the mass of material which confronts him. When the instructor leads the group through diverse methods in case analysis, the student may be left floundering. He does not know where to start and how to proceed in orderly fashion. One may find him entangled in peeling the onion from the inside out rather than from the outside in. The orderly procedure which has been started in the beginning course should now be systematized further and made a more conscious process. Thus through repetition the student gets a sense of security. There is a way of doing on which one can rely to become competent. Both the prospect of competence and the case-to-case attainment of it ease anxiety.

Fifth, at this stage the method of comparative study of cases is particularly needed. We have arranged the cases in pairs which lend themselves to significant comparison for the formulation of principles. Also, comparison is made from certain cases to those studied in the first quarter, somewhat as has been indicated in our discussion of the first and last cases in the two courses. Retrospective comparison gives a sense of continuity and of progression. Students get a sense of their own movement as they find the old expanded and deepened in the new. When this occurs, discouragement gives way to hope, and thereby resistance is lowered. Often it is possible to project continuity and movement into the future through envisaging that this idea, this situation, this formulation, will recur next quarter. One may predict that we will probably go further with it then or that we will find ourselves modifying our thinking about this or modifying our use of that principle later. As in the beginning course, in order that learning may become a conscious process, the instructor

9. Helen H. Perlman, "The Lecture as a Method in Teaching Case Work," *Social Service Review*, XXV (March, 1951), 19–32.

continues the practice of closing each case with consideration of what has been learned here for use elsewhere. Repetition helps develop this as a habit of mind—the habit of searching for foresight through hindsight, the habit of generalizing to the extent that the experience lends itself to formulations, the habit of noting certain things to note. Thus we have one means to the end that professional education inculcate a habit of self-directed learning, which hopefully may wax strong with time.

In summary: Why have we selected the cases which we have described for this second stage of learning? The reasons constitute criteria for continuity of experience with greater complexity, criteria for a larger learning demand than prevailed in the beginning course.

First, one begins where the learner is in his current experience. The student is now well launched in field work in a family agency. He is motivated to learn about people who manifest problematic attitudes or whose disturbed feelings are creating social problems which take them into social agencies. The cases selected are rather typical of the clients now being worked with.

Second, the clients are sufficiently within the range of the normal, with sufficient adversity to justify some of their feelings and attitudes, that the student can identify, can feel with them, and can comprehend the logic of many of their responses. Furthermore, now one can expect a widened span of identification in the student through the learning experience of the first quarter. He has greater knowledge of the conditions of life which make for or inhibit growth, so that he can, to a greater degree, understand differences from himself. In relation to his reform motivation, he should have begun to differentiate between helping people change and making them over. Some of these clients resemble those of the first quarter in having considerable capacity for change as social stresses are alleviated and as they get limited help with their feelings about the stresses.

Third, these cases move ahead of those in the first quarter in presenting a few individuals who have limited capacity to use help. This frustration for the social worker makes a new emotional demand, but one which he is already meeting in the field, so that he needs the support of knowledge as conveyed in the classroom. This knowledge may enable him to begin to see many failures as implicit in the client rather than as the result of his own ineptitude. The abandonment of futile striving and mounting need to succeed may protect both client and worker from wasteful endeavor and additional frustration.

Fourth, the client's need for service which the agency has to offer permits the student, through identification with the worker, to be engaged in activities which he can envisage himself as learning and performing. Thus the learning in the beginning course is repeated and extended. The disturbed emotions of the client do not become the central focus of the helping relationship.

Fifth, there is an enlarged demand for greater precision in study and diagnosis, in order that it may serve as a basis in teaching differential help. The sources for understanding the individual are widened. He must now look more closely into the past, into family relationships, and beneath the surface for motivation. The emotional demand steps up markedly, for now the student's own underlying conflicts may be activated. As indicated previously, he will need the support of educational measures which diminish the affect which otherwise may interfere with integration. At least the intellectual process of case study need not leap ahead if cases are selected so that inductive thinking is possible and so that speculative inferences are not demanded.

Sixth, these clients often bring great emotional need to the relationship, so that the demand in this area may be considerably greater than with the clients in the beginning course. To safeguard against teaching more complexity than the student's background warrants, one selects cases which show workers who focus on the services sought and who do not become involved in meeting the client's need beyond the limits which he has set in seeking certain kinds of help.

As in the beginning course, the case selection has been guided by concern for the student's integrative capacity in relation to the integrative task. We have been less concerned to have it exceed the task. Knowing that the demands must mount rapidly, we accept as inevitable temporary phases of imbalance. One of the manifestations of imbalance is the student's tendency to discard the external stress factors for the internal ones. For mastery of the new he may become absorbed in the deeper implications, to the exclusion of more simple obvious factors in causation. We rely, therefore, on the student's resilience and on his capacity in the long run to integrate, even though his learning proceeds somewhat unevenly. We rely also on the educational measures described earlier to aid him in the ups and downs of learning. At this stage we expect him to have more negative affect to express than he readily or appropriately can express. However, the learning experience of the first quarter should have made him less fearful of his feelings in so far as, throughout, it has conveyed knowledge with which he may understand them and a consistent intent to understand on the part of the faculty. Presumably more secure than at the start in his relationships with field supervisor and faculty, he should become increasingly free to express doubts, fears, and disagreement. Field supervisors and faculty should help the student as an individual and in the group to express his reactions to case situations, to subject matter, and to educational demands, with a view to gaining understanding of his reactions, in order to regulate them in the interest of the client. There is variation in the time at which different students find learning traumatic, but the second quarter is one in which the student commonly shows growing pains, at which time faculty can elicit responses with the purpose of helping the student meet the demand that his feelings not be projected onto his work with clients and agency colleagues.

IV. THE COURSES IN THE SECOND YEAR

1. *The Selection of Cases for Progression in Learning*

The second-year case-discussion course extends over a period of the first two quarters of the second year. The student has had an interlude of one quarter, during which he has not had a casework course, the first two basic courses having accompanied the first two quarters of the three-quarter assignment in basic field work. He has thus had time for some assimilation of the knowledge and theory of his first casework and psychiatry courses in his three quarters of field work. The student has taken his comprehensive examination to qualify as a candidate for the Master's degree. He is now launched on his second year and now thinks of himself as "advanced" or at least as over the first big hump.

In contrast to the two first-year courses, the second-year course meets once a week rather than twice a week. Consistent with our concept of progression in learning, we think it desirable that the classes be more widely spaced, to permit time for reading and for the student to work on his own between sessions. The student is now beginning advanced field work in a "specialized" setting—child welfare, medical or psychiatric social work, etc.—in which the nature of the work approximates that of this course. Each class is composed of a cross-section of students placed in a number of settings. Cases are selected from the various settings rather than from the specialized setting of the individual student's field practice.

The cases are selected for the second-year course with the same criterion of simplicity or complexity, namely, the individual's relationship to his problem. We move forward from people who are applying for specific social services to people who in a social agency or clinic are applying primarily for help with a disturbed relationship or some form of social maladjustment due to emotional disturbance. They all present personality problems which are interfering with their family, social, school, or work adjustment. These people may also need help through social services which the agency has to offer, such as help in securing medical care, child placement, financial assistance, employment, and the like. The range in personality difficulties is from mild to gross pathology. The clients are like those in the second course of the first-year sequence, in that they are emotionally disturbed, they are having social difficulties as either cause or effect of their personality difficulties. A few have in common the need for social services. The decisive difference between the two groups is in the nature of the help sought. The former group saw their need for help as the social difficulty. The present group seek help either for themselves or for someone in a relationship in which they are deeply implicated so that they have a near-realization of their own involvement in the problem. The individual's own emotional disturbance or personality problem is in the foreground in the request for help.

Why does this factor of difference in nature of help sought make these cases a more advanced learning experience for students? The most notable reason is that these cases make a demand which requires deeper understanding of the worker-client relationship and its management. In this course there is a major emphasis on this area of learning. The nature of this demand and its educational implications will be discussed shortly.

If such cases as these are advanced, then the logic of having the advanced courses made up of a selection of cases from a variety of casework settings is obvious. It is logical because in current practice these clients are being helped by social workers collaborating in the traditional psychiatric clinical team, by social workers using psychiatric consultants, and also by social workers functioning alone without benefit of psychiatric help. One of the aims in including all the types of settings in which work of this nature is practiced is that the student may begin to differentiate the help given under one of the foregoing sets of circumstances from the help given under another set of circumstances. In this course there is sharpened focus on the ways in which agency function and professional function fashion diagnostic and treatment activities.

The following case typifies the teaching of this area of learning at this stage:

> The mother of an adopted child applies to a state child welfare agency in a western state, where there are no psychiatric resources, for help with her disturbed relationship with her child. The worker, through understanding the mother and through giving help of a guidance nature, nicely oriented to the mother's feelings and emotional capacities, contributes to an improved relationship. This case has great value in affording discussion of treatment measures of a more deep-reaching nature, which might have been possible in a clinic or in a social agency with close psychiatric consultation, had these resources been available. The student is given an appreciation, however, of the knowledge, understanding, and skill involved in the service rendered. The point is established also that, had the woman gone to a clinic, the initial exploratory procedure might have yielded a diagnostic formulation which would have indicated the appropriateness in a psychiatric clinic of the same kind of help given in the child welfare agency.

Knowledge and understanding of community resources and their use should become only a minor refrain in these courses for two reasons. First, since the cases are being treated largely through the interview in one agency, there is a minimum use of community resources. Second, where there is use of other resources, the records do not show the process whereby complexities in interagency relationship are handled, the thinking which prompted division of responsibility between agencies, or the choice of particular agencies.[10]

Orderly thinking in study, diagnosis, and treatment remains a major refrain in these courses, as in the first-year courses. Within this area, exploration of the past to explain the present and to predict the future continues throughout the first part of this course. In the last part we begin to infer tentatively more of the past from the present. The study of the interplay of family life continues, and its part in fashioning the personality structure becomes more precise than in the first-year courses. For example, in considering ego-super-ego development and integration or lack of integration, the signifi-cance of parental relationships is thought through more explicitly. There is a revived focus on social factors and external circumstances for their causative role and for their import in treatment. In the beginning course the focus was largely on external circumstance as the basis of emotional difficulty. In the second course and con-tinuing into the first part of the second year, the student, in spite of the instructor's efforts to keep the external and the internal to-gether, becomes absorbed in seeing and accepting the idea that the social problems were being created by the individual's inner conflict and disturbance. Many students could include both only on an "either-or" basis. In the latter part of the second-year course the two become better integrated through the student's focusing again on situational factors. This is particularly noticeable in his appraisals of case movement. Instead of attributing the client's progress wholly or largely to the inner change produced by the worker's direct-treatment efforts, he spontaneously emphasizes the sustaining social factors. In fact, he often puts the individual back into his environ-ment to such an extent that he is skeptical about, or at least mini-mizes, the benefits of the direct treatment. When the student has

10. For teaching, this is a glaring omission in records in all types of social service. If schools are to extend and deepen learning in this important area over that imparted in elementary courses, this recording is essential. When one recalls the basic function of social work as the science and art of effecting relation-ships, interpersonal and intergroup, the import of this omission is obvious for practice at all operating levels, from caseworker to administrator to community organizer. When one recalls also that much of the unique contribution of the social worker in many multidiscipline teams lies in this area, it is apparent that the field of practice collaborating with schools of social work could well develop teaching records in which this material is not omitted.

reached the point of questioning the values of "psychotherapy" in an untenable social situation, the instructor heaves a happy sigh and feels some gratification in having helped to "born" a social worker.

In this area of orderly thinking, the inductive method begins to give way to a larger use of the deductive method. We begin to infer more and to postulate tentatively, but more daringly, from evidence at hand. Cases are studied from the point of view of what can be inferred from the individual's response in the interviews. The inferences are then looked at in the light of the data on life-experience, development of the difficulty—in short, the historical background. Thus the practice of adhering to one method of approach in the study of a case, as in the basic casework courses, gives way to some variation determined by the use that is being made of the case in relation to other cases. For example, as just indicated, the initial focus in certain cases may be on what the treatment response tells us tentatively of the individual's need, personality, and capacity to use help. Then, in the light of the other data, we question the significance of the response. Is this perhaps deceptive movement, or is the movement consistent with what one could well anticipate? There is a continuation of the practice of thinking from case to case currently and retrospectively, with the same values indicated previously. In class discussion as well as in assignments there is, throughout this course, a progression in the demand that the student evaluate, summarize, and formulate for use in the particular case and elsewhere. Thus, in terms of intellectual discipline, he repeatedly learns to analyze, in order later to synthesize and generalize.

The student's knowledge and understanding of human behavior as derived in psychiatry courses, previous casework courses, and readings must be drawn on heavily and supplemented throughout the last part of the course. The student has developed a basic understanding of the individual's needs and the import of nurture, of gratification, and of deprivation and frustration for personality development. He brings also considerable understanding of the import of his behavior; that is, he has learned to focus on understanding its purpose in the present life-situation, as determined by the past and in relation to the individual's plans and aspirations for the future. This basic understanding of ego development and of the ego's resources for adaptation and defense is now systematized.

There is an attempt to teach more precisely various personality structures in terms of the relationship of superego to ego and to consider differentially the treatment import of specific mechanisms of defense. There is a fuller consideration of the ego's failures than there has been in preceding courses; but throughout there is still a focus on what can be done to help this individual use his personality more productively, hence a focus on his inner resources, in relation to the reality factors.

In this course we are helping the student to individualize the knowledge acquired in psychiatry courses. Inevitably those courses leave the student thinking in terms of types of disorder and personality types. These stereotypes must be broken down in the social casework courses. A major concern of these courses, now that the student is becoming steeped in psychiatric knowledge, is that he may see mental and emotional illness as a deviation from normal behavior in which individual differences obtain within disease categories. In each condition there is individual development to be understood. That study, diagnosis, and treatment must be individualized has been taught from the early stages of the beginning course, but it still needs to be worked on assiduously to the last lap of the final course. This is a greater problem in teaching today than it was some years ago. A great deal has been formulated in the literature, and instructors bring to class a wealth of categorical thinking built around age groupings, problem groupings, disease groupings, situation groupings, and culture groupings. This creates an immediate learning problem for the student, though it may facilitate learning in the long run. We bring to the student today generalized knowledge that vital life-experiences create common problems in relation to common human needs. Likewise, certain kinds of life-situation create common problems, as the states of poverty, being an immigrant, being an orphan, the state of unmarried motherhood, growing up in a delinquent environment, being a prisoner, being a soldier, or being a displaced person and once an enemy alien. Each situation creates a special state of being, often inducing common problems in personality development and social adjustment. This heritage of learning may serve the student as a means to easy and fallacious assumptions that obstruct his understanding of the individual. It may, on the other hand, sensitize him and sharpen his thinking, thus enabling him to get more quickly to the heart of the matter, if he learns habitually to individualize within the context of the general. This implies holding the student strictly to account to focus on such individual factors as age, prior life-experience, specific circumstances surrounding the onset of a problem, specific conditions that give purpose to responses—in short, the timing of the difficulty in relation to a variety of individual factors. By reason of the fact that in our teaching we stress comparative thinking, we take great care to focus on difference as well as to see likeness. A distinguishing mark of the second-year course over beginning courses is the increased demand for individuation.

It was stated previously that a major emphasis in this course is on understanding the client-worker relationship and its management. It was said that the nature of help sought by the people in the cases selected heightens the individual's need and complicates his response in the relationship with the helping person. Why is this and what are its educational implications?

Inasmuch as the individuals primarily seek help with their own disturbed feelings, their behavior in relationships, and their personality difficulties, the feelings about asking for help may be more intense. This experience may be more deeply humiliating because the problem connotes to the individual: "There is something wrong with me." In so far as he feels and sees the problem as being within himself, then something must be done to him, perhaps something drastic. There is greater fear due to fear of alteration of self. Attitudes commonly encountered among people seeking this kind of help include fears of mental disorder, which produce deep anxiety, about the stigma, the possible loss of management of self, and the small confidence in what can be done; and, importantly, feelings of guilt due to the conviction sometimes expressed: "I am responsible for my own behavior more than I am for what happens to me." Hence there may be marked anxiety due to anticipation of disdain, condemnation, or even punitive treatment. These dreads may express both wish and fear. Hostile attitudes may prevail—hostile feelings which are often at the root of emotional difficulties as well as the rage toward the helping person engendered by feelings of helplessness. These feelings in turn may inspire fear of retaliation.

Persons seeking this kind of help may carry such a burden of anxiety, due to acute fears, hostility, and guilt, that their ambivalence in the application process may be marked. They therefore may have to experience a change of feeling about the helping experience and about themselves in relation to their problem before they can move into using the help. This presents the educational task of teaching the student to understand and deal with anxiety and resistance at an early point in the case. This aspect of learning has been started in the beginning course. It is now extended and deepened, so that the student increasingly sees the diagnostic import of the individual's initial response, particularly in relation to what it says of his needs and inclinations in the use of the relationship.

As many of these individuals move further into treatment, the fear of change may persist and mount, causing strong resistance. The sense of guilt over sins of omission and commission may compel intimate confidences, the impulse to tell all, which may be followed later by fear and resistance. Since the problem is felt to be within the self, exploration of it invites intimate confidences which may cause feelings of inadequacy, resentment, anxiety, and resistance. Since with these individuals discomfort tends to be intense, the case records will reveal—more clearly than the records in the earlier courses—more marked escape reactions, such as projection, justification, and denial of reality. They may reveal, also, more bizarre uses of the problem in attitudes of self-blame, self-punishment, and dramatization of the difficulty, as well as more marked compensatory strivings. But withal they sometimes may show a stronger urge to face the problem, to pay the price through taking help. Anxiety may be handled through a strong impulse to get help and to use it productively in the solution of the difficulty, as attested in recent observations on the response of many individuals to brief psychotherapy.[11] In the light of all this, more extreme responses to, and uses of, the relationship can be expected, in deeper fear of succumbing, more stubborn resistance, more pronounced guilt, deeper dependency, more hostility, more marked ambivalence, and greater distortion of the identity of the worker. These responses may be overtly expressed or heavily disguised, so heavily, in fact, that the underlying feelings often are recognizable through the very vivid-

11. Franz Alexander and Others, *Psychoanalytic Therapy: Principles and Application* (New York: Ronald Press, 1946).

ness of disguise—for example, strong denials of feeling, repetitive protests against dependency or against being to blame, or strong assertions of positive attitudes. The deeper emotional import of the relationship re-creates more vividly the parent-child relationship, leading to a transference situation such as may not obtain in the casework relationship, where the problem is externalized to a greater extent.

The nature of the problems and of the help given results in responses which, when recorded discerningly, afford an opportunity for the more precise study of personality structure. In these cases the inner conflicts, the defenses, the ego adaptations, can be identified for study. Now that the student has the knowledge with which to look beneath the surface, the disguised responses, as indicated previously, are often patent.

In terms of progression in this area of worker-client relationship, the first-year courses afforded cases in which the management of the relationship presented no unusual problems in terms of client's excessive need, anxiety, or resistance. The student considered the professional relationship—its confidential nature, its respectful nature, its compassionate nature, but withal its dispassionate quality and something of the import of the worker's response in the client's response. By and large, the clients moved into taking help fairly readily; and, in those instances where termination occurred, there was a natural and uneventful tapering-off of the relationship. In these second-year courses, these individuals, in whom the problem from the onset is placed in some measure within the self or in some relationship in which a great deal of the self is invested, afford the learner early and recurrent encounters with marked anxiety and resistance. They present also extreme responses of dependency, hostility, guilt, and anxiety which persist but which gradually subside as clients experience help. Accordingly, there is opportunity to study the interplay of worker and client, to recognize transference manifestations, and to learn some of the ways of responding to the client, of clarifying the relationship, and of focusing and rendering help so as to limit the development of a transference neurosis. This involves more penetrative scrutiny and more precise consideration of the activity of the worker in each case, with reference to his own implied needs and strivings and the necessity for their regulation.

By reason of the fact that these cases involve some working with people in close relationship to the client or patient and some collaboration with members of other professions, there is considerable focus on the differential use of collaterals for diagnosis and treatment and on the social worker's function in a working relationship with other disciplines.

2. Criteria of Progression in Demand and of Growth in the Learner

The elements which make these courses advanced beyond the preceding ones have been both stated and implied. We summarize them to serve as criteria for "advanced" casework and to serve as criteria of the student's movement, as follows:

First, the student is studying exceptional people more than exceptional circumstances. These people present certain very real problems to the student, who needs to learn to feel *with* but not *like* them. Some of them, by reason of their pathology, are so different that they could well be difficult to understand. Others are near enough like all of us—in fact, they are ourselves magnified, ourselves a bit more so and sometimes hardly more so. The problem of relating objectively to those clients and patients would have been difficult earlier. Now, however, the student usually has not only the knowledge with which to understand but an attitude of understanding, a confirmed set of mind to the effect that he will say: "If the person is this way, there are reasons." The student now tends spontaneously to focus on explaining people in order to help them, rather than on reacting for or against them.

By now the student will have realized that he can at least convey an intent to understand and a wish to help, even though he cannot feel into and comprehend fully what an experience means to the client when that experience is beyond his own. This is discussed in the very first course and touched on repeatedly throughout the basic casework courses. We acknowledge a limitation, which often is also an asset, that we can consider only imaginatively what it would mean to be in the client's boots and that imaginative feeling may fall short of, or may magnify, what the client is really feeling. We can, however, develop a feeling of readiness to understand and to help. It is this feeling, rather than like experience and feeling, which the client needs to find in us. As the student's anxiety over the identification factor is diminished, his inclination to make learning a conscious process emerges, while his capacity to relate helpfully is increased. Normally, one encounters much less affect and less subjective involvement in client's problems at this stage of the game than earlier. However, the social worker is always subject to involvement with this or that individual. This possibility has been discussed, and some of the criteria for knowing when an individual has unusual import for us has been shared with the class. When affect mounts at this stage or when the student consistently gets involved for or against clients, the response is something to be understood. Sometimes he may need to get help elsewhere if he is to continue in social work.

Movement with the same significance as changing attitudes toward clients is shown in the student's attitudes toward the worker when the activity of the worker in the case is evaluated. In earlier courses the student is often harsh toward the worker who fails to perform competently, but sometimes he is identified defensively and shows strong feeling about criticism of the worker. Now normally there is no aspect of the case discussion which interests him more. Up against helping people in similar conditions, he knows the difficulties and is strongly motivated to learn why what the worker did was helpful or not helpful and also what else might have been done. The instructor has to guard against letting the course become a technique course in the sense that there is a tendency to lift ways of doing out of context for use elsewhere without reference to difference. The student still needs help either in defining or in being reminded to define the principles by which the worker operated.

In evaluations of the worker the student now tends to be sympathetic. He sees himself making the same mistakes. He is excited about work well done. Now with a look of self-satisfaction, he seems to say, "I would have done that," in which event the feeling of adequacy is expanded. Or, again, he may seem a bit threatened, as though discouraged in feeling the worker's great distance from him in skill. When this is marked, it suggests lags in the student's development or sometimes a hostile rivalry with colleagues. Normally the student is much less defensive of the worker. When fear of criticism of the worker is more than fragmentary or when it is a consistent response, its meaning must be assessed. It may be significant of the instructor's attitudes as she takes issue with students in the classroom and of the feelings she reveals toward the limitations of workers in case situations. In this event one would expect the response to be a fairly general one, involving the class as a whole. It may be significant of the experience in criticism which the student is undergoing in the field, due to his own lacks and basic problems regarding authority and dependency and/or to the field supervisor's attitude and methods in evaluation. Why cannot this student take criticism? This is the question which the classroom instructor should not let go unanswered but should endeavor to know the reasons.

The first criterion of "advanced" is the use of cases for study of exceptional behavior. If learning has proceeded normally, the behavior will not be reacted to as so exceptional that it cannot be understood.

Second, the problems of the people in the cases of this course, if well focalized, tend to be defensively focalized. "I only want help with my child's school difficulty" was the statement of one parent who struggled to constrict the clinic experience. Other individuals asked for help with problems which they had focalized in a given relationship or a given social difficulty, but in some instances they soon showed diffuse concern with many problems or revealed that the total personality was involved in the difficulty with which they sought help. This tendency to widen out, or the lack of focalization of the difficulty, is one reason why these cases are "advanced." The workers in the cases selected fairly consistently kept the helping relationship focalized. They did not endeavor to help the individual with everything that concerned him or to treat the total personality. They helped the client to work purposively in a well-defined area of the total need. With two exceptions, they worked gradually to lower defenses when clients tended to keep the problem so narrowly focused as to exclude help. These two cases and fragments in other cases serve the purpose of teaching *what not to do* along with a predominance of material with which to teach *what to do*. The criterion of "advanced" implied herein is that these cases, by the nature of the problem and the nature of the help, present the possibility of breakdown of defenses and the possibility of growing dependence as need unfolds, so that they could readily surpass the limits of casework help.

Throughout these courses the student will normally need considerable help in seeing the values of not going further faster. Sound focalization calls for knowledge and experience as a basis of diagnostic skill. These cases step up the demand for precision in diagnosis, for more exactitude than is attained in two years in school. Supervised experience will carry this learning forward if the individual is not too frustrated by limits in helping. In this course and in his field work we aim at having the student become aware of the importance of focalizing help and at giving him a small experience in the ways of doing it. The student normally will be showing some frustration at not being able to give more deep-reaching and more comprehensive help. Normally he will still be resisting the idea that in some instances even the psychiatrist could not help and might refer such a case to a social worker for a limited service. There is great range in degree of frustration shown around this point, and considerable protest is not necessarily a sign of neurotic need to cure or to reform as a projection of personal need. This response may bespeak the student who cares, the one who has willingness to give the much that he has to give. It also may bespeak the one who does not abandon hope readily. The more uneducable student may be most ready to accept the client's limited capacity to use help, for the simple reason that this verdict plays into his own hopeless feelings and his own anemic impulse to help.

Third, the cause-and-effect relationships in these cases are not simple and obvious. The behavior manifestations speak clearly to the student who can use his knowledge, the one who is not blocked by the concept of unconscious motivation and who can bear to hear more than the literal meanings of words. That the individual often talks and acts to conceal rather than to reveal is beyond the imagination of the student who dares not look beneath the surface. We think it has been made clear that the demand for orderly thinking is heightened in these cases. Normally the student takes this acceleration in his stride. His greater knowledge enables him to deal with the complexity of multiple causation, and one finds him less prone now than earlier to erect dichotomies. He thinks increasingly in terms of this and this and this. Earlier, some of the inferences would have been bizarre, but now they are logical and understandable. Normally there is some lag between the student's intellectual grasp of theory as he participates in the classroom and his ability to use it in the field, but this lag is not always present. Marked discrepancies present a problem to be understood. Particularly significant is the response of intellectual brilliance and seeming maturity in thinking in the classroom combined with poor ability to perform in the field. The reverse, of much greater ability to perform than to intellectualize, has sometimes seemed to result from a student's tendency to protect himself from taking on intellectually more than he can master. He therefore shuts out what he cannot use until he can use it. He may learn by doing, and his capacity to articulate his thinking may gradually show up as adequate in the field. His potentials for professional development will be limited if in the long run he cannot make his doing a conscious process.

The many variations in student capacities to learn to think for use in the way demanded in professional education are not fully understood. Likewise, the learning problems in this area are not understood completely. On the assumption that the student in a professional school has adequate intellectual capacity for the task, the tendency has been, when problems have arisen, to postulate emotional conflicts in relation to the subject matter or in relation to the authority of the educational situation which is demanding intellectual discipline. Certainly our explorations of learning difficulties have shown this to be the case in many instances. Instructors have found it helpful to note the point in the system of orderly thinking at which learning is interrupted. For example, occasionally one finds a student who can apply his knowledge of orderly procedure to see what is wrong. He is sensitive and keen in identifying the factors and forces which have produced the problem. He can identify the individual's needs and specify help. He blocks, however, at seeing the meaning of the problem or of the social situation to the individual as revealed in the purposes served by his behavior. Hence he falls down in evaluating and in conducting a differential helping process. The dynamics of the social milieu as well as the behavior dynamics of the individual stymie him. To figure out the interplay in family life or some other social situation or to appraise what purposes dependency, hostile aggression, chronic illness, a speech defect, or any other symptom may be serving the person is the point at which he stops. Sometimes the student is unable to express his feelings about this step in learning beyond flat statements of its difficulty for him.

The question often arises in the instructor's mind as to whether it is the extent of the complexity in relation to prior educational experience. If the student has not experienced discipline in thinking but instead has merely annexed the thinking of others without experiencing the process, he is indeed meeting a difficult demand now. The emotional significance of this learning problem often has been manifest both in the student who can articulate his feelings and in the one who shows them only in action. Discussion may reveal significant attitudes. One student explained that he did not like to think of people as being mechanical, their ways of reacting fixed by drives and purposes which could be figured out. He liked to think of them as being inexplicable rather than so explicable, more free somehow, with more freedom of the will. Another student reacted against the need basis of behavior, stating that people viewed thus are regarded as always suspect. Another student asked: "Who am I to judge why people do as they do?" For him condemnation was implied. The specific import of these attitudes could be given only through full discussion of each student as an individual learner. Suffice it to say that in each instance the attitude was emotionally determined and that in each instance learning was interrupted because of the intense affect stemming from underlying conflicts.

Yesterday, before the student brought to a school of social work preprofessional preparation in the social sciences, such attitudes were more common than now. Today, however, one encounters them often enough to regard them as within the range of the normal in the first casework course. By the second year the student has been subjected to knowledge which should enable him to think beyond this. Furthermore, he presumably has experienced attitudes in his relationships with those conveying the knowledge, with those instructing and advising him in school and field, to correct his feelings of the evil intent of understanding. Hence, in the second year, attitudes which express fear of understanding because of the fear of being understood suggest that the student has not been accessible to learning because of defenses which have not been lowered or perhaps have mounted. The fear of the feeling of helplessness implicit in having one's defenses recognized, an experience which would leave one defenseless, may well operate in these instances. Stoppage in learning at this point, or at any point, is a response to be understood. Always one must take into account the educational method and consider whether or not it has produced confusion and resistance through introducing complexity at too rapid a tempo. One must consider also the attitudes of instructors in classroom and field toward students and toward humans in general. In short, the learning situation must be appraised carefully in determining the significance of the student's response for his educability.

Fourth, the progression in understanding the client-worker relationship and its management has been stated rather fully. The criterion of "advanced" is the extent of the client's need—the degree of dependency, hostility, guilt, anxiety, which he brings to the relationship, the nature of his defenses in terms of whether or not they give way readily, and the nature of the help sought. At this stage the student in case study normally will show readiness to accept and understand the feelings shown by the client. He will still have some anxiety about his "know-how" in dealing with feelings and in managing the relationship so that the client does not become too dependent or so free in the expression of feeling that anxiety and resistance may be engendered. He is intent upon attaining some balance between eliciting feelings and meeting need—in short, between giving and setting limits.

The problem of freedom and restraint looms large realistically, for it hinges on diagnostic skill and relationship skill. Both await the integration of knowledge through wider experience than two years of schooling can afford. In the classroom the student will normally show movement in his intellectual grasp of this learning and movement in certain attitudes, notably his reactions to both client and worker in the case. The tendency to be strongly aligned with one versus the other should subside. The defensive identification with the worker shown in fear of hearing him criticized is significant in this connection because it shows development or lack of development of professional identity. Fear of inexpert activity out of concern for the client is normal, while indifference to this factor, coupled with a compelling urge to push ahead without regard for the limits set by the client's response, is a more problematic re-action. Concern for the client versus the striving for self-maximation may operate here. Excessive fear of worker's activity, a withhold-ing from relationship, which may be revealed more in the field than in the classroom, is a highly significant response to be understood. It may mean fear of the client's dependency, of his hostility, or of acting out one's own hostile impulses toward him. In the class-room this tendency may show up in uncertainty as to whether or not the worker has done the right thing and in expressions of fear over whatever has been done.

At the beginning of the second-year course the student often shows some sense of loss of the specific services rendered in the cases in the earlier courses. This may be manifested in wanting to inject them into these cases or in wanting the worker to help the client do, instead of helping him decide to do, or in restiveness over a feel-ing that not enough is being accomplished. Actually, the cases in the last part of the first year have prepared the student for this. His response is probably based on his inability at first to envisage him-self as being able, like the workers in the case, to function without the prop provided by having something specific to give. In many instances this anxiety has been reinforced by the advanced field work, which concurrently is making the same demand. This reaction, shown early in the course, generally subsides as the student through competent performance in the field gets a sense of helping without concrete giving.

At the close of the course the student is showing considerable facility in appraising objectively the worker-client relationship, in terms of both the client's responses and the worker's activity. The cases in the final quarter test this capacity rigorously, as do the assignments during the first quarter of the second year. There is more variation in the headway which the student may make in the field; but normally there will have been marked movement from the start of the fourth quarter of field work through the sixth quarter in establishing and sustaining a constructive helping relationship. As stated previously, movement in this area is a test of the student's total learning. It is a test of his capacity to grow into carrying the responsibilities of a mature adult. The student who carries a heavy emotional burden from the past, one who has not an ego-superego integration which enables him to function on his own, will need to repeat or to react strongly against his own earlier experience in giving and taking, in demanding and submitting. Thus he may be unable to meet the client's need because of his own dependency-authority conflicts.

Fifth, progression in use of the agency is characterized by sharpened evaluation of the part played by agency structure and function in fashioning both diagnostic and treatment activity. The criterion of "advanced" is that the cases call for knowledge of differences in agency function and for enough point of view about variations in practice to be able to see how agency policies and procedures affect both the worker's activity and the client's response. This aspect of study affords the student considerable security in relation to other demands made in the course. As he moves into the realization that considerable discrimination and much differential activity will be required of him as a social worker, he finds comfort in the thought that to some extent what he does will be blueprinted for him by the agency. That there will be bounds to activity may bring varied reactions in the student group. Authority-dependency attitudes show up clearly. More normally the student by now is acceptant of agency structure, even finding security in it. He becomes increasingly able to evaluate objectively the worker's activity in relation to the agency and to evaluate agency practices both negatively and positively. Authority-dependency conflicts show up in strong alignments with agency versus client or the reverse, or with worker versus agency and the reverse. They show up also in finding this aspect of learning difficult so that the student gets confused in his discussion of it or consistently overlooks it as a factor to be taken into account.

3. The Final Step—The Milieu of Practice

Following these courses, the students enter the additional social casework course mentioned earlier, one concerned with the study of the relationship of agency setting to casework practice. This is an integrative course, in that it serves both the administrative and the social treatment sequences and also in that it summarizes and formulates earlier teaching on agency structure and function as a determinant of casework practice, a recurrent area of learning throughout the casework sequence. The materials are selected and arranged with the aim of carrying forward rather than of merely repeating the earlier teaching. As a final course in the casework series, its focus and emphasis have the value of identifying the student with agency concerns and reality problems and issues at a time when he is intent upon learning what he will need to know in order to get along in agency practice. The authority-dependency alignments now become sharply focused, with opportunity to resolve conflicts as the student becomes increasingly identified as a professional person. The noteworthy element of progression is that this is a course in the classification and evaluation of agencies in relation to the philosophy and aims of the profession. One of the distinctive attributes of social work is its members' responsibility to work within the context of both agency and profession, with awareness of the identity of each but with an unwavering commitment to the aims of the profession. Students must be prepared for this, at times highly problematic, responsibility. This implies conviction of the importance of helping agencies become truly instruments of the profession. The culmination of the casework learnings in a course which centers in an evaluation of the administrative structures within which the profession operates has this important aim.

V. THE USE OF READINGS

Knowledge is stored in books and journals, and much knowledge may be conveyed through the literature of social work and related professions. Whether learning takes place through this resource or not varies with the character of the material, its timing, the instructor's guidance, and the student's capacity to read for meaning. There are moments when old-timers responsible for education long for the days well within their recollection when there was not much to be read in social work, casework, and psychiatry. In those simple times when one learned what one learned by hand and mouth, at least the learner stood a chance of knowing well what little he knew. The integrative task was relatively light, whereas today it can be overwhelmingly heavy, owing, in part, to the accretion of recorded professional experience to which every student is heir.

This resource constitutes a decisively important problem in professional education. The student's reading will be done in part in response to assignments, and we hope also in response to his own search for enlightenment. In professional education the emphasis should be that we read in order to use, hence we read selectively rather than promiscuously. Therefore, bibliographies in the beginning course are organized around cases to convey understanding of people and notably the meaning to them of certain kinds of problems and social stress, as well as the significance for social work help of the individual's response to stress. The early readings also focus on what it may mean to individuals to ask for and take help and also on methods of helping. All this entails beginning early to read on the study, diagnostic, and treatment processes of social casework. A few general readings aim to convey philosophy and trends in thinking and practice.

The common tendency of instructors to prepare reading lists of a length beyond the scope of the most prodigious reader can well serve as a deterrent. On such lists most important readings often are indicated. While this probably helps, there is a "you can never catch up" connotation to the unrealistic list which discourages participation. Bibliographies for future reference, for long-time use, could well be issued separately from a list for which students soon will be held accountable. Comprehensive lists of basic required readings for several closely related courses can well serve as an aid to integration. For example, such a list in the first year for casework, development of personality, and health and disease could well create awareness of their common core and motivate students to relate the three courses to one another.

In the first course the social casework student is encouraged to read selectively. He is warned not to read prodigiously. He is told that assimilation will be facilitated through purposive reading, that is, through reading to throw light on a case in classroom or field. At the start he is not held too rigidly to documentation of papers, nor is this emphasized as important. He should try to think through cases themselves rather than to try to use someone else's thinking. When he tries to fit a case into concepts derived in his reading, his own thinking may be constricted. Better to use a bit of basic knowledge to think as far as he can than to be so engulfed by knowledge that he cannot think. One other purpose here is to set a pattern of independent endeavor rather than to encourage dependence before he can be intelligently dependent on selected authorities. Examination questions on readings are not appropriate in the beginning course because the student cannot be expected to have assimilated his readings sufficiently to have them at his fingertips and also because he has not been held accountable for them during the course as he will be later.

The progression in the use of readings is that at the start the instructor takes more responsibility for suggesting readings, for focalizing them, for citing them. As the course series advances, this should taper off to less direction and to the encouragment of more extensive reading and more exploration of the literature. There is progression from little emphasis on documentation to demand for it and also from helping the student apply readings to holding him accountable for their application. This progression can be interfered with by such circumstances as the organization of the library and the availability of books. The professional student's heavy program, with long hours in the field, time spent on transportation, and class hours, operates against leisurely exploration of the literature. Readings must therefore be readily available if he develops the habit of going beyond specific assignments. In a complex library system such as may obtain in the large university, where there are long waits for books and journal orders, instructors are realistically driven to continue the infantilizing practice of active guidance as to what specifically to read for economical use of time and energy. This argues for the small professional library to supplement the central library. This progression toward greater self-dependence in reading is interfered with also by the character of the social casework literature, which makes it necessary that the instructor guide the student in his reading to a greater extent than is desirable, if he is not to squander his time.

In relation to the educational aim of setting in operation a learning process which will endure and wax strong throughout the years of professional activity, we are concerned to inculcate a habit of reading. This implies that the student has incorporated the challenge conveyed variously throughout his educational experience that he explore on his own, that he become self-dependent. Because it has been possible for the student in a professional school to learn a great deal with minimum reading, to learn as his predecessors learned, through doing and hearing, it has often been possible for him not to become a systematic reader. This may be likely to occur as a protective device in the interests of integration, now that the literature not only is assuming mountainous proportions but also that it is of an unmanageable nature. Professional educators in fields other than social work often comment on the common tendency of professional people not to keep abreast of practice through reading. Possibly, beyond time pressures and energy deficiency, this is because they can get a sense of progress through hearing and doing. Furthermore, in a field where knowledge changes at rapid tempo, often a work is out of date by the time it gets into print, or its major contribution may already have been experienced and learned by the reader in his practice. That the social worker can continue to learn through doing may operate against his extending and deepening his self-education through drawing on the experience of others as recorded in the professional literature.

Finally, perhaps a most important obstacle to making reading a habit is the character of social casework literature. It is difficult to help the student attain an orderly progression in reading which supports the orderly movement which can occur through case selection. As has been observed by Roger W. Little, if our literature were cumulative and structured rather than so largely an accretion, it could give unity and coherence to the efforts of individual thinkers (teachers and students).[12] Of medical social work literature Miss Goldstine comments:

> The numbers of descriptive articles of this type and the slimness of their analytical content bear eloquent testimony to the absence of a scholarly tradition in writing, as noted by Roger Little. In the case work articles of the last ten or twelve years, the two most distressing failings have been (1) the lack of any attempt to relate the writer's experience and ideas to the accumulated knowledge and thought of the past and (2) the tendency to describe and generalize superficially about a case or agency experience with no analysis of underlying premises or concepts and no evaluation of results.[13]

12. For statements significant for social work education see Roger W. Little, "The Literature of Social Casework," *Social Casework*, XXXIII (July, 1952), 287–91 (cited by Goldstine).

13. Dora Goldstine, "The Literature of Medical Social Work: Review and Evaluation," *Social Service Review*, XXVII, No. 3 (September, 1953), 316–28.

Thus the tendency in casework articles to generalize from one case or one situation supports, rather than counteracts, the limitations of classroom and field instruction which inevitably is centered on case-by-case teaching. The stage of development of casework literature does not readily support, therefore, what we attempt to teach of orderly thinking, of comparative analysis, and of sound generalization. It particularly does not support the mounting demand of the second year that the student increasingly synthesize and formulate his experience with individual cases in classroom and field. This imposes a responsibility, which some casework instructors have assumed, for questioning and testing the written word and drilling students all the more in comparing, in synthesizing, and in generalizing.

The great amount of repetition without progression noted by Little and Goldstine[14] in their studies could well deter the intelligent and creative student from making a habit of reading. Furthermore, with reference to their observations, if much of casework literature has been concerned with specialized practices and techniques rather than with general principles and processes, if also until very recently it has not been concerned with the relationship between processes within social work, much of the literature has been more of a burden than a resource as a means to the integration of learning. In these analyses of the literature one perhaps finds several answers to the educators' questioning complaint as to why it is so difficult to get students to become habitual orderly readers.

There is variation in the individual's need to read for creative work. It is well known that the obsessive reader is often not creative; in fact, he may be task-centered to a problematic degree and rigidly dependent. The reading habits of the creative student, by reason of the fact that he has not presented a problem in learning, are less well known. Motivation in reading varies widely, and prior educational experience operates in the student's response to this aspect of his program. There are those who have read largely for diversion, which may include pleasure in the artistry of the writing. They will find much professional literature unenjoyable, to say the least. There are those who have read for self-adornment. To be well read is to make a good showing. This motive interferes with

14. Little, *op. cit.*; Goldstine, *op, cit.*

professional learning, for it is liable to lead to the acquisition of useless, unrelated knowledge through reading which clutters rather than clarifies. There are those who regard reading as laborious rather than pleasurable. The movie, the radio, the current digests, which could have served as an impetus to read, may well have had the opposite effect with those whose learning pattern has essentially been that of reaching out to be fed rather than to feed. To be informed with a minimum effort drives them to great effort to pick up knowledge by word of mouth and by hand (trial-and-error doing). There are others, fortunately, who are habituated to reading critically for meaning, in order to get help in their thinking and doing, rather than merely to acquire knowledge because it is required or because it will enable them to pass some test. Because educational systems have fostered the latter attitude in many instances, the professional educator has the problem of helping the student become motivated to read for enlightenment and for use.

Some of the ways which may help the student read productively have been indicated. More specifically, each case discussion can present a stimulus to read, provided that the instructor consistently indicates facts, theories, and controversial opinions in the literature, which enlighten and clarify confusion. Again "the hows" are the use of focalization, of repetition, of comparative thinking, of synthesis, and of generalization. Through reading the student can be helped to focalize; to learn through repetition as ideas recur and as certain readings repeat but go further than earlier ones; to compare as implied in critical evaluation of various points of view; to generalize from what is well established and generally agreed upon. Important in the student's response to the instructor's help in this area, is the factor of identification. As a student reaches out to approximate the instructor's knowledge, if he gets the sense that her competence has been derived in part through a grasp of reading, if he finds that she draws on the literature critically, that is, appreciatively but not worshipfully, he may move toward the literature rather than away from it. In this aspect of learning, as in others, the student's personality development will be revealed; in fact, a treatise might be written on the emotional growth of the student as reflected in his attitudes toward reading and his use of this means to professional growth. The authority of the educational system and of the instructor, as well as of the printed word, is here to elicit the whole range of attitudes toward authority from acceptance through aggressive resistance through passive dependent submission and resistance. Likewise, motivation in terms of service aims and narcissistic strivings is manifested, as are dependency needs. The motivation desired is that the student should want within himself to read, in order to know in order to serve more competently. The motivations decried because they break down with time and also because they do not yield such great benefits are reading submissively, because required; reading out of fear of being found wanting; reading rivalrously, to outwit, to outdo others, to impress, to make a good showing. In a materialistic society the possession of knowledge can become an end in itself, a useless acquisition for which, with other materialistic strivings, there is small place in a profession.

We have presented the case selection, its arrangement for progression in learning as well as the use of readings throughout four of the five casework courses required of all students. These have been guided by concern for cumulative effect to bring about desired change in the learners, an objective which calls for measures to safeguard the integrative capacity of the learner. The desired changes are recalled, briefly, as developing a way of thinking, a way of feeling, and a way of relating purposively in order to help individuals and groups. We recall also the aim of furthering a strong identification with the conscience of the community and of the profession, which implies a constructively critical attitude toward the profession's principles and instruments. In discussing the integrative task implicit in these objectives, as well as the subject matter essential for their attainment, we have inevitably considered method. Recognition has been given to the reality that the aims of professional education cannot be attained fully in the training period. The changes, however, can be set in operation for the attainment of the aims through subsequent experiences. This is contingent in large measure upon educational method, as has been indicated throughout. We turn now to a consideration of the progression in other learning experiences and methods through which we attempt to teach so that learning may be facilitated.

CHAPTER 11

Faculty Collaboration and the
Instructor's Preparation

I. RANGE OF INSTRUCTION—ORIENTATION TO THE WHOLE

One measure for the attainment of progression in learning is that instructors teach the range of courses in the social casework sequence. It is not desirable, however, that one instructor carry the same students throughout the series. Change is essential for enriched experience through variation in point of view and method. It is essential, also, both for correction of an individual instructor's bias and emphasis and for confirmation of basic essentials which do not vary from instructor to instructor. Furthermore, growth is implied in terminating meaningful working relationships and making new ones. Teaching the series, however, enables the instructor to maintain continuity, to extend and deepen learning experiences sequentially and through close cross-referencing to aid integration. At the University of Chicago we have found that it is desirable that one instructor conduct a class through the first two courses of the first year and another through the second-year course. The final course, on the relationship of agency setting to casework practice, can well be taught by a third instructor or by one previously experienced by the students. Theoretically, it would seem sound for the student to separate from the first instructor at the close of the beginning course, in that it is a basic course which lays groundwork for all that follows, covering the whole of casework in rudimentary form. It would seem to be a *fait accompli* and a logical point for terminating the relationship with the first instructor. Here, again, logical sequence and the student's development are two different matters. With many students the factor of identification as a means to learning, as well as the factor of stability in proceeding with one way of teaching through the first year, makes one instructor for the two courses advisable. The latter course, it may

be recalled, steps ahead inevitably at rapid tempo. Continuance of
the same instructor has not always been possible administratively,
however, and so we rely on the close collaboration between members
of the social casework faculty to diminish the element of marked
difference in instruction.

It is very important for the progression in learning that the casework faculty collaborate in the structuring and teaching of the
courses. While one or two members may take major responsibility
for planning a given course, its prospectus should be discussed
in the group to determine its co-ordination with preceding, subsequent, and related courses. The aims of the course, the use made
of specific cases, its scope in relation to the aims and scope of the
sequence, as well as its significance for other fields of study, should
be well known by all members. It is desirable that the use of
specific cases throughout the sequence be sufficiently familiar to
each instructor that he can refer to them. Thus those instructors who
teach a part of the series are oriented to the whole. Furthermore,
all instructors can thus have a part in shaping the given course so
that it is not out of alignment in terms of continuity; so that its
repetitive elements are purposeful rather than chance ones; so that
it harmonizes with the whole. It is as the faculty work together
that students are assured of greater consistency in philosophy, in
method, and in faculty attitudes and demands as determined by
common understanding of the developmental stages in the learning
process. This is one measure to enable students to get a sense of the
school as an organic whole, stated earlier as desirable, for the integration of learning. In those courses taught by the same instructors, essentially the same cases are used with an agreed-upon purpose, the same bibliographies are used, and assignments are con-
ferred upon, so that, in general, the same kinds of assignment in
terms of purpose, are used. Since assignments have an educational
aim, as well as an evaluative purpose, they vary somewhat in relation to class need and movement. They are not standardized.

II. DIFFERENCES BETWEEN CLASSROOM TEACHING
AND FIELD-WORK INSTRUCTION

In contrast to the method in some schools of social work where
cases for classroom discussion are brought in from the student's

current field-work experience, our cases have been selected from the field of practice and prepared for the classroom by faculty members, in accordance with the use that is to be made of a particular case in the sequence of learning. These cases are used over a period of time; but, almost continuously, one by one they are being discontinued and replaced as they become outworn for one reason or another. There are many arguments among educators for and against each of these case-selection methods. Beyond the greater administrative simplicity, our choice has been determined by our educational conviction that the demands of professional education cannot be individualized. This implies that in any one course, determined by the steps of learning, there are certain areas of knowledge to be conveyed, certain habits of thought to be inculcated, certain methods to be known in a limited time span. The chance factors operating in the composition of the case loads of a group of students at a given time, as well as the variables operating in the student's need to present a given case, would make it impossible to select cases for adequate coverage, for orderly sequence in intellectual and emotional demand, for grouping with other cases for comparative teaching, for emphasis timed for cumulative effect as depicted in the preceding chapter.

Furthermore, to get the selection mimeographed and in circulation in order that both students and instructors may prepare in advance presents an administrative problem which would be insuperable. The unsuitability of the current field-work case for our classroom use is obvious when one considers the factor of the instructor's and the student's preparation.[1]

The instructor's preparation entails not merely the grasp of the individual case as an isolate, but relating it to what has gone before and sometimes also using it as a springboard to what is to come. His preparation entails, furthermore, indicating appropriate readings and planning assignments around certain cases so that the course sequence of assignments carries learning forward. In addition, our emphasis on faculty collaboration makes it important that

1. For more detailed statement on the instructor's preparation in both discussion and lecture methods see articles by Helen Harris Perlman, "The Lecture as a Method in Teaching Case Work," *Social Service Review*, March, 1951; and "Teaching Case Work by the Discussion Method," *ibid.*, September, 1950.

instructors in subsequent courses be familiar with the case material as well as the general learning of the preceding courses.

Time for the student's preparation is equally essential. In order that the student may retain as much management of his affairs in the educational situation as is possible, in relation to the demands made by other courses and field work, it is necessary that he know from the beginning the demands that the course is to make upon him. This is made more possible as he has the case records and bibliography for the quarter, so that he may proceed in his reading and in the study of the cases in accordance with his time and circumstance. While the quarterly time spent in field work is fixed, he cannot always rigidly adhere to the weekly allotment of time. Thus the activity demands of field work cannot be timed comfortably to other school pressures. Because learning in the field cannot pursue an orderly course in time, energy, and intellectual and emotional demands made on the learner, it is essential for the student's equilibrium that classroom learning be as orderly as it is possible for arrangement of content and demands to make it. At best, it will have its own disorder, in so far as the individual student's development does not gear with a logical sequence.

Furthermore, it is our opinion that classroom teaching and field-work instruction in social casework are different. The aims of both are attained best when they complement each other rather than when they duplicate each other. The current case brought into the classroom from the field affords a learning opportunity which closely approximates that of clinic or agency-staff conference. The case selected with reference to sequence and scope of a course as a whole presents a different learning experience. It has been said that knowledge and theory are taught predominantly in the classroom. The specific case under study has the purpose of making knowledge and theory meaningful for use elsewhere beyond the learner's field placement. In the field, "doing" is taught predominantly. Knowledge and theory are retaught as needed in order "to do" in a specific situation in a specific agency. Learning for use elsewhere can occur retrospectively; but at a given moment in field-work learning, as case activity is in process, the learning is inevitably focused on the here and now. The what and how and why we do as we do bear the deep imprint of the specific agency. While it is hoped that field-work instruction does not end with case-by-case learning, leaving each experience an isolate, it inevitably has a specific focus. Certainly, it is essential that field instructors, like classroom instructors, help the student look from case to case in order to formulate concepts and to generalize his experience, but this proceeds at a different tempo. The teaching afforded through a given case in the field often extends over a period of time. A decisive point is that the learning afforded in a case as a whole does not have to be extracted in one or two sessions. In the classroom the student presenting the current field-work case will be intently focused not only on learning what to do with it in his specific agency but also on measuring the field-work instructor against the classroom instructor or the reverse. Colleagues will be drawn into the same focus and issue. In so far as the classroom instructor focuses on or emphasizes different elements in the situation as important or subordinates specific agency considerations to general practice considerations, the student may become confused. In so far as difference in any respect with the field instructor arises, the conflict in authority of knowledge and skill may heighten the affect in learning before students are ready to weigh and reconcile difference in professional thinking and emphasis. It is stressed that this implies discrimination based on knowledge and experience. Hence conflict between authorities may produce confusion and conflict even for the mature student. The less mature student may have his educational growth impeded because, out of his need to depend on someone, he may be driven to align himself with classroom or field instructor, a division which operates against the integration of learning. The neurotic student will often find in these differences between authorities a channel for the enactment of his ambivalence and a support to his defenses against learning. In both these instances field work, because it engages the emotions most deeply, may be most strongly aligned with or against, in accordance with the individual's need to defend himself against emotional involvement or his propensity to seek entanglements.

In the field, following a staff conference, the student has individual sessions with the supervisor to help him understand and reconcile differences in thinking about "his case." For integration he has also the support of identification with the supervisor's ability in these conferences to take criticism or to differ without being threatened. The classroom does not provide this resource for the immediate individualizing of the student's response to having his case discussed. Hence we are loath to introduce into the classroom an experience, the response to which is not readily dealt with through classroom measures.

In conclusion, since the classroom is primarily concerned with imparting knowledge and theory in a situation in which the doing is intellectual rather than actual performance, it is a place for reflective and imaginative consideration of varied aspects and possibilities. The field-work case introduces a greater pressure of specific what and how in this case as unique, rather than this case as a means to learning much that will be relevant elsewhere. Just as the classroom instructor must extricate himself from practice in order to teach beyond the confines of his particular experience, so the classroom material should afford students emotional detachment from their field experience and a certain perspective on it in preparation for the near day when they will move into another agency experience.

III. HELPING THE CASEWORK PRACTITIONER BECOME A TEACHER

1. *The Conduct of Consultation Sessions with New or Prospective Classroom Teachers*

Social casework teachers generally are experienced practitioners with a competent grasp of their subject. This they should be first and foremost. No nicety of method would compensate for this lack, even if it were possible to sustain any method with such a basic deficiency. To become something more than or other than a practitioner need not be a chance development through a slow trial-and-error process, if the new instructor can be given and can take the experience of his seniors through help focused on his function as a teacher. Identity as an educator will come about in part through his relationship with those from whom he learns something of teaching. Our experience shows that it is important that a new instructor have individual consultation sessions with a senior member of the faculty during his first teaching of each course. This is in order that his work may be geared into the aims and the movement of the whole. The instructor who is to teach for the first time may profit by auditing and observing an experienced instructor's course in advance of teaching it himself. On the whole, we are in favor of help given concurrent with the initial teaching rather than in advance of teaching, for reasons which will be given shortly.

a) Timing, method, and content of the sessions.—In advance preparation for teaching, our experience has shown that the following procedures are helpful. Observing and auditing a course should be accompanied by conferences with the instructor, for which the student teacher prepares. In these sessions after discussion of the aims, scope, and structure of the course as a whole, he is given points upon which to focus his observations of the first case discussion. This is followed by a retrospective consideration of what was taught and how taught. There is also some discussion of the whys of the instructor's method and selection. Thereafter, he is asked to delineate in advance of several case discussions what one might teach from a given case, why he would teach it now, and how he envisages doing it, also what responses he anticipates from the students in relation to the major issues in the case. The hows include the focus and progression, as well as his anticipated use of didactic instruction, readings, and assignment. Evaluation follows the class session on the instructor's use of the material and conduct of the class in which the learner is encouraged to identify problems which emerged.

In the evaluative sessions the instructor can well be autocritical, so that the learner is freed to question and to identify problems, as well as reassured through the fact that the seasoned instructor makes mistakes. A learner can hope to approximate the instructor who falls short of perfection. Furthermore, it gives him security to see that slips can be retrieved within the session or in subsequent sessions. It is comforting to observe also not only that an instructor does not have to have all the answers but that he can acknowledge in the classroom some of his sins of omission and commission, for example—"I think I should have shelved our discussion of this matter at this point. We've got ahead of the game, so that the relevance of all this is not clear. We'll return to it later when we've thought the situation through more carefully." Or: "Last session we got bogged down, and, on reflection, I think it would have helped had I directed you to consider the situation from another angle." Or, on growing aware that his elaboration has been tangential, the instructor may acknowledge that he apparently has failed to get the import of a question. Consideration in class of students' production on an assignment may seek their criticism and result in the instructor's acknowledgment that the assignment made an unrealistic demand or pushed them too little or that the demands were not sufficiently clear. The decisive point is that the prospective instructor gets the sense that teaching is a problem-solving venture in which one continuously learns as one goes. It is important that the tutorial sessions, in so far as it is possible, instil the foreknowledge that, as he gets experience, his present fear of the trial, error, and correction process implicit in teaching will diminish.

Actual teaching of the course worked on should start the following semester or quarter. It is not advisable that there be a prolonged observation and discussion experience covering a sequence of courses without practice.[2] In the first teaching quarter the learner will need to confer fairly regularly as he attempts to put to use the knowledge acquired in advance. There will be considerable variation in amount of help needed, depending on the degree of security afforded the learner through advance preparation and the degree of assimilation that has occurred.

When it is not possible for the new instructor to audit and observe in advance, the same helping procedure is conducted. He goes from the tutorial session to teach, rather than merely to listen and see. The "post mortems" are on his version of how his class went, in which he is free to confer on the problems which concerned him for help in their solution. There is much to be said in favor of concurrent teaching. For some learners great anxiety is built up through prolonged observation, discussion, and delayed action. For them learning is assimilated more readily as it is put immediately to use. The preview of all that is involved frightens and may inhibit learning. It is to be remembered also that social workers are habitu-

2. This produces a problem in post–Master's degree programs, where experienced students are preparing to teach. Unless practice teaching can be offered, the amount of time spent on educational theory and observation must be limited.

ated to learning through immediate use of theory. Mounting anxiety will be manifested in varied ways in the learner's discussions with the instructor, so that in these instances the instructor may well avoid the too much in too great detail, thus keeping the analysis of case material and the evaluation of sessions focused on major points and issues and adhering to the learner's tempo in developing and elaborating them. Other learners find a great sense of safety in the advance rehearsal. Weighted with a sense of responsibility for the conduct of a class and fearing ineptitude in the conspicuous position of leader of a group, they feel they cannot be too well prepared.

Individual motivation in teaching varies widely. The configuration of determinants which prompt one social worker to teach and another to eschew it are doubtless highly individual. It is probable, however, that there is a relationship between what teaching signifies to the individual and the use he is able to make of help in learning to teach. Some individuals seemingly enter teaching out of their urge to convey what they have learned to others. Their dedication to their work, their need to multiply themselves in order that their mission may be widely extended, makes them ready to plunge into teaching unself-consciously, with small concern as to the educational process. In fact, they may be contemptuous of and irked by a demand that they focus on method. It is only as they get into the situation and encounter problems with which they need help that they may be dynamically motivated to learn to teach. Awareness of the much to be learned in this area may come as a shock to produce the anxiety responses previously mentioned. They may well learn best as they perform. Many a pioneer social work educator has been of this group. He has learned to teach through trial and error and to solve his problems as best he could. In so far as he has not failed his students, it has been because of the reliability of his knowledge, the clarity of his thinking, and his ability to articulate it, as well as the contagion of his enthusiasm for his subject matter and the strong motivation of his students to learn, even the hard way. Granted other causal factors, that we pioneers have not been highly satisfying teachers, that something has been lacking in our part in the educational process, is suggested by the few followers who have felt the inner call to follow in our wake. It would seem that great teachers would beget teachers.

Other individuals equally possessed of knowledge, understanding, and skill to convey to others and equally dedicated may not have envisaged themselves as teachers. Perhaps because of intellectual grasp of the scope of the task and the special skills involved, perhaps also because of an overevaluation of what it takes to teach, they have assigned this function to others as a "natural gift" which they do not possess. That there have been many such individuals in social work is suggested by the fact that recruitment of teachers has been difficult. Many able social workers, seemingly well endowed for the task, have been loath to teach. Many factors have doubtless operated in this reluctance, but the current response to educational opportunity in this area suggests that some of them have hesitated out of their keen comprehension of what is involved, perhaps also out of a well-developed conscience in relation to responsibility, as well as out of sensitivity to the needs of students. In this connection it is possible that some disappointment in their own mentors or frustration in their own educational experience has operated. They accordingly have held back from this venture until opportunity has presented itself for them to learn to do what they have not dared undertake without special preparation.

Social work educators are now assuming that, given certain qualities, specified above, teaching capacity may be developed. From consultation with and direction of supervisors in their student and staff casework supervision, our first understanding of the learning process and our early formulations of educational methods were derived. Much of what is learned here is used in the training of classroom teachers, in which we have made a bare beginning. It is clear that certain principles in the education of social work students apply in the education of professional teachers, a notable one being that the demands of teaching cannot be individualized but the learning process can be to some extent. As yet, differential methods are not formulated. It seems probable, however, that one differentiation dictated by our experience may be sound—that some individuals will use help more productively when it is concurrent with teaching. Others will need and want advance preparation, in which an intellectual process wherein they are relatively safe precedes actual performance of the intellectual doing of the classroom.

The teacher new to a school but not new to teaching will also need conferences with a senior instructor, in order to gear her work into the sequence and aims of the courses taught by others. To what extent she will need the systematized help afforded through some focused observation and regular individual conference sessions will depend on the extent and nature of her previous experience. Many casework teachers have not prepared for their class sessions as envisaged above. They have gone to a class as to a staff conference, well versed in the case, but with no prior thought given to teaching it as an integral part of an educational process which has continuity and changing emphasis. It may be found, therefore, that a new staff member with teaching experience will need some of the same systematic help as an individual new to teaching.

In helping the beginner learn to teach, as in all learning, there should be as much orderly progression as is possible. The progression of the cases in the classroom, previously described, through which she is moving on the teacher level rather than the student level will assure this in some measure. On the other hand, when the first teaching experience is in the beginning course, the novice does not start with the simple in terms of the needs and demands of the learners and in terms of the importance of the course as a beginning experience. As such, it must lay groundwork for all that is to follow, in establishing basic methodology and in setting in operation the process of change in feeling and thinking envisaged earlier. Since the demands are lighter in an advanced course, there may be instances when it is advisable for the new teacher to start teaching such a course rather than the beginning course. This depends on the individual concerned and on the amount of time and competent help a school faculty has available for tutorial sessions. When and if an instructor later undertakes the teaching of the beginning course, he may well use to advantage some help from an instructor experienced in inducting students into social casework learning. In the Chicago school, in spite of the reversal of the progression in the demand on the teacher, we have chosen to start new instructors in

the beginning course. Because we believe it has a necessary ante-
cedence, we go along with Whitehead in holding that the easier
task cannot always precede the harder.[3]

The fundamentals of teaching and learning are more deeply
understood as one teaches the basic course. As the teacher proceeds
up the line, she will be a more competent instructor when she understands the learning process from the ground up. What social work
learning means to students stands forth in bold relief at the start,
unobscured by adaptation or defense. The defenses of a later date
will be more discernible to a teacher who has seen them in the
making. An instructor in an advanced course will be more competent when she has mastered the conduct of herself in the conduct
of the beginning class. Hence she should be more free to engage
in the greater complexity of knowledge in the content of advanced
courses. The nature of social work learning dictates that its hardest
teaching task comes first. When this is postponed, the educator is
less well equipped to help the students navigate the widening and
deepening stream of learning. Obviously, the educational practice of
starting the novice in the beginning course is sound from the point
of view of teacher and students, only when enough help can be
afforded to make this initial teaching charge a productive learning
experience for the teacher.

b) Preparation as a way of life for creativity in teaching.—
The educational process of helping social workers learn to teach
should be infused from the start with concern to help them become
self-dependent teachers. There are two dangers in the process envisaged: the first, obviously that of engendering dependency on the
senior instructor; the second, the danger of imposing an imprint
which interferes with the learner's own style. Individuality within
limits is to be cherished in teaching, as in all creative work.

One might question the imprint of the old on the new and prefer
that nature take its course for a new slate, since we old teachers
are none too good. Actually, however, we might get more of the
weaknesses of the senior generation of teachers repeated in the jun-
iors if the latter were to proceed alone to develop themselves as their

3. Alfred North Whitehead, *The Aims of Education and Other Essays* (New
York: Macmillan Co., 1929).

predecessors did. For many of the weaknesses of the former are due to long, slow, hit-and-miss learning efforts. Through giving her self-confidence, through helping her become aware of and analytical of educational process, the support given the young instructor today may well free her and inspire her to fashion the new rather than to duplicate the old. History repeats itself when its makers do not learn from the past. Our practice of structuring courses jointly and of using the same materials with the same purpose might well raise the protest of too much standardization. It has been a great misconception that, since teaching is creative, each instructor must be a law unto himself in a world of his own making. This is an "art for art's sake" concept which has no place in professional education, which is education for use. Since it engages the total person deeply, teaching is not readily standardized. Personality wrinkles are not easily ironed out. The enriching effects of interchange of thinking and experience, together with the discipline implied in a scheme of carefully organized planned work, will modify the individual's use of his abilities without necessarily constricting his individuality. Marked differences in teaching still obtain.

Orderly progression in the young teacher's learning process demands that her teaching responsibility proceed from light to heavy in terms of the size of the total load of work. It is not uncommon for the faculty member new to teaching to be saddled with from two to four courses at the start; and sometimes, in addition to a very heavy teaching load, she is given other responsibilities, such as administering a field-work program, supervising field practice, counseling students, and serving on school committees. When she has more to do than she can master, she is driven to depend on others. Since her relationships are not well established in the current faculty group, she is prone to turn to the past and teach from her notebooks what she was taught, in the ways she was taught in so far as she can recapture these ways. This duplication of the old not merely fails to correct the limitations of the past but even falls short of it. As the individual embarks upon professional teaching, she should have time and energy for reading, for reflection, for imaginative consideration, for clarifying thinking as it is challenged in class, for assimilation of the new experience as it proceeds. She should have time for self-inquiry, to determine what of

344   The Learner in Education for the Professions

what she knows is suitable and relevant to give and for finding and noting ways of doing which are effective. We have found it highly desirable for the new faculty member, even when she has had teaching experience, to have a light teaching load, not more than one full credit course, for the first six months and a relatively light load for the first year. This enables her to work productively on her own and also to become a part of the school as a whole through knowing its point of view, practices, and procedures. This is attained through consultation time with the dean and other instructors, as well as through participation in group activity as the admissions committee, the examinations committee, and the curriculum committee. The productiveness of new faculty members under this plan has convinced us of the inestimable value of a gradual induction to teaching and an immediate induction to the school as a whole. In this context the individual instructor who is receiving considerable help from a senior faculty member is less prone to become dependent on her consultant than she might otherwise be, were she both overburdened and unrelated to others.

Progression in the process of learning to teach implies a tapering-off of the help given. In the learner's second teaching experience of the same course, consultation should be available for her to use as she needs it rather than through regularly scheduled sessions. She should need less anticipatory help and less specific help. She should see more clearly the import of class developments. It is advisable that she teach the same course two successive quarters, for in the immediate repetition of the first experience her learning is intrenched and her errors corrected. When she continues to need as much or more help on the repeat experience, there is a problem to be explored and understood, and action taken to solve it.

In an individual's second new teaching experience in which she proceeds to another course in the sequence, she can well start by presenting her plan for the course as a whole, and be expected to develop the plan for her class sessions more fully on her own. Tutorial help might at times precede next steps or might often be retrospective as she encounters problems with which she needs assistance. The sessions should be on a consultation basis as she seeks them. The premise is that the systematic help with the first course should have intrenched a method of preparation which she can use on her own as she proceeds into new teaching experiences. In the third new experience she might conceivably need to confer only for orientation to the aims, scope, and structure of the course and for intermittent discussion, in order that her work may be geared into the aims and movement of the course sequence and oriented to the students' developmental stage. The assumption here is that the mature social worker who is ready to teach in terms of knowledge and motivation and who has requisite aptitude for the task will not need prolonged tutoring. She will carry forward her basic learning into the new fact situations of other courses, developing them in her own style.

c) Summary of aims in the preparation of the classroom teacher. —In summary, individual supervisory and consultation sessions with new faculty members have the basic purpose of helping them change from social casework practitioners haphazardly teaching to educators systematically teaching social casework. These sessions will have attained their aim if the following objectives are realized in some measure:

First, the learners should have incorporated a method of preparation for class sessions beyond familiarity with the case. This implies that they feel the necessity for preparation and do not regard it as a time-limited discipline for the apprentice. There will be depth to their acceptance, in so far as the method to which they have been habituated has enabled them to be competent, that is, has been more useful than burdensome. There will be permanence to their acceptance of the need for preparation in so far as they have become conscious of its values, for instance, that careful preparation frees them to conduct the class in terms of relating to students individually and collectively. It releases them from a defensive position, in that imaginative consideration enables them to anticipate events and responses. Thus they are in a state of readiness enough of the time to handle the unexpected and the emergent with equanimity. It enables them to attain continuity. It frees them to observe and to understand learning responses and to attend to the import of their own activity. It makes possible a consistent approach, so that the students know what is expected of them, and, furthermore, it enables the instructor to give appropriately and to make realistic demands consistently. Furthermore and very important, it serves not only to motivate students to prepare but at times also to convey what constitutes preparation and proper working methods.

Of the import of the instructor's preparation for students, Albert Schweitzer records that, on entering the gymnasium, he was at first a poor scholar. Of this he says: "It was only when my form master . . . showed me how to work properly and gave me some self-confidence that things went better. But Dr. Wehmann's influence over me was due above all to the fact, of which I became aware during my first days in his form, that he most carefully prepared beforehand every lesson that he gave. He became to me a model of fulfillment of duty."[4] But Albert Schweitzer was then in early adolescence, at the stage when the young learner is being repatterned for adulthood. This concern to serve as a model of fulfilment of duty might seem less necessary in adult professional education than earlier. Again, one recalls the vital part played by identification in professional learning, owing to the fact that the learner is entering a new culture and is being patterned to assume its responsibilities and to work in its distinctive ways. One might assume that the selected group of students in a professional school would be inwardly committed to work hard and bring good work habits with them. It has been noted earlier that they are strongly motivated and have high expectations of themselves. It is to be remembered, however, that the educational system often has not prepared students to become self-dependent learners. It may have patterned them more largely to acquire knowledge in order to intellectualize as an end in itself than as a means to well-defined ends.[5] Because they are deeply committed to the attainment of their aims, it is all the more important that they find in their mentors the way to professional competence. A basic purpose, therefore, of supervisory and consultation sessions with new faculty members is that they may become habituated to preparation as a way of life.

A second objective of help given to prospective or new teachers is that the learners may accept the responsibility to be consciously attentive to the import of their activity. In teaching there are always new elements to master. Automatic responses to familiar stimuli are not sufficient for this creative activity; hence teaching must be a conscious process. Because conscious attention and groping experimentation constitute a first stage in this learning, as in all professional learning, a troublesome stage of acute self-consciousness may be involved. This may be expected to subside as the instructor finds the knowledge of educational method acquired through work with an experienced teacher effective when put to use and also as she loses herself in her work. The behavior pattern of responsibly looking to the self is a charge which the teacher must accept along with the responsibility of teaching. Close collaboration with a senior instructor will bring the realization that the latter has not permitted herself the comfort of becoming deeply unconscious of self. As she measures herself against those from whom she learns to teach, she may experience criticism and freedom in self-criticism which lowers rather than heightens defenses, so that she, too, may become autocritical. One would expect her basic professional discipline to have laid the groundwork for the extension of this capacity into this new area of endeavor.

In the third place, it is the aim to set in operation the process of trans-

4. Albert Schweitzer, *Out of My Life and Thought: An Autobiography* (New York: Henry Holt & Co., 1949), p. 3.

5. See chap. 3, pp. 61–62; chap. 7, pp. 205–13.

ferring learning useful in social work to the educational situation. The social work educator can well draw on and adapt to classroom use her understanding of human behavior, of group dynamics, of interviewing. She has at hand for modified use measures which help people change feelings and attitudes so as to think and do differently, as well as measures which promote a purposeful working relationship.

Fourth, it is to be hoped that the working relationship with a senior instructor has not only helped the learner to meet the demands of teaching competently but also freed her to develop her own style and to become increasingly self-dependent. The close collaboration described may serve to identify the social worker with education, and it may serve as a corrective relationship in instances where the learner tends to repeat her own past instruction without making it her own so that she is free to use it differently. It may serve this corrective purpose also in instances where a learner is motivated to teach by the disappointment and frustration of her own educational experience.

2. *Preparation of Field-Work Supervisors To Become Teachers*

Field-work supervisors, like classroom instructors, are generally experienced practitioners with a more or less competent grasp of casework. They likewise must become teachers, and today this need not be a chance development if the new supervisor can be given and take help from his seniors, help focused on his function as a teacher. There are differences in point of view as to the qualifications for student supervision, in terms not only of years and types of experience but also of stages of development. Because of the important place of the field-work instructor in the outcome of the student's learning as well as in reliable appraisal of his progress and determination of educability, it is essential to select casework practitioners who are ready not only to contribute to the development of students but also to evaluate their development. The following indications of progress in professional learning have been formulated as a basis for appointment to these responsible positions.

a) Qualifications for assumption of supervisory responsibility.—A social caseworker is ready to supervise students when her grasp of the knowledge and skill essential for competent practice is sufficiently well integrated that she no longer needs supervision in her casework practice. The test of this would be a period of time, probably a year or more, in which she has been working on her own as a senior caseworker, using supervisory staff only in a consultative capacity in her casework. It is not advisable that a worker still under supervision in her casework undertake to learn to supervise a student, a common educational practice in the recent past, one which may persist because of staff shortages. This is not advisable, because a person cannot teach what she is currently being taught. Knowledge and skill cannot be passed from one head to another and on to a third head. It must have been assimilated so that it is conveyed from within the teacher. Furthermore, because of the authority-dependency elements implicit in supervisor-worker relationships, it is very difficult for an individual simultaneously to be a supervisee in one relationship and the supervisor in another relationship. It is highly essential that the supervisor's capacity for self-dependence be well intrenched through having experienced practice with consultative help, as differentiated from close supervision. She must be more than potentially self-dependent. A social caseworker who is to supervise should have shown in her final use of supervision an acceptance of the authority and dependency implicit in the relationship. This will have been evidenced in many ways, notably in her attitudes toward evaluation, in her use of it, and in her ability to terminate the supervisory relationship. An individual who has not basically accepted supervision and who thereby needs either to flee it or to cling to it will not make a competent supervisor, even though she knows enough to be one.

A social caseworker selected for student supervision should show a capacity to meet dependency without taking the management of affairs out of the hands of those who depend upon her, except as this is indicated through the tested incompetence of the dependents. Consistent with this capacity, one would expect to find the ability to identify with authority. This implies that she would not be fearful of authority, as shown in a capacity to use authority as differentiated from a need to be authoritative. These two attributes are appraised through the individual's work with both clients and colleagues. They are evidenced also in the worker's use of the agency, notably in her ability to accept the agency's policies and procedures, working freely within their limits to make the most of its provisions for the client.

With reference to the educational aim delineated by the needs and demands of social work as a profession in society—that its members have a high degree of social conscience and an unwavering intent to make the agency an instrument of the profession—it is decisively important that a worker selected for student supervision be a staunch representative of her profession. This implies that she is not worshipful of the agency in the sense of being noncritical or defensive of its policies and practices. It also implies readiness to participate in groups concerned with evaluation of the policies and routines of the agency in terms of their effects upon clients, personnel, and community relationships with a view to effecting change when indicated. Readiness to assume responsibility in making known need for change or in effecting it, through any avenues open to the casework practitioner, also should be manifested. This inclination is not to be confused with rebellion occasioned by self-centered strivings or needful alignment against authority. An attitude of caring for the client and for the agency, hence concern with what it does and how it operates, would be expressed as differentiated from an attitude of being generally against the agency and all its workings.

Unfortunately, administrative practices in some agencies, through not affording opportunity for caseworkers to participate in agency evaluation, make it difficult to know a caseworker's potentialities in those respects. At times administrative practices make it difficult also to differentiate realistic dissatisfaction from neurotic discontent. Therefore, the prospective supervisor's capacities or inclinations to deal constructively with the duality of agency and profession are often unknown until students call them into play, as almost inevitably they do sooner or later. Classroom teaching in both casework and administration courses, in envisaging desirable conditions of practice and the long-run aims of the profession, makes inescapable some conflict for students as they experience the realities of current conditions of practice and the hardships of their profession in a society which is both for and against social work. This conflict makes it all the more essential that the student supervisor have a philosophy of agency and profession in the community which enables her to help the student accept reality without loss of hope and breakdown in motivation to solve problems implicit in the situation. This implies, on the supervisor's part, a point of view that individual, social agency, and community are always, at a given point, in "the process of becoming." She then sees social work's task as that of beginning where each is and moving progressively toward next-step goals shaped by the nature of the needs to be met, the problems to be solved, and the inner potentials and external resources for participation and use in their solution. With this sense of things being in process, supervisors focus on helping students appraise potentials for growth and change, in individual, agency, and community. They also help them come to know the indications that an individual or situation is incapable of growth and not subject to change.

A social caseworker selected for student supervision should have demonstrated capacity for effective co-operation and collaboration with colleagues and with the members of other professions. This implies that she has shown a flexible ability either to assume major responsibility or to play a minor role, permitting others to play a major role. It implies a readiness to give and take and a respect for the functions of other professions and the authority of other disciplines. These attitudes are contingent upon a full-fledged respect for her own profession and the authority of its learning. Social work in the immediate past has been and currently to a large extent is more identified with, than related to, those from whom it has been learning while collaborating. Confused identity has led to unsound interprofessional practices and to a disorientation as to the distinctive functions of social work. While this problem is now widely recognized, it has not been solved in practice. The place of social work among professions in current interprofessional practice makes it difficult, therefore, to reconcile the teachings of the classroom and the learning experience of the field. It makes it difficult also to procure supervisors who have the attitudes specified and who are functioning as described. Early lags in social work education contributed to this problem in practice, while in turn the educational lag persists because of the conditions of practice. There is considerable evidence that the impasse is breaking and that it will be increasingly possible to lay the groundwork for a stronger professional identity during the educational stage. In this connection the recent union of psychoanalytic psychiatry and the social sciences is serving to give social workers a renewed respect for the social component in social work, the basis for social work's contribution as distinguished from that of other professions concerned to educate, help, and heal people. Thus tomorrow we may hold caseworkers applying to teach in the field accountable for more competent collaboration than we can today. In the meantime every effort should be made to bring the teaching of the classroom and the field together, in so far as it is possible to do so.

A social casework practitioner who undertakes supervision, particularly of students, must become a teacher. She must therefore have shown some capacity to formulate her thinking and to articulate it. These abilities will have been revealed in the worker's recording, particularly in evaluative summaries for supervisory and staff conferences. It will have been shown also in her preparation for supervisory conferences, in her participation in group discussions of various types, and in her interpretation of agency program and services to clients, colleagues, and others. This capacity to formulate and impart thinking will be developed greatly through teaching—in fact, a common comment of the new supervisor is to the effect that supervision has clarified her thinking. It pushes her to know what she knows and what she does not know to a greater extent than her casework practice under supervision. This is why, as preparation for supervision, it is important that the caseworker have had a period of relatively self-dependent practice in which she has been responsible for thinking and acting without benefit of regular supervisory support. In spite of supervisory methods which guard against fostering dependence in workers, the fact that in the last analysis the supervisor is held accountable for the casework performed under her administration makes it inevitable that workers rely to a considerable extent on the supervisor's responsibility to know precisely and to think sharply in order to guide or check the worker's knowing, thinking, and doing.

Because in many agencies workers have not had a period of full-fledged professional self-dependence before undertaking student supervision, the first experience in supervision has often been rough going and sometimes traumatic both for supervisor and for student. In these instances the supervisor often gropingly tried to repeat the supervision she experienced. In not being free to be herself and in trying to be someone else, she is unsure and ineffectual. Thus she is often not free to extricate herself from the role of casework practitioner to become teacher and supervisor. She can leave her casework practice for educational practice in so far as she has made it more fully and deeply her own through a period of self-dependence. Feeling insecure in her new role, she is prone to cling to her old areas of competence. The casework helping process is a less intellectualized one than teaching. Hence she may be prone to subordinate the knowing and thinking of an intellectual approach to those of a therapeutic one, thereby establishing an inappropriate relationship.

The social caseworker who does not have the intellectual qualities specified may have a difficult time becoming a teacher. It is a common observation that some highly skilled casework practitioners do not have aptitude for student supervision and even less aptitude for classroom teaching. As field-work supervision more and more approximates classroom instruction in stressing the teaching of the whys of professional performance rather than more largely what to do and how to do it, there is less difference in the qualifications for the two forms of instruction than obtained in the past. Field-work instruction at its best today may well pattern students eventually to become classroom teachers to a greater extent than it did yesterday. This may occur as it also attempts to develop the intellectual potentialities of the student.

The social caseworker selected for student supervision should show readiness to use help in becoming an educator. Increasingly, agencies and schools expect to help the new supervisor initially, with teaching, helping, and administering methods in order that supervision may contribute to the development of the student or worker. Student supervision is essentially an educational process in which the teaching and helping components are large. The profession has a body of educational knowledge and skill to convey to the new supervisor. Unlike her predecessors, she need not learn by trial and error. The caseworker's use of casework supervision in her practice is a major test of her readiness to use consultation or supervision in educational practice. This implies that she will be learning to understand the learner and the professional learning process, as well as what to select to teach and how to teach it, in order that learning may progress. It will also involve identifying learning problems and knowing ways of helping appropriate to the educational situation. The decisive point is that she will not be supervised on the casework knowledge and practice which she is teaching.

b) Individual variations in need for help to become a teacher of practice.—There is considerable variation in the amount of teaching help which new supervisors need in order to function competently. There is variation in practice among schools in the amount of help given the individual who is supervising students for the first time and in the faculty's conception of the process. In some schools it is envisaged as consultative help which the supervisor seeks as she needs it. It thus becomes help focused on problems as they arise. In other schools it is set up as regular individual supervisory sessions, in which the supervisee's procedures and practices are reviewed and evaluated systematically, with a view to giving help throughout in the prevention of problems. The values of this are obvious, one being the opportunity for the novice more quickly to gain an identity as a supervisor through the relationship with her instructor. In this connection the use of the group for study and discussion of supervision when two or more new supervisors are beginning work at the same time is advantageous. Learning together and from one another as well as from the experienced supervisor affords each learner greater freedom to develop individuality and offsets the imprint of the senior supervisor. The liabilities in supervision of supervisors are equally obvious, one being its prolongation, beyond a point of actual need for help in order to be competent. As we embark upon the supervision of the field-work educator it is important that we do not repeat the pattern of social casework practice, where overlong supervision is now coming to be recognized as one factor operating against the professional maturation of the practitioner, as well as against her status as she collaborates with the members of other professions. If an individual is ready to teach, she should not have to have supervision for long; in fact, systematic supervision sessions might well occur only in relation to her first unit of students. Thereafter, she could be expected to apply what she has learned, using an experienced field instructor in consultant capacity and using group meetings of field instructors conducted within the school to help her solve problems and to advance her learning.

Prolonged individual supervision is to be avoided, lest it interfere with the supervisor's development of professional self-dependence. In a responsible position, one which demands that she meet the dependence of students without fostering dependence, it is important that the young supervisor feel self-reliant. For this it is essential that she early learn through the give and take with colleagues, her contemporaries, and her seniors, rather than in a tutorial relationship, in which ordinarily she will be less free to develop her own style and to find her own way. Even though the teaching focus is on educational method and process rather than on the content taught, it is to be remembered that, because of the authority-dependency components implicit in supervisor-supervisee relationships, it is very difficult for an individual simultaneously to be a supervisee in one relationship and a supervisor in the other. In spite of this fact it is highly essential that current educators not have to repeat the past through learning by trial and error, as their predecessors did. The same principle holds as in the training of classroom instructors. The new generation of teachers will be more likely to move ahead of the past generation when they can start with what has been learned, provided that educational instruction is not imposed beyond its time or out of the senior educator's need to perpetuate herself through imprinting herself on her prospective successors.

Throughout this delineation of capacities and qualities essential for student supervision, professional maturity is implied. This means not only competent grasp of subject matter but also well-intrenched professional attitudes and responses, notably sustained self-awareness, capacity to regulate feelings, and capacity to assume responsibility with minimum anxiety over dependence and authority. With reference to the demand made by student supervision, two prevalent practices occasion comment: first, the procedure of having caseworkers learn to supervise staff through the supervision of students and, second, the procedure of removing the supervisor from casework practice when she undertakes supervision. The first practice connotes an assumption that student supervision makes a lower demand. This assumption has the vintage mark of the days when it was thought that, because the student knows less, the supervisor safely can have less knowledge and skill to impart. The second practice connotes the misconception that, once a caseworker attains skill and security in practice, she retains it through observing it and teaching it. While some social workers do retain firsthand feel and touch from the sidelines to a greater extent than others, this assumption ignores the fact that professional practice changes and grows and that its practitioners mature through participation in the process more than through intellectualization of the process.

c) *Supervision of students differentiated from supervision of staff.* —In the light of current concepts of the supervisory process as an educational process to be conducted in ways which pattern the learner for the profession and which promote personality development beyond the acquisition of knowledge and skill, the practice of qualifying for staff supervision through "learning on students" is outmoded and outworn. In view, also, of our current understanding of the pressures and stresses in professional learning and of the learning process, as well as of the significance of the relationships in which the individual learns, it is self-evident that student supervision calls for maximum professional maturity. We are increasingly of the opinion that a prerequisite could well be experience in staff supervision. One could well learn the rudiments of supervision with staff members, trained or untrained. In these instances the integrative task of the learner is lighter, through the fact that he is not concurrently having the same heavy impact of intellectual learning as is the student. Also the employed supervisee expects less of the supervisor and more of himself. Not only is the trained worker more self-reliant, but he expects less teaching and helping, often even feeling that he is not entitled to it. The untrained worker brings considerable dependency to the supervisory situation. There is, however, a slower tempo of learning and a lower aim. He is given enough knowledge and theory to enlighten the doing, but he is learning largely through doing, so that the integrative task is relatively light.

In contrast, the professional-school student is having a minimal amount of doing, a bare sufficiency to enlighten his classroom learning. Consequently, the integrative task is heavy, and his mastery of learning awaits his subsequent experience. The untrained worker reaches out for less because he is training for a job, and therefore he is striving primarily for enough help to get along in this specific situation. The student, in contrast, is training for the profession, so that the immediate situation is felt to be a temporary means to an end. He wants and seeks preparation in terms of remote goals and long-run aims. Consequently, he is more critical of the agency experience and restive with slow-tempo learning. Furthermore, he knows that he is being evaluated in terms of potentials for professional development rather than merely for adequate performance in the specifics of the current job.

This and other factors combine to make staff supervision a different and a less complex responsibility than student supervision. The caseworker with the qualities which have been delineated would have a more orderly progression of experience, were she to move into the supervision of junior staff workers as preparation for student supervision. She might be competent in staff supervision and still lack certain qualities essential for the different demands of student supervision. In agencies where the personnel practices are sound and where there is concern for staff development, she would have a maturing professional experience, however, which should stand her in good stead in student supervision. When the field of practice regains the sense of its place in professional education which it once had when it carried the sole responsibility for it, agency administrators may not depend on the school to train their staff for supervision through putting them prematurely to use in student supervision. They may instead afford caseworkers some staff supervisory experience as preparation for student supervision. When this practice prevails, the social services may get an appreciable number of better-trained social caseworkers from the schools. In the long run, this should make for conditions of practice essential to carry forward the professional learning which, at best, can be only begun in the schools. While the nature of these beginnings in the educational process is decisive for the intrenchment of a learning process which will endure, the nature of the individual's subsequent practice, particularly in the early years, is also very important for the integration and progression of learning.

d) Implications of current supervisory systems for social work as a profession.—In the light of current concepts of the supervisory relationship as one in which the student is patterned for practice in part through identification with his supervisor and as one in which he depends upon her security as a social worker to support him in the attainment of social work identity, the student supervisor's withdrawal from practice has considerable import for him. When the supervisor does not continue to apply and hence to integrate knowledge which she may continue to acquire through reading and through association with colleagues in practice, her teaching may lose a certain vitality, that life born of knowing firsthand whereof she speaks. Furthermore, as time passes, she may come to feel not merely rusty in relation to the old but also inexperienced in relation to new developments. A resultant loss of confidence may lead to dependency on colleague practitioners and importantly to undue reliance on practitioners in other fields. Thus she may not only increasingly look to others for knowledge and direction on casework procedure but also turn over to others some of her responsibility for teaching. When a supervisor gives herself over to the supervision of a psychiatrist rather than participating as a full-fledged collaborator or using him as a consultant, she turns her students over to psychiatry. The student, out of his eagerness to learn to put his learnings to use, is bent toward identification with those who not only perform competently but are the authorities on doing. Consequently, he may come to regard much that is social work function and responsibility as psychiatry's legitimate role. When this occurs, his identity as a social worker is weakened. He is not patterned to represent social work appropriately in relation to other professions. The widespread removal of the seasoned practitioner from social work practice, at that point of beginning readiness to represent the profession adequately among professions, constitutes a loss not only to those whom the profession serves but also to social work's contribution in the interprofessional scene. A noteworthy loss in professional education is the difficulty that social work students may have in developing early that sense of pride in calling which may motivate the individual to do work of a high order and to attain professional self-dependence. Pride in calling is derived through contact with a high order of competence in doing as well as in knowing. A field-work center where a seasoned social work staff, in collaboration with other professions, demonstrates skill in casework thinking and practice comparable to that which obtains in other professions should not have this problem.

CHAPTER 12

The Conduct of Class Sessions, Assignments, and Examinations

We are concerned here to depict how continuity, sequence, and integration may be attained through the conduct of the social casework class and through the use of assignments and examinations. These are means not only to contribute to progression in learning but also to evaluate the outcome of learning.

I. THE CONDUCT OF THE CLASS SESSIONS

1. Teaching, Timed and Focused

In the classroom several elements in learning move along together. The instructor is charged to impart knowledge, to inculcate certain habits of thinking, to foster appropriate feeling—all for the development of understanding for use. Although skills are developed largely in the field, much doing is taught in the classroom. In spite of the fact that it is difficult to separate knowing, thinking, and feeling, the instructor must be able to differentiate them. Continuously, she must be aware of knowledge, thinking, and feeling as separate elements, in order to see their relatedness in the learning response. For instance, she must be quick to recognize that *now* is the time to impart knowledge or to direct students to another source to obtain it; these are attitudes to be modified through the students' expressing and examining their feeling and/or through the instructor's own assertion of feeling; this student's thinking is logical in the light of his inadequate knowledge or the reverse; he has not grasped the thought-process, though he has annexed an array of knowledge. In short, the instructor must be aware of the class's need for help in specific areas, in order that she may emphasize particular aspects as learning proceeds. In presenting the means for teaching the learner to know, to think, to feel, to understand, and to do, it is from the standpoint that these elements are con-

357

tinuously interrelated but that *to know* comes first. Again we state: Students must have knowledge with which to think. Feeling as a professional person must come to feel is developed through and in response to knowledge. Understanding comes about through knowledge that has been integrated through emotional acceptance, which permits the faculties of knowing and thinking to function in the doing. The nature of the doing will therefore reflect integration or lack of integration of knowledge. We recall, furthermore, that the commonly noted anxiety in professional learning is often due to realistic lack of knowledge with which to think and to do. It is important, therefore, that knowledge be timed as far as possible according to the need created by demand for it for competent performance. The dangers of much knowledge imparted too fast have been emphasized. The equal danger of a lagging tempo, due in part to a poorly selected sequence, frequently has been overlooked.

The body of knowledge to be conveyed has been presented. It comes to the student in the casework classroom from the instructor, from books and journals, from case records, from his colleagues with their variations in age, experience, and cultural background, and, importantly, from his own mind, as old knowledge is recalled and widened, deepened and corrected, through connection with the new. It is taken in by the student through studying cases, through participation in and listening to class discussion, through reading, through working on assignments, through reviewing for examinations, and, throughout, through identification, as he enters into working relationship with the instructor and also with his colleagues. As has been stated, the what that is taught at a given time is determined remotely by the educational aims of social work education. It is determined more immediately by the scope of the course which has been delineated on the basis of assumptions as to stages of learning. Hence part of the what is what he needs to know now in order to get well started to proceed through this stage. Although cases have been selected for the attainment of remote objectives, the what is determined *very* immediately, by what he needs to know *now* in order to perform competently if he were a social worker in this case. The first *how* of teaching, therefore, is focalization. It is not teaching all we know, not encouraging reading of all there is to be read. It is putting first things first and knowing also what *not* to teach now.

2. *Discussion and Lecture as a Means to Learning*

Social casework courses have long been referred to as "case-discussion courses." Sometimes one has wondered whether they have aimed to teach social casework or discussion. Obviously, a method is a means to an end, not an end in itself. The case-discussion method, out of its very vitality as a natural and inevitable means to learn social casework, may become such an end. This has frequently happened when, among other determinants, the instructor has had an abiding faith that discussion will teach. It will not necessarily do so; in fact, it has been known to confuse and confound rather than to systematize and clarify thinking. Discussion which is not focused through the direction of a leader and organized and reorganized through intermittent summarization can become a flight into purposeless activity—activity which, in not attaining its aims, often breaks down into noisy fragments or sinks into silence. The instructor who has been blindly trustful of discussion as the major means to learning will be driven to lecture and to point the lesson, an uneasy task, first, because often she must bring order out of confusion and mental ease out of agitation; second, because she is prone to feel a failure when she finds herself unwittingly and unwillingly lecturing. To her, lecturing will somehow be a guilty "talking-at" when not en rapport with her group, and as such it will almost certainly fail of its aim.

Another factor leading to misuse of the discussion method has been the misconception of its therapeutic value. Social work educators, aware of emotional factors in learning, have been concerned to ease feelings and help students resolve conflicts in learning in order that resistances might be overcome so that learning might be assimilated. The instructor who relies heavily on discussion to teach also often has an abiding faith that it in itself will heal, in the sense of effecting change in feelings and attitudes. An elementary casework learning has been disregarded when this occurs. For just as the client's unburdening will not necessarily re-educate or heal, just as a caseworker must direct him to talk to a purpose and help him focus and relate his production toward activity in the solution of his problem, so similarly in the attainment of the school's re-educational aims the instructor is responsible for the conduct of case discussion. This implies discriminative use of the lecture method along with and within the discussion method. A decisive point is that as casework educators come to regard didactic teaching as something other than a defense for use when discussion gets out of hand, as they come to know its function, they will gradually give it its rightful place. When the instructor has made peace with herself on this matter, her lecturing will become a talking to and with the students rather than an attacking or uncertain "talking-at" them. Lecture and discussion go forward together, one now giving way to the other, each serving the other as integral parts of the learning process. It has been well said that "the lecture is a communication which either sows the seeds or garners the fruits of discussion."[1] It could also be said that discussion vitalizes the lecture, thus affecting its traditional limitations. We shall attempt to depict in broad strokes the function of didactic teaching in a discussion course and the interplay of lecture and discussion.[2]

The first responsibility of an instructor is to create conditions favorable for productive discussion. Students do not come to a course to discuss everything and anything. What to take hold of, where and how to start, are insistent inner questions which, when unanswered, leave them to flounder experimentally and often to feel helpless. In order that they may start out with a sense of competence, focus is essential, and certain knowledge which orients thinking is implied for this. In addition to an initial framework of knowledge, the instructor is concerned to relate to the students in ways which free them to participate in discussion. This is done through setting an example and a way of responding in her attitudes toward clients, toward workers and all professional col-

1. Helen Harris Perlman, "The Lecture as a Method in Teaching Case Work," *Social Service Review*, March, 1951.

2. Perlman, *op. cit.*; also "Teaching Case Work by the Discussion Method," *Social Service Review*, September, 1950; Charlotte Towle, "The Classroom Teacher as Practitioner," *Social Service Review*, Vol. XXII, No. 3 (September, 1948), also in *Social Work as Human Relations* (New York: Columbia University Press, 1949).

leagues in the case situations, toward social issues, and toward the student's contribution in the classroom.[3] The essential attitudes are that students are competent and ready to engage in learning until proved otherwise, that the instructor is here to help, that she is concerned that one learn rather than being bent on outwitting one, that she is intent upon one's success rather than one's failure. Implied throughout is our intent to understand, our readiness to think and feel with students, but not necessarily like them. This involves avoidance of condemning attitudes, caricaturing individuals, sarcasm in the critical evaluation of a part played by a worker in a case under discussion, as well as an objective response to the student's contribution. This does not rule out criticism or imply acceptance of the student's thinking and feeling when it is invalid and inappropriate in a given instance. His response may be accepted as understandable but not necessarily as useful here and now. An instructor frees students to express feeling when she herself shows feeling. As has been stated elsewhere—"professional integrity compels righteous indignation over social injustice, deep sympathy with the underprivileged, definite commitment of feeling and opinion concerning the right and the wrong . . . a teacher therefore passes moral judgments . . . in short he stands up to be counted in no uncertain terms. He acts however to understand through scientific inquiry and orderly thinking. . . ."[4] Since first sessions tend to be pattern-setting, these conditions which encourage productive discussion should obtain from the start. They provide knowledge which orients, direction which focuses, and attitudes which reassure.

3. *Teaching Patterned by Stages of Learning*

Each course has a pattern, that is, a phase of imaginative consideration, a period of disciplined analytic thinking, and an inte-

3. For further discussion see Charlotte Towle, "Emotional Elements in Professional Learning," in pamphlet entitled *Professional Education* (New York: American Association of Schools of Social Work, 1948); "The Classroom Teacher as Practitioner"; also in *Social Work as Human Relations;* "Teaching Psychiatry in Social Case Work," *Family,* Vol. XX, No. 10 (February, 1940).

4. Towle, "The Classroom Teacher as Practitioner," and in *Social Work as Human Relations.*

grative stage of generalization. Each case discussion recapitulates the pattern of the course as a whole.[5] The function of didactic teaching within this structure leads us to consider, first, its place in the opening sessions of a course and in the beginning of a case discussion. At this stage its predominant purpose is to give, in order that students may give—that is, to motivate thinking and to engage participation.

To establish a purposeful working relationship, every course opens with a presentation by the instructor in which the place of the course in the curriculum and in the casework sequence is depicted, its aims stated, its special emphases delineated, and the student's responsibilities specified. There is progression in this from course to course. At the start it is essential to make clear the purposes of the discussion method in learning social casework. Also, since a case record tends to be a story and little more when read for the first time, our first step is to prepare students to study a case. In so doing we institute a practice which persists throughout the first year and continues on occasion in advanced casework courses, that of indicating focal points around which the case is to be studied and its use in the sequence of learning. For example, in the first course the students are told we are using the first three cases to understand what it means to a person to ask for help and to be helped. This is identified as essential first learning, because what the individual feels about taking help influences his use of it. In the first case, therefore, they are to note what feelings Mr. B shows and be ready to cite the evidence for their impression from the description of how he acts, the account of what he says and what others say about him. In the second case this focus is repeated with the additional focus: In what ways does the individual deal with his discomfort? In what ways did the worker's activity ease or heighten discomfort? In the advanced courses the practice of focusing case study continues in those cases which we teach with a special emphasis or in which we teach a part rather than the whole, the assumption being that now students know how to

5. Alfred North Whitehead, *The Aims of Education and Other Essays* (New York: Macmillan Co., 1929); for application in teaching social work see Towle, "Teaching Psychiatry in Social Case Work," *The Family*, XX (February, 1940), 324–31.

proceed in situations where there is to be no departure from former practices.

The progression is that, at the start, students are given more direction in how to work and more help in focalizing their efforts. There is repetition from course to course, in that a frame of reference is always given and the working relationships defined in terms of the course demands and the implied responsibilities. There is movement in the repetition, in that the new elements are well pointed up and departures from former practices explicitly stated. Hence, as each course takes a step ahead which modifies the focus of case study, it is defined and identified as a step ahead. At the start of a course the nature of the case selection is described, and the focus that the selection will bring is defined, much as stated previously.[6] For the integration of learning it is essential that the learner have the guiding insight which enables him to adapt his goals to those of the situation and thus to have a sense of direction to serve him in self-directed purposeful activity. Therefore, from the start, we begin to make the educational process a conscious experience.[7]

This knowledge which orients represents the demands of the educational situation on the student, conveyed didactically by the instructor. Questions for clarification or reasons why may be raised, but this material is not designed to evoke discussion. It is a definition of what we will work on and and how we will work and our purpose in doing so. This is not debatable. Because initial stages tend to be pattern-setting, it is important that the early sessions of a course afford discussion. Our way of working together should therefore be instituted at the start.

For this some instructors introduce case material in the first session. The author found early in her experience that the students reacted more vitally to case discussion when they were helped to avoid becoming lost in the complexity of detail in case analysis, through a preliminary presentation of basic concepts, fundamental theories, and working principles which they would be using.[8] This

6. See chap. 10.
7. For further implications see earlier discussion of educational principles and measures, chap. 5.
8. Two sessions in Social Casework I and II. One session in Social Casework III and IV.

knowledge with which to think provokes many questions and some controversy. It immediately brings to the surface some resistance, which may be relieved in part by the statement of purpose. It is made clear that these concepts are selected because they are implicit in casework thinking and practice or have deeply influenced it. Our experience with these concepts and theories may tend to confirm or negate them, though we must, for the time being, think with them and through them. The student finds security here, in that he is helped to focus through having certain definite formulations from which to observe and around which to center his thinking. His interest is stimulated, and it matters little at this point whether he proceeds into case analysis fired with the impulse to prove or to disprove a point. The important fact is that he is fired and that he is set for imaginative consideration of the various general concepts and principles that must remain the lodestar if he is not to become confused by a welter of details. From course to course there is progression in the content of these initial sessions.

In the beginning course the basic needs and strivings and behavior motivations which the individual commonly brings to a helping experience are presented. They are identified as not new in their entirety but new from the standpoint of the context in which they are encountered. As the basic concepts and working principles of casework are presented and discussed, they are identified as old, in that they are the basic tenets of democracy as a way of life, but new, in that we will try to apply them in a professional helping relationship in which both individual and agency have certain rights and obligations. We are concerned that social casework be a democratic helping process. To what extent can it be? What are our ways of accomplishing this? These, among others, are lessons to be learned. In subsequent quarters the first sessions introduce concepts, theories, and working principles expanded and deepened, and they define where we are to go from where we left off. As earlier, discussion of this is important, in that the new that is being introduced can be related to the old by the students themselves. Imaginative consideration of change, of progression, is not threatening when one envisages working anew with the old. It is always exciting to find that one has what it takes for a new undertaking. Under these circumstances the learner is challenged to push forward and motivated to ingenious effort.

As indicated previously, every case discussion has a beginning phase of imaginative consideration. The frame of reference described, as well as the focal questions or points on which to concentrate in the study of a case, tends to have created a questioning state of mind, an attitude of reading to discover, to test, and to apply. In the first discussion of a case we take an over-all view of it for its general implications. We reflect on the nature of the problem, its social significance, its psychological import in terms of what such a problem commonly signifies and what it does to person and family. We often consider speculatively the person in terms of his response to the problem and his attitudes toward help. We think of the agency in terms of its function and procedures in relation to this person and problem. All this general reflection has the purpose of framing major considerations, decisive questions, basic issues, possibilities, and probabilities with which we need to be concerned as we proceed to discover through precise evaluation where the evidence in this particular case leads us and why we reach one set of conclusions rather than another. In the early courses the instructor naturally implants more knowledge and ideas at this stage than in the advanced courses, where students increasingly bring their experience and knowledge to more productive preliminary reflection. Why this phase of initial reflection, in which speculation and premature generalization occur? Beyond its purpose of alerting students mentally and of inciting interest, of fostering identification, and of focalizing study and discussion, it plays another important part. It makes conscious a mental process and exposes it to the discipline of individuation based on the particular configuration of factors in a given case. Given a client with a problem, students automatically generalize the problem and the reason, and it is easy to stop there. Hence, through bringing it into the open, we become aware of the fallacy of easy generalizations through experiencing their repeated correction. As we do this, we become habituated to exploring and correcting our initial responses, and thus our services become individualized rather than fashioned by our projections.

The lecture and fragmentary didactic teaching at the beginning of a course, or of a case, serves the several purposes of imparting knowledge with which to think, focusing discussion, and pointing the lessons to be learned. It serves, furthermore, to incite interest, to stimulate identification, and to prepare students for productive study through creating awareness of the unreliability of generalization unsupported by a careful weighing of evidence. It helps to establish a purposeful working relationship, through directions given and expectancies defined as well as through giving in several other forms. A notable gift is that the instructor has permitted the students to know her, her thinking, her feeling, her readiness to understand and to help. In short, she has permitted herself to be known as a person to whom they can safely and productively intrust themselves as learners. One limitation of discussion sessions in which an instructor refrains from didactic teaching is that she remains a more unknown quantity for a longer time. The resultant insecurity of students is manifested in various responses, as in withholding or in provocative participation which may be misunderstood. This may be mistaken for a productive response, particularly when the instructor has not clarified for herself the difference between an educational session and a group-therapy session. In this instance she may happily and optimistically receive expressions of negative feeling, attacking attitudes, challenging comments, and overt resistance as productive participation. She fails to see the hostility which she is eliciting as hostility which she has begotten through failing to give of herself and through failing to teach in ways which facilitate learning. She believes she is relieving hostility which would otherwise interfere with learning, when actually she is engendering it needlessly.

Throughout the aspects of disciplined analytic thinking, in which the course as a whole or the individual case-discussion session is centered on precise analysis, the lecture and fragmentary didactic teaching continue to play a vital part in the learning process, when well selected in content and rightly timed with reference to the learners' need.[9] The patient process of mastery of details, the pre-

9. For a rich orientation to the discriminative use of the lecture in relation to discussion see Perlman, "Teaching Case Work by the Discussion Method," and "The Lecture as a Method in Teaching Case Work."

cise analysis of a whole into its parts, the consideration of the parts
in relation to the whole, and the final synthesis of the parts into a
formulation for use require the illumination of knowledge at many
points. Without knowledge, some wholes cannot be broken down,
and some parts have no relationship to one another. Without knowledge, they do not fit together to comprise an intelligible entity. Hence
throughout this process the instructor will be imparting and evaluating knowledge with which to think, knowledge which brings order
out of confusion.

While social work educators are in favor of encouraging and
holding students accountable to acquire knowledge through their
own efforts, the fact remains that much that is needed is unattain-
abe except through the hand and mouth sources of experience, or
it is sufficiently inaccessible that it is not possible for the students'
acquisition to be nicely timed with classroom demands. The volu-
minous literature on social casework and its related disciplines is
unevenly developed, with much proffered in some aspects and
meager gleanings in other areas. Points of view change rapidly, sc
that some of the old is outdated while some of the new is untested.
The social work literature is largely dispersed through many journals over the years. The instructor or experienced social worker
knows the gaps in the literature, the trends in thinking and practice
over a period of time, the controversial issues, real and semantic,
all of which enables her to convey knowledge selectively and to appraise it. The timing of this contribution will be determined by
need, commonly apparent as follows: First, it will often be given in
anticipation of need, as preparation for next cases, next steps which
make a demand for new knowledge in one or more areas, such as
human behavior, psychopathology, community resources, structure
and function of agency, social casework process. Second, it may be
contributed retrospectively, to clarify confusion, to help students
relate and reconcile what they have taken on but not taken in.
Third, when a class is not participating productively, a decisive
consideration is whether they need to know, whether they have
reached a point of need to be given some wherewithal to break the
impasse, such as information, questions which enlighten, ideas
which redirect thinking, or summarization which clarifies. In such
instances the knowledge imparted for discussion sometimes bears

on learning process, on knowledge of selves as learners, on feelings and attitudes appropriate to social work, on working relationships. This is never focused on an individual but is given when it can be oriented to the group response or to a common problem.

Summarization concludes every case and every course. It is interspersed throughout the analytic process. It breaks the tedium of the stage of precision, even though it is part and parcel of it, in that it gives sense to the painstaking labors. What does all this add up to? What have we got to show for it? Such questions engage interest and participation, in spite of the difficulty of the task. Summarization is fruition.[10] Learning is manifested in this activity. Obviously, at the start the student's summary of a case is rudimentary. Often it is an adding-up without weighting the parts and relating them dynamically. From course to course one expects to see marked movement in students' capacity to synthesize. In that summarization is the fruition of the learning process, it is a major test of integration. The summary lecture is introduced to interpret the meaning of what we have, that is the interrelationship of the parts and the gist of the situation, with emphasis given to that which has vital import. It is the instructor's mission to inject, if need be, that something which makes the whole something more than the sum of its parts. It is her knowledge and experience which enable her to appraise the significance of a part in one whole which makes this total different from that in similar configurations. It is the instructor's responsibility to impart the knowledge which enables students to see the logic of the final inferences. Without certain knowledge, other inferences might well have been logical. Only as inferences make sense, will the process of summarization be intrenched for use through having proved useful. When summarization is unusually difficult for a student, it may indicate a lack of knowledge to differentiate the import of the parts. Having the knowledge, drill in the process of summarization is an important means to the integration of learning.

Just as every case closes with a summary session, every course terminates with a session in which the learning experience is summarized and evaluated. Prior to the closing session the students often will have been given an assignment in which they have been

10. Whitehead, *op. cit.*

asked to discuss the principles and concepts presented in the course which they have found useful or not useful, giving examples from their field experience. Or in the final course they will have been asked to summarize and evaluate their major learnings of the two quarters' advanced work. The instructor takes the major responsibility in the class session for course summarization. Her aim, unless contraindicated, is to supplement, to widen and deepen a bit the student's thinking, and to give a glimpse of where they go from here. In a course summary there are pauses for brief student participation, but it is important that these sessions do not break down into discussion typical of the everyday work session. This is a time for the instructor to give to the group as a whole, out of her knowledge and experience, a perspective to orient them for next steps. In a sense these are sessions for quiet reflection on the students' part more than for active participation, which may involve them. For assimilation they can work on it in subsequent sessions in terms of their individual need. The final course-closing session focuses on an appraisal of what students have for use in the field of practice, with emphasis on the fact that the means to learning have been given them for the pursuit of further knowledge, understanding, and skill. These means are identified and their continued use envisaged. In a sense, final sessions are nurturing sessions, in which, after the labors of each case and of the course as a whole, the students should be given sustenance as they go forth to meet the next demand.

The stage of generalization emerges from summarization. As the learnings of a given case or a course are synthesized, the professional learner wants to identify and salt down what out of all that he has learned will be useful, "come a rainy day or an hour of need." Whereas synthesis is fruition, generalization is the "garnering of the harvest" and the taking stock of what, in general, is on hand for the morrow and what specifically is on tap for the vicissitudes of the days to come.[11] The process of generalization has been taught through both discussion and the lecture by questioning and by using and formulating general concepts. Generalization has occurred throughout this learning experience, through studying cases comparatively, to see the import of variables and to formulate basic concepts and principles from common elements. It has occurred re-

11. Whitehead, *op. cit.*

peatedly as specific situations have been looked at in the light of generalizations in the literature; for example, this unmarried mother in the light of recorded thinking about individuals in this state of life; the parental roles and the interplay in this Italian family in the light of formulations about the Italian family; this adolescent against the background of what is known of this developmental period. In the final deliberations on specific cases and in the course summaries a more comprehensive and systematic attempt at generalization is initiated by the instructor. The lecture with or without discussion plays a prominent part. Whereas generalizations taught fragmentarily throughout class sessions have been spontaneous, these terminating sessions of case and course will often call for the planned lecture. It is emphasized that generalization constitutes professional wisdom only in so far as general concepts are questioned and tested in individual instances. This emphasis in didactic teaching will fall on receptive ears only in so far as students have repeatedly experienced, in case analysis in classroom and field, the testing, refining, and correcting of general concepts. It is through the lectures and didactic teachings in the sessions which terminate case or course, sessions which have the aim of integrating through summarization and generalization, that the instructor has an opportunity to demonstrate professional wholeness. Her philosophy, her attitudes, her ways of thinking and responding, are manifested with an entirety which can engage students deeply. As commonly occurs throughout life, it is on leaving an experience that the vestiges of resistance often give way. Thus final sessions are vitally important. It is our aim that students may take something of the whole rather than an array of parts to the next learning venture.

4. *Some Typical Responses and Their Significance*

The personality development of the student as well as movement in learning is revealed in the classroom through the part the student plays in discussion and in his response to didactic presentations. In the interplay of the group in relation to the instructor, the learning patterns of individuals are being manifested, sometimes in well-defined form but more often only sketchily.

One sees the student who can give and take freely and who therefore gives way undefensively. Reacting to criticism as help rather than as an attack, he responds to difference in thinking critically but not necessarily negatively.

One sees also the student who can give but not take. He cannot have his giving modified and responds to alteration of it, with angry persistence, giving way, finally, with a sense of being wronged or defeated. This student sometimes is challenged by didactic instruction to oppose his thinking forcibly, as though fighting the authority of the instructor and/or his knowledge.

There is the student who early in the course often needs to establish his identity through talking a great deal, whether or not he has anything pertinent to say. This need to seem adequate may or may not have the quality of attacking or outwitting the instructor through hair splitting and through pointing to discrepancies in the instructor's thinking, as though exerting every effort to find her wrong. In these instances of hostile attack it is soon clear that he is more concerned with the instructor than with the subject matter and that it is the relationship with the one who gives and demands which is involving him.

Of negativistic students at the college level, Bloom states:

> One of the major problems of a teacher in handling a discussion is recognizing the presence of these hypercritical individuals as well as in avoiding being lured into spending a considerable amount of the class time in following the false scents . . . especially when these are primarily to gratify the needs for opposition rather than because of their clear relevance to the problems being discussed. If their thoughts can be properly channeled, these individuals can be highly stimulating members of a discussion class; and if their negativism can be turned to ideas rather than people, they may, by virtue of this negativism, become highly creative and original in their problem solving. Thus negativism, if properly used, can become a very useful characteristic. To the extent that it is merely generalized opposition, it is frustration and tension producing for the individual and useless to the group.[12]

Then there is the student who can take but not give verbally. His silent but attentive participation, his expressive face, suggest

12. Benjamin S. Bloom, "Personality Variables and Classroom Performance," *Journal of the National Association of Deans of Women*, Vol. XVI, No. 4 (June, 1953).

the import of the learning for him, and often he may be learning more than the student who is very active in discussion through which he is defending himself aggressively.

There is the student also who gives fearfully and who is heartened when his thinking is affirmed but who beats a hasty retreat when taken issue with or when pressed for elaboration.

And, finally, there is the student who stays out, through being both verbally and attitudinally unresponsive.

Repeatedly one sees this range of responses as students come up against the pressure to participate implicit in the discussion group. It is the conviction of the educator who uses the discussion method that participation is essential for maximum learning and also for the development of professional responsibility. This is one of several working relationships through which the student may develop desirable patterns for professional relationship through growth in capacity to give and take responsibly and objectively. There is great variation in the import of the problematic responses. Sometimes they bespeak basic personality problems and deep resistance to learning. At other times they reflect prior experience. Some students have had more experience in discussion groups than others. Some may have been traumatized in an earlier group experience. Some have had experience in groups where the measure of adequate participation has been quite different from that of the social casework class, in which discussion and debate are not an end but a means. The purpose of class discussion may have to be clarified from time to time; and one fact of which some students need to be reminded is that we are discussing in order primarily to learn casework, not to learn discussion skills. Hence we do not have to win our arguments. We may contribute to class learning through losing as well as through winning, through being wrong as well as right in our thinking. If the instructor's response identifies the student's contribution as being useful in the day's progression, he may get a sense of achievement rather than of defeat and perhaps not need to adhere defensively to his thinking.

The experienced classroom instructor has developed ways of dealing with problematic responses which ordinarily help students change, so that learning progresses for the individual as well as for the group as a whole. The group itself deals with problematic responses, sometimes in ways which are helpful, at other times in ways which are not helpful, to the individual concerned, in that they may reinforce his defenses and thus produce a fallacious appearance of rigid hostile aggression. Or they may crash his defenses, causing a retreat into silence or pretensive agreement which covers inner rebellion. Sometimes, therefore, individual consultation on the student's response is indicated outside the classroom. When problematic responses do not give way to the instructor's ordinarily helpful efforts, often there is great rigidity and deep resistance to any modification in ways of relating and learning. Because there are limits to the help which a classroom instructor can give an individual in the group, it is often not possible to understand the import of the student's responses or to see clearly whether they represent a well-defined characteristic pattern or a more fragmentary and transitory response. Since field instruction permits more individualization of the learner in terms of teaching and helping, the rigidity or flexibility of the student's responses can be tested more reliably in field work than in the classroom.

The present impression is that there is great variation in the significance of the student's lack of movement as a participant in classroom instruction. It is a common observation that the student's professional development in the field and in subsequent practice often belies his inadequate response in the classroom. This does not argue for indifference to problematic responses. Many factors have operated for an easy acceptance by classroom instructors of wide variation among students in this area of performance and for a low expectancy of and demand on them. In this there have been two notable factors among others: First, the size of classes and the casework instructor's feeling of incompetence in understanding group process and in functioning as a leader of group discussion may lead the instructor to charge the student's lack of movement to her own lack of skill in dealing with the individual in a group. Second, a classroom instructor inevitably is focused on the movement of the group as a whole more than on the progress of any one student, and, consequently, problematic responses may be overlooked or appraised in terms of their usefulness to the group. A provocative student, even when obsessionally so, may stimulate the instructor and the other students to produce creatively, so that he is valued for contributing to learning. The import of his learning pattern, an anxious, aggressive attack to master opponents and to outdo others, for his development as a professional helper and collaborator should not be ignored. Since the social worker does not deal with ideas apart from people, Bloom's evaluation of negativism as a potential for creativity in problem-solving may not hold in professional education.[13]

It is important, therefore, that problematic responses should be noted and dealt with in so far as is possible in the group. For further understanding they should be checked with the student's responses in other classes, in contacts with the administration, and, most important, with his development in field work. In this way the faculty may gain an understanding of the individual as a learner. In so far as his problematic attitudes and responses are pervasive so as to limit his professional development, collaborative effort may occur to help him through a consistent approach.

Social work educators have identified some configurations of behavior which, when persistent, seem to constitute patterns of learning that have varying import for education for social work. These tentative formulations need to be tested through systematic comprehensive observation of the learner throughout the educational experience. For reliable educational diagnoses and predictions, recorded observations of the individual's response to specific experiences in field work and to the educational measures used to help him learn are most important. As stated earlier, research into the learning process both of normal and of problematic learners is needed to establish criteria for use in the selection and elimination of students and for the improvement of educational methods. Beyond the contribution to professional education, such research should throw light on the normal adaptive functions of the ego.

5. Summary

We have envisaged an instructor intent on helping students learn and intent on imparting what they need to know now for current use in order to know more next time. The *how* of teaching has been

13. Bloom, *op. cit.*

a discriminative use of the lecture method along with and within the discussion method. Specifics within this have been her responsible, purposive, and well-timed use of the student's activity, of focalization and of repetition, as well as of comparison for generalization, and of progression in giving and demanding. Other specifics have been her efforts to make the student's learning a conscious process and to establish and sustain a constructive working relationship, through giving as well as demanding and through enabling the student to function responsibly through knowing his obligations and responsibilities. The areas of knowledge for understanding which have been conveyed, stated broadly, are: subject matter per se in knowledge of human behavior, community resources, agency function and administration, and social casework process. There has been conveyed knowledge of the learning process, the scope of the course, ways to proceed in order to get along, how to study, how to think, and what feelings and attitudes are appropriate to social work. Both directly and indirectly some knowledge and understanding of self as a learner have been imparted. In short, knowledge of thinking, feeling, understanding, and doing has been conveyed in ways which have aimed to extend the individual's integrative capacity. Throughout, there has been concern to lower the anxiety and tension in learning and to help the individual develop his potentials for dealing with it constructively, so that learning may progress.

II. THE USE OF ASSIGNMENTS

1. *Evaluative and Educational Aims*

The fourth and final test involved in planning and in conducting an educational program is that of evaluating the effectiveness of the program in attaining its objectives through appraising the progress of the students. Of this Tyler states:

> The common practice is to appraise the knowledge of the students and certain of their technical skills. In addition, many professional schools appraise the students' ability to solve problems as these are presented in verbal form. Few institutions provide for careful, systematic appraisal of problem solving in the professional situation, and appraisal of professional interests and attitudes. Hence the School does not have a compre-

hensive picture of the achievement of its students in terms of its own purposes.[14]

Tyler states further that a comprehensive program of evaluation uses varied devices for obtaining evidence of educational progress and that these devices should include not only written tests and examinations but also observations, interviews, questionnaires, reports from the field, samples of the student's work—in short, any device which gives evidence regarding the significant behavior of the student. For light on the immediate effectiveness of the school's educational program and for evidence of the permanence of learning and the extent to which it has achieved some continuity with professional experience, Tyler recommends three appraisals—one early in attendance at the professional school, one near his graduation, and one after several years of service in the profession.

In relation to these devices it can be said that social work education has until recently relied less on written tests and examinations than have some other professions. It has made wide use of written assignments and problem-solving projects. Its evaluative process has started early and been continuous through the students' school residence. It has not followed them into practice through the conduct of follow-up studies on representative groups of students from a cross-section of practice, as suggested by Tyler. In the recent establishment and expansion of programs for advanced education, we are now having the opportunity to observe the outcome of learning in a selected group of students, after considerable service in the profession. A distinctive feature of the social work evaluative process has been the full records kept on the student's performance in the field. These records are focused on progress in specific areas of learning, on identifying problems in learning, on defining what to work on and the means to the solution of the problems, as well as on evaluating the student's response to the teaching and helping measures of supervision. A notable feature is that it is common practice for the student to participate in the evaluation of his work and for the supervisor to share her appraisal with the student, orienting criticism as much as possible to norms for stages of learning. A good deal of thought has been given to the formulation of

14. Ralph W. Tyler, "Distinctive Attributes of Education for the Professions," *Social Work Journal*, April, 1952.

principles of criticism, in order that evaluation may facilitate rather than impede learning. This procedure is structured as to content and systematic in terms of timing, since field reports commonly must go to the school, mid-quarter or semester, while more comprehensive ones are sent in at the close of every quarter or semester. Thus the student commonly experiences five or six comprehensive evaluations of his performance while in the school. It is common practice, also, for evaluative conferences with advisers and classroom instructors within the school to bring together the learning progress and problems of the classroom and of the field.

Perhaps a distinctive attitude of social work education has been the social work educator's awareness that evaluative measures in and of themselves must be educational if they are not to deter learning and if they are to yield valid findings. Consequently, evaluation has been rather highly individualized, first, in terms of the student; second, in light of the fact that an orderly progression in learning cannot be maintained consistently through case assignment, it has attempted to individualize in terms of the variations in demand which field practice has exerted on the student; and, third, there has been variation in terms of the supervisor's or teacher's evaluative methods. The many variables resulting from this have complicated the situation for systematic research into the learning process and the educational programs. In spite of this fact, considerable headway has been made in some schools in the establishment of some common evaluative practices in terms of focus, agreement on what is significant to observe and record, and adherence to certain basic principles in teaching and helping. Records of performance are therefore becoming increasingly reliable indexes of the student's progress. Increasingly the reports lend themselves to comparison, so that research for the more precise establishment of criteria of progress is indicated.

Since professional education is education for use, the teachings of the classroom undergo their most meaningful test in field practice, where the changes which education has aimed to effect in the learner are more convincingly demonstrated. They are tested to some extent also as certain casework learning is put to use in the research project. It is not surprising that evaluative procedures have been developed and formalized and norms tentatively indicated to a greater extent in the field than in classroom teaching. More recently, thought is being given to criteria of movement, progress, and regression in the classroom, as well as to the structuring of assignments and examinations so that they may be more reliable measures of change in the learner. The attempt to select and arrange learning experiences for an orderly progression in the attainment of objectives, the attempt, also, to identify evidence of specific change in relation to objectives delineated in the preceding chapter and in the discussion of the use of readings is now being carried on with reference to written assignments, course examinations, and comprehensive examinations. Each of these has a twofold purpose, to advance learning and to test learning. The test element may serve either to facilitate or to deter learning, depending upon the degree of negative affect—that is, acute fear, resentment, chronic anxiety, feelings of helplessness—which a test situation may incite. The prior educational experience and habits formed in relation to evaluative procedures will operate in the student's response. Since the class assignment makes a different demand and does not present the same problem as a deterrent to learning, we discuss it first.

2. *Educational Principles for the Attainment of Aims*

In furtherance of learning, class assignments, which are usually two or three papers each quarter in the casework sequence, should make it necessary for the students to seek information, that is, acquire knowledge beyond that conveyed in the classroom, and to use knowledge, imparted and acquired, through applying it in the solution of problems typical of those which they will encounter in practice. The assignments aim to test knowing, thinking, feeling, and doing through questions which call for imaginative consideration, for analysis, for synthesis, and for comparison for generalization; they aim, also, to test through the presentation of concepts which students are asked to apply specifically in a given case, or in citations from their field practice or through the demand that they identify concepts and working principles in a given case situation and evaluate their use. Throughout, therefore, questions aim to test their grasp of the casework process. Some instructors give out the quarter's assignments at the beginning of the course, in order that students may know exactly the what and the when of the course demands. This is in order that they may become habituated to planning their time and effort. Other instructors make assignments as the course proceeds, but always with what is considered ample time for the student to do thorough and competent work.

These assignments are among the best measures for engaging the student actively in learning. They can well push him a bit but nòt so far beyond where he should be that he does not have a chance to do a competent piece of work. Students for the most part are challenged by the assignments. They clearly identify them as learning experiences, as well as evaluative measures. Accordingly, on both counts, they are concerned to receive criticism, in fact, to know exactly where they measure up to standards and where they fall down. It is our practice at the University of Chicago to discuss the majority of these assignments very specifically in the classroom and also to write rather full comments on each paper. In these comments the attitudes which should prevail in the classroom should be expressed in the marginal notations. Whenever more than fragmentary negative comments are made or when a learning lag is discernible, there should be suggestions as to what the student needs to work on in order to solve his learning problems. Appointments for help are often proffered. Since each instructor keeps an evaluative record of each paper, it is often possible in conference with the student to comment specifically on movement or on lags which persist. These records of class written work serve as a basis for comparison with field-work reports and for consultation between classroom instructor and field supervisor. They serve as a basis also for individual advisory work with the student.

The progression in assignments is as follows: At the start, more help is given in guiding students in their search for information and in how to proceed in handling the subject. To sketch the progression specifically and comprehensively would be to repeat the criteria of the progression as shown in the discussion of case selection and arrangement.[15] The same criteria for simple and advanced guide the instructor in the demands conveyed in assignments. Assignments vary also with the movement of the class, so that while often they would be focused forward and constitute preparation for the next step in learning, at other times they would look backward. When

15. See chap. 9.

the going has been rough and instructors want to help students clarify and tack down certain aspects which have been difficult, an assignment may in a sense be repetitive drill. Briefly, the distinguishing mark of advanced assignments over early assignments would be that the student, within limits, could increasingly be expected to infer soundly from smaller evidence through ability to select decisive evidence; to recognize the need for more evidence; to see beneath the surface. Other characteristics of the advanced assignment would be greater precision in the student's use of knowledge, an increased capacity to focalize, to individuate, to integrate, and to formulate. In relation to integration, he could be expected to bring some things together through seeing their relationships. There should be less either/or in his evaluations. He should be able to take more factors into account than earlier.

In evaluating the learner's integrative capacity, instructors must orient their appraisals to the knowledge which the student could be expected to have attained. He cannot see relatedness beyond his knowledge, and sometimes beyond knowledge tested through experience. Hence all the implications of a case situation may not be grasped at the close of the final casework course. With reference to formulation, inexperienced students do not acquire great facility in this in two years of study. This capacity awaits experience. The educational aim with reference to both these developments is that of setting in operation a habit of trying to integrate and to formulate. Appraisal therefore relates to the learner's propensity to put two and two together and to look for what a case or an experience teaches in terms of principles for use elsewhere, rather than to richness and precision in his production. Instructors must guard against using their own capacities in these areas as a measuring stick. One of the values of repetitive use of the same materials in the classroom is that it enables the instructor to establish norms.

Written assignments which do not exceed the student's capacity to expand may increase his integrative capacity. This is because there is time for calm deliberation and the opportunity to discharge affect through activity in preparation, which may include discussion with colleagues. There is also the chance to use what he has learned of where and how to find out, as well as the time to pull forth assimilated learning to use in solving a problem, in the process of which further assimilation may occur. Repeatedly one gets evidence that knowledge shelved in the upper story is drawn on for use as the student actively engages himself in meeting fully the demands of the assignment. Class assignments can thus be a vital educational measure when designed with close reference to the learning progression and when students can accept them as a means to growth. When the student is more intent on grading well than on learning, when he is content in seeming to be rather than in being, he has the opportunity to get an inordinate amount of help from others. This is one of the limitations of the classroom assignment both as an educational measure and as a testing device. This behavior in students in a professional school is significant. In each instance, it raises questions about the student's capacity for the work and the student's personality development. Perhaps he is basically too immature to engage responsibly in the educational process. Finally, does this behavior bespeak the total impact of a system which is promoting regression rather than growth? Why so much anxiety about evaluation? What is wrong with the relationship between the student and the school? Why do people who have committed themselves to a goal shed responsibility for its attainment? These and other questions bedevil us.

III. THE USE OF EXAMINATIONS

Whereas the very word "assignment" connotes self-activity, a task to do, examination connotes being "done to." It has been said that one of the demands of a profession, out of its responsibility to the community, is that its members give evidence of capacity to use the body of knowledge and skill essential for competent practice. Within some professions, the examination has been the traditional method of establishing proof of competence. Examination systems vary widely between professions and within some professions. In social work education, examination systems for the field as a whole are a recent development. Several discernible factors have operated here. Social work education in its early years was more agency-centered than school-centered. The evaluation of a student's competence rested on his performance in practice, and it was difficult to test this performance in a written examination. Social work educators, on the whole, have been skeptical of the examination as a reliable means to gauge professional competence. With reference to these attitudes, it is important to bear in mind that social work educators have largely been social work practitioners who did not experience comprehensive examination systems in their own professional education.

The fact that social work education until fairly recently has consisted in training for special functions rather than for the field as a whole has resulted in separate course examinations determined by the inclinations and educational convictions of the individual instructor rather than in comprehensive examinations administered by the school through the interrelated work of an examination committee composed of faculty members from the several fields of study. Perhaps because the profession itself is not subject to the procedures of licensing and registration through examinations administered in the community, social work educators have been able comfortably to evade the issue of comprehensive examinations. They have not been regarded as essential preparation for subsequent examination experiences. Whatever the causes may be, very important is the fact that evasion has resulted in many social work educators not having studied examination methods to determine what can be tested. Ineffectual experimental trials have yielded bizarre returns, which have argued against the measure rather than for intelligent use of it. The recent great development in the public social services, in which applicants must take civil service examinations, has perhaps operated to induce some schools to establish more systematic examination procedures. More influential determinants in this trend, however, could well be social work's increasing sense of identity as a profession, which engenders a feeling of responsibility to exert group discipline in various forms. The university setting doubtless has exerted the pressure of its ways on schools of social work. Within professional schools, because social workers have a conception of themselves as educators with a responsibility to develop students oriented to the profession as a whole rather than as practitioners teaching students to perform a specific function, they are drawn toward traditional educational methods and mores. It is well that these be not embraced uncritically but, instead, that they be put to use experimentally with readiness to adapt them to social work's educational aims.

1. The Examination, a Problem in Learning

In schools of social work where the educational emphasis and the curriculum content are focused on training for the profession as a whole and where the regimes would adequately meet the criteria established for professional education as differentiated from technical training, some educators are skeptical of the comprehensive examination system and of examinations in general. They are loath to institute them, out of their awareness of the many problems which they present. They see them as a deterrent to learning and as having dubious value in testing learning. Sometimes they are apologetic for not having them, feeling that perhaps they should for respectability in the university setting and among professions; but their conviction that social work education is different, that certain elements in its process in relation to its aims would be endangered, leads them to hold back. This reluctance, in the writer's opinion, is not purely resistance to change or inertia in problem-solving. The social worker's understanding of the human learner, his concept of this educational process as being student-centered rather than subject-centered, his awareness of the emotional elements in learning in relation to the size of the integrative task to which social work students are subjected—these insights among others, make him discerning of the import of examinations in the learning process. The writer dares to presume that social work educators have an essential awareness in this area lacked by their colleagues in some other professions, where examination systems are a heritage which they have taken over without reference to recently acquired insights into behavior motivations and the integrative task in professional learning. If the author were to choose between some examination systems and no examination system, she would unhesitatingly choose the latter.

It is noteworthy that in medicine, where the student has traditionally been subject to course examinations at frequent intervals and to rigorous comprehensive examinations periodically, some medical educators are becoming concerned to modify their examination procedures. Whereas one of the important final objectives of medical training as a whole is the development of skills in dealing with people, and in view of current recognition that changes to be effected in the learner should be set in operation early, these medical educators are currently critical of the preclinical program, which for the first two years fosters the idea in the student that he is expected to be wholly a scientist, essentially unrelated to people. Among the means identified as important for the development of a mature professional perspective and a social approach to medical problems is that of reducing the feeling of competition that burdens the students at this stage of learning. Accordingly, some schools are modifying their grading and examination systems. Of this, one report states: "In a few schools grades are entirely de-emphasized and the student is only informed that he is passing or failing. In other schools only general categories of levels of achievement are given at the end of the year; in still others, written examinations are optional and are taken by the student largely to indicate to him what progress he is making."[16] The bulletin of one medical school states its educational emphasis as being on "teaching basic principles, methods, scientific evaluation of data and on the student's attitudes, understanding and performance in handling problems of the patient as related to health; to prevention, diagnosis and care of illness; and to the patient as a person and a member of society." Among the methods specified for the attainment of these aims, it is stated: "The student will be given an increasing responsibility for his own education *during the four years* by providing him with free time, to be used with the advice of a tutor, and with the opportunity to perform certain long range projects which will require independent thinking by the student. It is anticipated that the student will be graded as pass or fail, and that final examinations will be held approximately once a year, with interim examinations being held as voluntary and anonymous exercises to permit students and instructors to appraise their progress."[17]

In social work education where some schools have de-emphasized grades, only to return to traditional grading systems, and where schools have known little or no emphasis on examinations, only to

16. *Psychiatry and Medical Education: Report of the 1951 Conference on Psychiatric Education, Cornell University* (Washington: American Psychiatric Association, 1952), p. 23.

17. "Requirements and Courses for the Academic Year, 1952–53," *Bulletin of Western Reserve University, The School of Medicine,* LV, No. 10 (June, 1952), 87.

develop them, we are of the opinion that we do not prepare the student for the competition of professional life through attempts to eliminate it in the professional school. Competition is there, whether or not we grade or examine students. Our grading and examination systems therefore may serve as a means to help students compete with integrity and less anxiety. Anonymous course examinations may foster insecurity rather than lower the student's anxiety, because they remove the support implicit in being known, for better or worse, by those who are responsible for helping him master problems in learning. Also, de-emphasizing grades does not necessarily imply less precise evaluation of the student. In so far as it does, however, anxiety may mount through the student's inability to appraise himself in relation to learning norms. Because, as is increasingly recognized, examinations operate for good or evil in the learning process, it is essential that their limitations and potentials be appraised and that their import for students be understood. Let us consider, first, some of the problems which the comprehensive examinations present. Why do some social work educators fear them? What is to be said in their favor? What are some of the ways in which they may be made a constructive experience, one which may aid rather than obstruct integration?

The attitudes which adult students bring to examinations are, by and large, unfavorable ones, apparently in part as an outgrowth of their earlier educational experience. This is in spite of the fact that we encounter a group of students who have successfully survived previous examination systems. Why so much anxiety about them? Why the depleting cram sessions through which learning is fragmented more than it is integrated? One answer is that many students have been traumatized through experiencing examinations which it was possible to survive by just such means. Examinations often have been an endurance test, a girding the brow for a battle of wits, more than an educational experience. Many students have developed a kind of technique for studying for and passing certain kinds of examinations, so that they may have reached a point of little anxiety about subject tests in college or even about comprehensive examinations in college. The course examinations in the professional school provoke much less anxiety than the comprehensives, first, because there is only one course at stake and, second, because to assimilate the content of one course is relatively easy as compared with grasping the whole of social work through relating its parts. It has been observed that comprehensive examinations given under certain conditions are preceded by a period of interrupted learning in the field, that students manifest marked tension, fatigue, and emotional disturbance in many forms, in one or more areas of their work. It has been noted also that the review process in carrying them backward removes them from vital contact with current learning and often is not integrated with it as a basis for subsequent progression at accelerated tempo.

In considering the meaning of this, it is essential to recall the possible meaning of the experience to the student. First, this is a life-work situation with much at stake emotionally in success or failure for the young adult. He has committed himself to certain goals and anticipates deep frustration if he should fail. Where comprehensive examinations are given at the close of one year of effort and when these alone determine whether or not he is qualified to continue his work for the professional degree, he has a great deal at stake. All that he has learned in classroom and field may go down before one set of examination questions. A high demand is made on his feeling of trust in himself in relation to his newly acquired competence, as well as on his feeling of trust in those who now have this power over him. Will they test him fairly, or is it their intent to find him wanting, if humanly possible? The nature of the .relationship he has had up to now with the school as an administrative entity as well as with individual instructors will do much to stabilize him or to produce uncertainty. We refer here to the previous formulation of the integrative task—"I want something very much"—wish strong; "I fear greatly the consequences"—fear strong. The integrative task is heavier when the intensity of affect is heavy. We refer also to the fact that negative affect increases the integrative task, whereas positive affect lightens it. Hence dread and resentment obstruct, whereas hope facilitates.[18] In connection with the factor of resentment, since it particularly tends to beget fear of failure, it cannot be overlooked that students often resent the *heavy* weighting of the comprehensive examinations as unjust, in that their total record does not operate in the final judgment as to their

18. See chap. 4, pp. 94-95.

educability. Also out of the past, students often equate an examination with an inquisition. How often in oral examinations, at the start, students react defensively, as though attacked. This response often gives way as they experience a helpful attitude, an intent to understand their discussion of questions, and a concern to affirm the student's stance rather than to trip him or corner him.

Second, from an early point the student has become aware of the difference in professional learning from earlier academic learning. Peripheral learning has not been so possible, because the process has engaged him deeply; hence old ways of getting by through giving out selectively have been disturbed. The profession's scale of values has not been sufficiently incorporated that he knows what is less important and what is most important.[19] Will he be safe in the examination without knowing everything equally well? On what shall he focus for preparation? For what will he be held accountable? Not knowing, he may know nothing to do but to attempt to recapture everything—hence cram sessions, which become a flight to the past, with loss of contact with learning as it progresses.

Third, the timing of the comprehensive examinations is important. In this educators can be guided only by the developmental progress which commonly obtains. At Chicago the qualifying examinations which admit the student to candidacy come at the end of the third quarter. The final comprehensives occur two or three weeks before the completion of their work in the sixth quarter. The qualifying examinations mark the point when the student moves into advanced casework, field-work, and classroom courses. The assumption based on norms established through observation of students is that toward the end of his second quarter, stabilization and greater self-dependence are manifested, while in the third quarter the student has been relatively free to learn, so that some integration has occurred. Therefore, this seems a desirable point for the first comprehensives. It is to be remembered, however, that there is great variation in when learning proves to be traumatic and that many factors produce this variation. It is therefore always possible that certain individuals will undergo this stress when the integrative function of the ego is being worked to such a maximum that they are in a phase when their resources for dealing with

19. See chap. 3, p. 60.

anxiety are below par. Consequently, it is not possible for an examination to be an equal test of all individuals merely because it is given at the same stage of their schooling.

In relation to timing, it is pretty generally agreed that the second year is one in which, after the initial resistances have been worked through, the student has found his footing and is ready to progress; that the affect which has made the integrative task large in the first year is normally decreasing; and that ordinarily the student is ready to give himself over to the enjoyment of learning. The concern of some educators is that when comprehensive examinations occupy the foreground at the close of each year, the student's energies are again spent in fighting anxiety and in recapturing the past, at a time when he might have moved ahead smoothly because he was at an integrative stage. It is generally agreed that, with few exceptions, the students whom the school expects to fail are the ones that fail and that the others come through alive, probably with their egos intact and perhaps even with a sense of achievement in having survived an ordeal. Some educators question whether the time might have been spent more productively by the students who pass. Certainly, it is clear that every effort must be made to have the examination experiences in these decisively important developmental periods carry learning forward rather than impede it. It is also clear that the attainment of this aim will be costly in terms of faculty time and energy for study of the examining process and for construction of questions which serve their intent and which are oriented to the limits of the examination as a means to test professional development.

2. *The Examination, a Means to Learning*

Those who are convinced that social work education should use this measure both for evaluation and to further learning, those who have tried and are still experimenting for its productive use, think as follows:

Since social workers increasingly face the reality of examinations which test their professional competence as they qualify for positions, the professional school should prepare them for this experience, through affording a similar experience. In this connection it is recognized that the examination experience in the professional school should be a corrective one, that is, should modify in so far as possible the attitudes and the responses which have been formed in earlier educational experience toward the examination itself and toward preparation for it. If these examinations are to be a learning experience, one aspect of the learning might well be to learn to prepare responsibly rather than opportunistically for an examination.

Since professional life brings many situations in which the individual must marshal his resources and perform competently under stress, the examination procedure offers an opportunity to develop the capacity for self-mastery. The conviction is that the ego develops as the individual *masters* difficult situations. This is quite different from precariously surviving them by hook or crook.

Preparation for examinations in looking backward, reviewing the past for current use, and in looking horizontally across the board for relatedness can further integration rather than impede it if done under favorable conditions. Elsewhere it has been said that we are making an unrealistic demand when we expect a nice integration of content on the part of students within the two-year period. If this is so, the primary purpose of the qualifying examinations cannot be to test for more than rudimentary integration. One of its major purposes can be, however, to set in operation an effort to integrate. As the student takes with him the imprint of his preparation for the examination and the questions on which he has worked, it may be expected that he will move into the second year conscious of the need to integrate, which may induce an integrative focus. It is a controversial question whether this measure best serves as an integrator of learning or whether a series of assigned written projects in which the student has the task of relating areas of learning within courses and between courses would be more effective. Such projects could be accompanied by evaluative conferences and could require revision.

The problem throughout is *to diminish* the anxiety element and the hostility element. The task is to afford the student a corrective examination experience, one in which he can feel emotionally secure and be free to produce productively rather than fragmentarily. If he can come out of examinations with a feeling of having mastered his fears rather than merely having survived an ordeal, he may have grown through the experience and can reasonably be expected to

meet the demands of the next examination with greater resourcefulness and integrity. There are several means for the attainment of this
aim in varying measure, depending upon faculty wisdom and skill
and upon the student's capacity for modification of habitual attitudes
and ways.

First, if comprehensive examinations are given, course examinations also must be given as preparation. This implies in social casework, as in each field covered, that the basic course examinations
should have questions which test for the same abilities through the
same means.

Second, students should be prepared for the comprehensive examination through knowing in advance its scope and the kind of
demands which it will make, notably use of knowledge and interrelationships in areas of study. This preparation can occur through
two means, both of which are desirable. A comprehensive written
statement given to each student shortly after admission to the
school which gives (1) the examination requirements; (2) the registration procedures; (3) the content of each examination in terms of
fields of study by courses; (4) a description of the committee activity in preparing and testing questions; (5) the grading system
and procedure, for example, what he will be graded on, who in
terms of school function will read what parts, that his identity will
be unknown to the grader, and the provision made for below-
standard and marginal papers to be reviewed by several instructors;
(6) the regulations for repeating the examination a second time; and
(7), finally, the kind of preparation necessary. It is essential that students know the examination demands from the start, in order to
govern their note-taking, their class participation, and their study
accordingly. They thus know the grounds on which they stand,
and their footing may not become unsteady through the earth's
beginning to quake suddenly at a later point.

It is desirable also that, following the registration for the examinations, the group to be examined have an opportunity to meet with
members of the school faculty, in order to raise questions and to
discuss the concerns they may have. Contact with those who are
about to have them in their power can reassure, in so far as feeling
is understood and as they convey an intent to be helpful through
clarifying confusion and through specific suggestions which focalize

preparation. The decisive point here is that faculty should not minimize the ordeal but instead help the individual face it realistically through emphasis on preparation and through help in how to prepare. It is desirable throughout that students be helped to see and feel this experience as one which can contribute to learning rather than wholly as a test device. It is recognized that the threat of its test function may make some students inaccessible to its other aspect.

Third, it is the writer's opinion that if we are intent on making the first comprehensive examination a corrective experience, if we regard it highly as a learning experience and want it to serve our educational aims as well as yield valid test findings on the student, the faculty, and the curriculum, then we will not give it undue weight in the total educational experience. It is important that we adapt this educational method to the nature of our learning experience, regardless of practices which may obtain elsewhere. Again, we recall the nature and tempo of our learning, our integrative task, the variation in students in the timing of the integrative stress, and, finally, our educational aim, which is concerned, perhaps to a greater extent than in some professions, with the development of the personality for professional use. This implies that the educational process strengthen the ego and further the integrity of the individual. In the author's opinion a measure for diminishing the anxiety and the hostility, which often have a disintegrative rather than an integrative effect, is to weight the first comprehensive examination not more than half. In short, the student's field-work standing should be averaged with his production on the comprehensive examination, even though the learning of field work is being tested to some extent in these examinations.[20] If this were done, he might well function better in preparation for the examination as well as in writing it. We cite Tyler's opinion that written tests and examinations, useful as they are, cannot serve as a basis for comprehensive evaluation and that evidence from field performance which gives valid evidence of the significant behavior of the student should be included. In so far as current field-work

20. For a statement concerning the importance of a comprehensive program of evaluation see Ralph W. Tyler, "Distinctive Attributes of a Profession," *Social Work Journal*, Vol. XXIII, No. 2 (April, 1952).

observations do not constitute reliable evidence, perhaps it is
indicated that we develop more precise evaluative procedures and
reports rather than concentrate largely on the development of skill
in the conduct of written tests and comprehensive examinations. If
professional education is education for use, the test of professional
learning is the individual's use of it. An examination can test some
forms of doing, but it cannot appraise competence in actual social
work practice. An examination can test the possession of knowledge
with which to think, the ability to think with knowledge presented,
and, very important, the capacity to communicate thinking under
stress of time and circumstance. It can gauge intellectual grasp of
what and how to do, as well as the student's thinking as to the
whys. It can test also whether a student knows what attitudes he
should have or whether he has appropriate attitudes toward people
on paper. It is one thing to be sympathetic with the troubled person in a case problem and another matter to feel with him in the
flesh when the impact of his need exerts pressure. An examination
cannot indicate how the student actually would use what he has
learned. For example, would the objectivity evidenced in a written
case discussion be sustained in actual contact with the individual
concerned? Would the steps correctly recounted as essential in the
handling of a community organization or administration problem
be carried out effectively in practice? In short, an examination can
test whether or not a student has the wherewithal for competent
practice, but it cannot reveal his competence in practice.

It could be argued that since a high degree of competence cannot be attained during the six quarters of a social worker's educational experience, the valid aim of its educational system is that of
conveying the means for competence as the student gains experience.
Accordingly, it is consistent that the student's proof of educability be
based on the findings of an examination system. The field experience,
however, reveals potentials for development or the lack of them
which many believe should be weighed in the school's appraisal.
It seems clear that the determination of a student's educability
through giving field-work performance equal weight with examination performance would not lower the school's demand on the student. It would, moreover, given a more comprehensive picture of his
development. It would also not ignore the variation which obtains

among students in the sequence of development of certain capacities. With many students, intellectual grasp precedes facility in the use of learning. Others gain their intellectual grasp through putting knowledge to use, bit by bit. In many instances the security afforded through having one's field work count would mean that there would be less at stake for all students, hence less negative affect surrounding the examination experience.

The examination system cannot be taken lightly by a school faculty. As has been indicated, there is knowledge of examination process to be acquired. Faculty members must learn not only what uses can be made of an examination but also its limitations. As delineated previously, how far can it test feeling and doing in testing knowing and thinking? Faculty members constructing questions in each field must have some developmental norms to guide them in what can realistically be expected at this point. In view of the fact that an examination can test only what the student has "on tap" for use under pressure of time, this implies knowing what the students should have assimilated by now. Knowledge not assimilated, which he might draw on for use in solving a problem in a class assignment, where calm deliberation, review of notes, and reading are possible, cannot be tested here. In view of the fact that the student's early days of practice rely heavily on resourcefulness in using what he knows of where and how to find out, he might appear more incompetent on an examination than he would be in practice. Hence questions must be closely focused on norms for assimilated learning. In social casework, norms have only recently begun to be defined, and they are tentative as yet. The importance, therefore, of using examinations as one means to establish norms argues for not weighting them too heavily.[21] Educators in social work can well turn to specialists in the field of education for help in constructing examinations. They can assist us in learning to formulate questions so that they fulfil their intent. Such factors as clarity, balance, appropriateness of demand, and adequacy as a discriminating test will be taken into account only as we study and work on examining.

21. At Chicago the student's field-work record is taken into account. The student who fails in practice does not get a degree, even though his rating in the final comprehensive is high. Also if the student's over-all average is low but passing on the final examination and his field-work grades superior, he would not be requested to take another examination for the degree.

At Chicago we have been conscientious in this regard. It is our conviction that the expenditure of time and energy can yield gains beyond more effective conduct of examinations, namely, greater clarity as to the learning progression for the selection and organization of learning experiences; more cognizance of the relatedness of fields of study; and a greater urgency to convey this awareness so as to help students integrate areas of learning.

The research project or thesis also often serves not only to promote continuity, sequence, and integration but also as an evaluative measure. It reveals the extent to which the student has grasped and assimilated various learnings for use. Social casework and social research have in common the method of scientific inquiry, both draw on contents of knowledge of human behavior. As stated elsewhere, sound social research uses psychological insights in gauging an informant's deliberate deception and self-deception. The social researcher depends on it also in appraising his own blind spots as well as in interviewing skills. One test, therefore, of social casework learning is in the student's use of it in social research.

In concluding the discussion of evaluative means, there is one aim which we should attempt to attain in their construction and conduct. They should not serve as a deterrent to learning. They should be an integral part of the educational process. In field work we long have regarded evaluation as a way to teach and to help, as well as to measure. Accordingly, we have developed principles of criticism and methods of engaging the learner's participation which have been fashioned by the nature of the learning experience and serve its ends. Our other test procedures should be conducted with the same intent. Only thus will they yield valid findings.

CHAPTER 13

Summary of Indications of
Movement in Learning

The appraisal of the learner's responses is necessarily based on observations in social work education. While education in each profession has distinctive attributes and social work education some highly individual features, we anticipate considerable carry-over from profession to profession in this matter of signs of movement in learning. This is, in part, because, wanting essentially the same level and kind of personality development in our students, we probably have sought by similar means to effect some of the same changes in behavior. It is in part also because, in common, our students are learning to serve people. It may therefore be expected that growth and change will be manifested similarly as young adults learn to assume responsibility in the lives of others.

I. THE CLASSROOM LIMITS APPRAISAL OF LEARNING

It is more difficult to appraise the import of the individual student's movement in the classroom than it is in field work. In both situations learning proceeds through swings forward and backward. In the long run, those responses which we term "regressive" may be aids to integration. Or what appears to be progress may be intellectual grasp without readiness or capacity to put it to use. Through the evaluative measures of the classroom, namely, observation of the student's response, written assignments, and examinations, we can determine whether or not he has attained essential knowledge; whether or not he can use it in orderly thinking and communicate it; whether or not he manifests appropriate attitudes —in short, our evaluative measures can enable us to know whether or not a student has the wherewithal for competent practice, but it cannot reveal his competence in practice. There are three noteworthy features in the appraisal of classroom performance to be borne in mind.

First, behavior in the classroom may conceal rather than reveal the potentials for professional performance. Thus the nonparticipating student may be educable, whereas the one who participates may not be educable. This is to say that the student's response in the classroom is not to be taken at face value and that it must be appraised not only in terms of its nature and timing but also in relation to his educational background, his performance in the field, his behavior in other classrooms as well as in relation to his response to the administrative procedures of the school. In short, educational diagnosis and prognosis involve reckoning with a configuration of factors over a period of time. The time element will be shortened as we systematically attempt to understand the significance of configurations.

Second, learning may proceed at an intellectual level but may break down when put to use. The student can change his thinking but not his doing. While intellectual grasp is a first step, from the standpoint of the aims of professional education, the student has not changed until he can do differently.

Third, one of the most significant means for appraising the student's educability is his response to help given as learning problems arise. The classroom does not afford the same opportunity as the field for him individually to experience understanding and help. Social work instructors need a better grasp than many have had of group process and more skill in dealing with the individual in the group within the limitations of an education situation than many have had. They also need a margin of time for the careful preparation of assignments and for the evaluation of written productions in relation to the educational purposes of the assignments. They need time, too, for individual counseling of students as learning problems are suspected or recognized.

II. NOTEWORTHY RESPONSES IN THE CLASSROOM

In spite of the limitations implicit in the classroom situation for the appraisal of movement in learning, there is much that can be known of the student as a learner through his classroom response. It is a significant fragment. Since the normal individual is more or less of one piece, what he does in one situation tells us something of him as a whole. The disturbed personality or the neurotic individual is more prone to be segmented in terms of discrepant responses. Hence his response in the classroom may be a less reliable indicator of his professional potentialities than those of more normal persons. We have become particularly alert to the following responses as worth weighing and as meriting continued observation, though no one of them taken alone may signify incapacity for social work.[1]

1. *Responses Suggestive of Problems in Learning*

Marked discrepancy between attitudes and feelings which are shown in written work in contrast to the more spontaneous verbal responses in class discussion should be noted. Remarkable also is the student who negativistically attacks instructor or colleagues more than the subject matter under discussion. The significance of this behavior increases when it does not give way with time or when it is not modified through the responses of those attacked. With reference to subject matter, if the student is rigid in defending his point of view when instructor and colleagues take issue with him, serious question as to his educability arises. It is worth noting also when certain attitudes, alignments, and ways of thinking and relating persist rigidly and do not change in response to knowledge conveyed and classroom drill in thinking. Examples of this are numerous. Strong identifications with agency and worker versus client persist or the reverse continue. The imposition of himself and his own value-judgments do not give way so that he becomes able to permit the client rather than himself to be the center of activity. Perhaps he persists in fitting facts into theory rather than applying theory to facts.

One notices also a compelling need to talk circumstantially and irrelevantly or no movement from fragmentary comments to more sustained discussion, as well as withdrawal from participation in class discussion. One is alert to sudden overwide swings in attitude and response. While marked resistance sometimes mounts, only to crumble suddenly into genuine conversion, this response frequently indicates that the subsequent complete acceptance is more pretensive than real. Basic change in attitude tends to occur slowly as

1. The possible import of these responses has been indicated earlier and is not elaborated again. See chap. 10, pp. 315–23; see also chap. 12, pp. 370–74.

learning is integrated. With reference to precipitous change, one observes particularly the relationship context in which it occurs. In some instances one finds that the student handles his anxiety in new learning experiences through an attack upon the conveyor or medium of the learning—teacher, supervisor, school, agency, and/or subject matter, those individuals and the systems which represent authority. In these instances the aggression essential for learning is hostile aggression, an angry attack upon the seemingly unattainable goal or against the individual who is the means to its attainment and who thereby has the power to block his strivings. This aggression later subsides as the individual feels competent and thus is assured of success or as his mistrust of the authorities lessens. It may collapse, however, as his guilt over hostility mounts and/or, more likely, as his hostility begets fear of failure. He may then identify as a defense. The limitations of this solution lie in the fact that he submits to, rather than accepts, learning, a factor which operates against its integration.

2. Responses Which Evidence Progress in Learning

From the positive standpoint, progress in the classroom is inferred as the student's attitude toward the client changes. This may be seen, as pity and blame give way to respect, as he increasingly reaches out to understand and to explain people in order to help them, instead of being committed for or against them. It is shown also in modification of the reform motivation, from that of wanting to make people over to realizing that he can only help them change. Progress is shown, too, in readiness to identify with the client, readiness to give rather than to withhold, that is, willingness to give unconditionally that to which the client is entitled. In this connection one notes the extent to which the student envisages giving in terms of the clients' need rather than in terms of his own need. One observes also whether he can accept the reality limits in giving and whether he reacts positively rather than negatively to giving within limits.

Likewise, one infers progress as the student's intellectual participation changes. As he attains knowledge, he increasingly puts it to use in dealing with more factors and is less inclined to erect dichotomies. He puts it to use also in inferring more soundly from material at hand and in recognizing gaps in knowledge which limit sound inferences. We assume progress as the individual is able not only to analyze, that is, break a situation into its parts, but also to synthesize, build it up again toward the solving of a problem. We see progress in the student's increasing urge to apply the learning in one situation to another, particularly when this is not done through impulsive use of fragments but instead through an attempt to formulate principles. We see intellectual progress, too, as the student's emotional acceptance of new knowledge permits him to be less dependent on stereotypes, so that he can individualize people and situations.

One infers lowered anxiety and emotional growth as the student's attitudes toward workers and agencies undergo change. This may be shown through change from being hypercritical of workers in cases and of agencies' policies and services, or from being fearful of criticism of workers and agencies, to readiness to evaluate the positives and negatives in each. The capacity to criticize work poorly done or to identify with work well done and to look at it, in either instance, for what it teaches suggests emotional acceptance of evaluation, a major means to professional learning. There is implied sufficient integration of knowledge to feel competent and to be competent, a prerequisite to freedom in autocriticism and criticism.

One assumes emotional growth as well as the integration of knowledge as the student increasingly is not frustrated through not being able to proceed faster toward the attainment of his goals in helping people and as he also can accept "not knowing" through the limits set by his profession's stage of development. An absence of resistance to these limits in himself and in his profession and an overreadiness to use them, however, may bespeak weak motivation to help and a tenuous identification with the aims of the profession.

We regard as progress the student's increasing courage to look beneath the surface and beyond the literal meaning of words in order to understand those whom he is helping and those individuals with whom he is working. In this connection a growing readiness to make learning a conscious process and a capacity to move from spasmodic self-consciousness to sustained consciousness of self mark the development of professional capacity to establish and maintain constructive working relationships. This development is shown more clearly in field work, but some evidence of it may emerge as the student participates in class discussion.

Finally, the student's growing freedom to take issue, to disagree, to stand by his point of view until it is thought through carefully with him, is regarded as progress in developing capacity for professional self-dependence and in being patterned for creative thinking and doing. One notes here whether or not the individual takes issue with ideas more than with people. One observes further whether his intellectual stand is well taken or constitutes futile hair splitting. This propensity is not always immediately differentiated from the provocative negativism described earlier; and often it is not differentiated by the instructor, who either fears opposition or is deeply committed to controversial discussion as a means to learning and is reassured by a battle of wits. These responses soon are differentiated, however, by the experienced instructor, who neither fears nor overvalues controversy and who responds to disagreement in ways which test it.

III. NOTEWORTHY RESPONSES IN FIELD WORK

The selective process of the admissions evaluations conducted by schools of social work has, within the limits of its lights, ruled out unpromising applicants. The student admitted to a school is therefore assumed to be educable until proved otherwise. While the spirit of the educational approach as he embarks on learning is not that of testing his educability but instead that of helping him learn, his capacities are tested in a teaching-helping process. It is as the student performs in the field, a situation in which he is related to the administrative, helping, and teaching functions of supervision, that, in the last analysis, his educability is determined. In determining educability the supervisory situation must be taken into account. The learner's response must always be evaluated in relation to the knowledge, understanding, and skill in the subject matter which the supervisor has at hand to convey. Her knowledge and understanding of the learning process, her skill in conducting it to productive ends, as well as her capacity for objective evaluation, must be taken into account.

Assume that one has a student who is not making progress and who *normally* is showing signs of great discomfort as he is not attaining his goals; assume also that the situation is one in which an experienced supervisor has done all that ordinarily helps, that is, she has taught when indicated, has used the usual measures to allay anxiety, and has performed her administrative functions in ways ordinarily not disturbing to students. In such an instance one suspects lack of aptitude for social work, which may or may not stem from basic personality difficulties. Before concluding this, however, one must determine, first, whether the work assignments exert exceptional demands in relation to the individual's age, experience, and stage of learning; second, whether there are exceptional stresses in his current life-situation, including health factors. Having ruled these out, the noteworthy features for educational diagnosis and prognosis will be not only the nature of the learning problem, in terms of its onset and development, but also, very importantly, his ways of dealing with his discomfort and his use of help in defining the problem and in making known available means to its solution.

1. *Responses Suggestive of Interruptions in Learning*

It has been recognized that the uneducable worker tends to remain in the beginning stage of learning.[2] This stage has been described as one in which the student normally has considerable anxiety due to feelings of incompetence and also to his realistic dependence on others for instruction and help, as well as to the threat of change implicit in learning. For a brief period the student may be diffusely confused, but normally he immediately becomes absorbed in the mastery of routines as a realistic means to the mastery of the situation and to the attainment of greater self-dependence. The uneducable student, in remaining in the beginning stage of learning, shows some or all of the following tendencies.

As his dependence is met, he does not become more self-dependent. In this he is unlike the educable beginner, who quickly makes some constructive use of help. The uneducable student's dependence persists and often mounts. He may make regressive use of help. In so far as there is discomfort over this dependency, he may deny it through evading supervision or through combating it. Dependency-authority conflicts fraught with hostility persist and do not respond to the measures ordinarily helpful in resolving them.

2. Bertha C. Reynolds, *Learning and Teaching in the Practice of Social Work* (New York: Farrar & Rinehart, 1942).

The uneducable student may become absorbed in routines, not as a means to an end but as an end for safety. This reaction may constitute an escape from other activity, out of his resistance to learning which threatens or a way of "binding" his anxiety. In the learner who fears authority it may be an expression of submission to supervision. On the other hand, the uneducable student may avoid routines and fail to master them. He thus remains helpless and dependent through his inability to get along without help or to progress into the assumption of greater responsibility.

With the uneducable student, new intellectual awareness does not bring change in his feeling, thinking, and doing. He thus does not put it to use in sustained fashion through attempting, more than spasmodically, to relate the facts he is learning to the needs and demands of the situation. Consequently, the general or diffuse confusion of the early period extends and deepens. Instead of a focalized problem, his upset may be reflected in several areas of his work. Or if problems are focalized, new ones replace the old as help is given.

Threatened by the pressures which compel change, the uneducable student shows marked resistance to change, often in defending his old thinking and doing and often in hostile attitudes and responses to new ideas and to those who convey them. This hostility may bring a collapse of defenses against learning, as guilt over hostile resistance mounts or as fear of failure is engendered. When this occurs, he may not participate in learning so much as submit to it. Such submission may be characterized by a demanding dependency of an unrealistic nature. The educable beginner submits in the sense of giving himself over to learning in which he participates. The uneducable student's submission is characterized by increased demand and expectancy that the supervisor be active in meeting his need for help in varied ways, often to an unrealistic degree.

These reactions suggest dependency-authority conflicts. When they persist one may expect progressively marked repetition of family patterns in his work relationships with supervisors, colleagues, and clients. This is shown in alignments, dependencies, and rivalries. It may be shown also through projection onto the client of what he gets or fails to get from the supervisor. While fragmentary and transitory transference reactions normally obtain in the early stages of the relationship between professional learner and teacher, the "transference relationship" often characterizes the uneducable student's response to those from whom he learns and with whom he works.

The regularly scheduled tutorial sessions of field instruction in which a student is being helped with insurmountable learning problems which frustrate him deeply are prone to induce a neurotic repetition, with relation to the supervisor, of stereotyped unsuitable behavior patterns based on the student's past. This reaction either to supervisor and colleagues or to clients, as though they were not themselves but some person in the student's past, often signifies that learning is obstructed, and, in turn, this response impedes learning. When this reaction does not respond to discussion focused on its import in the current educational situation, most notably its implications for the client, it is highly probable that the student's personal needs call for help of a kind beyond the scope of the educational situation. One of the characteristics of the uneducable student is that he and his relationship to the supervisor and the agency remain more important than services to the client. This constitutes a handicap in the establishment and maintenance of constructive working relationships. Progress or lack of it in this area is one of the major criteria of educability in social work learning.

While it has been stated that the uneducable student tends to remain in the beginning stages of learning, it is to be remembered that he is essentially unlike the beginning learner. Responses which are normal for the beginner persist; thus he differs markedly in his ways of dealing with his discomfort and in his use of help, rather than in his initial behavior manifestations. If the early responses of students in field work were to be studied systematically and comprehensively in relation to subsequent development, it is possible that certain initial behavior configurations would prove to be an index of the outcome of training. For example, at the start, students show marked difference in this matter of the weight which they give to the importance of the relationship with the supervisor and the agency, as compared to the relationship with the client. Some students are centered at the start on services to the client, showing an urgency to give and to do. They will err on the side of serving inadvisedly, thus risking mistakes which bring the disapproval of agency and supervisor. Other students are markedly concerned not "to do wrong," sometimes for the client's sake and sometimes for their own sakes in terms of their status strivings. Many such proclivities merit study for their possible significance.

2. Responses Which Evidence Progress in Learning

The educable student will have marked discomfort and become disturbed when his learning is obstructed. His ways of dealing with his discomfort and his use of help will be in marked contrast to the uneducable student. Full portrayal of his characteristic responses would involve specifications which are implied in the criteria of lack of progress delineated above. We therefore briefly summarize the nature of his responses. Prominently he shows reaction formation against professionally unacceptable impulses rather than an inclination to indulge them. Out of expectancy of success, often stemming from having *felt* successful and having been conditioned to learning as a pleasurable adventure, he has minimum discomfort over the dependency implicit in learning. Therefore, he early takes responsibility for seeking help as he needs it, unless normal dependencies have been tabooed through a supervisor's high evaluation of self-dependence out of her own fear of and hostility toward those dependent on her. As problems arise, he thus takes responsibility not only for seeking help with them but also for striving to cope with them himself. At times when learning is impeded or interrupted, his breakdown in competence is kept within narrow limits. It is focalized in the sense that it does not involve his total production and many people. He tends to keep difficulties somewhat centered in himself. His initial response will be a self-questioning one—Why am I not getting along? What is wrong with me? What can I do about it? He is slow to involve others predominantly and does not do so unrealistically, except momentarily. This is to say that his projections are not rigid. Instead, he is accessible to evaluation of them.

The educable student is concerned for the client. He is slow to take out his discomfort on the client by becoming neglectful of him, hostile toward him, or defensively aligned with him as his own needs are not met in the educational situation. Instead, in an effort to solve the problem, he first directs his expressions of dissatisfaction realistically toward those who are failing him and who are responsible for helping him. It is only as these efforts fail of their aim that the client may bear the brunt of his frustration. At such times he is more prone to align with the client than to deprive or to punish him. In these instances it is as though he unconsciously makes known to the supervisor and the agency—"you may fail me but you cannot fail him." Or from another standpoint it might be said that, feeling inadequate as his learning is not progressing, he compensates through outreaching himself and the agency lest the client suffer through his incompetence. The student who is a productive learner makes the most of supervision, even when it has definite lacks. He learns in spite of odds for a number of reasons.

First, in relation to the authority-dependency conflicts implicit in adult learning he is able to take help without so much discomfort that hostile rivalry is engendered or collapse into submissive dependency precipitated. Thus, as he is deprived, he is free to make his wants and needs known. He is not driven to retaliate because the supervisor who fails him is not felt and seen to be a parent or other person in his past who failed him. In short, current failures and frustrations are not repetitive ones; hence transference reactions of a negative nature are minimal.

Second, he makes productive use of help given in response to his need for help. As his realistic dependency need is met, he does not feel categorically dependent and hence inadequate. He is therefore free to become more self-dependent. As this occurs, he learns increasingly on his own. Thus he bridges gaps and seeks to supplement in accordance with his unmet needs. The educable student learns freely from his colleagues, from staff members in agency conferences, from his own experience. He is not narrowly tied into one relationship, demanding all or nothing therefrom. The supervisory relationship can fail him in some measure and not fail him completely. Again one notes that transference reactions are minimal.

Third, the educable student is not hypersensitive to criticism. He even welcomes it, equating it with help rather than with an attack. There will be some protectiveness at times, but it will be temporary. With reference to criticism, as with all learning experiences, it is to be remembered that the healthy ego protects itself against too much all at once in the interest of integration. The educable student does not react to criticism with wide or persistent projections or with abject self-criticism. Instead, he is motivated to reckon with it bit by bit and to take action in solution of the difficulty. His momentary projections will serve to prevent discouragement and thus operate against dependency or submission to failure.

Fourth, the educable student will make productive use of supervision, out of his readiness to make learning a conscious process. His urge to know how to get along for the attainment of his goals, together with his potentials for self-dependence, motivates him not only to learn what to do and how to do it but also to seek the whys of the doing. His hope of success operates against fear of independent functioning. Therefore, throughout his dependence on supervision, he is pushing toward emancipation through knowing why as well as what and how. Thus at some point he spontaneously begins to seek the wherewithal for responsible doing, including

"Why do I do as I do?" Consciousness of self may not be attained with equanimity, but he shows capacity to weather this stress through readiness to keep this focus, a means to the end of understanding others in order to help them. In other words, absorption in self does not exclude the client. The emotionally dependent student who fears guiding insight and emancipation is more prone to seek direction in what to do and how to do it, excluding the whys.

A supervisor narrowly centered on "technique teaching" may reinforce this tendency in the dependent learner. She also may fail the educable learner in his quest for whys, if she has not formulated them herself or if she has a need to imprint herself on others. In the latter instance she may unconsciously convey that the whys are unnecessary. The "do-as-I-do" attitude, with the implication that it is right because I do it, which is in essence dogmatic teaching, obviously has no place in professional education. The supervisor's gratification in a worker's unquestioning dependence on her ways of doing may cause the educable student to act dependent in his effort to meet the supervisor's need in order to get along with her. When this occurs, learning may be impeded—at least, the student will have been deprived of the opportunity of laying the groundwork for creative activity while in school. The student's progress in making learning a conscious process is peculiarly contingent upon the supervisor's capacity to make her activity a conscious process. In other words, the supervisor's unconscious is an instrument for helping or hindering the learner throughout the fieldwork experience.

3. *Major Differentials for Use in Appraising Educability*

Finally, with reference to the matter of the relative importance of the student's relationship to the supervisor and the agency as against the importance of his relationship to the client and concern for the agency's services, all students have in common some self-centered strivings. All desire to perform their work competently for their own satisfaction and for status in the educational situation, which, in the last analysis, is a struggle for survival. This desire stems from a combination of needs: the need to feel secure and safe in competition with others in that area of life in which his potential means to a livelihood is at stake; the need to fulfil his ideal of himself as an adequate person. Through self-respect he feels secure in commanding the respect of others and more confident of gaining desired status in the group, as well as in the eyes of the educational authorities, who have it in their power to rate him and thus to determine whether or not he attains his aims. Consequently, it is to be expected that all students will have a marked need to perform competently and to stand high in the eyes of their instructors. Normally, all students will be concerned with their status and show anxiety as they measure themselves against their colleagues and their mentors. The difference between the educable student and the one who is not educable often lies in his concern to be genuinely competent as distinguished from a concern to seem to be doing well. The uneducable student is often compelled to be content with "getting by." This difference is often manifested in responses to criticisms and evaluation, a point to which we return shortly.

As motivation for the profession, all students admitted to social work education are expected to bring a strong desire to serve people competently, to help them rather than to harm them. One would hope that this desire might stem from their concern and liking for people and from their capacity to live beyond narrow absorption in self. This expectation is not fulfilled in every instance. There is wide variation in the degree of concern and liking for people and in the capacity for object love brought to the educational experience. As indicated earlier, the motivation to help people may stem from personal experience in having been hurt or in having failed in some of their own life-relationships. The marked desire to help and not to hurt may be composed more of fear of hurting and failing people out of repressed impulses and reaction formation against doing so than out of a positive impulse to give help and to relieve suffering. When the student is motivated to help out of his own need for help more than out of his readiness and capacity to help, the helping process will not be well sustained. In these instances the individual's need for gratification and for self-maximation will predominate. A marked desire to succeed, to perform competently for his self-interest, is a common denominator among students, whereas the nature of the need and desire to serve the client varies widely. Furthermore, normally the motivation to serve fluctuates to some degree with success and failure in attaining competence. It is difficult to sustain one's liking and concern for people who do not respond to one's well-intentioned efforts.

As training progresses, therefore, the quantitative balance which obtains between these two strivings, as well as the quality of each, has import for educational diagnosis and prognosis. The uneducable student's striving for success often has a self-centered quality. He and his aims are more important than the client. He is prone to react to evaluation as to an attack. He is strongly defended against negative criticism, and often he is extremely dependent on approval in order to function. Sometimes his response is essentially narcissistic in its self-loving aspect, which at times ill conceals the self-hatred evoked by failure. His hostility may be momentarily turned against himself, but frequently it is projected onto those who hold him accountable through evaluation of his performance.

In the last analysis, the test of educability for social work lies in the extent to which the learner can subordinate his self-concern, his need for status and self-realization, to the needs, desires, concerns, and the welfare of the client. This implies readiness to seek help, to assume responsibility for learning, and to accept criticism as shown in sustained effort to put it to use. The evaluation process in social work education is rightly regarded as a teaching-helping process. The student's response to evaluation, a decisive criterion of his educability, is shown more largely through his inclination to be taught, to be helped, and to exert effort to learn than through his immediate reaction to the failure implied in criticism.

IV. CRITERIA OF EDUCABILITY CONTINGENT ON EDUCATIONAL
OPPORTUNITY AND CONDITIONS OF PRACTICE

The decisively important place of the field-work supervisor in the outcome of the student's learning as well as in reliable appraisal of progress and determination of educability has been indicated. Repeatedly, it has been implied and stated that the learning which leaves the deepest imprint is that which occurs in field practice in the context of the tutorial relationship with the supervisor. We trust that this portrayal of progress and of lack of progress in learning has made it clear that appraisals must always be of a student in situation, not of a student per se. This implies that there must be continuous close reference to the qualifications, abilities, attitudes, and practices of those who have attempted to teach and to help him.

Now, as programs for advanced education beyond the Master's degree are being established and expanded, as these programs give us an opportunity to know the outcome of earlier learning in several years of practice, we are having an opportunity for the third appraisal recommended by Tyler. Our early observations of a selected, rather than a representative, group of graduates disposes us to say that the aims of advanced education as determined by the demands of practice are having to be reconciled with a long line of shortcomings in preprofessional and professional education, as well as in practice. Headway is being made not only in the identification of problems but also in recognition of possible means to their solution, in preprofessional and professional education.[3] As students return to schools of social work from several years in practice, it has become clear that, under educational systems highly favorable for the attainment of the profession's educational aims, the two short years afforded the learner may not make possible thorough grasp and integration of learnings so that he is able immediately to use them freely for their further intrenchment. Therefore, his subsequent experience has been decisive in carrying forward, in arresting, or in breaking down the development of his professional learning.

For instance, as indicated earlier, it is possible in the Master's program to set in operation a habit of orderly thinking for problem-solving. This does not become so deeply ingrained, however, that it may not break down in subsequent practice in those situa-

3. Katherine Kendall, "Professional Education: A Responsibility of the Total Profession," *Social Casework*, January, 1953; Helen R. Wright, "The Professional Curriculum of the Future," *Social Service Review*, Vol. XXV, No. 4 (December, 1951); Grace Coyle, "The Role of the Teacher in the Creation of an Integrated Curriculum," *Social Work Journal*, Vol. XXIII, No. 2 (April, 1952), and "New Insights Available to the Social Worker from the Social Sciences," *Social Service Review*, Vol. XXVI, No. 3 (September, 1952); and papers by Eveline Burns, Eleanor Cockerill, and Charlotte Towle in *Guiding Principles* ("Social Work Education in the Post Master's Program Series," No. 1 [Council on Social Work Education, January, 1953]).

tions where pressures operate for emergent rather than planned doing. Pushed by necessity from hour to hour and day to day, the social worker may, in time, delegate his thinking to the expert consultant, called in to solve problems which might not have arisen had conditions of practice sustained and carried forward his school learning. Accordingly, the advanced student often needs to review his habits of orderly thinking before he can extend and deepen his knowledge.

A common concern of social workers returning for advanced work is to clarify their place as social workers in relation to other professions in the community and in multidiscipline programs. In spite of the fact that the faculties of schools of social work, by and large, have not been more committed to man's psyche than to his soma or to his social circumstances, uncertain identity often has been engendered in the student's subsequent practice. It is to be hoped that, tomorrow, advanced social work education will not have to be concerned with reorienting students to the nature and function of social work. The recultivation of professional identity is a repetitive process for both student and educator, one which will be unnecessary when the conditions of practice nurture the beginnings made in the educational experience. When this occurs, the distinctive contribution of social work to other professions and disciplines may be maximized rather than minimized or even lost. Furthermore, its members, out of their need for a sense of adequacy, may not be driven to identify with others who have a well-defined role to play in the give and take of interprofessional practice.

Many other illustrations could be delineated to show the significance of the conditions of practice for the eventual fulfilment or failure of each of the aims of social work education. Let it suffice to say that the vitality of social work education stems not only from the quality of the profession's practices but also from the degree of its participation in carrying forward the teaching and learning of the professional school. Among other measures, there is a recognized need for the field of practice to share the responsibility of professional education through agency programs which afford students a period following completion of their Master's degree work when they would be regarded as interns for whom there would be a planned progression of work with well-defined educational aims.

A profession is a product of civilization. In society each profession is charged with making certain benefits of civilization available to mankind; and, among professions, one of social work's distinctive attributes is that it has a "breadth and wholeness" of concern with unmet need.[4] The social worker in the performance of his threefold function, of helping the individual deal with stresses which threaten to master him, of removing the stresses, and of preventing their occurrence, must be responsibly engaged in effecting change in individuals within social situations. This implies change in either or both of them. Furthermore, to effect change, one must have an inner readiness to incorporate change, an intelligent fearlessness of it. For the conduct of individual helping relationships, for the organization and administration of social services, and for research, the social worker needs not merely to acquire knowledge, understanding, and skill but to be able to use them creatively, as he can do only when he has made them his own to the extent that he is free to depart from the established order of thinking and doing. This implies a depth of integration of learning which can occur only through an enduring learning process. The integration of learning proceeds with experience. Progression is contingent on the patterns imprinted in the professional school and on the conditions of practice. The profession as a whole is responsible for professional learning. Social work's place in society in comparison with that of other professions makes this a peculiarly difficult, but challenging, charge.

When one views the character of the charge in relation to our capacity to fulfil it, our aims are idealistic, in that they are not possible of immediate attainment. We would hesitate, however, to square them with necessity—that mother more often of "futile dodges than of invention." Again in the words of Whitehead: "When ideals have sunk to the level of practice, the result is stagnation." In so far as we are motivated by something akin to divine discontent with conditions of practice in social work and in education, we will progressively set our aims to determine the direction of our striving, even though they may not measure our current attainment.

4. Wright, *op. cit.*

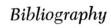

Bibliography

Bibliography

ACKERMAN, NATHAN V., and JAHODA, MARIE. *Antisemitism and Emotional Disorder*, Foreword by CARL BINGER. ("Social Study Series," No. 5.) New York: Harper & Bros., 1950.

ALEXANDER, FRANZ. *Our Age of Unreason*. New York: J. B. Lippincott Co., 1942.

———. *Fundamentals of Psychoanalysis*. New York: W. W. Norton & Co., 1948.

ALEXANDER, FRANZ; FRENCH, THOMAS M.; et al. *Psychoanalytic Therapy: Principles and Application*. New York: Ronald Press Co., 1946.

ALEXANDER, FRANZ, and ROSS, HELEN (eds.). *Dynamic Psychiatry*. Chicago: University of Chicago Press, 1952.

ALLEN, RAYMOND B. *Medical Education and the Changing Social Order*. New York: Commonweath Fund, 1946.

ALLPORT, GORDON W. "Attitudes." In CARL MURCHISON (ed.), *Handbook of Social Psychology*. Worcester, Mass.: Clark University Press, 1935.

AMERICAN PSYCHIATRIC ASSOCIATION. *Psychiatry and Medical Education: Report of the 1951 Conference, Ithaca, New York, on Psychiatric Education*. Baltimore: Lord Baltimore Press, 1952.

ASHDOWN, MARGARET, and BROWN, S. CLEMENT. *Social Service and Mental Health: An Essay on Psychiatric Social Workers*. London: International Library of Sociology and Social Reconstruction; Routledge & Kegan Paul, Ltd., 1953.

BABCOCK, CHARLOTTE G. "Social Work as Work," *Social Casework*, Vol. XXXIV, No. 10 (December, 1953).

BERENGARTEN, SIDNEY. "A Pilot Study To Establish Criteria for Selection of Students in Social Work." In *Social Work as Human Relations: Anniversary Papers of the New York School of Social Work and the Community Service Society of New York*. New York: Columbia University Press, 1949.

———. "The Pilot Study," *Alumni Newsletter, New York School of Social Work*. New York: Columbia University Press, 1950.

———. "A Pioneer Workshop in Student Selection," *Bulletin of the New York School of Social Work*. New York: Columbia University Press, 1951.

BINGER, CARL. *The Doctor's Job*. New York: W. W. Norton & Co., 1945.

BLOOM, BENJAMIN S. "Personality Variables and Classroom Performance," *Journal of the National Association of Deans of Women*, January, 1953. Published by the Association of Department of Deans, National Education Association, Washington, D.C.

BROSIN, HENRY N. "Psychiatry Experiments with Selection," *Social Service Review*, Vol. XXII, No. 4 (December, 1948).

415

CAMERON, NORMAN. *Human Ecology and Personality in the Training of Physicians in Psychiatry and Medical Education: Report of the Conference on Psychiatric Education, Ithaca, New York, 1951*, pp. 63–96. Baltimore: Lord Baltimore Press, 1952.

CANNON, WALTER B. *The Wisdom of the Body.* New York: W. W. Norton & Co., 1932.

CAUDILL, WILLIAM. *Japanese American Personality and Acculturation.* (Department of Anthropology, University of Chicago, "Genetic Psychology Monographs," Vol. XLV [1952].) Provincetown, Mass.: Journal Press, 1952.

COLWELL, ERNEST CADMAN. "The Role of the Professional School." In RALPH W. TYLER, *Education for Librarianship*, pp. 13–21. Chicago: American Library Association, 1949.

COUNCIL ON SOCIAL WORK EDUCATION. *Papers by Members of the Curriculum Committee on Advanced Education.* ("Social Work Education in the Post Master's Program.") New York, 1953.

COYLE, GRACE L. "The Role of the Teacher in the Creation of an Integrated Curriculum," *Social Work Journal*, Vol. XXXIII, No. 2 (April, 1952).

———. "New Insights Available to the Social Worker from the Social Sciences," *Social Service Review*, Vol. XXVI, No. 3 (September, 1952).

DOLLARD, JOHN, and MILLER, NEALE E. *Personality and Psychotherapy: An Analysis in Terms of Learning, Thinking, and Culture.* New York: McGraw-Hill Book Co., Inc., 1950.

DUMMER, ETHEL S. *Why I Think So: The Autobiography of an Hypothesis.* Chicago: Clarke McElroy, n.d.

Education for Professional Responsibility: Report of the Proceedings of the Interprofessions Conference on Education for Professional Responsibility, papers by DR. JOHN ROMANO and LON J. FULLER. Pittsburgh: Carnegie Press, 1948.

EMERSON, ALFRED E. "The Biological Foundations of Ethics and Social Progress." In A. D. WARD (ed.), *Goals of Economic Life*, chap. x. New York: Harper & Bros., 1953.

———. "Dynamic Homeostasis: A Unifying Principle in Organic, Social, and Ethical Evolution," *Scientific Monthly*, Vol. LXXVIII, No. 2 (February, 1954).

ERIKSON, ERIK H. *Childhood and Society.* New York: W. W. Norton & Co., 1950.

EVANS, LESTER J. "Medical Education for Insight," *American Journal of Orthopsychiatry*, Vol. XIX, No. 4 (October, 1949).

FRENCH, THOMAS M. "Psychodynamic Analysis of Ethical and Political Orientations," *American Journal of Economics and Sociology*, Vol. XII, No. 1 (October, 1952).

———. *The Integration of Behavior*, Vol. I: *Basic Postulates.* Chicago: University of Chicago Press, 1952.

FREUD, ANNA. *The Ego and the Mechanisms of Defense.* London: Hogarth Press, 1937.

FREUD, ANNA, and BURLINGHAM, DOROTHY T. *Infants without Families.* New York: International University Press, 1944.

GAIER, EUGENE S. *Selected Variables and the Learning Process.* ("Psychological Monographs," No. 349; "General and Applied," Vol. LXVI, No. 10, ed. HERBERT S. CONRAD.) Washington, D.C.: American Psychological Association, 1952.

GERARD, RALPH W. "The Biological Basis of Imagination," *Scientific Monthly,* June, 1946; republished in BREWSTER GHISELEN, *The Creative Process: A Symposium.* Berkeley and Los Angeles: University of California Press, 1952.

GHISELIN, BREWSTER. *The Creative Process: A Symposium.* Berkeley and Los Angeles: University of California Press, 1952.

GOLDSTINE, DORA. "The Literature of Medical Social Work: Review and Evaluation," *Social Service Review,* XXVII (September, 1953), 316–28.

GRINKER, ROY R., and SPIEGEL, JOHN. *Men under Stress.* Philadelphia: Blakiston Co., 1945.

HAMILTON, GORDON. "The Interaction of School and Agency," *Social Work Journal,* Vol. XXX, No. 2 (April, 1949).

———. "The Role of Social Casework in Social Policy," *Journal of Social Casework* (October, 1952).

HARRISON, GEORGE R. "Faith and the Scientist," *Atlantic,* Vol. CXCII, No. 6 (December, 1953).

HENDERSON, L. J. "Physician and Patient as a Social System," *New England Journal of Medicine,* CCXII (May 2, 1935), 819.

HENDRICK, IVES. *Facts and Theories of Psychoanalysis.* New York: A. A. Knopf, 1938; 2d ed., enl. and rev., 1948.

HILGARD, ERNEST R. *Theories of Learning.* New York: Appleton-Century-Crofts, Inc., 1948.

HUTCHINS, ROBERT M. *Education for Freedom.* Baton Rouge, La.: University of Louisiana Press, 1941.

KENDALL, KATHERINE. "Professional Education: A Responsibility of the Total Profession," *Social Casework,* January, 1953.

KERRIGAN, IRENE H. (ed.). "Selection of Students for Training in Social Case Work with Emphasis on Essential Personality Criteria," *Institute Proceedings.* New York: American Association of Medical Social Workers, 1950.

KIDNEIGH, JOHN C. "Social Work Administration," *Social Work Journal,* April, 1950.

KIMPTON, LAWRENCE A. "Growth through Change: Alumni Day Address, University of Chicago," *Tower Topics,* Vol. XX, No. 1 (1953).

LEE, PORTER R., and KENWORTHY, MARION E. *Mental Hygiene and Social Work,* pp. 184–263. New York: Commonwealth Fund, 1929.

LEVY, DAVID M. *Maternal Overprotection.* New York: Columbia University Press, 1943.

LEWIN, KURT. *Resolving Social Conflicts: Selected Papers on Group Dynamics,* see paper on "Conduct of Knowledge and Acceptance of New Values" (1945). New York: Harper & Bros., 1948.

LITTLE, ROGER W. "The Literature of Social Casework," *Social Case-work*, XXXIII (July, 1952), 287–91.

MACDONALD, MARY E. "Curriculum in Social Work of the University of Chicago," *Social Service Review*, XXV, No. 4 (December, 1951), 459–65.

MEANS, J. H. "The Clinical Teaching of Social Medicine," *Bulletin of the Johns Hopkins Hospital*, LXXVIII, No. 2 (February, 1946), 96–111.

PARSONS, TALCOTT. "Psychoanalysis and the Social Structure," *Psychoanalytic Quarterly*, XIX (1950), 371–84.

PEABODY, F. W. *The Care of the Patient*. Cambridge: Harvard University Press, 1927.

PERLMAN, HELEN HARRIS. "Generic Aspects of Specific Case Work Settings," *Social Service Review*, XXIII (September, 1949), 293–301.

———. "Teaching Case Work by the Discussion Method," *ibid.*, XXIV (September, 1950), 334–46.

———. "The Lecture as a Method in Teaching Case Work," *ibid.*, XXV (March, 1951), 19–32.

PRESCOTT, DANIEL A. *Emotions and the Educative Process*. Washington, D.C.: American Council on Education, 1938.

RALL, HARRIS FRANKLIN. "Social Change." In *Religion and Public Affairs*, p. 217–40. New York: Macmillan Co., 1937.

REYNOLDS, BERTHA C. *Learning and Teaching in the Practice of Social Work*. New York: Farrar & Rinehart, 1942.

ROBINSON, VIRGINIA P. *A Changing Psychology in Social Case Work*. Chapel Hill: University of North Carolina Press, 1930.

———. *Supervision in Social Case Work*. Chapel Hill: University of North Carolina Press, 1936.

———. *The Dynamics of Supervision under Functional Controls*. Philadelphia: University of Pennsylvania Press, 1949.

ROSENHEIM, MARGARET KEENEY. *Readings in Law for Social Workers*. Published for the University of Chicago School of Social Service Administration by the University of Chicago Press. Advance preliminary draft.

ROSS, HELEN. "A Contemporary Concept of Family Welfare," *Marriage and Family Living*, Vol. XV, No. 3 (August, 1953).

Russell Sage Foundation Annual Report, 1951–52. New York, 1952.

SCOTT, LYNDELL. "The Function of Field Work in Professional Education," *Social Service Review*, Vol. XXV, No. 4 (December, 1951).

SIMMONS, LEO. "The Manipulation of Human Resources in Nursing Care," *American Journal of Nursing*, LI, No. 7 (July, 1951), 452–56.

SMITH, OTHANEL. "Social Perspective as the Basic Orientation of the Curriculum." In VIRGIL E. HERRICK and RALPH W. TYLER (eds.), *Toward Improved Curriculum Theory*, pp. 3–16. ("Supplementary Educational Monographs," No. 71.) Chicago: University of Chicago Press, 1950.

SWIFT, SARAH H. *Training in Psychiatric Social Work*. New York: Commonwealth Fund, 1934.

"Symposium: Interdisciplinary Collaboration in Medical Education and Total Patient Care," *Journal of Psychiatric Social Work*, Vol. XXIII,

No. 1 (October, 1953), papers by JOHN B. YOUMANS, EDWARD HARPER, ARTHUR L. DREW, JR., and DOROTHY ROBINSON.

TAFT, JESSIE. "A Conception of the Growth Process Underlying Social Casework Practice," *Social Casework* (October, 1950); also in *Social Work in the Current Scene: Selected Papers, National Conference of Social Work*. New York: Columbia University Press, 1950; also in *Principles and Techniques in Social Casework: Selected Articles, 1940–50*, ed. CORA KASIUS. New York: Family Service Association of America, 1950.

TOWLE, CHARLOTTE. "The Individual and Social Change," *Social Service Review*, Vol. XIII (March, 1939).

———. "Professional Skill in Administration," *News-Letter, American Association of Psychiatric Social Workers*, May, 1940.

———. "Teaching Psychiatry in Social Case Work," *Family*, Vol. XX, No. 10 (February, 1940).

———. *Common Human Needs*, Part III, pp. 95–122. ("Public Assistance Reports," No. 8.) Washington, D.C.: Government Printing Office, 1945.

———. "Social Case Work in Modern Society," *Social Service Review*, Vol. XX, No. 2 (June, 1946).

———. "Emotional Elements in Professional Learning." In pamphlet entitled *Professional Education*. New York: American Association of Schools of Social Work, 1948.

———. "Curriculum Development," *Social Work Journal*, Vol. XXX, No. 2 (April, 1949).

———. "The Classroom Teacher as Practitioner," *Social Service Review*, Vol. XXII, No. 3 (September, 1948); see also in *Social Work as Human Relations*. New York: Columbia University Press, 1949.

———. Discussion of "Multidiscipline Approach to Child Development," by PETER B. NEUBAUER and JOSEPH STEINERT, *Social Service Review*, XXIV, No. 4 (December, 1950), 466–68.

———. Discussion of *Why a Nurse Mental Health Consultant in Public Health*, by KATHERINE B. OETTINGER, *Journal of Psychiatric Social Work*, Vol. XIX, No. 4 (spring, 1950).

———. "The Contribution of Education for Social Casework to Practice," *Social Casework* (October, 1950); also in *Principles and Techniques in Social Casework: Selected Papers, 1940–50*, ed. CORA KASIUS. New York: Family Service Association of America, 1950.

———. "The Distinctive Attributes of Education for Social Work," *Social Work Journal*, Vol. XXXIII, No. 2 (April, 1952).

———. "The Learners." In *Guiding Principles*. ("Social Work Education in the Post Master's Program," Vol. 1.) New York: Council on Social Work Education, 1953.

———. "The Place of the Autobiography in the Selection of Students." Publication pending.

TYLER, RALPH W. "Educational Problems in Other Professions." In his *Education for Librarianship*, pp. 22–28. Chicago: American Library Association, 1949.

TYLER, RALPH W. "Basic Principles of Curriculum and Instruction," *Syllabus for Education 360*. Chicago: University of Chicago Press, 1950.
———. "Distinctive Attributes of Education for the Professions," *Social Work Journal*, Vol. XXXIII, No. 2 (April, 1952).
WAGGONER, R. W., and ZIEGLER, T. W. "Psychiatric Factors in Students Who Fail," *American Journal of Psychiatry*, C, No. 3 (November, 1946), 369–76.
WHITEHEAD, ALFRED NORTH. *The Aims of Education and Other Essays*. New York: Macmillan Co., 1929.
Widening Horizons in Medical Education: A Study of the Teaching of Social and Environmental Factors in Medicine: Report from the Joint Committee of the Association of American Medical Colleges and the American Association of Medical Social Workers. New York: Commonwealth Fund, 1948.
WRIGHT, HELEN R. "The Professional Curriculum of the Future," *Social Service Review*, Vol. XXV, No. 4 (December, 1951).
WRIGHT, HELEN R., *et al. Reply to the Questionnaire on Community Needs*. ("Preparatory Commission Documents," No. 087, of the 1951 Conference on Psychiatric Education, Ithaca, New York. Washington, D.C.: American Psychiatric Association, 1952.)

Index

Index